T0321474

Applying Methods of Scientific Inquiry Into Intelligence, Security, and Counterterrorism

Arif Sari
Girne American University Canterbury, UK

A volume in the Advances in
Digital Crime, Forensics, and Cyber
Terrorism (ADCFCT) Book Series

Published in the United States of America by
    IGI Global
    Information Science Reference (an imprint of IGI Global)
    701 E. Chocolate Avenue
    Hershey PA, USA 17033
    Tel: 717-533-8845
    Fax: 717-533-8661
    E-mail: cust@igi-global.com
    Web site: http://www.igi-global.com

Copyright © 2019 by IGI Global. All rights reserved. No part of this publication may be
reproduced, stored or distributed in any form or by any means, electronic or mechanical, including
photocopying, without written permission from the publisher.
Product or company names used in this set are for identification purposes only. Inclusion of the
names of the products or companies does not indicate a claim of ownership by IGI Global of the
trademark or registered trademark.

Library of Congress Cataloging-in-Publication Data

Names: Sari, Arif, 1986- author.
Title: Applying methods of scientific inquiry into intelligence, security,
    and counterterrorism / Arif Sari, editor.
Description: Hershey, PA : Information Science Reference, 2019.
Identifiers: LCCN 2018057672| ISBN 9781522589761 (hardcover) | ISBN
    9781522589785 (ebook) | ISBN 9781522589778 (softcover)
Subjects: LCSH: Cyber intelligence (Computer security) |
    Cyberterrorism--Prevention.
Classification: LCC QA76.9.A25 A675 2019 | DDC 005.8--dc23 LC record available at https://
lccn.loc.gov/2018057672

This book is published in the IGI Global book series Advances in Digital Crime, Forensics, and
Cyber Terrorism (ADCFCT) (ISSN: 2327-0381; eISSN: 2327-0373)

British Cataloguing in Publication Data
A Cataloguing in Publication record for this book is available from the British Library.

All work contributed to this book is new, previously-unpublished material.
The views expressed in this book are those of the authors, but not necessarily of the publisher.

For electronic access to this publication, please contact: eresources@igi-global.com.

Advances in Digital Crime, Forensics, and Cyber Terrorism (ADCFCT) Book Series

ISSN:2327-0381
EISSN:2327-0373

Editor-in-Chief: Bryan Christiansen, Global Research Society, LLC, USA & Agnieszka Piekarz, Independent Researcher, Poland

MISSION

The digital revolution has allowed for greater global connectivity and has improved the way we share and present information. With this new ease of communication and access also come many new challenges and threats as cyber crime and digital perpetrators are constantly developing new ways to attack systems and gain access to private information.

The **Advances in Digital Crime, Forensics, and Cyber Terrorism (ADCFCT) Book Series** seeks to publish the latest research in diverse fields pertaining to crime, warfare, terrorism and forensics in the digital sphere. By advancing research available in these fields, the **ADCFCT** aims to present researchers, academicians, and students with the most current available knowledge and assist security and law enforcement professionals with a better understanding of the current tools, applications, and methodologies being implemented and discussed in the field.

COVERAGE

- Database Forensics
- Malicious codes
- Global Threat Intelligence
- Malware
- Vulnerability
- Cyber Warfare
- Digital Crime
- Computer virology
- Network Forensics
- Telecommunications Fraud

IGI Global is currently accepting manuscripts for publication within this series. To submit a proposal for a volume in this series, please contact our Acquisition Editors at Acquisitions@igi-global.com or visit: http://www.igi-global.com/publish/.

The Advances in Digital Crime, Forensics, and Cyber Terrorism (ADCFCT) Book Series (ISSN 2327-0381) is published by IGI Global, 701 E. Chocolate Avenue, Hershey, PA 17033-1240, USA, www.igi-global.com. This series is composed of titles available for purchase individually; each title is edited to be contextually exclusive from any other title within the series. For pricing and ordering information please visit http://www.igi-global.com/book-series/advances-digital-crime-forensics-cyber/73676. Postmaster: Send all address changes to above address. ©© 2019 IGI Global. All rights, including translation in other languages reserved by the publisher. No part of this series may be reproduced or used in any form or by any means – graphics, electronic, or mechanical, including photocopying, recording, taping, or information and retrieval systems – without written permission from the publisher, except for non commercial, educational use, including classroom teaching purposes. The views expressed in this series are those of the authors, but not necessarily of IGI Global.

Titles in this Series

701 East Chocolate Avenue, Hershey, PA 17033, USA
Tel: 717-533-8845 x100 • Fax: 717-533-8661
E-Mail: cust@igi-global.com • www.igi-global.com

Table of Contents

Detailed Table of Contents

Chapter 1
Taxonomy of Cyber Attack Weapons, Defense Strategies, and Cyber War
Incidents 1

Arif Sari, Girne American University Canterbury, UK
Ugur Can Atasoy, Girne American University, Cyprus

Cyber security is the newest internal concern of this century where different technologies developed through telecommunication, computers, and internet are used in the international arena as cyber-weapons. This chapter provides in-depth information about up-to-date cyber-attack methods and mechanisms used in the cyber war, and it focuses on the cyber war incidents starting from 1982 with Siberia Natural Gas Explosion until 2015 Russia-Turkey cyber-attack conflict and between variety of developed and developing countries in detail. In addition to this, cyber-weapons developed by Russia, USA, and Israel targeting critical infrastructure are elaborated. The chapter concludes with the use of cyber-attack methods and tools with their taxonomy and elaborates the fundamentals of cyber defense strategies to these proposed attacks with existing solutions from the literature.

Chapter 2
Android Application Security 46

Marwan Omar, Saint Leo University, USA
Derek Mohammed, Saint Leo University, USA
Van Nguyen, Saint Leo University, USA
Maurice Dawson, Illinois Institute of Technology, USA
Mubarak Banisakher, Saint Leo University, USA

Android is a free, open source platform that allows any developer to submit apps to the Android Market with no restrictions. This enables hackers to pass their malicious apps to the Android Market as legitimate apps. The central issue lies at the heart of the Android permission mechanism, which is not capable of blocking malicious apps from accessing sensitive phone resources (e.g., contact info and browsing history); it either allows or disallows apps from accessing the resources requested by the app at the installation time. This chapter investigated the scope of this issue and concluded that hackers use malicious apps as attack vectors to compromise Android smartphones and steal confidential data and that no security solutions exist to combat malicious apps. The researcher suggested designing a real time monitoring application to detect and deter malicious apps from compromising users' sensitive data; such application is necessary for Android users to protect their privacy and prevent financial loss.

Chapter 3

Open source intelligence (OSINT) is one of the most confrontational topics in cyber security in today's world where technology and data transfer methods are highly developed. It is known that many organizations and individuals use OSINT as an information gathering tool during data transfer over the internet and provide many personal or corporate information access. OSINT is a systematic method that is produced by official and private organizations via sources such as the internet or the media. In recent years there has been some debate about the security and privacy of this information, especially with the widespread use of social media. In this chapter, the control of information obtained by OSINT the security will explain the positive effects on this control mechanism.

Text analytics applies to most businesses, particularly education segments; for instance, if association or university is suspicious about data secrets being spilt to contenders by the workers, text analytics investigation can help dissect many employees' email messages. The massive volume of both organized and unstructured data principally started from the web-based social networking (media) and Web 2.0. The investigation (analysis) of messages online, tweets, and different types of unstructured text data constitute what we call text analytics, which has been developed during the most recent few years in a way that does not shift, through the upheaval of various algorithms and applications being utilized for the processing of data alongside the protection and IT security. This chapter plans to find common problems faced when using the different medium of data usage in education, one can analyze their information through the perform of sentiment analysis using text analytics by extracting useful information from text documents using IBM's annotation query language (AQL).

Chapter 5

Ibrahim Firat, University of Reading, UK

It is undeniable that technology is developing and growing at an unstoppable pace. Technology has become a part of people's daily lives. It has been used for many purposes but mainly to make human life easier. In addition to being useful, these advancements in technology have some bad consequences. A new malware called botnet has recently emerged. It is considered to be one of the most important and dangerous cyber security problems as it is not well understood and evolves quickly. Communication of bots between each other and their botmaster results in the formation of botnet; this is also known as a zombie army. As botnets become popular among cybercriminals, more studies have been done in botnet detection area. Researchers have developed new detection mechanisms in order to understand and tackle this growing botnet issue. This chapter aims to review working principles of botnets and botnet detection mechanisms in order to increase general knowledge about botnets.

Chapter 6

Acheme Odeh, Girne American University, Cyprus

The internet technologies have made it even easier for terrorist activities to migrate smoothly to the internet. Nations are now benefiting from the act of cyberterrorism, making it more difficult to successfully fight this monster. This chapter aims to draw up a review on various published work addressing the financial benefits of cyberterrorism. The question is to know if economic benefits alone is significantly strong enough to encourage more cyberterrorism activities. Should this be the case, what can be done to curb this deadly cancer from spreading further? Scientific methods could prove to be a much efficient solution to the issue of cyber terrorism. But how is that going to happen and for how long should we wait to see this happen? Would it ever happen? Considering that the internet is an ever-growing technology with endless possibilities for both attackers and crime investigative specialist, do we forsee a cyber war between nations who can boost of better fighting and defending technologies? These questions and many more are discussed based on recent literature.

Chapter 7

Joshua Chibuike Sopuru, Girne American University, Cyprus
Murat Akkaya, Girne American University, Cyprus

Improved technology has led to significant changes in society over time. This has been accompanied by significant changes in the economy. The improvement in technology has also been accompanied by significant changes in the modeling of network-based systems. This is comprised of significant updates of computer and mobile operating systems. The development of mobile phones and operating systems have endangered essential individual and corporate data over time by making it vulnerable and prone to viruses, worms, and malware. This chapter focuses on reviewing literature that serves as guides for modeling a network flow-based detection system for malware categorization. The Author begins with an in-depth definition of mobile devices and how they have eased the spread of malicious software. Identifying Android OS as the most used operating system, Android OS operating system layer was explained, and the reason for user preferability unveiled. The chapter continued with a review of known malware and their behaviors as has been observed over time.

Chapter 8

Thanks to the internet, the distances between the countries are easily overcome and the communication network rapidly expands. This situation also affects the cyber security of the countries to a great extent. Attacks on critical infrastructures, companies, and public institutions can be magnitude that make great harms. These developments in cyber space bring new problems. One of them is cyber terror. Cyber terror does not have a certain and well-known definition. Cyber terror is the realization of terrorist acts in the field of cyber war. In addition, cyber space is a place of display for terrorist acts. The effects of cyber terror attacks have reached a level to scare all countries. There is not enough information about the definition, characteristics, methods used in cyber terror attacks and cyber terror groups. It is important for national administrators and staff to become conscious and to become informed about cyber terror. In this chapter, information will be presented, endeavors on awareness-creation will be made, and a role of guiding the future studies will be taken.

Chapter 9

Improvements in the technology unequivocally aids everyday life. These advancements lead states to save time and money. The crucial point is the facilitation that the internet and cyber services offer. Internet can be used for providing services to the citizens and can be benefitted while storing massive amounts of data. Nevertheless, cyberspace comes with serious problems too. The security of the data that have been transferred to the digital space ought to be protected in absolute terms. In cases of lack of securitization, cyberspace becomes vulnerable to attacks and, obviously, terrorist organizations can benefit from this. The Middle East, too, is an arena for such actions. But, the particular importance of the region reveals itself via its affiliation with the most widespread and dangerous terrorist organizations. Their ability to use the internet for propaganda and organizing attacks should not be disdained. Referencing these, this chapter will focus on the transfer of conventional terrorism to cyberspace in the Middle East.

Chapter 10

Internet has become the most unavoidable phenomenon in our daily life. Together with it has risen the most unfathomable aftermath of anonymity exploitation. The internet available for the normal users are limited to the sites that are directly indexed by common search engines. But apart from these contents, a major portion of the internet lies hidden from regular search engines and is not available to users resorting to ordinary browsers. This part forms the deep web and within it lies the darkest part also known as dark web. Several illegal activities take place in this darkest part, including child pornography, financial fraudulence, drug deployment, and many others. Thus, countermeasures to put a curb on these activities are very much required. The chapter focuses on the most relevant research areas and possible research scopes in the area of the dark web.

This chapter is a literature review of intermediate system to intermediate system (IS-IS) routing protocol to provide basic security mechanisms against cyber-attacks and enhance network security. IS-IS was originally developed by the International Organization for Standardization (ISO) as a link state routing protocol. It was first built with the ability to route CLNPs or connectionless network protocols according to the OSI standard equal to IP. IS-IS is also developed so that it can accommodate routing for any layer three-based protocol. Internet Engineering Task Force (IETF) in 1990 specified the support for IP and introduced IPv6 extensions in 2000. IS-IS protocol implementation was written as modules in order for it to be distributed freely and easily installed on the GNU routing software. SourceForge.net supported the project and gave access for developers to easily contribute to the project. The chapter elaborates the ISIS routing protocol for network security and proposes a critical survey on security routing protocols.

Chapter 12
    Merve Şener, Girne American University, Cyprus

Critical infrastructures ensure that activities that are vital and important for individuals can be safely delivered to the society uninterruptedly. The damage on these critical infrastructures caused by cyber-attacks whose control is carried out through computers and network systems is very large. Cyber-attacks directly or indirectly affect companies, institutions, and organizations economically and cause great financial losses. In this chapter, two different categories, energy and finance sector, which are described as critical infrastructure, are discussed; cyber-attacks carried out on these sectors, cyber-attack weapons, and economic losses caused by these attacks are examined.

Preface

Interdisciplinary and multidisciplinary research is slowly, yet steadily revolutionizing traditional education; however, multidisciplinary research can and will also improve the extent to which a country can protect its critical and vital assets. The field of intelligence requires focus on the assessment and resolution of complex problems. The disciplines form the basis of the protection of a nation; au contraire, the dynamics of the intelligence field lead to the necessity of raising awareness and placing a priority on the fostering of more improved ideas through the use of interdisciplinary and multidisciplinary connections. The intelligence is not only linked to the scientific discipline as a result of the necessity to counter nuclear, radioactive, or other similar attacks, but the underlying basis of science knowledge can further improve intelligence activities. To ensure that there are improvements in security and intelligence matters, the necessity of attaining a strong scientific knowledge must be highlight. This book, "Applying Methods of Scientific Inquiry into Intelligence, Security, and Counterterrorism," has been established in order to provide a detailed discussion wherein the ways in which science can be applied to the intelligence field are explicated.

Each chapter has focused on highlighting the necessary blend of science and intelligence activities. Furthermore, detailed examples given in the chapters provide readers with a thorough understanding of the specific aspects of intelligence activities that can be improved through the relevant application of science concepts.

ORGANIZATION OF THIS BOOK

In this book, we present 12 chapters aimed at emphasizing necessary blend of cybersecurity, science and intelligence activities in today's society. The topics covered in this book are briefly listed and explained below.

Chapter 1, "Taxonomy of Cyber Attack Weapons, Defense Strategies, and Cyber War Incidents," provides in-depth information about up-to-date cyber-attack methods and mechanisms used in the cyber war and subsection of this chapter focuses on the cyber war incidents starting from 1982 with Siberia Natural Gas Explosion until 2015 Russia-Turkey cyber-attack conflict and between variety of developed and developing countries in details. In addition to this, cyber-weapons developed by Russia, USA and Israel targeting critical infrastructures are elaborated. The chapter concludes with use of cyber-attack methods and tools with their taxonomy and elaborates the fundamentals of cyber defense strategies with existing solutions from the literature to these proposed attacks.

Chapter 2, "Android Application Security," investigated the Android operating systems permission mechanism which is not capable of blocking malicious apps from accessing sensitive resources thus hackers use malicious apps as attack vectors to compromise Android smartphones and steal confidential data and that no security solutions exist to combat malicious apps.

Chapter 3, "Cyber Security and Open Source Intelligence Techniques," presents Open Source Intelligence (OSINT) techniques which is one of the most confrontational topics in cyber security in today's world where technology and data transfer methods are highly developed. In recent years there has been some debate about the security and privacy of this information, especially with the widespread use of social media. The details of the chapter provide information to control of information obtained by OSINT and explained the positive effects on this mechanism.

Chapter 4, "Intelligent Strategy and Security in Education, Big Data (Text Analytics)," focuses on the field of big data analytics in education and improvement issues for educationist and professionals). The Information analysis techniques provided through the performing of sentiment analysis using text analytics by extracting useful information from text documents using IBM's Annotation Query Language (AQL to find common problems faced when using the different medium of data usage in education

Chapter 5, "Inevitable Battle Against Botnets," elaborates the Botnets that can perform a number of different cyber-attacks and malicious behaviors such as DDoS attacks or email spamming. As botnets become popular among cybercriminals, more studies have been done in botnet detection area. Researchers have focused on development of new intelligence mechanisms to support detection mechanisms to understand and tackle this growing botnet issues.

Chapter 6, "A Review of the Economic Benefits of Cyber Terrorism," aims to draw up a review on various published work addressing the financial benefits of cyber terrorism. The question is to know if economic benefits alone are significantly strong enough to encourage more cyber terrorism activities and should this be the case, what can be done to curb this deadly cancer from spreading further. Considering that the internet is an ever-growing technology with endless possibilities for both attackers and crime investigative specialist. Do we for-see a cyber-war between Nations who can boost of better fighting and defending technologies? These and many more are discussed based on recent literatures in this chapter.

Chapter 7, "Guide for Modelling a Network Flow-Based Detection System for Malware Categorization: A Review of Related Literature," focuses on reviewing literature that serves as guides for modeling a network flow-based detection system for malware categorization since the development of mobile phones and Operating systems have endangered essential individual and corporate data over time, by making it vulnerable and prone to viruses, worms, and malware.

Chapter 8, "A Review of Research Studies on Cyber Terror," presents the definition, characteristics, methods used in cyber terror attacks and cyber terror groups. It is important for national administrators and staff to become conscious and to become informed about cyber terror.

Chapter 9, "From Conventional to Sophisticated: A Cyber Guise to Terrorism in the Middle East," presents significant findings about activities of cyber-attack groups in the Middle Eastern countries. One of the major findings exposes the categorization of cyber-attack groups in Middle-East and demonstrates the amount of effort exerted by the terrorist groups to prove themselves to world in cyber space. Their ability to use the Internet for propaganda, and organizing attacks should not be disdained. Referencing these, this chapter focused on the transfer of conventional terrorism to the cyberspace in the Middle East.

Chapter 10, "Dark Web and Its Research Scopes," devotes to the identification of research scopes in the dark web. The chapter emphasizes the real dark web scenario, complex problems in dark web that are unaddressed, research challenges, existing research developments and possible research directions in connection with dark web.

Chapter 11, "Enhanced Security for Network Communication With Proposed IS-IS Protocol," elaborates the Intermediate System to Intermediate System (IS-IS) routing protocol in order to provide information about basic security mechanisms against cyber-attacks and enhance network security.

Chapter 12, "Economic Impact of Cyber Attacks on Critical Infrastructures," presents latest cyber-attacks generated against critical infrastructures in Energy Sector and Finance Sector. It elaborates the investigation and categorization of attacks that causes critical damage and economic loss.

Arif Sari
Girne American University Canterbury, UK

Chapter 1
Taxonomy of Cyber Attack Weapons, Defense Strategies, and Cyber War Incidents

Arif Sari

ⓘ https://orcid.org/0000-0003-0902-9988
Girne American University Canterbury, UK

Ugur Can Atasoy
Girne American University, Cyprus

ABSTRACT

Cyber security is the newest internal concern of this century where different technologies developed through telecommunication, computers, and internet are used in the international arena as cyber-weapons. This chapter provides in-depth information about up-to-date cyber-attack methods and mechanisms used in the cyber war, and it focuses on the cyber war incidents starting from 1982 with Siberia Natural Gas Explosion until 2015 Russia-Turkey cyber-attack conflict and between variety of developed and developing countries in detail. In addition to this, cyber-weapons developed by Russia, USA, and Israel targeting critical infrastructure are elaborated. The chapter concludes with the use of cyber-attack methods and tools with their taxonomy and elaborates the fundamentals of cyber defense strategies to these proposed attacks with existing solutions from the literature.

DOI: 10.4018/978-1-5225-8976-1.ch001

Copyright © 2019, IGI Global. Copying or distributing in print or electronic forms without written permission of IGI Global is prohibited.

INTRODUCTION

In recent years, global importance and interest of cyber security has been intensified. Countries started to perform specific operations in cyber security and cyber defence concepts. Due to these breakthroughs, customized approaches have been raised in the cyber world and countries started to form new customised cyber-attacks along with their defence mechanisms. Among all these expansion, cyberspace started to recognise as a fifth aspect of war concept. Distinctly from classical war concepts, main actors of this war concept are telecommunication and computer technologies. Since these technologies became a vital part of both the daily and professional life, the corresponding assets used as cyber weapons in international connections. Thus and so, cyber security concept become newest internal concept for the countries.

Cyber weapons and their countermeasures which are advanced in territorial researches, started to take a part in transnational cyber-attacks for the purpose of national interests. Nowadays cyber war strategies and cyberspace started to use as a deterrent force both in offensive and defence in international relations in case of disagreement situations. Newest technologies are improving the opportunities in the cyberspace; these opportunities are accepted as a threat both for institutions and countries. Cyber war is defined as a major threat in the cyberspace. International organizations are started to prepare themselves for these situations and coordinate their military forces against cyber war cases. In the near future, the cyber war results will be similar to the classic wars, by capturing the critical infrastructure's management and abusing them against to the target, there are expected specific attacks like destroying communication lines, barrages and nuclear power stations (Yayla, 2013).

The incidents are showing that; the cyber war is real, but the cyber weapons, which used until this time, are primitive cyber weapons and the contracting countries not showed their real abilities and cyber weapons yet (Clarke & Knake, 2010).

Cyber war accepted as fifth dimension of the war, so the cyberspace used through cyber-attacks in order to support conventional wars. Cyber war has a variety of methods and mechanisms such as; espionage, manipulation, propaganda, damaging the systems via Viruses and Trojans, sabotage, fraud, etc. Therefore, the cyber-attacks which are targeting countries, especially those are aiming the critical infrastructures became critical point of the counties in the brackets of cyber defence.

Success of the cyber-attacks are mostly depending on up-to-date attack perspectives, coding and configuration flaws, systems and hardware glitches, precaution inadequacies, human vulnerabilities, lack of education and usage of legacy systems/products. Up-to-date attack patterns and structures which are used in cyber warfare would be discussed in the scope of this chapter, while subsection of this chapter also focuses on the cyber war incidents starting from 1982 with Siberia Natural Gas Explosion until 2015 Russia-Turkey cyber-attack conflict and between variety of developed and developing countries in details with effects of cyber wars on the international balance. In addition to this, this chapter elaborates the critical infrastructure targeted cyber-weapons developed by Russia, USA and Israel (Stuxnet, Duqu, Gauss, Tinba etc.). The chapter concludes with use of cyber-attack methods and tools with their classifications and elaborates the fundamentals of cyber defence strategies with existing solutions from the literature to these proposed attacks.

CYBER SECURITY FUNDAMENTALS

There are varieties of definitions for the cyber security concept. United Nation's (UN) authorized information technologies media organ, International Telecommunication Union's (ITU) cyber security description is; usage of tools, policies, security concepts and recommendations, risk management approaches, actions, education and trainings, applications and the whole technological concepts in order to protect user's and organizations' assets in cyberspace. The cyberspace involves persons and organizations assets, hardware, structures, applications, services, communication services and information (Çeliktaş, 2016; ITU, 2008).

There are several functions and aspects of cyber security in the literature. The summarized definition is; Specifying the security risks and vulnerabilities which are existing in the cyberspace and ensuring the confidentiality, integrity, availability principles along with taking precautions and activating the required reactions in order to protect system and reversing the system conditions to "safe" during any kind of cyber security issue. Other than cyber-attacks and threats, cyber security concept involves decreasing the vulnerabilities which originates from the manufacturers, administrators and users as well (Sağıroğlu, 2011; Atalay, 2012: 43; BTK, 2009; ITU, 2008).

Cyberspace

Cyberspace is a global information environment which is created by connecting communication networks, computer systems, control mechanisms and their sub connections. So, the cyberspace is providing a world-wide connection without geographical border limitations (Ercan, 2015; Hildreth, 2001).

The main element of cyberspace is the internet but there is other essential element which are; computers, energy transportation networks, mobile phones, transmitters, satellite systems, robotic systems, drones, network components, electromagnetic systems and all networks of these systems along with their communication structures and software are cyberspace elements as well (Akyazı, 2012: 56; Çifçi, 2013: 5).

The population of cyberspace is daily users, criminals, malicious mannered people, organizations, institutions, international organizations, spy agents, governments, national cyber armies and intelligence services (Hundley & Anderson, 1997; Çifçi, 2013: 5).

As described above, the population of cyberspace is crowded and there are both malicious mannered people's and non-malicious people's actions on the cyberspace (Kara, 2013).

Cyber Attack

Entire planned and coordinated attacks against critical infrastructures and systems by interrupting services, stealing data, spying, exposing and infecting are called cyber-attack. The attacks could be conducted by hackers and criminals on the users who have low awareness. Ultimately, cyber-attacks are violating the data principles like confidentiality, privacy and integrity (Çakmak & Demir, 2009;; Kara, 2013)

The crowded population nature of cyberspace makes it a perfect target for a variety of attacks. The attacks may occur both in digital and physical shapes. As a result of these attacks there would be damage and panic on the target system and users (Ercan, 2015; Vasilescu, 2012).

Cyber Crime

The main difference between cyber-crime and known crime is that the cyber-crime is conducted through computer systems and networks. It is done by illegal actions such as; accessing to system, modifying data, blocking access to system and recording the communication without permission of the owner are examples of cyber-crimes. Ultimately, the cyber-crime is usage of information systems and digitally stored data for a malicious purpose. These actions could occur inside and outside of network (Corell, 2000; Çakmak & Demir, 2009).

Cyber crimes could be conducted through daily used digital products such as computers, credit cards and mobile phones. The danger and importance of cyber crimes rose in 2010s and some countries made investments in order to get benefit from this field. Attackers who are supplied by countries and self groups conducted critical attacks which threaten target states national cyber security. There are some attacker groups who made the cyber crime commercial and featured advertisements in digital platforms (Ercan, 2015; Tabansky, 2012).

Cyber Deterrence

Deterrence is taking extensive precautions as a country or community against any possible attack launch, which could the attackers the ability to control even the military forces. There are two essential points in application of deterrence strategy; firstly having intense defence strategies and capabilities. Secondary requirement is retaliation capacity and ability to handle any kind of attack (Haley, 2013).

Possession of nuclear weapons creates the intimidation towards other countries and communities but possession of cyber weapons impresses the same population too. Nuclear power is attack oriented while cyber weapons are defence oriented, so another aim of the cyber deterrence is persuading the attackers that the systems are extremely secure in order to stop the action by demonstrating the system will not be affected from the attacks. Ultimately since the cost of cyber-attacks are lower than cyber security establishment costs, some countries will follow retaliation and punishment methods against attackers rather than securing the critical infrastructures and digital systems (Lupovici, 2011).

Cyber Intelligence and Espionage

Intelligence and espionage were used throughout the history by opposing countries and communities in order to gain advantages against their opponents. Even though the importance of these concepts is not changed, the method of administration is. In earlier times, running the intelligence and espionage actions were dangerous and costly but with the development of the technology, actions became more secure and less dangerous. In addition to this, the gathered information content is a lot more than what old-fashioned methods provided. By using variety of hacking methods such as analysing the attack and threat specifications of the opponents by conducting cyber-attacks for the continuity of the state is the key concept of the cyber intelligence and espionage (Çifçi,2013; Keleştemur, 2015; Clarke & Knake, 2010).

Finally, these intelligence and espionage concepts are used for collecting the critical data from political, military and economic fields by leaking with illegal means without authorization of the owners of the systems and information. These services will create a great supremacy and information knowledge against opponents during a possible cyber war. So, cyber intelligence and cyber espionage implementations are a must for the continuity of the state in a possible cyber war (Keleştemur, 2015; Singer & Friedman, 2015; Çifçi, 2013)

National Cyber Security

National cyber security is surveillance and security of the information and communication services which are serving in the boundaries of a country. As we described above, any cyber-attack targeting the national security of a country also possesses the power to interrupt majority of services in the corresponding national area. The recent attacks on Estonia and Georgia demonstrated the magnitude of the threats. These attacks also highlighted the necessity of cyber defence strategies and precautions (Kara, 2013).

CYBER WAR

Basically, cyber war is leaking action from one country's computer to another country's computer, communication networks and systems in order to damage or disable the operation of target country's systems. Cyber war concept has two essential points; firstly, defending the country's civil and military's information technologies against enemy countries' attacks, then conducting organized attacks to opposing countries' through information and communication technologies. The enemy targets are selected through economic, politic and military issues (Çeliktaş, 2016;Yazıcı, 2011). There are variety of military force branches that dedicated to work on national cybersecurity. Some of them does not officially reflected in the press, however the existence of corresponding cyber teams are known through global cyber operations signs. Cyber defender military forces and national CERT's (Computer Emergency Response Team) are representing the official defending line while unidentified actor groups are pointing offensive side.

Especially after the cold war and technological advancements, countries are struggling in the technological field. Countries started to attack target countries with electronic and digital weapons in order to crash their systems, expose confidential information and blackmail. There are variety of attacks and purposes in the cyber war concept, but the cyber war is secret, real and includes whole world and it is spreading rapidly (Lupovici, 2011).

Cyber war concept is divided into strategic and operational subjects. Strategic cyber war is; completed attacks against governments and their people in order to change the governments' attitude while the operational cyber war is attacking into target country's systems with the military conventional attacks (Libicki, 2009).

Cyber War Incidents

Cyber war is accepted as the fifth dimension of the war, (after land, air, sea, and space) so the cyberspace is used through cyber-attacks in order to support conventional wars. Cyber war has a variety of methods and mechanisms like; espionage, manipulation, propaganda, damaging the systems via Viruses and Trojans, sabotage, fraud, etc. Therefore, the cyber-attacks targeting the countries, especially those aiming the critical infrastructures became critical point of the countries in the brackets of cyber defence (Çeliktaş, 2016, Kara,2013).

The methods and mechanisms, which are used in the cyber war will be discussed in next sections. This section will focus on cyber war incidents and effects of cyber wars on the international balance.

Siberia Natural Gas Explosion (1982)

In 1982, the explosion occurred in Siberia is accepted as the first attack which was done by the usage of cyber technology. The cyber-attack caused an explosion, which was the biggest non-nuclear explosion at the time. During the cold war, there are known espionage operations between United States of America (USA) and Soviet Union. In 1982, Russians started to steal a natural gas pipeline controller software from Canada, the corresponding software was used in the Canada region and it was a CIA (Central Intelligence Agency) trap, the USA injected a Trojan into the corresponding software. The Russians thought they were stealing a software from USA, but the USA gave them a Trojan which allowed them to steal it. On the other side of this explosion, the story goes on like this; in the beginning of the operation Russia started stealing the corresponding software, but the USA noticed the leak, so USA injected a Trojan into corresponding software rather than breaking the operation. Thereby, the stolen software broke down and increased the gas flow to unstable levels and caused a pipe to explode (Kara, 2013; John, 2013).

This is the first cyber-attack example that proves the espionage operation field must be improved. The explosion did not cause any casualties but it caused economic and material damage (Kara, 2013; Karakuş, 2013). As a result, the espionage and other war concepts must shift into digital fields immediately because the cyber intelligence as explained in this incident proves that cyber intelligence could change the international balance.

Iraq (1990)

In 1990, US commandos and cyber soldiers worked in collaboration for the gulf war. The collaboration decided to destroy Iraq's wide range radar and missile systems in the first attacks rather than their chief of staff, which was located in Bagdad. With this strategy bombing, Iraq which has the 5th biggest army would have been easier to deal with and the US would hold air superiority against Iraq. Accomplishing these was depending on bombing the radar, defence and missile systems which caused lack of communication and coordination between army and air forces of Iraq (Kara,2013).

US army intelligence unit appointed the Iraq's communication systems and listened their radio channels secretly. After a while the US army started to communicate with Iraq army through Iraq's communication systems. Therefore, the Iraq army switched communication to auxiliary channels but US army detected this as well and leaked into these channels too. After that, Iraq switched into embedded telephone network, but the US army used the same method and leaked to this communication too. Iraq army then used the hard copy delivery method as a final solution. The hard copied orders were being delivered through army trucks. This method empowered the communication and coordination of the Iraq army units, but US army interfered communication again by bombing the Iraq army trucks. Due to this move, some of the drivers refused carrying orders to commanders and some of the commanders began disobeying the orders and switched off the devices in order to stop possible location exposure. Finally, the Iraq's command and control systems were destroyed due to loss of communication (Kara, 2013; Mitnick & Simon, 2013).

The Iraq war is the first massive war which prompted the importance of cyberspace abilities and winner specification power during war (Kara, 2013). Iraq incident shows that the cyberspace abilities both in offensive and defensive aspects are more important than a crowded army; the ability of the cyber offensive and defensive techniques and methods determines the winner. as explained above, capturing the cyberspace during a war can state the winner.

Hainan Island (2001)

In 2001, a USA spy plane and China aircraft crashed and the Chinese aircraft crashed while US spy plane was damaged and forced to land to Hainan Island. After this crash, around 80 thousand Chinese cyber attackers started a "Defence operation against USA aggression". The New York Times magazine qualifies this incident as a "First World Wide Web War" (Çeliktaş, 2016; Çifçi, 2013; Smith, 2001).

Second Iraq War (2003)

In 2003, before the conventional war, USA leaked into Iraq's army network and sent thousands of e-mails through Iraq ministry of defence in order to stop affiliating of the soldiers by surrender calls. This propaganda attack accomplished successfully and enemy's defences was weakened and psychological and demotivational results occurred as well such as surrendering or leaving the duty place. When USA started attacking Iraq, they saw parked tanks rather than an offensive army. In other words, the USA hackers psychologically demotivated the Iraq's soldiers by leaking into system and sending e-mails. Old-fashioned brochure spreading methods is now replaced with e-mails and other digital materials. So, the propaganda actions demotivate the enemy with cyber war methods and effects. In this incident, there is not any information based on manipulation and technological damage, some of the specialists accepted this incident as a psychological war inside of cyber war (Çeliktaş, 2016; Kara, 2013; Clarke & Knake,2010; Çifçi, 2013).

Estonia Case (2007)

Estonian government decided to remove the red army statue, which symbolizes Soviet soldiers who died in the World War II while fighting against German Soldiers. After the statement of removing the statue, Estonia internet infrastructure, press, law, government websites, and banking services was cyber attacked three weeks in a row. The attack vector was DDOS attack, thousands of zombie nodes was attacking Estonia. Estonia was the pioneer country in Europe on the usage of e-government systems and internet technologies depended on country's system. Estonia had higher usage of the internet and information technologies than any other countries in Europe so the effects of the attack was doubled. As a result of the attacks, the biggest two banks, government parliament and presidency, political parties and ministries, three of six communication foundations received critical damage and ceased operation. Estonia requested help from NATO (North Atlantic Treaty Organization) and the Cyber Defence Excellence Collaboration Centre was created in Talin. Until today, world public opinion is not clear whether the attack origin was Russian government or intelligence services. Estonia suffered from cyber-attacks due to high dependency on the information technologies and being one of the internet consumer countries in both government and private sectors. Estonia case became a turning point of accepting the usage of the cyberspace for politic issues and competition between countries. In addition to this, this incident created questions marks on cyber war concept like; "In which conditions cyber-attacks will be accepted as cyber war?" and "How to response the cyber-attacks?" (Çeliktaş, 2016; Çakmak & Soyoğlu, 2009; Aydın, 2013).

Israel and Syria-Operation Orchard (2007)

In 2007 Israel conducted the Orchard Operation with F-15 and F-16 aircrafts which were designed and manufactured in 1970's, and bombed Syria and North Korea collaborator nuclear facility in Syria without being caught to Syrian advanced technology air defence applicances and radars. On the night of the operation, Israel leaked into Syrian defence systems and captured the management of the systems along with uploading modified resources into detection systems. So, the Russian made air defence systems and radars were not able to detect the Israel war crafts in the Syrian airspace. After this operation, rumours surfaced about the operations success and manipulation of both defence and systems. This incident proved that the latest technology products, which was promoted as provider of extremely high security measures, could be inoperable as a result of a cyber-attack and it is an absolute example of a cyber-attack. Figure 1. shows the conditions of the target (Çeliktaş, 2016; Clarke & Knake, 2010).

Georgia Case (2008)

In 2008, Russia and Georgia connections were finalized with conflicts because of the South Osetya field, which is known as a Georgian place but exist with the monetary support of the Russia. In 7 August 2008, Russia started their cyber-attacks towards Georgia's information and communication systems along with critical infrastructures. The day after the cyber-attacks, Russian army moved on to South Osetya. The attack vector was DDOS, and it was conducted through zombie nodes from Turkey, China and Canada. Zombie nodes were being controlled by a master computer, which was located in Moscow. The Georgia press and community services suffered from the attacks and as a result of the damage, outer world connection of the Georgia was interrupted. Having low internet dependency of information and communication technologies, the overall effect did not damage Georgia too much. The significance of this incident is that due to the usage of cyber weapons with conventional methods, this incident constitutes as an operational war example (Çeliktaş, 2016; Çifçi, 2013; Aydın, 2013).

Figure 1. Before and after the Orchard operation (Çeliktaş, 2016)

Stuxnet (2010)

Stuxnet case is accepted as a turning point of the cyberspace and cyber security in terms of the biggest evolvement performed. Stuxnet spread the affect around whole world but it focused especially on Iran. It leaked into Iran's nuclear facilities and disabled almost 1000 centrifuges. It interrupted the uranium enrichment programs for 2 years. The corresponding Trojan spread with Microsoft Windows OS's zero day vulnerability and was designed to target specific motherboards, thus it did not damage the standards users. This spread method and political usage makes the Stuxnet different from other malicious applications. The Trojan upload and spread case is still uncertain. The thoughts are focused on two cases; the upload could have been done by an employee with unintended manners or someone who works for Mossad could have had uploaded the Trojan through USB drive on purpose and activated it (Hagerott, 2014; Mueller & Yadegari, 2012, Aydın, 2013)

Stuxnet did not just aim the nodes, which were connected to the network, it was aimed to ICS (Industrial Control Systems) which were close to outer world too. This criteria has a critical importance and it carries an exemplary situation for the countries which does not have adequate preparation or are underdeveloped against cyber-attacks. The size and complication of Stuxnet malicious prompts that there is at least one country support behind it. The fact that even the world press could not find the real attackers, majority of the strong resources speculates that; the corresponding malicious was produced by US and Israel union. Critical point of Stuxnet is; the nodes, which were not connected to the network, could have been infected by a malicious software with the help of the human intervention. So, the cyber defence awareness creation must include the personnel who are working in their respected branches in order to ensure the cyber security and cyber defence quality (Çifçi, 2013; Mueller & Yadegari, 2012).

Shady RAT (2006-2011)

Shady RAT (Remote Access Tool) attacks was created in 2011. McAfee security firm's report explained the attacks and stated the attack periods as a 2006-2011. The attacks were APT (Advanced Persistent Threat) class espionage actions. Nowadays, considering that the international strategies and company secrets have critical importance on the economic success rates, the effect of such an action on the world's market is obvious. Evaluating the

Shady RAT in terms of size and time period, it is the most extensive cyber-attack in the cyberspace history (Çeliktaş, 2016; McAfee, 2011).

BlackEnergy and KillDisk Trojans (2014)

BlackEnergy Trojan was created in 2007 with simple DDoS attacks. Later on, corresponding Trojan started to be used for spam and online banking frauds. In 2014, BlackEnergy capabilities were; data capturing from hard drives, network exploration and RAT functions in order to control the infected node remotely. It was also detected in the specific computers in both Poland and Ukraine such as government institutions, private institutions and civil organizations computers. In 2015 BlackEnergy and KillDisk Trojans usage was specified in the cyber-attacks, which caused power failure in Ukraine. KillDisk Trojan deletes the system files in order to stop rebooting on the infected system, and it specifically designed against ICS and other critical infrastructures. Due to detection of these Trojans in the specific countries, which are against Moscow, politics prompts that; Russia behind the secene of these attacks. There are some thoughts by cyber security analysts such as; these attacks was done by some hacker groups in order to accomplish the Russian geopolitical purposes (Çeliktaş, 2016, Dean & Herridge, 2016; Lipovsky,2014).

Russia and Turkey (2015)

In 2015, Turkey was the target of one of the biggest cyber-attacks in the history of the country. The targets were 6 different DNS (Domain Name System) servers and the DDOS attacks was done in two days in a row (15 and 16 December) in order to inhibit the internet services. As a result of these attacks; 400 thousand Turkish webpages including "edu.tr", "gov.tr" and "com.tr" could not be accessed steadily for a 1 week period. Although the Anonymous hacker group undertakes the attacks, several specialists argue about this massive attack that it couldn't be accomplish by a hacker group without the support of a country. Due to time sequence between cyber-attack starting date and war craft crisis between Russia and Turkey, analysts support the idea that there could have been a possibility of country support behind the attacks (Çeliktaş, 2016).

Cyber War Preparations of Countries

Due to the rise of internet and information technology dependency and the critical results of cyber war incidents, both of the cyber power' and cyber war concepts' importance was recognized by countries and several of them started investing on this field in terms of preparing cyber security policies, building cyber armies and institutions, creating awareness and providing educating in cyber arena. Designation of national cyber strategies and developing national cyber security concepts along with products are included in this preparation aspects. Other than these main fields, cybercrime, cyber war procedures, cyber defence, cyber security practices and cyberspace standards are common concerns of the countries. Turkey, US, Russia, China, Israel, Iran, France, ITU, EU, NATO are the states which are working in cyberspace, cyber security and cyber defence areas. There are specific details of each country's strategies and methods for the areas which were titled above and each of them are capable of research content. Since this study is focusing on the cyber-attacks and cyber weapons which are invented in the purpose of cyber war, this section is not elaborated.

For the final thoughts of this section, obviously, the cyber war concept is real and it has worldwide effects, even the conventional wars are supported with the cyber intelligence services by using information and internet technologies. When consider the worldwide dependency of the information and internet technologies, the cyber weapons of the countries have critical aspects. In particular, in case of extensive cyber war, the world balance could change in terms of politics and economics.

Cyber Weapons

Almost every country has rules and regulations in conventional weapon production and usage. These rules and regulations are guideline for both internal and external connections and are continuously updated according to the requirements and developments. Modern day laws do not state certain definitions on cyber weapons, it just states weapon description. Weapon is; every single tool which used in purpose of harming systems, constructions and humans. Weapons used in order to killing, lamming, outmanoeuvring and defeating people or opponents. The weapons can be used both as offensive and defensive purposes (Brown & Metcalf, 2014; Intoccia & Moore, 2006; Mele, 2013).

The cyber weapon development is continuous, so determination of cyber weapons is not depending on security papers since the cyber weapon concept includes methods and software. Almost any software and digital service could be used as a cyber-weapon in malicious manners. Except the specific ones, the main point of stating software or method for being a cyber-weapon is the usage method, purpose, scope and results rather than official purpose of the product. Due to this inference, the majority of the information and communication technologies and services have the potential to be a cyber weapon. For instance, the social media platforms could be abused in terms of cyber espionage, information exposure and location tracking.

There is no international agreement on cyber weapons, however most of the time cyber weapons are defined as part of conventional weapons as well as computer codes which are developed in order to damage, affect, break, destroy, and threat critical infrastructures, human, plus information and communication technologies directly. Another definition of cyber weapon is; software, devices and methods which are used to destroy the enemy's information systems or target data integrity, privacy and availability which is stored in the enemy's information systems in order to destroy and interrupt the corresponding systems and services. Many of the cyber weapons are produced by governments but there are non-government agents who are producing cyber weapons as well. When we consider the volume of the cyber weapon usage and production by non-government actions in this intricacy, it is hard to compromise the cyber weapon development, spread and usage by governments and international organizations. The developers of these cyber weapons, especially those carrying high damage rate, are developed by people who are experts and have ultra-high technical knowledge with target oriented special methods which requires time and significant financial power (Rid & McBurney, 2012; Çifçi, 2013; Mele,2013; Arimatsu, 2012).

Cyber weapons are easy to produce than most of the conventional weapons in terms of time, cost and operability. Rather than conventional weapons, cyber weapons can be re-produced with lower costs, remain hidden without physical risks and spread into information and communication technologies for longer periods. Due to these advantages, non-government agents commonly use these cyber weapons. In addition to these, there are some disadvantages of cyber weapons. When a cyber-weapon is used against an opponent, in case of a second attack the attack could fail if the opponent evolved their security capabilities by taking required precautions. So, the second attack's success rate could be lower than the first attack. Due to this, a cyberweapon, which was produced against a specific target, is single use only. So, it is very difficult to anticipate the same intensity in the means of performance for next targets. Therefore, selection of time and place of the cyber weapon have critical importance on the success rate of the cyber-attack (Çeliktaş 2016; Mele, 2013).

This section identifies most common cyber weapons which are being used instead of conventional weapons. Following sections will divide the cyber weapons in two main titles as **non-specific** and **specific cyber** weapons.

Non-Specific Cyber Weapons

Common purpose of all cyber weapons is the same; harming a system, gaining superiority, having remote access, destroying the system or hardware and inhibiting the stability. These non-specific cyber weapons are not harmless, they are capable of destroying systems but they were not developed specifically against unique targets such as SCADA (Supervisory Control and Data Acquisition) systems. There are varieties of these cyber weapons available in the cyberspace. The specific cyber weapons are enhanced, customized and branded varieties of these cyber weapons.

Malicious Software (Malware)

Definition of the Malware is; a software which was developed for a malicious purpose which is used as a common cyber weapon. These are; viruses, worms, Trojans, backdoors and spywares. There are varieties of spread and infection methods of these cyber weapons, but usually the user faults, system vulnerabilities and deception methods are used for infection of target node (Çeliktaş, 2016; Ercan, 2015).

Virus

Virus is a malicious software, which embedded into a non-malicious software, in order to harm system and files. Viruses are capable of spreading through shared/copied files and software. Transfer can be done through online sharing and external storage units. Usually, viruses need human interaction to start working. There is a confusion between a Virus and a Worm, which are the most common cyber weapons. Worms are capable of working independently from software and human interaction; viruses are depended on these factors. The method embedding viruses into software is getting better day by day. So, detection of these infected files became harder, due to this evolution; users started to use security products which are capable of detecting complicated software infrastructures in order to inhibit infection (Çeliktaş, 2016; Çifçi, 2013; Keleştemur, 2015).

Worm

This is an independent malicious, which is well known and commonly used. It is capable of reproducing itself and spread into the network. To accomplish this action, it uses systems vulnerabilities and deception methods. Worms harm the systems and rapidly increase by reproducing itself, infect other nodes via e-mails and files and jam the infected node. To accomplish these actions it does not require any human interaction. (Çeliktaş, 2016; Ulaşanoğlu, 2010, Ercan, 2015; Guinchard, 2011).

Trojan

Trojans are software or software pieces which appear like non-malicious and harm the computer it installed on, in background actions. Rather than Viruses, Trojans cannot copy themselves into other computers. Trojans wait for the user interaction to start working. Trojans are designed to create backdoor in infected node in order to allow remote access. Even if the Trojan is copied to another node, it cannot do any malicious activity without user interaction (Çeliktaş, 2016; Çifçi,2013; Keleştemur, 2015; Ercan, 2015; Turhan, 2010).

Backdoor

This malicious type is designed to connect to the information and communication technologies remotely. It could be pre-installed in the systems, could install manually or embed into software. So, there are various methods to spread it. Backdoors allows connection to the system without standard authentication steps. The installation can be done due to exploitation of the systems vulnerabilities as well (Çeliktaş, 2016; Ercan, 2015, Çifçi, 2013).

Logic Bomb

This malicious is programmed to work in specific time and it mounted to software for this purpose. It waits hidden in the background of the system until the time comes, then it takes action. Logic bomb harms the system with the pre-recorded information and it can take action by the attackers' instruction as well (Çeliktaş, 2016; Ercan, 2015, Robillard, 2004).

Rootkits

These malicious hides the malicious software or code from the user and OS by modifying corresponding OS in order to inhibit the detection of these malicious applications. Rootkits allows the malicious applications to work on the OS without being detected. Due to its nature of working on the core level of OS, detection of Rootkits is tough (Çeliktaş, 2016; Çifçi, 2013; Keleştemur, 2015; Ercan, 2015).

Spyware and KeyLogger

Spyware is the common name of the applications that collect information about the person, institution or foundation without user allowance. There are varieties of Spyware malicious such as internet activity recorders and commercial software variety sender, which provides involuntary application promotions. KeyLoggers are keyboard record applications, the application records every single keyboard hit, so it could easily capture the passwords, e-mails and other personal information (Ercan, 2015; Çifçi, 2013; Keleştemur, 2015; Özdemir, 2007).

Zombie

Information and communication technologies can be controlled with small sized applications. The structure, which covers computers that are infected and controlled by attackers in order to attack to specific targets, called zombie computers. These computers controlled by the real attackers with specific software varieties and they are ready to use. Frequently, the Zombie computers are used in large scaled attacks (Ercan, 2015; Arora, 2012; Güngör, 2015).

Attack Kits

The toolset, which is able to conduct several cyber-attacks and malicious attempts without requiring any cyber skill or knowledge are called an Attack Kit. There are varieties of these toolsets in the market such as free ones and paid ones. These toolsets can transform a normal user into an effective attacker (Çeliktaş, Symantec, 2011).

Zero Day Vulnerabilities

Zero Day Vulnerabilities are new vulnerabilities of systems, which are not known by the society including security firms and producers. Usually, all systems which are being used as corresponding products, are exploitable too. These are critical vulnerabilities which can be activated with an attack or a cyber-weapon. Due to its importance, it is available on vulnerability stores and sometimes security firms and governments purchase them. While security firms are using these vulnerabilities in order to provide a more secure environment for their customers, there are some agents who buy these vulnerabilities in order to create cyber weapons. (Singer & Friedman, 2014; Shakarian et al, 2013).

Ransomware

These malicious locks the computer in order to leak money from the user via blackmailing. The locking phase depends on the type of Ransomware; some of the varieties locks the system at startup and some of them encrypts data and files which are located in the infected system. Strong encryption mechanisms are used in order to inhibit the decryption of the files by the user. After the encryption or lock, attackers request an amount of money and give time for the payment. If the user don't obey the time limitation, attacker increases the ransom amount or deletes data and files on their computers. These malicious varieties usually spread by security vulnerabilities and Trojans (Çeliktaş, 2016; Symantec, 2015).

Advanced Persistent Threats (APT)

These are cyber threats which are designed against specifically aimed targets. The production aspects of this cyber weapons are specific for a certain target and purposes are stated explicitly. Due to these privatizations, these cyber weapons are capable of conducting impactful cyber-attacks. APT's involve long-term threats and they are developed for cyber war. APT's are used for advanced threats and specially developed attack methods. So, APT's could work on the target system without being detected for a long period. Usually

APT's are developed with support of government or groups. APT's usually aim governments' critical infrastructures (Kara, 2013; Çeliktaş, 2016; Bircan, 2012).

Critical Infrastructure Targeted Cyber Weapons

As explained in the beginning of this section; specific cyber weapons are depended on non-specific cyber weapons. These are enhanced, customized and branded varieties of these non-specific cyber weapons. Being unique and specific usually depends on the target. For instance, a malicious which affects just a particular OS does not have to be a specific cyber weapon. Being a specific cyber weapon depends on target oriented customization of a malicious which is capable of destroying the target at least in one critical point such as social, economic, politic and military. For instance, the zero day vulnerabilities was commonly used to create specific cyber weapons.

Stuxnet

As explained before, it is the first known complex software. After analysing, security experts stated that it is not a basic worm. Several experts with great scale investments professionally built it. The aim of this cyber weapon is critical infrastructures and it is designed to capture management of industrial systems by passing through Windows systems to special systems which are used in management of the critical infrastructures. It destroyed the Iranian nuclear centrifuges in order to stop uranium enrichment project (Kara, 2013).

Duqu

Duqu malicious was created a year after the Stuxnet and there are major similarities between them. Due to these similarities, the developers of Stuxnet and Duqu may be considered the same or developers of Duqu might have seen the Stuxnet resource code. Both of them were seen in Iran. The common points of these two malicious are; both of them spreaded through zero day vulnerabilities and targeted critical infrastructures. The difference between Stuxnet and Duqu is; Stuxnet is destruction oriented while Duqu is information gathering oriented. Unlike Stuxnet, Duqu deletes itself from the infected system after 36 days. In addition to this, Duqu indicates the prudential threats. Gathering information from SCADA systems means determination of strengths and weaknesses of the system, which means a variety of different Stuxnet version could be developed (Kara, 2013).

Flame

Flame malicious was designed in 2012 and it is 20 times effective than Stuxnet. This complex structured malicious specifically targeted Middle Eastern area and the purpose of this malicious is information leakage. The countries affected from this malicious are; Iran, Israel, Sudan, Syria, Saudi Arabia and Egypt, there are more than 1000 computer which was infected with Flame (Kara, 2013).

Gauss

Gauss malicious was created in 2012. It was deigned to spy on online banking actions in order to steal critical information and banking account details. There are some similarities between Gauss and Flame; Gauss targeted the Middle Eastern area like Flame but it was designed to steal different information than Flame. The countries which were affected from this malicious, are Lebanon, Israel and Palestine, there are more than 2000 computers were infected by Gauss (Kara, 2013).

Tinba

Tinba malicious was discovered in June 2012 by Denmark security laboratories In September 2012, TrendMicro security company release the Tinba analyse report. According to these reports Tinba is specialized specifically for Turkey and it is capable of stealing information, listen to network traffic and conduct MITM (Man In The Middle) attacks. There are more than 60 thousand users affected from this malicious (Kara, 2013).

Shamoon

Shamoon is a malicious targeted for energy sector and it operates with the purpose of damage. Discovery of Shamoon happened through a cyber-attack which targeted Saudi Arabian petrol company Aramco in 15 August 2012. As a result of a few hours cyber-attack; 30.000 computers were damaged and become unserviceable. A hacker group undertook the attacks and the group stated that the reason of the attacks was politicalally rhetorical in nature (Kara, 2013).

As a result of this section we can state that the war concept became a more effective and silent method in cyberspace. Due to the existence of cyber weapons, technologies and concepts, it is obvious that cyber war concept will be more destructive in the future. So all users, including countries will be more concerned about cyberspace and will consider it as a place of war.

CYBER WAR ATTACK AND DEFENCE CLASSIFICATIONS

This section focuses on cyber-attack methods which are used in cyber war concepts. The classifications are applied methods of the cyber weapons which are being used by security professionals, attackers and intelligence services along with military forces.

There are several attack vectors and strategies in cyber world, but the backbone of these attacks is depending on classical and most known strategies which will be discussed in this chapter. However, whereas majority of the sophisticated attack vectors and strategies are evolved and improved varieties of these structure, there are new methods and styles discovered on current technologies of the century.

Attack Methods

These methods and concepts are used by both security professionals and attackers but their purposes are different; while security professionals focus on the vulnerability patching, the attackers focus on exploiting the vulnerabilities in order to acquire profit or inflict damage. There are several steps for taking over a specific system. They are; (Akyıldız, 2013).

- Information Gathering
- System and Network Exploration
- Vulnerability Scanning
- Exploiting the Vulnerabilities
- Obtain System
- Clearing Logs

Information Gathering

This is the foundation step of the system analysis. Due to the results of the information gathering process, the attack methods, tools and results. The information gathering can be completed by open source tools passively or by interaction with the system directly (Akyıldız, 2013). There are varieties of passive information gathering tools, which provide detailed information about the target system. The tools can be helpful for finding IP (Internet Protocol) range, DNS (Domain Name System) records, along with user details. The advantage of these tools is; these methods will not leave a trace because there is no communication with the target. Several open source information gathering tools are listed below; (Akyıldız, 2013;Burlu, 2015; Elbahadır, 2016).

- http://whois.domaintools.com
- http://www.ripe.net
- http://www.centralops.net
- https://www.shodan.io/
- https://www.arin.net/
- Google Search
- Maltego
- Wireshark
- Nmap

There are various tools for these services such as **Maltego, Wireshrak, Nmap** and etc. which provides detailed information about specific targets. Apart from these, there are varieties and script variations of these services which was made both by security researchers and attackers. Due to the usage of these kinds of tools and services, collection of information is required such as mail lists, social media information, network path, service version, ISP (Internet Service Provider), Domains and DNS details. This gathered information is enough to conduct several attacks to a specific target.

Physical Attacks

Data signal transferring starts in the physical layer like cables and transmitters. So, with the help of external tools it is possible to execute malicious activities on signals such as obtaining and manipulating. The attack would be able to collect whole traffic between connected nodes (Akyıldız, 2013, Çeliktaş, 2016; Yıldız, 2014).

Social Engineering

Social Engineering is human deception art and in this attack, the attacker is called a social engineer. The social engineering hacks humans. Rather than computer hacking, it depends on persuasion methods and exploitation of human vulnerabilities like; communication methods, ways of thinking, trust, assistance and other emotions. Social engineering is an effective way of attacking and it could help with passing cyber security processes or get over some procedures. These all depend on the creativity of the social engineer. The most known social engineering methods and techniques are; creating fake scenarios, introducing himself/herself as a trustable person and offering rewards in order to leak information. (Yıldız, 2014; Bican, 2008 Keleştemur,2015, Çifçi,2013).

The success of a social engineering's attack depends on the attacker's skills such as deception, trust and impression. Having these qualifications and creating real-like scenarios will provide outstanding results. Since humans are the weakest point of the security, the attacks of a social engineering will always be a critical threat. Human factor is always critical both in positive and negative ways. For instance, a million dollars' worth security device may not notice a leakage or attack which is out of the product's scope. Or there may be a zero-day attack. But the human factor is able to notice these attempts. Another side of this advantage is, due to human emotions and mistake rate of humans, a person could damage a system on purpose or by mistake. Since attack methods and scenarios are depending on the attacker's creativity, there could be combination of different attack methods as well.

Digital Manipulation

This method is commonly used by intelligence and security units. The aim of this attack is deceiving or misleading the public opinion by modifying any image or video files by using computer tools and software (Çeliktaş, 2016; Gürkaynak & İren, 2011; Türkay, 2013).

Cryptologic Attacks

These attacks are aimed to break a password and code in order to obtain, access and manipulate the protected data and communication. There are several attack varieties like; MITM attacks, Brute Forcing, Dictionary Attack, WEP, WPA/WPA2, Chipper Text Only, Known Plaintext, Adaptive Chosen Plaintext and Related Key Attack (Keleştemur, 2015; Canbek & Sağıroğlu, 2007).

Man In The Middle Attacks (MITM)

This attack allows the hacker to operate between target and communicated platform. So, the communication traffic flows through attacker and the attacker acquires entire communication. There are varieties of this attack, ARP poisoning method is explained below: ARP (Address Resolution Protocol) analyses the IP address in order to find the MAC (Media Access Control) address. Gratuitous ARP packages informes packages that they are sent in case of MAC address alteration of IP address. Attackers sniff the traffic by exploiting these protocol's functions. (Akyıldız, 2016; 2013). Figure 2. illustrates MITM attack models;

MAC Flooding Attacks

CAM (Content Addressable Memory) table holds all IP and MAC addresses which are present on the switch. There is a capacity of corresponding table and MAC flooding attacks aimed to fill this capacity by facing the MAC addresses in order to force the switch to work as a hub. In this case, switch lose its feature and start using all ports for delivering packages. So, attacker would be able to capture the packages and get important information of the users by listening to the ports (Akyıldız, 2013; Wilkins & Smith, 2011).

DNS Attacks

DNS is the name converting system of IP addresses. The web addresses would be catchier, due to hardness of remembering IP addresses. DNS system uses word-masking method for IP addresses and when a user types a specific web address, the word phases are converted to IP address, thus the user sends request to corresponding page. DNS systems hold the IP and name conversion records. Due to this important functionality of DNS, the

Figure 2. MITM attack models illustration

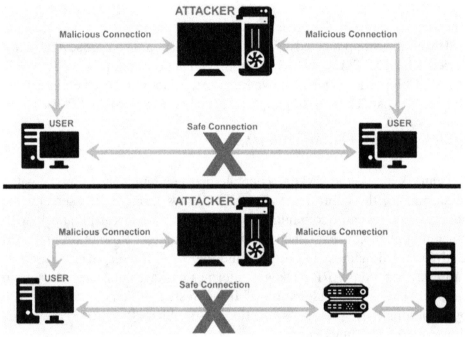

attacks that target DNS systems could manipulate the route to fake web pages in order to gather information of the rerouted request host. Searching a web page represents a DNS request and there are two types of DNS requests; Recursive and Iterative. Iterative requests are the requests between last user and DNS server. Iterative requests are the requests between DNS servers. There are several attack methods which targets DNS, most popular DNS attacks are listed below. (Akyıldız, 2013; Northurp & Mackin,2011). Figure 3 illustrates DNS working mechanism;

Phishing

Phishing is copying a specific web page or creating a fake one and re-routing the last users to these malicious web pages through DNS. The aim is stealing personal information of the user. There are several known scenarios for this attack; like asking information or providing a link and request following of the instructions as a competent authority (Akyıldız, 2013; Northurp & Mackin,2011; Çifçi, 2013). Conducting this kind of attacks was not easy until the automatized attack tools become popular. Now there are varieties of automatized tools which do not require any programming skills to conduct

Figure 3. DNS structure

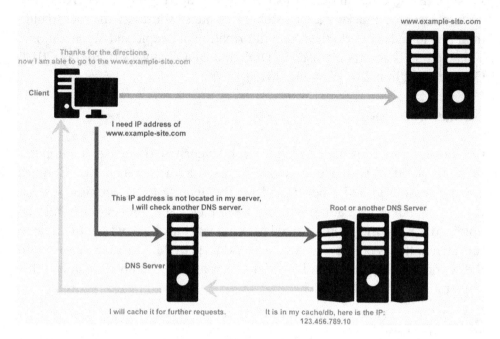

such attacks. For instance, SET (Social Engineering Toolset) is capable of various attacks such as mentioned above.

Pharming

Pharming is changing the DNS conversions in order to attack the last users. So, when the user makes a request towards the official trustable website they will be redirected to another website because of manipulation (Akyıldız, 2013; Northurp & Mackin,2011).

DNS Spoofing

By conducting MITM attacks in LAN (Local Network Area), the attacker could inhibit the DNS server's request to the last user and answer to the request through fake DNS in order to reroute the last user to a specific website (Akyıldız, 2013; Northurp & Mackin,2011).

IP Spoofing

IP spoofing is hiding the source IP address of the attack vector. IP Spoofing is done by changing the IP addresses of the packet's header with secure systems IP addresses in order to show the package is coming from a secure system. Usually, attackers use trustable website IP addresses in order to hide their real id and access to the secret information of people and organizations. This method is commonly used in DOS and DDOS attacks (Çeliktaş, 2016; Girkaynak & İren, 2011; Aydın, 2013).

Cookie Injection

Cookies are tiny files which are placed by websites to the user's computer in order to identify the corresponding user as a member. So, Cookies contain session id and other user data. By stealing these cookies, session of corresponding user along with personal pages and information could be obtained. Lately, the popular social network site Facebook was vulnerable to this attack. It was possible to steal user Cookies by MITM attack and obtain the session of the corresponding user. After a while Facebook patched this vulnerability (Akyıldız, 2013).

SQL Injection

SQL (Structured Query Language) organizes the data recording system that works by recording the data in tables and calls the data from tables when it is required. It is possible to acquire the database and locate a backdoor in the system by exploiting the SQL vulnerabilities. Rather than SQL vulnerabilities, there could be logical vulnerabilities in the system if the required precautions are not taken by the responsible authorities. Most common logical vulnerability finding statements are; "Admin ' or 1=1 " and "having 1=11--" (Akyıldız, 2013; Gupta, 2006). There are varieties of these logical tests which are more advanced. Usually, the usage of the attack vectors and vulnerabilities are directly proportional with the attacker's imagination, so stating all of the methods is almost impossible.

XSS Vulnerabilities

XSS (Cross Site Scripting) vulnerabilities depends on the coding mistakes in the web level. There are varieties for XSS attacks but usually the XSS attacks are cookie targeted in order to steal the session of the target. XSS attacks are done by manipulating the scripts, which are sent by the server to the last user and due to this modification, the attacker could steal the Cookies and session information of the target. The server asks for provided Cookies in order to identify the user and attacker's aim is to obtain this cookie (Akyıldız, 2013, Demir, 2013). Figure 4 illustrates XSS attack model (Exploiting the XSS vulnerabilities).

Reflected XSS Attack

This attack is performed directly with the help of the target user. The attacker sends a malicious link to a specific user through a vulnerable website and when user follows the link, they are redirected to the malicious website and attacker obtain the session and login details (Akyıldız, 2013; Demir, 2013; Stuttard & Pinto, 2011).

Stored XSS Attack

In this attack, the attacker targets the website and inserts malicious codes to a specific point or a page of the XSS vulnerable website. When the target visits the corresponding page, the attacker obtains Cookie information (Akyıldız, 2013; Demir, 2013; Stuttard & Pinto, 2011).

Figure 4. XSS attack model

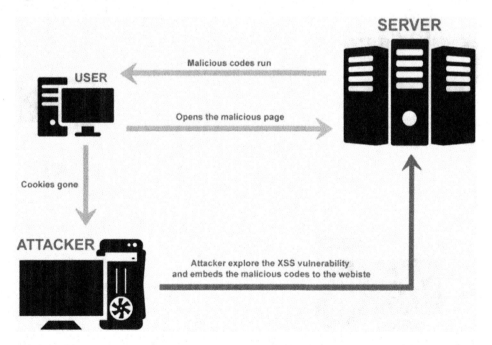

CSRF Attacks

This attack is similar to XSS attack and it's done via sending links like in XSS attacks. The major difference between XSS and CSRF is; XSS attacks conducted through trusted websites of the users and CSRF attacks conducted through trusted users of the website. As a result of CSRF attack, there may be varieties of results that could be obtained by the attacker such as session information and most importantly, the attacker can easily manipulate the user actions by a single link as shown below (Elbahadır, 2016).

```
<IMG SRC="http://VulnerablePage/?Command">
<SCRIPT SRC="http://VulnerablePage/?Command">
<IFRAME SRC="http://VulnerablePage/?Command">
```

The commands can be for purchasing a specific item or money transfer, as mentioned before, the command section is up to attacker's imagination and purpose. Figure 5 illustrates the CSRF attack model.

Figure 5. CSRF attack model

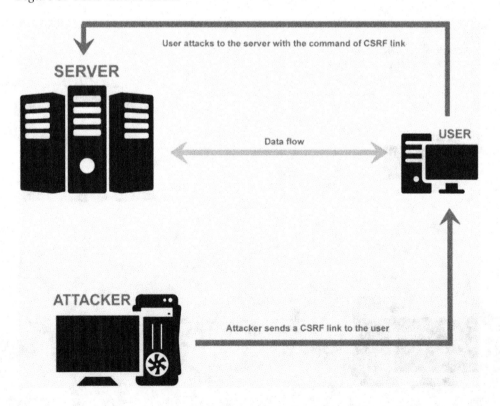

DOS and DDOS Attacks

This is one of the most effective attacks which does not require considerable technical skill and knowledge. Usually, attackers use DOS and DDOS attacks when they cannot access the system with an unauthorized id. Purpose of conducting these attacks are stopping the system services by overloading so attackers hinder the usage of the corresponding system for everyone. DOS attack sends packages in order to overload the bandwidth of the system. If the incoming requests bandwidth is greater than the target system, target service could stop working and there aren't any solutions for this case. DDOS attack is conducting the same attack methodology with one difference; DDOS attack sends the requests collectively with zombie nodes. So, the resistance time of the target will decrease and the damage rate will increase. DDOS attacks are conducted through zombie nodes and botnet in a disperse why so detection of the sources becomes a harder task. Due to this advantages usage of DDOS became frequent. Botnet attack is a variety of DDOS attack which is controlled through IRC (Internet Relay Chat) channels and websites. Botnet systems depends on zombie nodes as well. While there are varieties of botnet types, there are different DOS attack method as well (Akyıldız, 2013; Burlu 2015; Keleştemur,2015). Figure 6 illustrates the DDOS attack model.

SYN Flood Attack

In this DOS attack type, the attacker sends SYN packages (SYNchronize Packages contain system information of the requester node) through spoofed IP addresses in order to fill the firewall's state table. After that, the system could be inaccessible with bandwidth overflow (Akyıldız, 2013; Burlu, 2015).

ACK Flood Attack

In this attack, the system is accessed by inhibiting extreme numbers of sent ACK packages (Akyıldız, 2013).

UDP Flood Attack

The aim of this attack is inhibiting the system usage by sending UDP (User Datagram Protocol) packages. There is no confirmation mechanism in UDP so IP spoofing is more effective in the UDP used systems (Akyıldız, 2013).

Figure 6. DDOS attack model

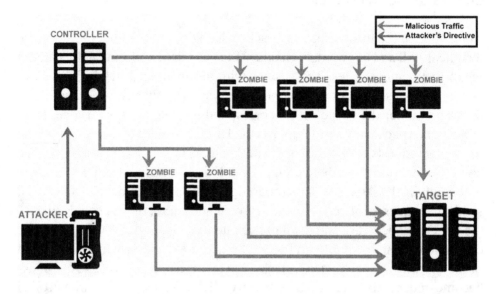

HTTP Flood

In this attack, the system services are ceased by sending consistently massive HTTP requests (Akyılız, 2013; Burlu, 2015).

Smurf Attack

In this attack, attacker sends massive ping packages to several systems but replaces the packages' resource IP addresses with the target's IP addresses, so the systems attack to the attacker's target while replying the ping package requests (Burlu, 2015).

Ping of Death Attack

65535 byte is the upper limit of a ping package, the bigger sized packages can divided and transferred but the main point of these structure is; a system have to reply the package with the received size. Due to structure rules, the attacker sends the target 65535 sized ping packages until the target cannot handle it and become inaccessible. The replying case of these massive ping packages is not an issue, attacker could replace the resource IP address with another system IP address and the attack could be in two ways without receiving any massive ping package (Burlu, 2015).

File Inclusion and Remote Code Execution

Unsecure programming methods, lack of experience, knowledge and lack of attention causes vulnerabilities in webpages such as File Inclusion, Command Injection and Remote Code Execution which are critical vulnerabilities. When an attacker exploits one kind of these vulnerabilities, the server will be a target for a threat as well as the website. Due to the importance of these vulnerabilities, there is an opportunity to run commands in order to get the server and manage or manipulate the whole server along with hosting websites (Elbahadır,2016; Burlu, 2016). Figure 7 illustrates the corresponding attacks (Remote Code Execution/ File Inclusion).

Cyber Defence

Cyber defence is the security and precaution actions of the cyberspace products such as; software, hardware, network, and the products which are made by combinations of these systems along with the sub systems, equipment and infrastructures in order to defend them against any possible cyber threats. These systems and services faces the problems like operating slow or shutting down. So taking the precautions is important and with the supports of the precautions, the system could work consistently against some attacks which means, the stress handling rate increases. Supporting the system just with cyber actions is not enough. The officers or employees must be able to re-

Figure 7. Remote code execution/ file inclusion attack model

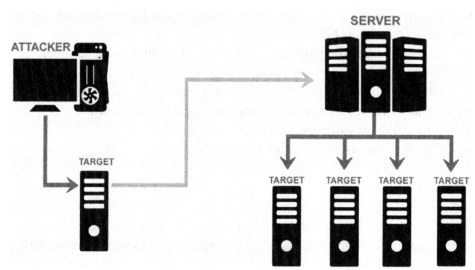

operate the damaged products and services (Ercan, 2015; Kararslan et al., 2008; Çifçi, 2012).

Cyber defence is a critical aspect like the attack aspect as well. Some authorities do not focus on the cyber defence area and covering the defence concept with empowering the attack capabilities. There are several methods and concepts which provides more secure cyber environment for the users. In this case, the users could be a state, organization or an individual user. Depending on the dependency of the cyberspace and information technology products, it is obvious to say that the attack methods and cyber weapons which are explained in previous sections are capable of affecting every single online node in the world. Due to these critical points of the cyber war reality, the countermeasures of these attacks and threats must be taken before any attack by every single user and authority because there is no absolute security in the cyberspace and depending on the attack and attacker, the precautions could stop or reduce the damage rate.

Fundamentals of Cyber Defence Concept

Main qualifications of the cyber security methods and strategies are listed below; (Ercan, 2015; Çifçi, 2012; Keleştemur,2015; Çeliktaş,2016).

- Capability of cyber threat analysis,
- Defending the information technologies against any cyber-attack,
- Blocking unauthorized access attempts both in physical and digital aspects,
- Developing the information technologies and their infrastructure as durable to against physical attacks,
- Determining and blocking the cyber-attacks with instant respond,
- Vulnerability analysis and patch,
- Global malware, malicious activity and zero day vulnerability analysis,
- Conducting security assessments and taking precautions,
- Improving the awareness and education grades,
- Creating coordination with required authorities.

Firewall

Firewalls are connection filters of the systems. These products analyses every single package that interacts with the system in order to keep the connection under control to inhibit the unauthorized access attempts. There are varieties of scanning methods of the Firewalls such as data transferring, web filtering, port filtering and content filtering. Setup aspect of these products is important and must be completed by a well-versed people in order to adjust the security configurations to stand against any possible threats (Arora, 2012; Ercan, 2015; Kaya & Öğün, 2009).

Intrusion Detection: Prevention System (IDS/IDP)

This product works concertedly with firewall systems in order to reprogram the firewall and stop the attacks in case of malicious and suspicious activities. IDS/IDP systems monitors the network activity and packages in order to take action against any threat.

Data Loss Prevention DLP

This is a hardware nod software combination system which monitors the network activities with blocking abilities in order to inhibit the data leak actions through network.

Network Access Control (NAC)

Corresponding system controls and verifies the node which is about to connect to the specific network in terms of security policies and required provisioning. If the node meets the requirements, the system permits the connection request and if it doesn't meeting the pre-requirements, the system directs the corresponding node to the concerned servers in order to complete the pre-requirements (Çeliktaş, 2016; Çifçi, 2013; Keleştemur 2015).

Honeypot

Briefly, Honeypots are trap systems which looks like a part of the main system. The aims of the Honeypots are detecting the attackers and the attacker's methodologies in order to decrease the attacks which damages the system, in addition to this, it takes precautions against detected attacks. As it can be seen, Honeypot's strength and benefits comes from attacks and vulnerabilities which are not fixed on purpose so the attackers will try to leak to the systems through Honeypot and will get caught by the security staff (Çeliktaş, 2016).

Antivirus

These are malicious detection and clearing software systems. Antivirus software monitors whole activities of the node and detects the malicious varieties before accessing to the systems and automatically deletes them. Another feature of the common Antivirus software is; detecting and deleting the malicious varieties which are inside the systems, warning the users about the suspicious files and blocking the access to the malicious files. Antiviruses must be up to date in order to work properly and provide secure digital environment. However they are not capable of protecting the system alone, there is a need for another fundamental security concept like firewall etc. (Çifçi, 2013, Ercan, 2015, Keleştemur, 2015).

Content Filter and Anti-Spam

This system filters whole traffic and disables particular websites, words, pictures, e-mails and applications in order to block the undesirable contents (Çeliktaş, 2016; Ercan, 2015).

Endpoint Security

This integrated system holds several security mechanisms such as Firewall, Antivirus, IDS/IDP, DLP and NAC in order to manage the whole security operations of the corresponding authority from one platform (Çifçi, 2013; Keleştemur, 2015).

Digital Forensics

In any legal status, the information which is located in the information and communication systems must analysed in order to impartial enforcement of laws. These systems allow collection and analysis of evidences without damaging the information security concepts from information and communication systems (Çeliktaş, 2016, Ercan, 2015).

Cryptography

Cryptography includes all of the used mathematical algorithms and methods in order to provide entire security principles of the information security. In other words; the methods which are protecting the transferred data between sender and receiver against any attack. In addition to this securing aspect, it also covers hiding the receiver and sender information from malicious attempts too (Çeliktaş, 2016).

Digital Signature

Digital Signature is common name of the digital authentication systems. There are varieties of digital signatures such as cryptology methods, biometric methods and signature files. Especially the cryptology methods are commonly used and these methods support the reliability, integrity, and nonrepudiation qualifications of the information security (Ercan, 2015; Ermiş, 2006; Yılmaz & Salcan, 2008; Gennaro & Rohatni, 2001).

Vulnerability Scanners

These are automated systems which provide variety of attack tests and reports about the systems. The analysis could be conducted against computers, network, operating systems and applications (Çeliktaş, 2016).

Cyber Awareness

The all security concepts could fail if the human factor ignored so the improvement of the human factor threats is the key concept of the cyber defence. There is a correlation between weakest points and the attack strength, so the education and cyber awareness has critical importance. The social engineering attacks could manipulate the human ideas with malicious purpose. So, the precautions must be taken by supporting the digital and physical products with education (Yıldız, 2014).

CONCLUSION

Information and communication technologies development is rising rapidly. As a result of this rapid development and flexible structure, the dependency of these technologies is increasing both in user and country aspects. Effective usage ability of these technologies without limitations creates the requirement of cyber security and national cyber security concepts.

Countries and security professionals accept the cyber war concept as a new generation war zone. Therefore, cyberspace became an investment point of war. Nowadays, majority of the countries and several groups are taking action in the cyberspace in order to solve political conflicts and accomplish other connections. Cyber war concept is a continuous progress, when the opponents are not fighting with each other, they are trying to leak information in order to gain advantage or develop specific cyber weapons. Consequently, the importance and value of information have increased. Evolved security concepts and mechanisms provide safer cyberspace for the users, but since the attack and defence concepts are interconnected new solutions bring stronger attack methods after.

Specific cyber weapons developed by evolving and customizing nonspecific cyber weapons against particular targets. Critical infrastructures are common target of the specific cyber weapons. Cyber weapon choice depends on the advantages like; low cost and high damage rate, ease of appliance, flexible structure and non-life threatening. Almost all technological developments, products and investments have a potential to be a cyber-weapon. Cyber weapon trading operations continue in the background both in country and group aspects. In time, the varieties of cyber weapons will increase with the migration of real life war methods and strategies into cyber war concept.

Usage of expensive security systems and products cannot be accepted as a successful solution, there must be investment on the national products and systems along with methods in order to stay safe and steady in the cyber world. The investments must be divided into several points such as education, awareness, developing and producing hardware, software and qualified person.

The scope of cyber war indicates that the development of a national operating system, national hardware and national network infrastructure is inevitable. It is not a smart move to rely on technologies that are developed by different countries which contains variety of vulnerabilities that might affect entire country's critical infrastructures, communications and securities. To put in different way, outcome of usage non-national products indicated that the vulnerabilities of the services leads to variety of issues such as personal data theft, organizational data security, data leakage and violation of personal privacy. There must be specific precautions that must be taken into consideration while using non-national OS varieties. Further studies can be carried out to expose different service vulnerabilities of these OS varieties and propose several patches for them to prevent country-wide infections.

Ultimately, since the cyber war continues secretly even than before, there are several precautions which must be taken by country authorities and users; like increasing awareness and education levels, implementing national hardware and software solutions, settling national policies, applying decisive supervision, investment and evaluation. The mentioned domains' synthesis is the major necessity of proactive security. Proactive security concept is new generation solution for both offensive and defensive aspects and it is highly depended on being up-to-date and ready in terms of background, technology, structure, competence and cyber maturity. The corresponding concept always focus on ultimate analysis and predict the future and possible threats before they happen. This perspective always helps the implementer sides to be "one step ahead" against the threats, so it gives an opportunity to take required actions before the attack instead of running recovery actions after the attack. All the utilized solutions are defensive actions which need to be implemented at country level. The other precautions include international agreements about cybercrime and cyber war criteria and concepts. The combination of cyber dependency and growth of cyberspace along with contents of cyberspace prompts that cyber war and weapons going to be much more capable and influential than today and it is obvious that the cyber war actions will keep increasing and became significant power of the countries in terms of changing the balance of the world.

REFERENCES

Akyazı, U. (2012). *Siber Harekât Ortamının Siber Güvenlik Tatbikatları Kapsamında Değerlendirilmesi.* İstanbul: Harp Akademileri Basımevi.

Akyıldız, A. M. (2013). *Siber Güvenlik Açısından Sızma Testlerinin Uygulamalar İle Değerlendirilmesi* (MSc thesis). Süleyman Demirel Üniversitesi Fen Bilimler Enstitüsü.

Akyıldız, M. A. (2016). *Uygulamalarla Siber Güvenliğe Giriş (2nd ed.).* Ankara: Ltd. Şti.

Arimatsu, L. (2012). A Treaty for Governing Cyber-Weapons: Potential Benefits and Practical Limitations. In *4th International Conference on Cyber Conflict*. Talinn: NATO CCD COE Publications.

Arora, M. (2012). E-Security Issues. *International Journal of Computers and Technology*, *3*(2), 301–305.

Atalay, A. H. (2012). *Kurumsal Bilgi Güvenliği*, Siber Güvenlik. *Mimar ve Mühendis Dergisi*, *68*, 42–47.

Aydın, M. (Ed.). (2013). *21.Yüzyılda Siber Güvenlik, 1.Baskı*. İstanbul: İstanbul Bilgi Üniversitesi Yayınları.

Bican, C. (2008). *Sosyal Mühendislik Saldırıları - Ulusal Bilgi Güvenliği Kapısı*. Retrieved from https://www.bilgiguvenligi.gov.tr/sosyal-muhendislik/sosyal-muhendislik-saldirilari-3.html

Bircan, B. (2012). *Gelişmiş Siber Silahlar ve Tespit Yöntemleri*. Tübitak Bilgem. Retrieved from http://docplayer.biz.tr/1142152-Gelismis-siber-silahlar-ve-tespit-yontemleri-bahtiyar-bircan uzman-arastirmaci-siber-guvenlik-enstitusu.html

Brown, G. D., & Metcalf, A. O. (2014). Easier Said Than Done: Legal Reviews of Cyber Weapons. *Journal of National Security Law and Policy*, *7*(115), 115–138.

BTK (Bilgi Teknolojileri ve İletişim Kurumu). (2009). *Siber Güvenliğin Sağlanması: Türkiye'deMevcut Durum ve Alınması Gereken Tedbirler*. Retrieved from https://www.btk.gov.tr/File/?path=ROOT%2F1%2FDocuments%2FSayfalar%2FSiberGuvenlik %2Fsg.pdf

Burlu, K. (2015). *Bilişimin Karanlık Yüzü (5th ed.)*. Ankara: Sinemis Yayın Grup.

Çakmak, H., & Demir, C. K. (2009). Siber Dünyadaki Tehdit ve Kavramlar. In Suç, Terör ve Savaş Üçgeninde Siber Dünya (pp. 23-54). Ankara: Barış Platin Kitabevi.

Çakmak, H., & Soyoğlu, İ. K. (2009). Doğu Avrupa ve Asya'dan Siber Saldırı Örnekleri. In Suç, Terör ve Savaş Üçgeninde Siber Dünya (pp. 111-136). Ankara: Barış Platin Kitabevi.

Canbek, G., & Sağıroğlu, Ş. (2007). Bilgisayar Sistemlerine Yapılan Saldırılar ve Türleri:Bir İnceleme. *Erciyes Üniversitesi Fen Bilimleri Enstitüsü Dergisi, 23*(1-2), 1–12.

Çeliktaş, B. (2016). *Siber Güvenlik Kavraminin Gelişimi Ve Türkiye Özelinde Bir Değerlendirme* (MSc thesis). Karadeniz Technical University Social Sciences İnstitute.

Çifçi, H. (2012). Her Yönüyle Siber Savaş. TÜBİTAK Popüler Bilim Kitapları, 37, 134-135.

Çifçi, H. (2013). *Her Yönüyle Siber Savaş*. İstanbul: TÜBİTAK Popüler Bilim Kitapları.

Clarke, A. R., & Knake, K. R. (2010). Cyber War: The Next Threat to National Security and What to do About It. New York: Academic Press.

Corell, H. (2000). *The Challenge of Borderless Cyber-Crime*. Symposium On The Occasion of The Signiing of The United Nations Convention Against Transnational Organized Crime, Palermo, Italy. Retrieved from http://legal.un.org/ola/media/info_from_lc/cybercrime.pdf

Dean, M., & Herridge, C. (2016). Patriotic Hackers' Attacking on Behalf of Mother Russia. *Fox News*. Retrieved from http://www.foxnews.com/politics/2016/01/16/patriotic-hackers-attacking-on-behalf-mother -russia.html

Demir, B. (2013). Yazılım Güvenliği Saldırı Ve Savunma. Dikeysen Yayın Dağıtım, 423.

Elbahadır, H. (2016). *Hacking Interface. In KODLAB Yayın Dağıtım Yazılım ve Eğitim Hizmetleri San*. İstanbul: Ve Tic. Ltd. Şti.

Ercan, M. (2015). *Kritik Altyapilarin Korunmasina İlişkin Belirlenen Siber Güvenlik Stratejileri* (MSc thesis). Gebze Technical University.

Ermiş, K. (2006). Sayısal İmza ve Elektronik Belge Yönetimi. *Bilgi Dünyası, 7*(1), 121–146.

Gennaro, R., & Rohatni, P. (2001). How to Sign Digital Streams. *Information and Computation, 165*(1), 100–116. doi:10.1006/inco.2000.2916

Guinchard, A. (2011). Between Hype and Understatement- Reassessing Cyber Risks as a Security Strategy. *Journal of Strategic Security, 4*(2), 87. doi:10.5038/1944-0472.4.2.5

Güngör, M. (2015). *Ulusal Bilgi Güvenliği: Strateji ve Kurumsal Yapılanma* (PhD thesis). Uzmanlık Tezi, T.C. Kalkınma Bakanlığı, Bilgi Toplumu Dairesi Başkanlığı.

Gupta, S. (2006). *Foundstone Hacme Bank v2.0™ Software Security Training Application User and Solution Guide*. Retrieved from http://www.mcafee.com/us/resources/whitepapers/foundstone/wp-hacmebank-v2-user-guide.pdf

Gürkaynak, M., & İren, Â. A. (2011). Reel Dünyada Sanal Açmaz: Siber Alanda Uluslararası İlişkiler. *Süleyman Demirel Üniversitesi İktisadi ve İdari Bilimler Dergisi, 16*(2), 263–279.

Hagerott, M. (2014). Stuxnet and the vital role of critical infrastructure operators and engineers. *International Journal of Critical Infrastructure Protection, 7*(4), 244–246. doi:10.1016/j.ijcip.2014.09.001

Haley, C. (2013). A Theory of Cyber Deterrence. *Georgetown Journal of International Affairs*. Retrieved from http://journal.georgetown.edu/a-theory-of-cyberdeterrence-christopher-haley/

Hildreth, S. A. (2001). *Cyberwarfare*. CRS Report for Congress, Congressional Research Service, *Order Code, RL30735*, 2.

Hundley, R. O., & Anderson, R. H. (1997). Emerging Challenge: Security and Safety in Cyberspace. In Athena's Camp, Preparing for Conflict in the Information Age (pp. 231-251). Santa Monica, CA: RAND Corporation.

Intoccia, F. G., & Moore, J. W. (2006). Communications Technology, Warfare, And The Law: Is The Network A Weapon System? *Houston Journal of International Law, 28*(2), 467–489.

ITU. (2008). *Overview of Cybersecurity*. ITU-T Recommendations. Retrieved from http://handle.itu.int/11.1002/1000/9136-en?locatt=format:pdf&auth

John, M. (2013). *Old Trick Threatens the Newest Weapons*. Retrieved from http://www.nytimes.com/2009/10/27/science/27trojan.html?_r=2&ref=science&pagewanted=al

Kara, M. (2013). *Siber Saldirilar - Siber Savaşlar ve Etkileri* (MSc thesis). İstanbul Bilgi Üniversitesi.

Karaarslan, E., Akın, G., & Feath, V. (2008). *Kurumsal Ağlarda Zararlı Yazılımlarla Mücadele Klavuzu*. Ulusal Akademik Ağ ve Bilgi Merkezi, Döküman Kodu:ULAKCSIRT-2008-01, 1, 2.

Karakuş, C. (2013). *Kritik Alt Yapılara Siber Saldırı*. İstanbul Kültür Üniversitesi. Retrieved from http://ylt44.com/bilimsel/siber.html

Kaya, A., & Öğün, N. M. (2009). Siber Güvenliğin Milli Güvenlik Açısından Önemi ve Alınabilecek Tedbirler. *Güvenlik Stratejileri, 18*, 8–27.

Keleştemur, A. (2015). *Siber İstihbarat*. İstanbul: Yazın Basın Yayınevi Matbaacılık Trz.Tic.Ltd.Şti.

Libicki, M. C. (2009). *Cyberdeterrence and Cyberwar*. Santa Monica, CA: RAND Cooperation.

Lipovsky, R. (2014). *Back in BlackEnergy: 2014 Targeted Attacks in Ukraine and Poland*. Retrieved from http://www.welivesecurity.com/2014/09/22/back-in-blackenergy-2014/

Lupovici, A. (2011). Cyber Warfare and Deterrence. *Military and Strategic Affairs, 3*(3), 49–62.

McAfee. (2011). *Revealed: Operation Shady RAT*. Retrieved from http://www.mcafee.com/us/resources/white-papers/wp -operation-shady-rat.pdf

Mele, S. (2013). *Cyber-Weapons: Legal and Strategic Aspects, Version 2.0*. Machiavelli Editions. Retrieved from http://www.strategicstudies.it/wp-content/uploads/2013/07/Machiavelli-Editions-Cyber- Weapons-Legal-and-Strategic-Aspects-V2.0.pdf

Mueller, P., & Yadegari, B. (2012). *The Stuxnet Worm*. Retrieved from http://www.cs.arizona.edu/~collberg/Teaching/466566/2012/Resources/presentations/2012/topic 9-final/report. pdf

Northrup, T., & Mackin, J. (2011). *Configuring Windows Server 2008 Network Infrastructure*. Washington, DC: Microsoft Press.

Özdemir, B. (2007). Zararlı Yazılıma Karşı Korunma Kılavuzu. *Tübitak Uekae, 12*.

Rid, T., & McBurney, P. (2012). Cyber-Weapons. *The RUSI Journal, 157*(1), 6–13. doi:10.1080/03071847.2012.664354

Robillard, N. (2004). *Global Information Assurance Certification Paper, 1*(4), 2.

Sağıroğlu, Ş. (2011). *Siber Güvenlik ve Türkiye*. Ankara: Siber Güvenlik Çalıştayı.

Shakarian, P., Shakarian, J., & Ruef, A. (2013). *Introduction To Cyberwarfare A Multidisciplinary Approach.* Elsevier, Inc.

Singer, P. W., & Friedman, A. (2014). Cybersecurity And Cyberwar What Everyone Needs To Know. Oxford University Press.

Singer, P. W., & Friedman, A. (2015). Siber Güvenlik ve Siber Savaş. Ankara: Buzdağı Yayınevi.

Smith, C. S. (2001). 6-12; The First World Hacker War. *The New York Times.* Retrieved from http://www.nytimes.com/2001/05/13/weekinreview/may-6-12-the-first-worldhacker-war.html

Stuttard, D., & Pinto, M. (2011). *The Web Application Hackers Handbook.* Indianapolis, IN: John Wiley & Sons, Inc.

Symantec. (2011). *Symantec Report on Attack Kits and Malicious Websites.* Retrieved from http://www.symantec.com/content/en/us/enterprise/other_resources/b- symantec_report_on_attack_kits_and_malicious_websites_exec_summary_21169172_WP.enus. pdf

Tabansky, L. (2012). Cybercrime- A National Security Issue? *Military and Strategic Affairs, 4*(3), 117.

Turhan, M. (2010). Siber Güvenliğin Sağlanması, Dünya Uygulamaları ve Ülkemiz İçin Çözüm Önerileri. *Bilgi Teknolojileri ve İletişim Kurumu, 42.*

Türkay, Ş. (2013). *Siber Savaş Hukuku ve Uygulanma Sorunsalı. İstanbul Üniversitesi Hukuk Fakültesi Mecmuası, 71*(1), 1177–1228.

Ulaşanoğlu, M. E. (2010). *Bilgi Güvenliği: Riskler ve Öneriler.* Bilgi Teknolojileri ve İletişim Kurumu. Retrieved from http://docplayer.biz.tr/632957-Bilgiguvenligi-riskler-ve-oneriler.html

Vasilescu C., (2012). Cyber Attacks-Emerging Threats to the 21st Century Critical Information Infrastructures. *Pobrana a Strategıe/Defence & Strategy, 1.* 7199.12.2012.01.053-062 doi:10.3849/1802

Wilkins, S., & Smith, F. (2011). *CCNP Security Offical Exam Cert Guide.* Indianapolis, IN: Cisco Press.

Yayla M. (2013). Hukuki Bir Terim Olarak —Siber Savaş —Cyber War As A Legal Term. *TBB Dergisi,* (104), 177-202.

Yazıcı, A. (2011). *Siber Güvenlik ve SAHAB*, Retrieved from http://www. emo.org.tr/ekler/fad64faae21db53_ek.pdf

Yıldız, M. (2014). *Siber Suçlar ve Kurum Güvenliği* (Thesis). Republic of Turkey Ministry Of Transport Maritime Affairs And Communications, Department of Information Technologies.

Yılmaz, S., & Salcan, O. (2008). *Siber Uzay'da Güvenlik ve Türkiye.* İstanbul: Milenyum Yayınları.

Chapter 2
Android Application Security

Marwan Omar
Saint Leo University, USA

Derek Mohammed
Saint Leo University, USA

Van Nguyen
Saint Leo University, USA

Maurice Dawson
ⓘD https://orcid.org/0000-0003-4609-3444
Illinois Institute of Technology, USA

Mubarak Banisakher
Saint Leo University, USA

ABSTRACT

Android is a free, open source platform that allows any developer to submit apps to the Android Market with no restrictions. This enables hackers to pass their malicious apps to the Android Market as legitimate apps. The central issue lies at the heart of the Android permission mechanism, which is not capable of blocking malicious apps from accessing sensitive phone resources (e.g., contact info and browsing history); it either allows or disallows apps from accessing the resources requested by the app at the installation time. This chapter investigated the scope of this issue and concluded that hackers use malicious apps as attack vectors to compromise Android smartphones and steal confidential data and that no security solutions exist to combat malicious apps. The researcher suggested designing a real time monitoring application to detect and deter malicious apps from compromising users' sensitive data; such application is necessary for Android users to protect their privacy and prevent financial loss.

DOI: 10.4018/978-1-5225-8976-1.ch002

Copyright © 2019, IGI Global. Copying or distributing in print or electronic forms without written permission of IGI Global is prohibited.

ANDROID APPLICATION SECURITY

Smartphones are becoming a more integrated and prevalent part of people's daily lives due to their highly powerful computational capabilities, such as email applications, online banking, online shopping, and bill paying. With this fast adoption of smartphones, imminent security threats arise while communicating sensitive personally identifiable information (PII), such as bank account numbers and credit card numbers used when handling and performing those advanced tasks (Wong, 2005; Brown, 2009). Traditional attacks (worms, viruses, and Trojan horses) caused privacy violations and disruptions of critical software applications (e.g., deleting lists of contact numbers and personal data). Malware attacks on smartphones were generally "proof of concept" attempts to break to the phone's system and cause damage. However, the new generation of smartphone malware attacks has increased in sophistication and is designed to cause severe financial losses (caused by identity theft) and disruption of critical software applications.

Research has shown that current defense measures, such as virus scanners, are not effective to withstand emerging smartphone security threats, simply because they are signature-based, so they can only detect known malware (e.g., worms, viruses, and Trojan horses)((Chen & etal.. 2017), (Hernandez and Butler. 2018), (Reshetova, Bonazzi, and Asokan. 2017), . Malware writers are writing malware that can easily bypass signature-based virus scanners and enetrate the operating system to execute malicious code. New and unknown malware presents serious security threats on smartphones; therefore, there is a critical need to design robust security countermeasures to rebuff evolving malware attacks (Schmidt, A-D., Bye, Schmidt, H-G., Clausen, & Kiraz, 2009). Solutions are expected to protect smartphones by first hardening the security of applications installed on smartphones, such as Bluetooth and web browser settings; turning off unnecessary or unused services (i.e., GPS); and using an integrated security system that ensures protection on more than one level, such as encryption standards and access control mechanisms.

GOOGLE AND THE ANDROID OPERATING SYSTEM

It was Andy Rubin who created Android with other founders with a vision of revolutionizing the mobile industry. Android was initially built with focus on digital cameras. When Google acquired Android in 2005 and since then it was Larry Page, the Google co-founder who fostered it and made it what it is today with the Andy Rubin. By 2005, one of Page's visions was to put handheld computers with access to Google in the pocket of every person on the planet. So, that year, Page directed Google corporate development to buy a small startup with the same ludicrously huge ambition. This startup was Android. Its CEO and co-founder was Andy Rubin, a former Apple executive who had also developed a failed but once-popular Internet-connected phone called the Sidekick (Quora, 2018)

ANDROID ARCHITECTURE

Android is designed as a stack of three main components or layers: the applications layer, the libraries layer, and the Linux kernel layer. The following diagram shows those three main components of Android's operating system:

Figure 1. Android component stac; the three main layers of Android's operating system Android Developers (2016)

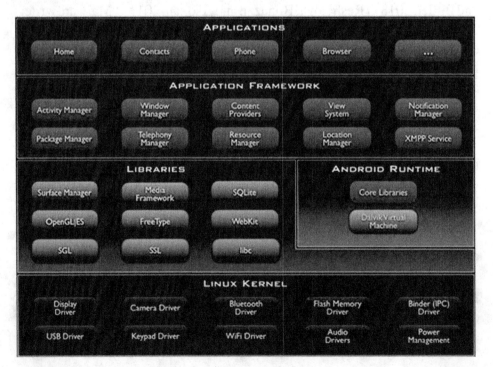

Application Layer

This is the top layer of the platform that acts as the interface between users and the Android platform and provides core applications written in Java programming language; such applications include email browser, SMS, phone, contacts, calendar, and Google maps. This layer includes the application framework, which is a software framework used to provide a rich set of services and extensions, such as Activity Manager (which manages the lifecycle of applications) and Content Provider, which allows for data sharing and access between and within applications (Android Developers, 2010). The most important feature of this layer is that it allows users to run applications simultaneously, such as listening to music while surfing the web; this in turn, contributes to users' productivity, interaction, and satisfaction (Speckmann, 2008).

Libraries Layer

Android provides a set of libraries written in C/C++ language. They are usually used with components in other layers (such as Linux and Application layers). Some of the core libraries include SQL database engine, 2D and 3D graphics, Web Kit (web browsing engine), and Media Framework (i.e., MP3). These capabilities can be developed by users through the application layer using a Java interface. This layer also includes the Run Time, which consists of the Dalvik Virtual Machine (DVM) and a set of core libraries written in Java. Dalvik VM offers the capability of running multiple VMs on a single device and better memory management by relying on the kernel to provide such functionality. It is important to note that the Dalvik VM is a very important component within this layer because it acts as the translator between the applications and the operating system, where it translates programs written by users in the Java programming language (which is not understood by the OS) to an executable program that can be run on the OS (Speckmann, 2008).

Linux Kernel Layer

This layer serves as the abstraction between the hardware and the rest of the software stack and provides system-level capabilities and services such as memory management, security, networking, devise drivers, and process management (Android Developers, 2010). A fact that gives the Android framework an advantage over other operating systems such as Symbian and Windows is that it offers a rich and innovative application-development environment where third party applications, technologies, and services can be developed using Java programming capabilities, which enables portability across other platforms as well. This underlines the popularity of Android among users, developers, and businesses and asserts the statement made by Andy Rubin, Google's director of mobile platforms: "There should be nothing that users can access on their desktop that they cannot access on their cell phone" (Speckmann, 2008, p. 11).

THE ANDROID SECURITY MODEL

Android is a multi-process system where each application (and parts of the system) runs its own process. The standard Linux facilities enforce security between applications and the system at the process level; those applications are assigned by users and group IDs. Applications are restricted in what they can perform by a permission mechanism, called permission labels, that uses an access control to control what applications can be performed. The permission labels are part of a security policy that is used to restrict access to each component within an application. Android uses security policies to determine whether to grant or deny permissions to applications installed on Android OS. Those security policies suffer from shortcomings in that they cannot specify to which application rights or permissions are given because they rely on users and the operating system to make that guess. They are therefore taking the risk of permitting applications with malicious intentions to access confidential data on the phone. Ongtang, McLaughlin, Enck, and McDaniel (2009 b) best described this security shortcoming by their hypothetical example of "PayPal service built on Android. Applications such as browsers, email clients, software marketplaces, music players, etc. use the PayPal service to purchase goods. The PayPal service in this case is an application that asserts permissions that must be granted to the other applications that use its interfaces" (p. 1). In this hypothetical scenario, it is unknown whether the PayPal application is legitimate or not because there is no way to determine whether this is the actual PayPal service application or another malicious program. Again, Android lacks security measures to determine and enforce how, when, where, and to whom permissions are granted.

ANDROID'S PERMISSIONS

Android uses permission mechanisms to determine what users are allowed to do in applications; this is achieved via the manifest permission that grants permissions to applications independently, which in turn, allows applications to run independently from each other as well as from the operating system. This could be a good security feature since the operations run by one application cannot interfere or otherwise impact operations within other applications. For example, users sending email messages will not be allowed (by default) to perform any operation within an application (such as reading a file from another application) that could adversely impact the email application. Applications achieve that using the "sandbox" concept, where each application is given the basic functions needed to run its own process; however, if the sandbox does not provide the needed functions to run a process, then the application can interfere with the operations of another process and request the needed functions to run a process. This capability of allowing applications to request permissions outside of their sandbox capabilities could be harmful to Android smartphones because it opens a window of opportunity for malware to exploit the privilege of accessing sensitive data on Android handsets and thus install malicious software (Vennon, 2010).

ANDROID'S SECURITY THREATS

The most recent studies about the Android Google framework reveal that there are imminent security threats associated with the use of this mobile operating system; this is because Android is open-source software that allows the development and programming of third-party software programs, in addition to being used as a tool to handle e-commerce tasks and perform online banking activities. Furthermore, Android was designed with the unique challenge of providing a customer-oriented, open-source, mobile operating system and addressing security challenges associated with an open-source programming environment. This, in turn, makes Android vulnerable to various attacks that can lead to identity theft (and financial losses), privacy violation, compromised confidentially of user information, damage to the telecommunication infrastructure, and disruption of important applications (i.e., email and internet surfing). The existing literature on Android security research identifies risks and vulnerabilities and presents some security

Figure 2. Android Application Mechanism. Dialog box depicting permission mechanism and Application permissions to users (Chu, 2016)

solutions, such as malware detection. Also, there has been research on investigating current security mechanisms (such as access control, intrusion detection systems, and antivirus software) used to protect Android and the sensitive information. However, literature lacks any research endeavors on a "high scale" to fully address the security shortcomings of Android and design a comprehensive protection approach.

Evolving Threats Pertaining to Android

The Android framework is susceptible to imminent security threats due to its open-source, free, and available Linux operating system. Linux contains some undocumented functions that allow the execution of various native

Linux applications, and those applications, in turn, can be used to write malicious code and ultimately launch attacks on Android devices. Permission mechanisms can always raise threats and make applications as well as Android phones more susceptible to attacks. Ongtang et al. (2009b) best described the threat associated with applications and permissions by introducing a hypothetical PayPal service built on Android (this is the same scenario that was discussed above regarding legitimate and malicious applications). Some applications, such as web browsers and email, utilize the PayPal service to make online purchases. In this instance, any of those applications may request permissions from PayPal to use its interfaces, which ultimately means that some users with malicious intentions could exploit permissions granted by the core application (PayPal) and execute malicious code.

Android phones are becoming more vulnerable, and hence becoming attractive targets for hackers, because battery life and resource constraints (i.e., limited memory and processing power) considerably limit the capability and feasibility of using traditional protection measures (i.e., antivirus and encryption methods) to defend against potential attacks. Vennon and Stroop (2010) reported on a malicious application that offered a trial period of a calculator program. Although the application looked benign and presented the user with permissions to install on the phone, the main intent of that application was to access private user data, monitor email traffic, and modify email addresses.

Android applications can always be a source of threat because Android relies on applications to interact with each other and assumes that they can request resources and permissions from each other in a secure manner without enforcing any security policy to verify the legitimacy of applications. This could be a security flaw if a malicious application was able to gain permission to access other core applications or services that involve confidential data. Enck, Ongtang, & McDaniel (2008) pointed out this security vulnerability and stated that Android is incapable of distinguishing malicious applications from legitimate ones because it relies on preset security permissions. If attackers exploit this vulnerability, they can use their applications' permissions to disable other applications or even the device itself. Moreover, malicious writers can extend their damage, exploiting this vulnerability, to disrupt other network devices or the network itself, such as abusing costly services (dialing prime numbers and sending SMS), compromising private contents, redirecting phone calls, sending spam, or infecting and eavesdropping on other devices. Poorly designed applications can always expose Android phones to attacks because they help attackers identify security flaws within the applications' security policies. For example, researchers have shown that some of Android's applications, such as SMS, location service, and voice, present vulnerabilities due to insecure application policy configuration ((Chen & etl.. (2017), (Hernandez and Butler. 2018)).

Android Threat Model Analysis

The first threat cluster involves exploiting the permission mechanism discussed earlier; a hacker can deliberately take advantage of permissions granted to an application during installation time and execute malicious code, which could ultimately impact the Android's integrity and confidentiality as a device. The second threat cluster arises from the possibility of an application exploiting vulnerabilities found in Linux kernel or other core applications within Android's operating system. The third threat cluster reveals vulnerabilities within the confidential content, such as the content of the SD card. Those contents are not protected by any means of access control; thus, private contents could be compromised. The fourth threat cluster involves the possibility of draining Android's resources, such as memory or processor because there are not any storage restrictions on applications. The fifth threat cluster deals with threats that could undermine and bring down network services by using a compromised Android device as an attack vector to attack other Androids within the network; this could be achieved using email applications, SMS and a variety of tools provided by a single Android device.

Android Vulnerabilities

It is important to point out that the first Android browser bug that was a serious vulnerability was identified and exploited by Miller, Daniel, and Honoroff (2009), independent security evaluators who discovered an exploitable bug in the multimedia subsystem used by Android's browser. The researchers did not think that the bug was as serious as they had thought in the beginning and mentioned that, "while the bug can be activated by the browser, the actual code that would be executed by a successful attack would run in the media player, not the browser" (Miller et al., 2009.para.4). According to this vulnerability, if Android users visit a malicious site, attackers would be able to run any code, escalating web browser privileges. Thus, attackers could have access to any information used by the web browser, such as saved passwords, cookies, and any other information entered into web applications.

MMS/SMS Vulnerabilities

Multimedia messaging service (MMS) and short message service (SMS) are some of the most popular, useful, and enticing services provided by cellular networks to their users. The functionality and structure of MMS/SMS is complex, which increases potential security flaws because the more complex a system is, the more likely to find software bugs. In turn, this makes Android smartphones open to serious vulnerabilities, which could render smartphones useless.

ANDROID MALWARE

Hackers first started to design malware for smartphones in early 2004 when the Cabir worm came to the scene. Despite the fact that Cabir was only a "proof of concept" attack form and did not cause any serious damage to affected smartphones, it brought hackers' attention to smartphones. Android, as a smartphone, is no exception when it comes to mobile malware attacks. Some of the first Android malware was devised by a group of security researchers as an attempt to bring attention to possible malware attacks on the Android platform because Android offers an integrated set of services and functionalities, such as internet access. The researchers were able to create the first Android running malware by exploiting undocumented Android Java functions and using them to create native Linux applications.

The most dangerous Android malware is the one that exploits security flaws within the operating system (Linux) to gain root-level access with root privilege. One of the first security flaws was discovered in Android in November of 2008 when security experts found a bug that would allow users and potential attackers to run command-line instructions with root privilege. Moreover, the bug, if exploited, would make the Android platform read and interpret actions based on the input text. For example, if an Android user input a simple text message, such as "Hello," it could be interpreted by the operating system as "reboot," which surprisingly reboots the Android device (ZDNet, 2010). This security shortcoming and many other vulnerabilities were discovered in Android over the last two years and have thus continuously raised pressing concerns about the credibility and effectiveness of security controls deployed in Android. Most of those vulnerabilities stem from Android's open-source nature, which allows development of third-party applications without any kind of centralized control or any security oversight.

Malware Evolution and Effects in Android Platform

The first academic work on Android malware appeared in 2009 (Schmidt, Bye et al. 2009). Android would be the next target for malware writers due to some vulnerabilities found in the Android operating system (Linux), which could be used to execute malicious payload and bypass the permissions mechanism. In fact, the researchers were able to create the first running malware on Android by exploiting some undocumented Java functions and thereby circumvent Linux for malicious purposes. Subsequent malware attacks have always targeted the operating system (Linux) and attempted to gain system-level access to take control of the device and execute malicious payload. The following graphical display depicts mobile (smartphone) malware evolution (from 2004 until 2009) and shows a steady increase in malware appearance.

THE CURRENT STATE OF SECURITY IN ANDROID PHONES

Google has carefully designed some strong security features and tools and integrated them into Android devices to provide a secure environment for users and developers, protecting phones and their contents from malicious attacks. A review of the collection of security-related mechanisms that are inherently integrated into the Android framework reveals that security mechanisms embedded in Android would address a whole host of security threats associated with the use of Android phones. One of the most critical and robust security measures deployed by Google includes the Portable Operating System Interface (POSIX) for preventing different applications from affecting each other. Google has also implemented a permission-based mechanism that dictates what operations can be performed by any particular application. Signing applications and application certifications are other significant security features that complement existing features. In applications signing, all files, along with their meta-data, are signed in the apk, including all the permission requested and provided by each application (Shabtai & Elovici, 2010)

Figure 3. Mobile malware; growth in number of known modifications 2004-2009 (Juniper Networks, 2015)

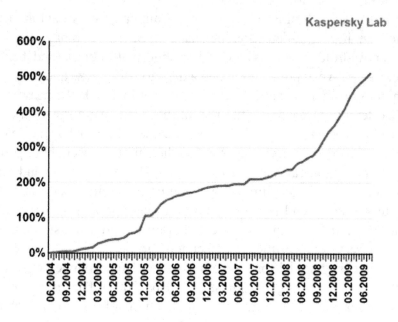

CURRENT DEFENSE SOLUTIONS

Over the last few years, security researchers have made inroads into Android's security by devising security solutions and proposing protection techniques to make Android smartphones as secure as possible to both developers and end users (Enck, Ongtang, & McDaniel (2008), Chen & etl.. (2017), (Hernandez and Butler. 2018). Some of the early attempts to secure Android smartphones started by studying the feasibility and applicability of security solutions deployed on desktops and laptops, such as access control, firewalls, antivirus programs, and encryption algorithms. It appeared that the effectiveness of those solutions was limited by resource constraints and processing power built into Android smartphones. Then, after memory and power constraints were realized, researchers started to think about designing mobile-specific, light-weight, collaborative approaches, such as intrusion-detection systems. As research on Android security matured and more schools of thought emerged concerning enhanced solutions for Android protection, security researchers proposed more effective techniques, which better addressed the security shortcomings of the Android open platform. Some of the emergent solutions targeted securing applications within the Android system, rather than tackling the platform as a whole.

Schmidt, A., Schmidt, H., Clausen, Camtepe, & Albayrak, (2008) designed an intrusion-detection mechanism called "anomaly detection" to protect Android phones by detecting abnormal patterns and behavior. Their collaborative approach included a detector to analyze and monitor the system in its normal state and an external server to handle the heavy task of statistical learning (reasoning the normal behavior of information). When specific events occur and their behavior is deemed abnormal by the detection mechanism, the detection manager would then alert the user about potential intrusion via a graphical user interface (GUI). The effectiveness and success of this security solution is limited by resource constraints (such as memory and battery energy) and is based on monitoring and detecting anomalous behavior on Android. It involves a collaborative approach, using on-device and remote server capabilities to detect anomaly.

A new security model for protecting Android smartphones was devised by Portokalidis, Homburg, Anagnostaki, & Bos (2009). The researchers used a virtual remote server to mirror the execution of software on the phone in a virtual machine. With this approach, they were able to use an unlimited number of attack detection techniques simultaneously. According to their applied technique, an Android phone would record a minimal execution trace and transmit it to the virtual security server in the cloud; the server then would replay the original message in exactly the same way as the phone would. The main purpose of this security approach was to address security shortcomings of Android smartphones due to resource constraints (e.g., battery life and limited memory), and it appeared to be effective in that it allowed the implementation of multiple defense techniques within a comprehensive security model that provides insights about hackers' attack mechanisms. Moreover, this architecture was proven to be suitable for protecting Android phones against zero-day attacks.

Chaudhuri (2009) proposed a language-based security solution for Android applications; this study was aimed at addressing some of the security concerns for both users and developers when using Android applications. This application-based security solution guarantees data integrity and secrecy by tracking data flow inside an application; this is performed by designing a core formal language that analyzes and describes the safety of Android applications and then notifies users whether it is safe to use applications from other users. Furthermore, this approach uses type-checking criteria (derived from the designed core language), that users can run on their Android phones to determine whether or not to deal with applications developed and sent by other Android users.

Kirin is a tool designed by Enck, Ongtang, & McDaniel (2009 a) to address security concerns associated with granting permissions to applications running on Android phones. Kirin is a log-based tool that allows permissions to be granted to applications if they satisfy a certain global safety invariant. Kirin extracts an application's security policy from its manifest file to determine whether the requested permissions are compliant with the phone's security policy. This approach is effective for controlling or banning permissions that may cause unnecessary data flow across applications. However, some applications may include several components that require a different set of permissions. Therefore, Kirin may not fit well with those applications because it does not track data flow within each application. Instead, it looks at the application and its different components as a one component and determines the safety of the underlying application.

Schmidt, Bye et al. (2009) made an interesting addition to Android security by performing static analysis on executables to detect malware in a collaborative manner. First, they performed the static analysis on executables by extracting their function calls in the Android environment using the command "readelf." Then they classified call function lists with PART, Prism and Nearest Neighbor algorithms after comparing malware executables to call function lists. Later, they used a collaborative malware detection approach to extend their results. The benefit of this enhanced approach stems from using simple classifiers to detect the presence of malware on Android devices without the need to rely on external servers to perform these tasks, in addition to the advantage of not being resource-consuming. This security solution was different from other previously proposed solutions for Android in that it did not use any signature-based techniques (e.g., antivirus) to detect malware. Instead, it employed a collaborative security technique to detect new and unknown malware in an efficient manner, thereby enhancing malware detection techniques for Android phones.

One of the most extensive and comprehensive security research endeavors for Android security was conducted by Shabtai, Fledel, Kanonov, Elovici, Dolev, & Glezer (2010). The researchers employed a methodological, qualitative risk analysis to identify five of the high-risk threats for Android devices and proposed mitigation strategies based on the likelihood of those threats occurring. In addition, they surveyed additional security mechanisms that can be integrated into Android-powered devices. They tested several of these mechanisms and evaluated them in their mobile device security laboratory. For instance, they ported SELinux into Android and activated a security policy for enhancing the protection of system processes. They also enabled a netfilter-based firewall that could be configured via a user-friendly, Android-compliant interface. An anomaly-based Intrusion Detection System (called Andromaly) to detect malware on Android applications was another mitigation technique they devised to harden the security of Android phones.

Android Malware, Risks, and Threats

Android devices are exposed to and vulnerable to a variety of threats, which can be exploited by hackers. Examples include threats of rogue and malicious apps, which can abuse their capabilities when accessing the phones' resources and thus send users' private information to remote servers without users' knowledge or consent. Most recently, there was an Android Trojan that was capable of sending SMSs and recording phone calls from victims' smartphones (Elish, et al, 2015).

Android phones are vulnerable to malicious software that usually comes with downloading apps that are not are officially approved by the manufacturer or service provider (Zhou, et al., 2014). The rise of mobile malware is becoming a reality as we see malware targeting smartphones constantly, and attackers are gearing their efforts toward this "soft target" that does not seem to have robust security technologies. This, in turn, poses great security risks to sensitive information. It is exceedingly likely that hackers will target Android smartphones, especially because the Android Market does not enforce any stringent security policies to weed out potential malicious apps to only allow the legitimate and secure apps to be made publicly available for Android users. To make matters worse, Android smartphones are turning into full-fledged computers with almost the same functionality and features as any laptops or desktops. This means that attackers can apply similar attack strategies, which have previously proven successful in targeting traditional computers, and apply them on mobile platforms.

Android malware was increased four-folds only within the year 2010. Examples of malware attacks in the form of rogue apps that access users' confidential information and work in the background without users' knowledge or consent permeate the literature. The latest one was an app that was called the Tap Snake game (it turned out to be a spying tool), which reported users' locations and accessed confidential information in an unauthorized manner. To demystify this inconsistency between respondents' responses and what the literature says, users may not always be able to determine which apps are rogue or malicious, even after installing them, because most of them (such as Tap Snake) do not make any visible changes on the Android smartphone immediately, but rather work in the background and access confidential information without making users aware (Hypponen, 2010).

Android Applications Security and the Permission Mechanism

Since Android is a free, open-source platform, it allows any developer to submit and upload apps to the Android Market with no restrictions enforced to determine the legitimacy of those apps. On one hand, this is a great benefit of having an open-source system that encourages developers and users to interact and exploit the advantages of this platform. On the other hand, this provides an opportunity for hackers to mask their malicious apps and submit them to the Android Market as benign and legitimate apps and make some of them freely available for download by end users. The central issue lies at the heart of the Android permission mechanism, which is not capable of blocking malicious apps from accessing sensitive phone resources (contact info, browsing history credentials, and bank login credentials). The current permission technique either allows or disallows apps from accessing the resources requested by the app at the installation time, but it fails to reverse the granted permission if the underlying app was deemed malicious or illegitimate (Grace, et al, 2013). It must be noted, however, that Android's sandboxing mechanism makes Android one of the more secure platforms by separating applications and processes from each other and enforcing each app to be executed in its own sandbox, thereby minimizing the risk of unauthorized access by other apps to sensitive phone resources (Zhou, et al., 2016).

Android users download and install apps on a regular daily basis, and they have a level of uncertainty about their confidence in the security of apps they download ((Enck, Ongtang, & McDaniel (2008) ((Zhou, et al., 2016)), Chen, et al.. (2017), (Hernandez and Butler. 2018). The current permission mechanism is discretionary in nature, meaning that Android users have to decide whether to grant apps the permissions they need to be installed, which increases the security burden on users. Stueckle (2011) stated that the rapid increase in the number of apps downloaded every day makes the current security system unable to cope with the malware risks, and therefore, it becomes very easy for hackers to develop and distribute malicious content that seems to be in its infancy stage. Although mobile malware that targets smartphones has been around since 2004, there have not been any major malware outbreaks yet. However, there have been many security incidents targeting Android phones recently, and since business organizations, government agencies, and academia are increasingly allowing their employees to access network resources using smartphones as a tool to enable productivity, this will certainly appeal to hackers and motivate them to shift their efforts towards this growing and rich industry.

Android Security Model Echoed

The previous discussion undoubtedly exhibits the fact that both the security industry and academia have come to realize and acknowledge the various security issues associated with the use of Android smartphones. Unlike traditional mobile phones, Android smartphones have become an integrated component of our daily lives and are increasingly used for a variety of tasks, such as financial transactions, online purchases, entertainment, and computing. This in turn, makes Android smartphones a repository for highly sensitive data, such as credit card numbers, contact lists, calendars, and phone locations. Those are certainly compelling reasons for hackers to gear their efforts and design malware to target this relatively immature platform. The researcher finds it a bit alarming that the Android platform has only been around for a little over three years, and yet the number of exploits, vulnerabilities, and security flaws identified so far exceeds expectations and highlights a rift in the effectiveness of the current Android security system. The latest security vulnerability was identified by a group of German researchers at the University of ULM (ULM University, 2011), where they demonstrated that any Android phones connected to open Wi-Fi networks transmit data in clear text. In particular, they proved that Android's calendars and contact lists can be intercepted and ultimately impersonated by attackers.

Research has clearly shown that there has been an explosive growth in Android smartphone usage and adoption by industries, academia, corporations, and government agencies. What has significantly helped in this regard is the fact that the Android platform is an open-source system, meaning that developers can freely develop and distribute apps to the Android Market and make them readily available for public use. Also, Google Android imposes very few restrictions on network operators and device manufactures, which has made Android smartphones the "the device of choice" for millions of smartphone users. As a result, it is expected that Android will soon become the prime target for malware writers, especially if they want to abuse the freedom given to developers by Google in the ease and flexibility of uploading apps without any approval or vetting process. On the flip side, it must be noted that Google's open source has certainly helped discover and patch many security flaws; for example, security researcher Charlie Miller has been a pioneer in identifying security vulnerabilities in the way Android played MP3 files. He also discovered a security flaw in the way Android processed SMSs (McMillan, 2009). Google has been very open to accepting those facts and worked diligently to patch those vulnerabilities in a timely manner.

CONCLUSION

Research has clearly shown that there has been an explosive growth in Android smartphone usage and adoption by industries, academia, corporations, and government agencies. Google Android imposes very few restrictions on network operators and device manufactures, which has made Android smartphones the "the device of choice" for millions of smartphone users. As a result, it is expected that Android will soon become the prime target for malware writers, especially if they want to abuse the freedom given to developers by Google in the ease and flexibility of uploading apps without any approval or vetting process. Android smartphone users tend to download and install apps frequently-In 2016 the number of both iOS and Android app (on Google Play store only) downloads reached 90 billion, 13 billion increase from the previous year (Business of Apps, 2018)., as all kinds of apps dominate the marketplace; apps usually require access to certain areas of the phone to function, and they ask users to grant permissions at installation time. Many apps tend to request permissions more than they really need to be fully functional. Also, many apps are seemingly benign to users and do not seem to pose any threats to confidential information. Therefore, Android users normally get distracted by enjoying all the features and added functionality offered by apps and do not give adequate attention to the security aspects of those apps. To make matters worse, hackers target popular apps, modify their source code, and then upload them again to the Android Market after injecting their malicious piece. Unfortunately, Google is not proactive in this area in that it does not remove potentially malicious apps until they receive complaints or until apps have already caused disruption and compromised sensitive data. Therefore, the researcher strongly believes that the greatest security risk lies at the heart of Android apps, where attackers are most capable of passing their malicious apps to end users through the Market and gain unauthorized access to confidential data to achieve financial gains. Furthermore, hackers are known to use attack strategies that tend to send expensive SMS messages and dial prime rate numbers as a quick and efficient way to gain money illegally.

REFERENCES

Brown, B. (2009). *Beyond Downadup: Security expert worries about smart phone, TinyURL threats: Malware writers just waiting for financial incentive to strike, F-Secure exec warns.* Retrieved, February 11, 2012 from http://business.highbeam.com/409220/article-1G1-214585913/beyond-downadup-security-expert-worries-smart-phone

Business of Apps. (2018). *App Download and Usage Statistics.* Retrieved from http://www.businessofapps.com/data/app-statistics/#1

Chaudhuri, A. (2009). *Language-based security on Android.* Retrieved from http://www.cs.umd.edu/~avik/papers/lbsa.pdf

Chen, Li, Enck, Aafer, & Zhang. (2017). Analysis of SEAndroid Policies: Combining MAC and DAC in Android. In *Proceedings of the 33rd Annual Computer Security Applications Conference* (ACSAC 2017). ACM. 10.1145/3134600.3134638

Chu, E. (2016). *Android Market: a user-driven content distribution system.* Retrieved February, 11, 2012 from http://android-developers.blogspot.com

Developers, A. (2016). *Android developer guide.* Retrieved February 11, 2012 from www.android.com

Elish, K., Yao, D., & Ryder, B. (2015). *User-Centric Dependence Analysis for Identifying Malicious Mobile Apps.* Retrieved from http://people.cs.vt.edu/~kelish/most-12.pdf

Enck, W., Ongtang, M., & McDaniel, P. (2008). *Mitigating Android software misuse before it happens.* Retrieved from http://siis.cse.psu.edu

Enck, W., Ongtang, M., & McDaniel, P. (2009a). On lightweight mobile phone application certification. *Proceedings of Computer and Communications Security (CCS'09)*. Retrieved from http://www.patrickmcdaniel.org/pubs/ccs09a.pdf

Grace, M., Zhou, Y., Zhang, Q., Zou, S. S., & Jiang, X. (2013). *RiskRanker: Scalable and Accurate Zero-day Android Malware Detection*. Retrieved from https://www.csc2.ncsu.edu/faculty/xjiang4/pubs/MOBISYS12.pdf

Hernandez & Butler. (2018). Android Escalation Paths: Building Attack-Graphs from SEAndroid Policies. In *Proceedings of the 11th ACM Conference on Security & Privacy in Wireless and Mobile Networks* (WiSec '18). ACM.

Hypponen, M. (2010). *Mobile security review. F-secure labs* [Video file]. Retrieved from http://www.youtube.com/watch?v=fJMLr8BDQq8

McMillan, R. (2009). *Android security chief: mobile-phone attacks coming*. Retrieved from www.computerworld.com

Miller, C., Daniel, M., & Honoroff, J. (2009). *Exploiting Android*. Retrieved February 11, 2012 from http://securityevaluators.com

Networks, J. (2015). *Empowering Mobile Productivity*. Retrieved from http://www.walkerfirst.com/wa_files/File/tech/Juniper_Empowering_Mobile_Productivity.pdf?PHPSESSID=v6ocd0ep1lv71414v1ecie4ek6

Ongtang, M., McLaughlin, S., Enck, W., & McDaniel, P. (2009b). Semantically rich application-centric security in Android. In *Proceedings of the 25th Annual Computer Security Applications Conference (ACSAC'09)*. Retrieved from http://dl.acm.org

Portokalidis, G., Homburg, P., Anagnostakis, K., & Bos, H. (2009). *Paranoid Android: Zero-day protection for smartphones using the cloud*. Retrieved from www.cs.vu.nl/~herbertb/papers/trpa10.pdf

Rapheal, J. R. (2010). *Will Android Honeycomb come to smartphones?* Retrieved January, 25, 2012 from http://blogs.computerworld.com/17642/android_honeycomb_smartphones

Rash, W. (2004). *Latest skulls Trojan foretells risky smartphone future.* Retrieved January, 25, 2012 from www.eweek.com

Schmidt, A.-D., Bye, R., Schmidt, H.-G., Clausen, J., & Kiraz, O. (2009). *Static analysis of executables for collaborative malware detection on Android.* Retrieved from www.dai-labor.de

Schmitz, R. (2009). *Mobile malware evolution and the Android security model.* Retrieved January, 25, 2012 from www.kriha.de

Shabtai, A., & Elovici, Y. (2010). *Applying behavioral detection on Android-based devices.* Retrieved January, 25, 2012 from http://www.arnetminer.org/viewpub.do?pid=2955537

Shabtai, A., Fledel, Y., Kanonov, U., Elovici, Y., Dolev, S., & Glezer, C. (2010, March/April). Android: A comprehensive security assessment. *IEEE Security and Privacy, 8*(2), 35–44. doi:10.1109/MSP.2010.2

Shin, W., Kiyomoto, S., Fukushima, K., & Tanaka, T. (2009) Towards formal analysis of the permission-based security model for Android. *Fifth International Conference on Wireless and Mobile Communications,* 87-92. 10.1109/ICWMC.2009.21

Speckmann, B. (2008). *The Android Google platform.* Retrieved January, 25, 2012 from http://www.emich.edu

Stueckle, J. (2011) *Android Protection Mechanism: A Signed Code Security Mechanism for Smartphone Applications.* Retrieved January, 25,2012 from http://www.dtic.mil

University U. L. M. Germany. (2011). *Catching authtokens in the wild. The insecurity of Google's clientlogin protocol.* Retrieved from http://www.uni-ulm.de/in/mi/mitarbeiter/koenings/catching-authtokens.html

Vennon, T. (2010). *Android malware, 2010.* Retrieved January, 25, 2012 from http://threatcenter.smobilesystems.com

Vennon, T., & Stroop, D. (2010). *Android market analysis, 2010.* Retrieved January, 25, 2012 from http://threatcenter.smobilesystems.com

Wong, L. (2005). *Potential Bluetooth vulnerabilities in smartphones*. Retrieved, February 11, 2012, from http://citeseerx.ist.psu.edu

ZDNet. (2010). *Google fixes android root-access flaw*. Retrieved January, 25, 2012 from www.zdnetasia.com

Zhou, W., Zhou, Y., Jiang, X., & Ning, P. (2014). *Detecting Repackaged Smartphone Applications in Third-Party Android Marketplaces*. Retrieved from https://www.csc2.ncsu.edu/faculty/xjiang4/pubs/CODASPY12.pdf

Zhou, Y., Wang, Z., Zhou, W., & Jiang, X. (2016). *Detecting Malicious Apps in Official and Alternative Android Markets*. Retrieved from http://www.csd.uoc.gr/~hy558/papers/mal_apps.pdf

Chapter 3
Cyber Security and Open Source Intelligence Techniques

Onurhan Yılmaz
Global Banking Company, Turkey

ABSTRACT

Open source intelligence (OSINT) is one of the most confrontational topics in cyber security in today's world where technology and data transfer methods are highly developed. It is known that many organizations and individuals use OSINT as an information gathering tool during data transfer over the internet and provide many personal or corporate information access. OSINT is a systematic method that is produced by official and private organizations via sources such as the internet or the media. In recent years there has been some debate about the security and privacy of this information, especially with the widespread use of social media. In this chapter, the control of information obtained by OSINT the security will explain the positive effects on this control mechanism.

DOI: 10.4018/978-1-5225-8976-1.ch003

Copyright © 2019, IGI Global. Copying or distributing in print or electronic forms without written permission of IGI Global is prohibited.

INTRODUCTION

Developments in the information technology sector have enabled us to achieve accurate and adequate information faster by using technology. While these developments provide less labor and time savings, they make the virtual environment uncover to security problems. In addition to facilitating socialization of virtual networks, the threats and dangerous created by the transperancy of these environments are can not be ignored. To find old friends through social media, to acquire new friendships and socialize by communicating with them, sharing individual opinions and thoughts, personal behavior analysis. In this way people and institutions are acquiring new enemies and under threat. The social environment facilitates people's lives and socialization, as well as negative threats. Open source intelligence tools and cyber security vulnerabilities personal and private information about institutions and individuals is exploited.

This article will emphasize the negativities and threats brought about by their social networking advantages over the internet. How to use active and passive information using open source intelligence tools will be mentioned. The most used of the open source tools are examined will be compared. Finally, threats to be encountered in terms of personal and organizational data security and precautions to be taken will be mentioned.

CYBER SECURITY

The ease brought by the world that is developed and virtualized with technology is a lesser measure. From computers and smart phones to home appliances, everything from cars to cars can be connected via internet. But the biggest challenge this situation has is the safety of this infrastructure to be able to provide. Information and communication systems must be used to protect against cyber threats and cyber attacks in order to be safe in the virtual environment where many personal, institutional and national information is shared.

Cyber security is defined as the name given to the entirety of security concepts, tools, activities, policies and technologies to protect the data of institutions, organizations and individual users in the virtual environment. Cyber security aims to protect the data, institutional and individual users' data, infrastructures, applications and services, electronic communication systems and all data stored in cyberspace against security risks in cyberspace. The purpose of cyber security is to provide accessibility, integrity and confidentiality of information. The threats and attacks that can occur in cyber security layers are shown in Figure 1.

Accessibility information is when the systems and services are readily available in case of an unexpected error, in an extraordinary state, and in the face of a cyber attack, whenever they are needed. It is very important that the information is accessible in case of a damage to information and communication systems that will occur in other infrastructure systems.

Integrity means that the data is preserved in the system completely and unchanged throughout the entire life cycle.

Confidentiality means that the data stored in the information and communication system is protected from being seized by unauthorized persons. Confidentiality is essential during communication to protect personal privacy. These are listed as interdependent conditions for ensuring safety of the cyber security. In addition to this is another identity authentication. Authentication declared by people verification of credentials. Online shopping and internet banking etc. In systems where credit card information or username and password must be used, the contribution of authentication to security is a measurable measure (Mustafa Ü., Cafer C.,Ayşe Gül M.,).

Every method to be used for the safety of cyber security and the systems to be developed have some considerations. These relevant matters are explained in detail in Table 1.

According to the research, it is useful to pay attention to these matters in the provision of cyber security and any measures to be taken. These entities have general priorities everywhere (Seda Y., Şeref S.,). In addition to these

Figure 1.

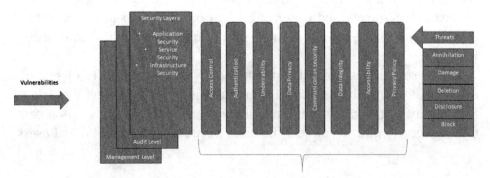

Table 1. Things to be considered in cyber security systems

Protection of citizens' rights and freedoms
To do what is necessary to ensure a society with equal rights
Ensuring the involvement of individuals from all walks of life in decisions affecting the country
Careful observance of the rules applied in other countries as much as possible
Taking common steps in this regard with other countries
To calculate and use the benefit to be earned and the loss suffered
Do not use this power to do much damage to the less powerful ones
Observance of the measure principle

items, other important points in defining the cyber security approaches are shown in Figure 2 and described in detail.

Development of National Policy Strategies

In order for the measures that can be taken against cyber attacks to be successful, the development of national policies and strategies in line with a certain objective of these studies must be complementary to each other.

There are some elements in the provision of national cyber security. If these elements are to be listed, national cyber security policies should be developed, skill and functional measures taken, international business cooperation should be ensured, the opportunities of the country should be developed, adequate support should be given and public awareness should be ensured, and awareness-raising activities should be carried out across the country as

Figure 2.

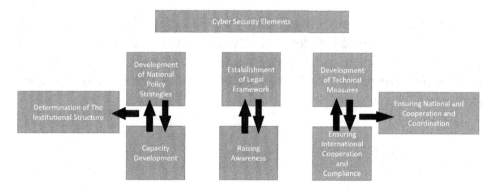

the determination of the institutional structure can be seriously hindered by the awareness of users against cyber threats and attacks (Mustafa Ü.).

Creating the Legal Framework

The cyber attacks have great physical and moral damages. It is thought that cyber security is ensured and the offenses that cause these harms are criminalized to deter the attackers. Considering the technological developments and the changes in the means and methods of cyber attacks, legal regulations which have a great deterrence against cyber attacks should be made.

Technical Measures Development

Legal measures are important in ensuring cyber security, but alone is not enough. It is necessary to take hardware and software measures against developing technology. Technical measures should be developed taking security standards into consideration for the security of software, hardware and business processes.

Determination of Institutional Structuring

Individuals, public institutions and organizations, private sector, non-governmental organizations have duties and responsibilities to ensure the safety of cyber security in a country. In short, all parties are responsible for the safety of the cyber security. However, the first thing that needs to be done is to establish an institution that provides cyber security. All facilities must be provided so that this institution can fulfill its mission.

National Cooperation and Coordination

All parties have their own responsibility for the safety of the cyber security. These sides provide security for themselves. However, they must be linked to each other for complete security. For this reason full co-ordination and union work is required within the framework of national strategies and policies (Mustafa Ü., Cafer C.).

Capacity Development

With the developing technology, the cyber attacks are developing in a direct proportion to the vehicles. For this reason, it is necessary to improve the knowledge of the persons and institutions providing security.

Awareness Raising

Personal users should be informed about the cyber attack and the threat. They must be aware of security.

International Cooperation and Coordination

It means that the global networks of internet networks can be easily reached to all the countries of the world. All of the national infrastructure systems are connected to this network system, allowing crime centers to be in different places. This network security is only possible with international cooperation. In this situation, international legal regulations should be adhered to.

Cyber Security in Turkey

Prior to the establishment of the Department of Criminal Crimes in our country, the Anti-Smuggling and Organized Crime Department was tasked with combating crime. The most common crimes in information crime are bank and credit card fraud, followed by interactive banking fraud. In Table 2, 2011 informatics crimes committed with statistics are given. (TUIK has not published the following events and suspicious statistics since 2011. The most recent statistical data obtained from the studies belongs to 2011.)

Table 2. 2011 Yearly Incidents and Number of Confessions

Crime Categories	Event number	Number of suspects
Bank and Credit Card Fraud	1819	1503
Interactive Banking Fraud	148	348
Crimes Against Information Systems	1791	1898
Qualified Fraud with Internet Brokerage	112	285
Others	31	123
Total	**3901**	**4157**

The increase in cyber attacks and cyber threats and the widespread use of information technology have increased the use of the internet. Consequently in Turkey began to take part in a national cyber security strategy. As a result of the studies made on the strategies of the developed countries in the beginning, some common points attracted attention. More reliable business environments and more reliable internet networks need to be provided through information systems. In addition to this, a more reliable infrastructure environment should be prepared by working on and strengthening the national infrastructure. It seems that current security strategies focus on these areas (Yrd.Doç.Dr.Hakan H.,Doç.Dr.Oğuzhan B.)

There is not much history of our country's work on cyber security. However, ensuring our country's national security and "e-transformation Turkey," the conversion path to the realization of the projects contemplated in the national information society must be given the importance of cyber security. In this context, there are basic principles, methods and steps that are important in the provision of national cigarette safety (Sedat A., Hamdi Murat Y., Zeliha Y.T).

The basic principles that will contribute to the provision of national security are the protection of fundamental human rights and freedoms, the establishment and observance of the equality order in society, the observance of the principle of proportionality, the determination of an approach within the scope of joint decisions of all institutions and individuals, to be proportionate in terms of technical and functional, and to provide international cooperation. According to the research, it is recommended to follow the precautionary principle to ensure safety.

OPEN SOURCE INTELLIGENCE (OSINT)

The intelligence word has taken its place from the Arabic-based intelligence word used to get news, to get new information. But the intelligence word means more to use the acquired knowledge, make it ready for use and use it as a power without knowing it (Serkan S.,Nurettin T.). According to this definition, intelligence has come to this day from the beginning of human relations. It is a kind of intelligence that human beings try to acquire unawareness about people that they are related or want to relate to. The way for states to learn their war strategy during the war and what to do next is a part of intelligence (Gökhan B.)

The rapid development of intelligence technologies changed the needs and working principles of intelligence services and brought new concepts to the intelligence world. A variety of these concepts is "Open Source Intelligence. Open Source Intelligence is the information that has intelligence value by making the information available to everyone easily available. With the development of information technologies, the open-source intelligence method that has entered our lives has taken the news to the table. Thanks to the developing technology, today, the intelligence desk from the beginning of the correct and fast way to reach the vast majority of the information requested. In other words, open source intelligence is public information in print or electronic environment. Information from the media (radio, television, print media and internet etc.) can be used as intelligence (Yavuz Ö.).

With the widespread use of the Internet, the use of media as news source in cyber intelligence has increased. While, the intelligence services used agents and spies as intelligence tools to learn the infrastructure of the enemy in hot war periods, today, open source intelligence is given more importance. Intelligence services use the media as a news source, but also media services in line with their own interests. The power of the media to change the perception structure of society is not to be underestimated. Thus, it imposes the actions and propaganda prepared for the internal confusion in the best manner to the people. But considering the unlimited possibilities of the cyber world, it has become almost impossible to censor new media elements. For example, it is possible for an individual to send the images that he / she has connected to the Internet to his / her computer or smartphone from the internet immediately. For this reason elements of new media, to human rights abuse in the cyber intelligence "freedom with security policy" must be maintained between the balance (Darren QuickKim-Kwang Raymond Choo).

When the Twin Towers were attacked, the images of the aircraft crashing into the towers were monitored by the world public opinion simultaneously. This attack had prepared the appropriate environment for the occupation of Iraq. In order to justify the occupation, the US and the UK have made public the information they provide from the intelligence services. This behavior raised the issue of public use of intelligence information, which was not used in the history of intelligence before. However, this practice created political debates in the UK government and the British Intelligence Committee in 2003. It has been learned that the intelligence report that was announced to the public through the media written about weapons of mass destruction in Iraq does not show the truth. It was understood that the government politicized the issue in order to support Saddam Hussein's regime and it did so to provide public support in possible operations against Iraq. Thus intelligence was used to provide public support to government policy (Gökhan B.).

INFORMATION GATHERING WITH OSINT TOOLS

There are many active and passive information collection methods with open source intelligence tools. Two of the active and passive information collection methods are the methods of collecting information from social networks and collecting information from search engines. In this century, where almost everyone uses social media accounts, individuals are actually unwittingly presenting information about themselves to the Internet. Malicious people have access to this information and use them for the purpose of news. In addition, since the vulnerabilities of the websites from the search engines can be detected, the attacker's target is to attack the website directly if it is an institution and it reaches to a lot of information including all the employees, customers and even the organizational structure of the company in a short time. In addition, when it discovers a system that is vulnerable, it can reach the server via the website and make it its own target on other sites on the server. The collection of information from the social networks, which are active and passive information collection methods, and the information gathering from the search engines are described in more detail in the following section (Heather J. Williams, Ilana Blum).

Collecting Information From Social Networks

Social networks are the virtual platforms in which individuals meet and communicate with people at the same cultural levels by introducing themselves to the society through the Internet. In this definition, besides social social gains, it brings with it many unnoticed dangers. While using social networks, they have negative aspects as well as useful aspects. In social networks, attackers exploit the personal information of individuals for the sake of their own personal interests and easily access this information through personal social accounts. Social networking sites are the most widely used in Facebook, Twitter, Instagram and Youtube. Apart from these sites, there are also many chat and dating sites available. But these sites are the most widely used and the first target of attackers. The attackers have access to the specific information they want about these sites. Information collection is divided into two types as active and passive. Initiatives to collect information on social networks are active attacks. Browsers, such as the name of the domain or the sub-domain to collect information from the sub-domain can be used on the social network page, and especially metadata content from the user information hervesting personal information can be accessed (Canbek G., Sağıroğlu Ş.).

It is possible to capture the access information of the target person in an attack that can be done over the social network. The personal information (name, surname, date of birth, etc.) that the attacker would obtain from the social media accounts of the target or institution will be useful to the attacker. Only the most widely used security question, 'What is mother maiden name?' may not reach the answer to the personal profile. This information can be easily learned from the account of the grandmother, grandfather and uncle of the person's friends list. The attackers have internet banking accounts at their target and are deemed to have access to the account at the rate of eighty percent. Today, in order to prevent this security weakness, a internet single-use password period has started in internet banking. The individual feels safe with a single-use password, but if the mobile phone or the sim card is stolen, the attacker can easily reach the goal by capturing the password (Uraz Y.,Şeref S.).

Gathering Information From Search Engines

As everyone knows, Google is the most widely used search engine in the world. When the searched word is written to the search bar, it finds and lists the relevant ones from more than 20 million data from the database. The Google search engine has its own parameters to make the calls more efficient, and it offers these parameters to the users. These related parameters make it easier for attackers to access their information easily and quickly. These parameters will be explained in detail in Table 3(Pompeu Casanovas).

In addition, there are symbols that Google offers to its users. In addition to the parameters, it provides additional features and convenience to the parameters by using these symbols. All parameters can be used with all symbols. The corresponding symbols are shown in detail in Table 4.

Using these parameters, attackers can access only those areas on the server where authorized persons can enter. You can ping anonymously to any computer, access the web servers, run shell commands on remote servers, and get more and more systemized.

If the target of the attackers is an institution, they infiltrate the website of the institution and obtain the necessary information. Most Web applications contain a security vulnerability. It is possible to search the Google search engine by filtering out those vulnerable applications. Attackers access

Table 3. Google search engine parameters

[all]inurl	This parameter can be used to search for a special word in the url. If more than one word is required in url, allinurl parameter is used.
[all]intitle	This parameter is used to search the title of the web page. If the header contains more than one word, the search is made by the allintitle parameter.
[all]intext	This parameter filters according to the words in the web page. As with others, if you search more than one word, allintext parameter is used.
site	Domain parameter filtering is performed with this parameter. For example, if we want to keep our limited search sites connected with Turkey's state sites: gov.t filter should be used.
filetype	This parameter is used to filter by the file type of the searched document. For example, if only MS World documents are requested, the filetype: doc filter should be searched.
ext	this parameter has the same function as the filetype parameter. However, if you want to reach more than one document that is different from one another, the OR logic operator is used. For example, the ext: doc OR ext: pdf filter is searched.
link	This parameter will display the pages with the desired link. For example, if the pages linking to www.gau.edu.tr are requested, link: gau.edu.tr filter is used.
cache	Some webpages may have been truncated or updated.Since Google keeps the old links of these pages in the index, this web page can be accessed with this parameter.

Table 4. Symbols used in the Google search engine

Symbols	Definition
-	The minus per-parameter of a parameter will have a negative function and will not display the results of the related parameter.
|	This symbol is used instead of the logical OR operator.
.	Any character can be used where the dot symbol is used.
*	Star symbol length is used to replace any character group that is not significant.

confidential information of customers and users that these sites have stored in their database (Emin İslam T.).

OPEN SOURCE INTELLIGENCE TOOLS

The aim of open source intelligence, is to gather information from the system or server before contacting the target institution or person directly. There are many tools on the Internet to collect intelligence based on various categories of information known as active and passive. While collecting information about the target in open source intelligence, the most frequently used tools are maltego, shodan, metagoofil, google hacking database and foca. The following subsections describe all the relevant vehicles in detail.

Maltego

Maltego is a new generation of advanced active and passive information collection tool. The biggest advantage of maltegon is that it shows the collected data as a table on the screen. Thanks to this feature, the relationships between information become more understandable. This feature, which Maltegon has provided, has facilitated the work of researchers who have performed several safety and weakness tests. Thanks to its efficient data analysis, it enabled testers to save time and work more accurately and more effectively. Maltego is a software developed in JAVA language, so it is compatible with Windows, Linux and Machintos operating systems. Maltegon's information includes domain names, IP addresses and records, collecting email addresses, and associating with people, whois information is in question. When querying with Whois, the results are graphically shown, and the admin information (phone number, e-mail addresses and IP addresses) is shown relationally (Matthew Marx).

Shodan

Shodan is a search engine for finding computers and servers connected to the Internet using various filters. You can access the FTP directories that are available on the Internet. In addition, the scan also detects open ports. The number of servers affected by vulnerabilities in the Internet can be learned. Shodan collects all its data from the metadata that the banner server sends to the client. This metadata shows all information about the software the server is using (Roland C. Bodenheim).

Web search engines like Google and Bing are great for finding websites. However, what if you are interested in finding computers running a specific piece of software (such as Apache)? Or, if you want to know which version of Microsoft IIS is most popular? Or how many anonymous FTP servers would you like to see? Maybe a new security vulnerability appeared and would you like to see how many hosts can infect? Traditional web search engines do not allow you to answer these questions (John Matherly).

Metagoofil

Metagoofil is an information gathering tool designed to extract official documents from the target companyMetagoofil searches the google to download the data to the computer and then makes the metadata debugging with libraries like Hachoir and PdfMiner. It generates a report with user names, software versions and server names to assist in the penetration test at the information gathering stage (Christian Martorella).

Metagoofil works with:

- Search for file types in the target area using the Google search engine
- Download all documents found and save them to local disk.
- Removing metadata from downloaded documents
- Save the result in an HTML file

Information that can be found using metadata is user names, path, MAC address, Software, Operating System, etc. This information can then be used to assist in the penetration testing phase.

Google Hacking Database

Google is the most used web-based search engine in the world. When the searched word is entered in the search bar, it searches billions of data from the google database and shows the relevant ones. With a wide range of search capabilities, Google is a favorite search engine. Attackers can access confidential files and password files that can be accessed by servers thanks to google. It is able to easily detect users' private information, access database server, and vulnerable sites (Emin İslam T.,).

Google cache is a powerful tool in the hands of the advanced user. It can be used to find older versions of pages that can normally disclose information that is temporarily unavailable. The cache can be used to highlight terms in a cached version of a page, even if the terms are not used as part of the query to find this page. The cache can also be used to anonymously display a Web page & strip = 1 URL, and can be used as a basic transparent proxy server. An advanced Google user will always pay attention to the details in the header of the cached page, because the date the page was scanned can be important information about the terms that are searched about whether the cached page contains external images. Links to the original page and the text of the URL used to access the cached version of the page. Directory listings provide unique views of Web servers behind the scenes, and directory navigation techniques allow an attacker to navigate around files not designed for an overview.

Locating Vulnerable Targets

Attackers are increasingly using Google to find Web-based targets that are vulnerable to specific exploits. In fact, it is not uncommon for public vulnerabilities to include Google links to potentially vulnerable targets.

Software vendors and security researchers regularly make suggestions about sensitive software that links to the affected software vendor's Web site. Not all referrals will list such a link, but a quick Google query should help you find the seller's page. Because our goal is to develop a query string to find vulnerable destinations on the Web, the vendor's Web site is a good place to explore exactly what the product's Web pages look like. Especially useful is the "Powered by... by search string.

In some cases, as we will see, it is not easy to find a good query, although the resulting query is almost identical to the construction. Although this method is further drawn (and can be short-circuited with creative thinking), it shows a typical procedure for detecting a complete study query to find sensitive targets. Here, let's take a look at how the hacker can use a program's source code to find ways to search for this software on Google. A phrase such as "powered by" can be very useful in finding specific goals because of their degree of uniqueness.

There are many ways to find the exploit code, it is almost impossible to categorize them all. Google may be used to search for Web sites that host the public interest; in some cases you may find "special" sites that host tools. Please note that many exploits are not published on the Web. New (or 0day) abuses are very closely guarded in many environments, and an open public Web page is the last place where a competent attacker can hide his tools. When a toolkit is online, it is most likely encrypted or at least password protected to alert the community and prevent the spread that will result in the eventual deadlock of potential targets. This is not to say that new, unpublished abuses are not online; however, it is easier to establish relationships with people they know clearly. Nevertheless, there is nothing wrong with having a nice hit list on public utilities sites, and Google is excellent at collecting those with simple queries that include abuse, vulnerability, or vulnerable words. Google can also be used to find source code by focusing on specific strings that appear in this code type. Finding potential targets on Google is a very simple process that requires nothing but a unique string presented by a vulnerable Web application. In some cases these strings can be removed from the show(Johnny Long Bill Gardner Justin Brown).

Foca

Foca shows the published documentation (PowerPoint presentation, Word document) of the target with search engines. These castantosian are called metadata. Foca related documentation is downloaded from the target system. Targeted information can be identified by extracting relevant data (Carlos Perez).

A very important part of any pressure is the metadata count, which collects information from the target network and the area that creates a lot of traction that will be attacked. I prefer to do most of my analysis locally, because all of my information is confidential and it is not allowed to share information with third parties. This tool analyzes metadata from Microsoft Office Documents, PDF files, Open Office Files, and WordPerfect files, EXIF images, and the best part is that you can manually add files you've manually collected using Google or find and download through web searches. The Witch of Live Search makes it extremely flexible for monks. Users enumerates the Software version used to create Folders, Printers, E-mails and file.

Comparison of Open Source Intelligence Tools

Active and passive information gathering work for each of the tools are used for different tasks and they all have separate facilities. Comparison between the most commonly used tools in open source intelligence, it is shown in Table 5.

According to research conducted on open source intelligence tools, maltego tool is among the most widely used tools in active and passive information gathering studies. The biggest advantage of this tool is that it shows the results obtained from the queries graphically, allowing the user to see the relationships more easily. Shodan, another intelligence tool, allows you to

Table 5. Comparative Open Source Intelligence Tools

Features	Tools				
	Maltego	Shodan	Google Hacking Dbase	Foca	Metagoofil
Acces to admin and user information	+	-	+	-	-
Access to Metadata	-	-	-	+	+
Detecting a vulnerability	-	+	+	-	-
Detecting open ports	-	+	-	-	-

find computers and servers connected to the Internet. Shodan detects the ports that are open by scanning. Attackers who want to extract the official documents obtained from the target company can access the information they want by using the Metagoofil tool. Creates a report containing the data obtained during the data collection phase. Vulnerable sites can be detected using the Google search engine. Research results from the site can be reached from the database server. Users who want to get metadata are targeted by using foca tool access documents.

Measures for Vulnerability in Open Source Intelligence

With the increasing use of social networks, institutions and individuals aim to reach faster their followers. Individuals and institutions are exposed to many threats if the data on the Internet is not controlled. The rates of these types of threats are not explain after 2011. Disclosure of these ratios will be an important decision lens in determining the order of priority in the measures to be taken.

Due to the weaknesses arising from corporate information security, the personal or corporate data that the institutions share over the internet contains more information than the level to be shared when adhering to the privacy and confidentiality principle. The examination of this issue should be done by information security personnel from a single source. Based on this issue, each institution should have its own information safe staff and this person should ensure that all necessary safety measures are taken. Systematic measures should be taken to ensure that the data of the institutions on the internet as well as the persons in the Internet is under control and trust. A high level of awareness should be given to managers and leaders. Measures to be taken in consideration of personal privacy and legal criteria should be made available.

Among the measures that can be taken in the personal accounts of people against vulnerability, the user name must be different from their own names, and the passwords used must contain letters, numbers and symbols. The priority should be given to accessing social accounts from unknown wireless networks. For transactions requiring internet banking or credit card, a single-use password must be requested for security reasons.

CONCLUSION

With the developing technology, it has become possible for smart devices to be more involved in our lives and individuals can connect to the internet whenever they want. When the photos and documents that are easily shared in the cyber world are downloaded, as a result of the metadata analysis, the private information of the individuals is reached in a simple way. In addition, when such information is shared by the institutions, the organizational structure of the institution also arises. Based on this information, it has become the first target of the attackers to obtain special information by means of the sense of trust that social media networks provide through their fake profile and friendship offers. Intelligence gathering software can be activated for many years without being noticed in the target system.

According to the findings obtained from the mingling of open source intelligence tools, the development of technology facilitated the life of the attackers as well as facilitating life. Thanks to the intelligence tools, the information that will decipher the personal life of people is easily reached. The data that people or organizations share contains confidential information about them. The attacker reaches this data through the intelligence tools and uses the information obtained for the purpose he wants.

Finally, according to the results obtained from the examinations, it is necessary to take measures to protect the metadata shared by the institutions. It is important to ensure that information system devices do not provide information about the institution or the individual. Cyber security is not only limited to a technical field, but with the development of technology, it is necessary to pay attention to security on the internet individually.

REFERENCES

Bodenheim. (2014). *Impact of the shodan computer search engine on internet-facing industrial control system devices.* Air Force Institute of Technology Air University Pompeu Casanovas. Open Source Intelligence, Open Social Intelligence and Privacy by Design Retrieved from: http://ceur-ws.org/Vol-1283/paper_24.pdf

Canbek, G., & Sağıroğlu, Ş. (2006). *Information and Computer Security: Spyware and Protection Methods.* Ankara: Graphic Designer.

Emin İslam, T. (2012). *Vulnerabilities Scan with Google.* Department of Computer Science, University of Mannheim.

Gökhan, B. (n.d.). New Requirement of Harbin Fifth Dimension: Cyber Intelligence. *Security Strategies Magazine, 20.*

Hakan, H., & Oğuzhan, B. (2013). *Turkey's Cybercrime and Cyber Security Policy.* Retrieved from http://www.acarindex.com/dosyalar/makale/acarindex-1423936102.pdf

Long, J., Gardner, B., & Brown, J. (2016). *Google Hacking for Penetration Testers* (3rd ed.). Elsevier.

Martorella, C. (2014). *Metagoofil.* Retrieved from http://tools.kali.org/information-gathering/metagoofil

Marx, M. (2014). *The Extension and Customisation of the Maltego Data-Mining Environment into an Anti-Phishing System.* Rhodes University.

Matherly. (2017). *Complete Guide to Shodan.* Leanpub.

Mustafa, Ü. (2014). *Awareness Study on National Cyber Security,* Academic Press.

Mustafa, Ü., & Cafer, C. (2010). *Cyber Security with National and International Dimensions.* Academic Press.

Mustafa, Ü., Cafer, C., & Ayşe Gül, M. (2009). *Ensuring Cyber Security: Current Situation and Cautions in Turkey.* Retrieved from https://www.btk.gov.tr/uploads/undefined/sg.pdf

Perez, C. (2009). *Metadata Enumeration with FOCA.* Retrieved from https://www.darkoperator.com/blog/2009/4/24/metadata-enumeration-with-foca.html

Quick & Choo. (2018). *Digital Forensic Data and Open Source Intelligence.* Big Digital Forensic Data.

Seda, Y., & Şeref, S. (2013). *Cyber Security Risk Analysis.* Threat and Preparatory Levels.

Sedat, A., Hamdi Murat, Y., & Zeliha, Y.T. (2011). *Cryptology and Application Areas: Open Key Structure and Registered Electronic Mail.* Academic Press.

Serkan, S., & Nurettin, T. (2016). *A New Dimension in Cyber Security: Social Media Intelligence.* Academic Press.

Uraz, Y., Şeref, S., & İlhami, Ç. (2012). Information Security Threats and Measures to be Taken in Social Networks. *Journal of Polytechnic Volume, 15*(1).

Williams, H. J., & Blum, I. (2018). *Defining Second Generation Open Source Intelligence (OSINT) for the Defense Enterprise.* Santa Monica, CA: Published by the RAND Corporation. doi:10.7249/RR1964

Chapter 4

Intelligent Strategy and Security in Education:
Big Data (Text Analytics)

Samson Oluwaseun Fadiya
The American University of Cyprus, Cyprus

ABSTRACT

Text analytics applies to most businesses, particularly education segments; for instance, if association or university is suspicious about data secrets being spilt to contenders by the workers, text analytics investigation can help dissect many employees' email messages. The massive volume of both organized and unstructured data principally started from the web-based social networking (media) and Web 2.0. The investigation (analysis) of messages online, tweets, and different types of unstructured text data constitute what we call text analytics, which has been developed during the most recent few years in a way that does not shift, through the upheaval of various algorithms and applications being utilized for the processing of data alongside the protection and IT security. This chapter plans to find common problems faced when using the different medium of data usage in education, one can analyze their information through the perform of sentiment analysis using text analytics by extracting useful information from text documents using IBM's annotation query language (AQL).

DOI: 10.4018/978-1-5225-8976-1.ch004

Copyright © 2019, IGI Global. Copying or distributing in print or electronic forms without written permission of IGI Global is prohibited.

INTRODUCTION

The examination of language and communication has been fundamental to the progression of text analytics as the astounding parts of semantics, which means, and the point must be to some extent motorised. To examine a past loaded with phonetics, one would consider pre-Socratic what's increasing, platonic eras (Gee, J.P., 2010). Notwithstanding whether oral or sign, language has been fundamental in the exchange and securing of data. One could see Discourse Analysis as a paste to connect phonetics to computation. It incorporates the examination of correspondence from any combination of sources with a real objective to recognise not just the typical structures to the exchange of data yet. Also, to distinguish more complex concepts, for instance, an exchange of partnership, distinguish, and activity (Clarke, Nelson, & Stoodley, 2013)

Notwithstanding the creating predominance of, development advancement in, and openings by text analytics, it had been transferred to somewhat cut of some current course, for instance, data mining. Research has, for the most part, focused on the structure, algorithms, and design (architecture) of text mining and related development (Goharian, Grossman, Frieder, & Raju, 2004) in courses offered from Software engineering divisions in Engineering schools. A review of educational or pedagogical techniques for data recovery (Fernández-Luna, Huete, MacFarlane, & Efthimiadis, 2009) was restricted to Software engineering and Library Information Science departments; Data Frameworks from Business colleges were rejected. In both the reported fields, the interest was in how to create tags, either for dictionaries and thesauri or to insert into software (Fernández-Luna, Huete, MacFarlane, and Efthimiadis, 2009). An illustration database for data mining (Gee, 2010) revealed that normal subjects here are often at the algorithmic. The business setting of how to utilise these thoughts and developments by examiners who can translate the results to impact essential proposals of business to regard has not been addressed. However regularly the setting has been on changing unstructured text into the quantitative edge(frame) to apply traditional quantifiable investigation. Working with databases will allow familiarity with structured data. Computers have been working with these systems for a very long time, be that as it may, the amount of stored structured data is less in nature when compared to unstructured data like some blog posts, tweets, documents created, and emails sent daily are all unstructured or semi-structured data. So, what can all this data do for us? For one, documents often contain facts.

In the meantime, these global changes are mounting on the foundations of advanced education; innovations (technologies) keep on having a critical effect on academic professions as research and teaching turn out to be more dependent on these advances' technologies (Glenn, & D'Agostino, 2008). During the most recent decades, a computerised upset related with improvements in new technologies, for example, ubiquitous computing devices, adaptable classroom outline and Massive Open Online Courses is fundamentally reshaping the mode and availability of learning and instructing. Likewise, numerous organisations are grasping new class formats and technologies intended to meet either developing student needs or as instruments to decrease operational expenses. Despite the developing changes occurring in nature of higher (advanced) education, the part of the information in aiding addressing to contemporary difficulties is frequently not regarded. As learning technologies keep on penetrating all aspects of advanced education, plenty of valuable 'information' (data) are created. This data can be used to advise establishments of higher education and practitioner to adjust better-considering changes occurring inside and outside their surroundings. These data can have a remarkable influence on the way we comprehend the frequently challenged nature of higher education administration (Clarke, Nelson, & Stoodley, 2013). Thus guarantee that establishments are not just ready to react viably to changes occurring inside and outside them, yet that they likewise stay pertinent to their motivation in the societies that they serve. In conclusion, this information (data) have infrequently been mined cleverly with the objective of enhancing learning and illuminating teaching practice. Despite the fact that proof from different divisions, for example, marketing, sports, retail, health and technology recommends that the viable utilisation of big data can offer. The education area the possibility to upgrade its frameworks and results (Manyika, Chui, Brown, Bughin, Dobbs, Roxburgh, & Byers, 2011.).

LITERATURE REVIEW

Structured and Unstructured Analysis

Enterprises are progressively inspired by getting to unstructured data and coordinating it with classified information (Gupta & Gosain, 2013). Unstructured data presents enormous difficulties for data researchers, regularly requiring an extreme measure of time to structure and get ready data for an investigation (Ise, O.A., 2016). Unstructured information (data) sources are high in volume. Along these lines, the challenges confronting data are: getting the correct data from it, changing it into learning, examining it to discover examples and patterns. Putting away data for quick and productive get to, dealing with the work process lastly, making important business shrewd reports (Sukumaran & Sureka, 2006). The below table showed the comparison between Structured and Unstructured Analysis extracting Information.

Examining, Table 1, the problem with unstructured data is that it was designed for human consumption in different ways or platform while structured data understand its attribute type, which is an integer, character, and decimal. Also, we know its use - whether it represents a salary, name, or postal code. With this data, our computer can process the information definitively. Be that as it may, unstructured data, by its extremely nature, does not have known attribute types or data usage. The best way to recognise that data depends on context. It is typical for people, however considerably troublesome for a computer program. Consider the expression "Tom Brown has brown coloured eyes." We can without much of a stretch recognise Brown as a formal person, place or thing (noun) and brown as a descriptive word (adjective). Be that as it may, to a program, the two words are same strings of characters.

Text Analytics and Emerging Technologies

The text analytics approach to deal with data extraction utilising supervised machine learning. The essential thought is to give data extraction issue a role as that of classification. A classification model, usually, comprises of two phases: learning and forecast(prediction). In learning, one endeavour to locate a model from the labelled data that can isolate the training data, while in prediction the learned model is utilised to recognise whether an unlabeled occurrence ought to be named +1 or - 1. There is sure accessibility of developing technologies and can be found in the present technology environments. The

Table 1. Analyzing and extracting information

Structured	Unstructured
Known Types • Integer • Character	**Unknown Types** • Strings in a document
Define Usage Name: Sam Black skin colour: black	**Usage-based upon the context** "Sam Black has brown eyes."

ideal solution of available technologies depends on requirements, below are types of data and technology environments.

1. Pig
   ○ High-Level Language programming designed for easy use
   ○ More extensible functions for user's flexibility
   ○ MapReduce for parallelisation
2. JAQL
   ○ It is suitable for highly semi-structured and nested data, e.g. JSON
   ○ Large Datasets is designed for parallel processing here, using, Hadoop MapReduce
3. AQL
   ○ It is familiar to Structure Query Language (SQL)
   ○ Words documents and pattern using an extractor
   ○ It has multilingual support and prebuilt extractor
4. Other Open-Source Options
   ○ Languages for Hadoop
   ○ Also, Python Natural Language Toolkit (NLTK) and General Architecture for Text Engineering (GATE)

Text analytics is a large and quickly extending field. There are numerous tools accessible. The perfect arrangement relies upon the sort of information; we want to extract, and technology environment. A typical utilise case is performing data mining and text analytics on vast datasets that are stored in a distributed document framework, for example, the open-source Apache Hadoop. It is naturally improved for a progression of MapReduce jobs, the centre Hadoop technology which takes into consideration colossal parallelisation. Another choice is JAQL, accessible open-source, yet additionally kept up in BigInsights, IBM's "enormous information" arrangement based upon Hadoop.

JAQL is intense for handling data stored in JSON (JavaScript Object Notation). Like Pig, the code is consequently streamlined for parallel computing. Next is AQL (Annotation Query Language). AQL is composed particularly for natural language processing and text analytics. Its syntax structure will be instantly commonplace to any individual who has worked with SQL. Exclusive of much of a stretch concentrate complex examples from less complicated building blocks, for example, words or regular expressions. AQL accompanies prebuilt extractors for some, regular use cases, and additionally broad language support. There are open-source options outside of Hadoop too. The perfect arrangement relies upon the type of information(data), the data you need to extract, and your technology condition. A typical use case is performing data mining and text analytics on comprehensive datasets that are stored in a distributed file system, such as the open-source Apache Hadoop. Hadoop accompanies Pig, which is itself given a high-level language called Pig Latin.

APPROACH FOR TEXT ANALYTICS

Text analytics can be separated into stages where it logically refines data until the point when it is left with something that can be utilised by using application has appeared in Figure 1. Amid the examination (analysis) stage, you recognise the type of data. It is proficient by marking (labelled) words and phrases in your sample documents. Now, we make rules that extract the data and verify that they function as proposed. This stage can be additionally separated or broken down. We create a regular expression to extract phone numbers. Moreover, after that, the extracted context for that basic block by combining them with the clues that are identified in the analysis stage. At long last, it moves onto execution or performance tuning, production, and all.

Figure 1. Text analytics phases

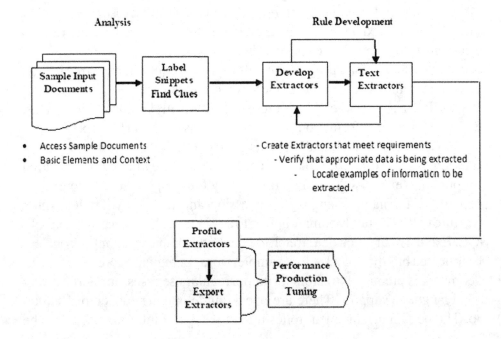

We will not broadly expound here; sufficiently only to make them compose writing and AQL modules.

Data Model for Annotation Query Language (AQL)

The data model for AQL is like that of an SQL database. To extract data, we create views. These are very similar to tables in a relational system. All data in AQL is stored in tuples, which is the same as rows. Each tuple is made up of attributes, which are like columns. All tuples in a view must have the same schema, meaning the name and type of each attribute must be the same for all tuples in the view.

1. Data Model
   - Standard Relational Model is like Data Model
   - It allows work with views which is like a table
   - Data are stored in the tuple (like rows in a table) and the tuples have attributes (like the column in a table)
2. Scalar Types
   - Text: Basically, this is a Unicode string which indicates the string that the tuple belongs in the metadata
   - Integer: It is a 32bits
   - Span: This is some characters in a text region object
   - Float: The Floating-Point number is a single precision
3. Execution Model
   - A collection of some views in Execution model is extracted by AQL, and each of this view defines a relation.
   - A document that is being annotated and is represented by Text (the textual content) and Label (the name of the document)
   - AQL contains files that must have. aql as a suffix
   - Statement are case-sensitive in AQL and ended with a semicolon
   - This (--) is used for a single line and (/**/) is for comments
   - Export and Import statements implemented can be re-used, and in a module, the code must be defined. AQL extractor consists of a collection of views, each of which defines a relationship. There is one view called Document. This view represents the document that is currently being annotated. The document is a reserved word and cannot create another view with that name to make use of any this views, dictionaries, tables, or functions, AQL file can contain the 'module' statement.

The text is basic for making on security choices. Security approaches regularly construct get to choices considering temporal context (e.g., time of day) and ecological context (e.g., geographic area). An Operating Systems get to control strategy as often as possible considers execution context (e.g., client ID, program contentions, past inputs). Security investigation for projects regularly utilizes contexts of control stream and data stream. In fact, there are numerous types of context considered in security. One type of context is as often as possible ignored: human desires, e.g., did a human anticipate that a specific usefulness will happen? This oversight may appear to be odd given that PC security is some of the time characterized regarding desire:

Computer is secure on the off chance that you can rely upon it and its software to carry on as you expect. The insufficiency in this definition is that human desires are frequently and casually characterize. Without a solid meaning of "expectation," the security of a framework can't be confirmed. People draw desires from numerous sources. One normal source is textual information. For instance, developers get security expectations from API documentation, remarks in code, and requirements documents. Clients derive security expectations from textual descriptions of program usefulness (e.g., portable application depiction).

USER-DEFINED FUNCTIONS

Allows the user to define the customers (educators) function properties to be used in the extraction rules. All the statements provide functionality for extracting essential features from the text. The statements make use of regular expressions, dictionaries, splits, blocks, parts of speech, and sequence patterns. All these are built-in functions provided in AQL, including predicate functions, scalar functions, and aggregate functions so that we can also code our functions to be used in extraction rules as seen in Figure 2.

TEXT MINING (ANALYTICS) IN BUSINESS AND SECURITY

The text analytics is the way toward discovering obscure or cover up the design from the data which is beforehand unfamiliar. On the off chance that the methodology is to find and concentrate content from different versatile textual materials for learning management, at that point it could be named as Text Mining (Gupta & Lehal, 2009), which gives the facility of overseeing

Figure 2. Modelling approach to data for AQL

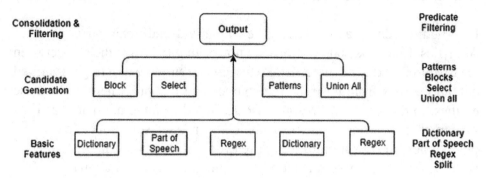

data framework for research and investigation (Nasa, 2012) and help the endeavors in better business administration. The data inflow for business association could be from different sources of uses like CRM, DB, centralized servers, printed documents, spreadsheets, which are dynamic and adaptable in nature. The arrangements of these adaptable sources of information tend to be disparate. This difference is a noteworthy obstacle for dealing with the data originating from these sources. The most important prerequisite is to make a Data Warehouse having brought together design dependent on which the information from these differed sources is coordinated into a single entity. To plan such information, Extraction, Transformation, and Loading (ETL) and data warehouse process is received to extricate unstructured data from changed sources, making brought together an arrangement for changing the data to fit business needs, lastly transferring the information into brought together data warehouse (Chhillar, 2015).

The sources of archives could be inward and outside to the enterprise contrasted with data Warehouse which supplies verifiable and current tasks and the data is internal to the enterprise (Samson, Serdar & Zira, 2014). The report document warehouse distribution center is involved to extricate the raw textual data to satisfy business needs according to the query in the setting of an occasion. It helps in content (text) mining with capable repositories for making on the profitable decision and business intelligence (Gupta & Narang, 2012).

MATERIALS AND METHODS

Unstructured data cannot merely be integrated and analysed using Text Analytics. Enterprise applications are now trying to bridge the gap between unstructured and structured data. This task requires extracting structured columns values from unstructured sources and mapping them to database entities. In this paper, we design unstructured data integration and analysis system that uses text analytic techniques in analysing educationist and practitioners in education to extract relevant information. The fundamental architecture of the system is based on Annotation Query Language (AQL) model. The system provides the user with the capability of using those building blocks to create intricate patterns. Moreover, removes HTML and XML tags from said document types which are learning and prediction to the database. The task begins by transforming unstructured nature of educationist and practitioners in education into a structured form that can comfortably fit into Text Analytics. The process of transformation is in two phases. In phase 1, which is the learning phase, the structure is added to unstructured data using ***Regular Expression***. The output of this phase is in eXtensible Markup Language (XML) format which in turn act as an input to Phase 2 where the data is a prediction of the Annotation Query Language (AQL).

Approach for Annotation Query Language (AQL)

As appeared in Figure 2, making AQL extractors is a multi-step, multi-layered process. We begin by making key segments that are certain, utilising the essential highlights of the language. These are along the lines of finding numeric strings in the data or finding every one of the organisations' division names in the document. These notable highlights are then utilised for Candidate Generation. At this level in the process, we utilise various essential highlights to discover events in education. Moreover, after that, utilising that data to find educationist and practitioners parameters that are related to divisions. Something it is discovered that the generating candidates extracted a more significant number of data that require. The third step is to consolidate or filter the hopeful outcomes with the goal that it extracts the desired data.

Extract Regular Expression

In the extraction of a regular expression, the create view statement defines a tuple with a single attribute, 'match.' Moreover, the tuples are extracted with a regular expression that matches any number (integer or decimal) in the document. Regexes are the bread-and-butter pattern matching tool, used to extract any text that conforms to the same structure in the documents, e.g., a phone number, proper noun, or IP address. AQL defaults to using Perl syntax for defining regular expressions. The regex is enclosed between forwarding slashes. The "d+" matches one or more digits. The next term in the parentheses matches a decimal point followed by another series of digits. The question mark indicates that the parentheses contain an optional term as it appeared in Figure 3.

Grouping Specification

Here we can specify groups to get specific parts of a regex match. Groups are enclosed by parentheses and read left-to-right, outer-to-inner. Group 0 is a select group that returns the entire match. Here we have a regex that matches phone numbers. This first group of parentheses is group 1 Next would be group 2, And this entire term is group 3 Now that we are done with the outer parentheses we move inward. It is group 4 This is group 5, And this is group 6 Here we see how groups are used in a 'create view' statement. We extract regex as before and assign each group as an attribute in a tuple using the 'return' clause, see Figure 4.

Creating Dictionaries

Dictionaries are a list of words that can be used in pattern matching. They are created with the 'create dictionary statement. There are two main types of dictionaries: inline and external. Inline is suitable when, the dictionary has only a few values, such as a dictionary of numeric scales. Here we see the syntax for creating an online dictionary. The language code is a string of comma-separated two-letter codes such as 'EN' for English or 'ES' for Spanish for the languages on which to evaluate the dictionary. Note that the dictionary will produce no results if an unrecognised language code is used. The default is English. The optional 'case' parameter specifies what type of case folding the dictionary performs when determining whether a given region

Figure 3. Regular expression (extract)

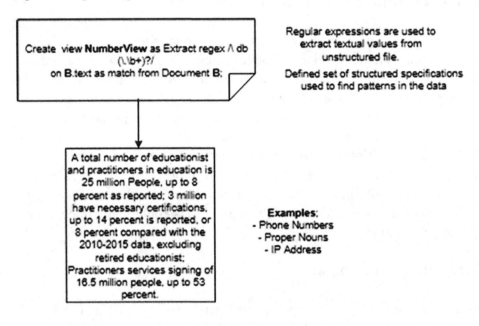

Create view **NumberView** as Extract regex ∧ db
(\.\b+)?/
on B.text as match from Document B;

Regular expressions are used to extract textual values from unstructured file.

Defined set of structured specifications used to find patterns in the data

A total number of educationist and practitioners in education is 25 million People, up to 8 percent as reported; 3 million have necessary certifications, up to 14 percent is reported, or 8 percent compared with the 2010-2015 data, excluding retired educationist; Practitioners services signing of 16.5 million people, up to 53 percent.

Examples:
- Phone Numbers
- Proper Nouns
- IP Address

Returned Span
- 813 - 888 - 6543
Group 0 is the entire match
- 813 - 888 - 6543
Group 1 is 813
Group 2 is -
Group 3 is 888 - 6543
Group 4 is 888
Group 5 -
Group 6 is 6543

Create view **PhoneView** as extract regex /(/b{4})(-)((\b{4})(-)(\b{5}))/
on **B.text**
return group 1 as area code and group 4 as exchange and group 6 as extension from Document B;

Figure 4. Specific parts of a regex

```
return
group <number> as <name>
[and group <number> as <name>]
Example:
/ (/b{4})(-)(\b{4})(-)(\b{5}))/
```

of the document matches. The choices are 'exact', 'insensitive', and 'folding'. 'folding' uses Unicode case folding. The default is 'insensitive'. The optional 'lemma match' parameter specifies that the dictionary is matched against the lemmatised form of tokens instead of their surface form. For example, the word 'better' has 'good' as its lemma. So, if the dictionary contained 'good', occurrences of the word 'better' would be considered as matches. Creating a dictionary from an external file differs in that there are no inline entry values but a 'from file' clause instead. The optional parameters are the same as with an inline dictionary.

External dictionary files are carriage-return delimited text files with one dictionary entry per line. Lines with a '#' character at position 0 are treated as comments. Dictionary Extraction Continuing with our theme of extracting company performance information from a quarterly report, we probably want to know the revenue generated by each division. Pulling out numbers, like '26.3', is going to be important, but you also need to know the numeric scale. Using a dictionary that finds all occurrences of 'million', 'billion', or possible 'trillion' will facilitate this endeavour. Our example here uses a single dictionary, but it is possible to create a view extracting from multiple dictionaries as seen in Figures 5, 6 and 7.

Detag

The detag statement strips HTML and XML tags from a document and creates a new detagged text document which can then be used for AQL queries,

Figure 5. Creating dictionaries

```
Create dictionary NumericScaleDict
        with language as 'en'
        and Case insensitive
        and lemma_match
                as
    ('million', 'billion', 'trillion');
-------------------------------------
Create dictionary NumericScaleDict
    from file '<path to dictionary file>'
        with language as 'en';


-------------------------------------
Create external dictionary <dict-name>
        allow empty [true, false]
[with] [languages as '<language codes>'] [and]
    [Case (exact | insensitive | folding)];
```

see Figure 6. In addition to stripping out the tags, the statement can also remember the original locations of the tags and their values. The format of the detag statement is as follows: The first clause provides the name of the input view containing the text and the tags. It also provides the name of a new output view where the detagged text goes. This output view contains a single column, called 'text'. Running non-HTML or non-XML text through a detagger can cause problems if the text contains XML special characters like pointed brackets or ampersand.

The optional 'detect content type' clause specifies whether to verify that the target document text contains XML or HTML content before attempting to detag it. 'always' will skip detagging if the document does not appear to be XML or HTML. 'never' will detag no matter what. The optional 'annotate' clause directs the system to remember information about the tags it removes, creating one or more views to hold the locations of the original tags, Figure 8.

Detag Example Here we have a simple detag statement and HTML document. The statement reads the document and creates two extractions: The first of which is DetaggedDoc, which contains the non-HTML text. There is also an 'annotate' clause which creates a view called Title consisting of tuples of a single attribute called 'match' which hold the text of the HTML elements.

Figure 6. Dictionary extraction

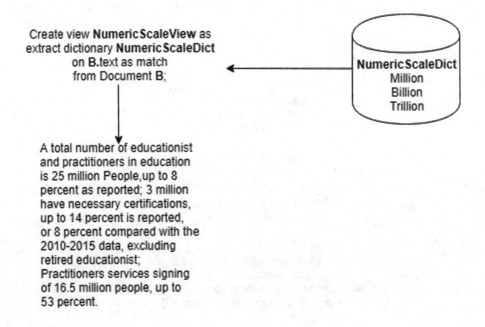

Figure 7. Having clause

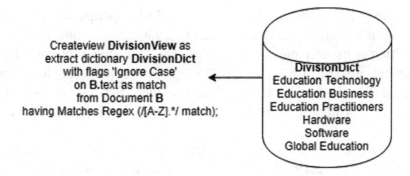

Figure 8. Detag

```
detag <input view name> <text column>
         as <output view name>
   [detect content_type (always I never)]
              [annotate
[element '<element name>' as <view name>
[with attribute '<attribute name>' as <column
                 name>]
[and attribute '<attribute name>' as <column name>]
             [element]]
```

Import and Export Statements

At this point, depending on the complexity of the project, we may find multiple modules. To use an object, like a view, dictionary, table, or function, we must include an export statement in its home module. Then, we import that object via the import statement, in Figure 9.

Figure 9. Statement

```
export <view I dictionary I table I function>
            <object-name>

import <view I dictionary I table I function>
            <object-name>
from module <module-name> [as < alias> ];
```

Blocks Specification

Blocks extraction can be used to identify blocks of contiguous spans across input text, as shown in Figure 10. A span is just a section of text specified by the position of its start and end characters. The 'with count' clause specifies the number of spans that make up the block. It can be an absolute number or a range. We also specify the acceptable distance between spans for those spans to be considered as contiguous. It can be some number of tokens or characters.

Blocks Example Let's look at an example of a block's extractor. Assume we have already created a view that returns all the capitalised words in a document. We would like to find blocks where there are two or three capitalised words within 100 characters of each other. Create view, called Block Capital Words. The extract blocks statement specifies a block size of 2 or 3 words, with a separation of 0 to 100 characters. The extraction performance on the existing view, Capitalized Words. The resulting view will have one attribute called caps words containing our blocks.

Performance Patterns (Sequence)

Sequence patterns can be used to perform regular expression matching over the document text itself, along with annotations extracted from the document.

Figure 10. Block specification

```
                    extract blocks
        with count [between <min> and ] <max>
       and separation [between <min> and ] <max>
                   (token I characters )
        on <name>.<column containing spans>
                   as <output name>
```

Example: Find blocks with 10-30 Capitalized words within 500 characters of each other.

```
            Create view BlockCapitalWords
                    extract blocks
              with count between 10 and 30
       and separation between 0 and 500 characters )
                      on cw.words
                      as capsword
               from CapitalizedWord cw;
```

It allows us to write complex extraction patterns involving alternation, sequences, and repetitions in a compact fashion.

The pattern specification is defined according to a context-free grammar. The rules of the grammar are necessarily quite complicated. Here is the basic format of a pattern extractor. The return clause functions the same as it does in an extract regex statement. Specify which groups to return and what to call. In the pattern, we saw that during this stage we might want to combine a number and a numeric scale to create a dollar amount. We can now accomplish this by using sequence patterns. Already we have seen a view that extracts numbers, as well as a view that extracts a scale value. The numbers representing amounts will all be preceded by a # (number sign). Thus, our view will look for the pattern of a dollar sign, followed by a number, followed by a numeric scale. Since the extraction returns only one group (remember that group 0 represents the entire match), the output view will have only one attribute in its tuples. Here is another example. Assume that we have a document that contains information about countries. It might be the country name, the longitude and latitude, the government type, population, its area, and climate. The steps involve in extracting the country name and the corresponding longitude and latitude. The first step would be creating a view called Countries that returns the extracted country names and a second view called Locations that returns all the longitudinal and latitudinal values. Next, create a sequence pattern that looks for a country name and a latitude/longitude pair near. We assume the Countries and Locations views have already been created. It looks for a Country name, followed by a latitude-longitude pair that is at least five tokens away but not more than 25 tokens away.

Union All

The union all operator allows the combination of the tuples from two views if the views have the same schema. To continue our example of extracting financial information from quarterly reports, dollar amounts by themselves are not the only financial indicators of interest. Knowing percentage increases or decreases can be useful as well. This example in Figure 12, assumes that we created a view that returns dollar amounts, like the one from our sequence pattern example, and another view that returns percentages. Notice that the same attribute name is used for both views. It is what we mean by having the same schemas. Each tuple must have the same number of attributes, with the same attribute names.

Figure 11. Sequence patterns

extract blocks
with count [between <min> and] <max>
and separation [between <min> and] <max>
(token | characters)
on <name>.<column containing spans>
as <output name>

Example: Find blocks with 10-30 Capitalized words within 500 characters of each other.

Create view **BlockCapitalWords**
extract blocks
with count between 10 and 30
and separation between 0 and 500 characters)
on cw.words
as capsword
from **CapitalizedWord** cw,

Figure 12. Union all

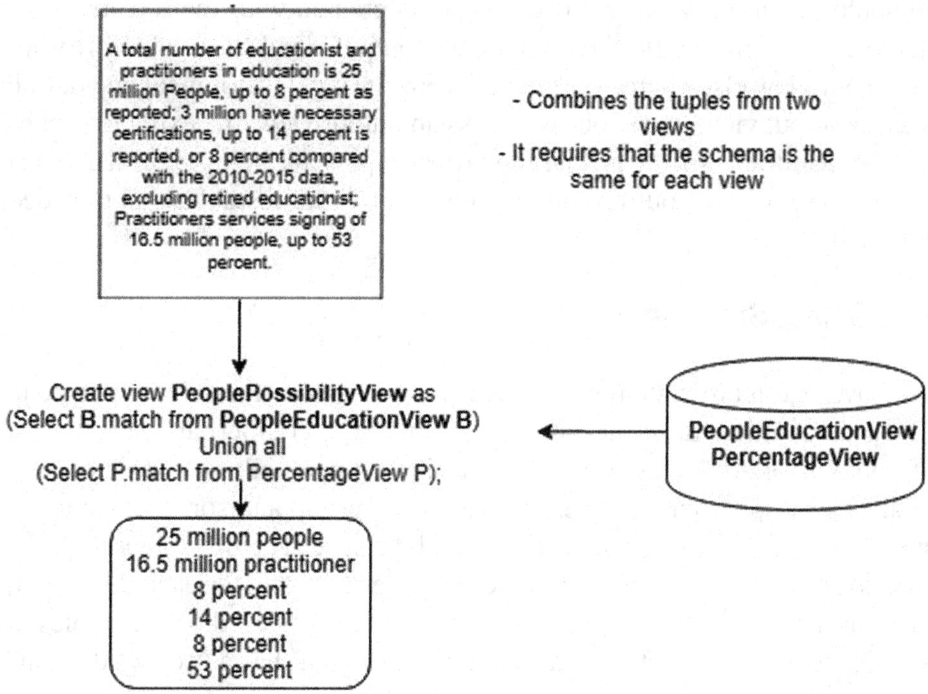
A total number of educationist and practitioners in education is 25 million People, up to 8 percent as reported; 3 million have necessary certifications, up to 14 percent is reported, or 8 percent compared with the 2010-2015 data, excluding retired educationist; Practitioners services signing of 16.5 million people, up to 53 percent.
- Combines the tuples from two views
- It requires that the schema is the same for each view
Create view PeoplePossibilityView as
(Select B.match from PeopleEducationView B)
Union all
(Select P.match from PercentageView P);
PeopleEducationView
PercentageView
25 million people
16.5 million practitioner
8 percent
14 percent
8 percent
53 percent

The Statement

Create View

Views are the critical components in AQL, akin to tables in SQL. There are several ways to create a view using the ‘create view’ statement. One way is to specify select or extract statements to populate the view. Using a ‘select’ statement, you can create a view by selecting attributes from a tuple defined in another view. Alternatively, with an ‘extract’ statement, you can extract directly from the text. Create a view by unioning together several previously defined views. Alternatively, get the set difference between two views with the ‘minus’ clause.

Output View

Views in AQL can either be an output view or non-output view. When an AQL extractor executes, it computes the result tuples for all output views.

The extractor only evaluates nonoutput views if their outputs are needed to compute an output view. By default, views created with the 'create view' statement are non-output. We must use the 'output view' statement if we want to use our view elsewhere. We create a view during development and define it as an output view to test our work. As an output view, the extracted spans will be displayed, so verify that the proper tuples are being returned. Then remove or comment out the output statement if the results are not needed externally.

The Select Statement

We have one more statement to cover in this lesson: the select statement. The statement is almost the same here as its SQL counterpart. Select a list of columns or attributes from a list of views. Optionally we can include a predicate by specifying a where clause. Also, group and sort the results by specifying a group by clause and an order by clause. The limit clause may be used to specify the maximum number of tuples returned for each document. Each of these clauses functions as we would expect based on their roles in an SQL select statement. One difference is that AQL has a "consolidate on" clause.

The Select List

The select list consists of a comma-delimited list of output expressions. If columns are listed, they must be qualified with a view name. They can be assigned a local name or alias; for example, viewname.colname as localname. The select list may include expressions as well. Expressions can be scalar function calls or aggregate function calls. It is also possible to specify a case statement as an expression.

Selecting From a View

The select statement allows us to create a view, based on a second view, and apply some filter criteria in the form of the 'where' statement. Suppose we have a dictionary, FalsePositivesDict, which contains values like 'increased, decreased, up, down.' In the quarterly report, there are these two statements: Assuming, the services signings of $17.8 billion, up 55%. Total gross profit margin was about 45%. The dollar amount and the percentages are returned in the AmountPossibilitesView; however, 'up 55 percent' just describes the services signings. It is not a value we want to be returned. We create a new view. The 'where' clause in the select statement says that we only want values where the token to the left of the span is not in the False Positives Dictionary. It eliminates our first candidate.

Filtering and Consolidation

The last step in creating an application is the filtering and consolidation phase, where the result is refined. Consolidation allows us to specify how we want to handle spans that overlap. Already we should see the use of the 'where' clause and predicate-based filtering. This lesson introduces set-based filtering, which uses the minus clause - essentially the opposite of 'union all.'

The 'Consolidate' Clause

The 'consolidate on' clause specifies what the system is to do if overlapping spans are returned. The format of the clause is "consolidate on <target> using '<policy>'." Note that the policy is enclosed in single quotes. The target is either a column or an expression composed of scalar function calls. There are five consolidation policies. ContainedWithin: If spans A and B overlap, and A completely contains B, then remove the tuple containing span B from the output. If A and B are the same, then remove one of them. The choice of which tuple to remove is arbitrary. NotContainedWithin: If spans A and B overlap, and A completely contains B, then remove span A from the output. If A and B are the same, then remove one of them. ContainsButNotEqual: Same as ContainedWithin, except that spans that are exactly equal are retained. ExactMatch: If a set of spans cover the same region of text, return exactly one of them. All other spans are left untouched. LeftToRight: Process the spans in order from left to right; when overlap occurs, retain the leftmost longest non-overlapping span.

RESULTS AND DISCUSSION

In this paper, we develop a system capable of transforming unstructured data in the form of educationist and practitioners using text analytics by extracting useful information from text documents. The system using text analytics techniques based on natural language processing technique can extract specific data from unstructured academic data, transform the data into structured data and Integrate the structured data into RDBMS for further analysis. we give an introduction to well-known systems and instruments of natural language processing (NLP) and text mining, and offer our encounters in applying text analytics investigation to security issues

Developing the system as an application based, built on IBM's Annotation Query Language (AQL). Model view All data extracted from unstructured educationist and practitioners are stored using performance production tuning which enables the system to recognise entities and extract features from develop and text extractors. We experimented with 40 randomly selected data from statements which were words and the punctuations. The dataset contains 25, million people, 16.5 million are a practitioner, 8 percent, 14 percent and 53 percent in the percentage view with union all. A sequence labelling Education and Level views have already been created. It looks for an Education Level, followed by a practitioner pair that is at least twenty-five tokens away but not more than 25 tokens.

REFERENCES

Abney, S. (1996a). Part-of-speech tagging and partial parsing. In S. Young & G. Bloothooft (Eds.), *Corpus-Based Methods in Language and Speech Processing* (pp. 118–136). Dordrecht: Kluwer Academic.

Abney, S. (1996b). Statistical methods and linguistics. The Balancing Act: Combining Symbolic and Statistical. *Linguistics, 23*, 597–618.

Chhillar, R. S. (n.d.). Extraction Transformation Loading – A Road to Data Warehouse. *2nd National Conference Mathematical Techniques: Emerging Paradigms for Electronics and IT Industries*, 384-388.

Clarke, J.A., Nelson, K.J., & Stoodley, I.D. (2013). *The place of higher education institutions in assessing student engagement, success and retention: A maturity model to guide practice.* Academic Press.

Daniel, B. (2015). Big Data and analytics in higher education: Opportunities and challenges. *British Journal of Educational Technology, 46*(5), 904–920. doi:10.1111/bjet.12230

Edgington, T. M. (2011). Introducing text analytics as a graduate business school course. *Journal of Information Technology Education, 10*, 207–234.

Fernández-Luna, J. M., Huete, J. F., MacFarlane, A., & Efthimiadis, E. N. (2009). Teaching and learning in information retrieval. *Information Retrieval, 12*(2), 201–226. doi:10.100710791-009-9089-9

Gee, J. P. (2010). *An introduction to discourse analysis: Theory and method.* Routledge. doi:10.4324/9780203847886

Glenn, M., & D'Agostino, D. (2008). *The future of higher education: How technology will shape learning.* New Media Consortium.

Goharian, N., Grossman, D., Frieder, O., & Raju, N. (2004). Migrating information retrieval from the graduate to the undergraduate curriculum. *Journal of Information Systems Education, 15*(1), 55.

Gupta, P., & Narang, B. (2012). Role of Text Mining in Business Intelligence. *Gian Jyoti E-Journal, 1*(2).

Gupta, V., & Gosain, A. 2013, May. Tagging Facts and Dimensions in Unstructured Data. In *International Conference on Electrical, Electronics and Computer Science Engineering (EECS)* (pp. 1-6). Academic Press.

Gupta, V., & Lehal, G. (2009, August). A Survey of text mining techniques and applications. *Journal of Emerging Technologies in Web Intelligence, 1*(1), 60–76. doi:10.4304/jetwi.1.1.60-76

Ise, O. A. (2016). Integration and Analysis of Unstructured Data for Decision Making: Text Analytics Approach. *International Journal of Open Information Technologies, 4*(10).

Manyika, J., Chui, M., Brown, B., Bughin, J., Dobbs, R., Roxburgh, C., & Byers, A.H. (2011). *Big data: The next frontier for innovation, competition, and productivity.* Academic Press.

Nasa, D. (2012, April). Text Mining Techniques - A Survey. *International Journal of Advanced Research in Computer Science and Software Engineering, 2*(4), 50–54.

Samson, O. F., Serdar, S., & Vanduhe, V. (2014). Advancing Big Data for Humanitarian Needs. *Procedia Engineering, 78,* 88–95. doi:10.1016/j.proeng.2014.07.043

Sukumaran, S., & Sureka, A. (2006). Integrating structured and unstructured data using text tagging and annotation. *Business Intelligence Journal, 1*(2), 8.

Chapter 5
Inevitable Battle Against Botnets

Ibrahim Firat
University of Reading, UK

ABSTRACT

It is undeniable that technology is developing and growing at an unstoppable pace. Technology has become a part of people's daily lives. It has been used for many purposes but mainly to make human life easier. In addition to being useful, these advancements in technology have some bad consequences. A new malware called botnet has recently emerged. It is considered to be one of the most important and dangerous cyber security problems as it is not well understood and evolves quickly. Communication of bots between each other and their botmaster results in the formation of botnet; this is also known as a zombie army. As botnets become popular among cybercriminals, more studies have been done in botnet detection area. Researchers have developed new detection mechanisms in order to understand and tackle this growing botnet issue. This chapter aims to review working principles of botnets and botnet detection mechanisms in order to increase general knowledge about botnets.

DOI: 10.4018/978-1-5225-8976-1.ch005

Copyright © 2019, IGI Global. Copying or distributing in print or electronic forms without written permission of IGI Global is prohibited.

INTRODUCTION

When it comes to talk about cyber security and its possible consequences, botnet is one of the most common word that pops in people's mind who are specialised in cybersecurity. Botnets can be considered as network of bots as they consist of more than one bot working together. Botnets use command and control (C&C) communication channels to talk with the cybercriminal who controls them. During this communication process, bots receive commands from the cybercriminal and then report back to that cybercriminal. This is one of the most distinctive characteristics of botnets which separates them from other malwares. Botnets have different architectures and cybercriminals choose any of these architectures depending on their purposes. Cybercriminals have a range of different options ranging from client-server model to peer-to-peer networks (Botnet, 2018). In general, botmasters try to collect more devices as possible to increase the strength of botnet. Through infection process, botmasters add new devices to their army. Botmasters infect new devices by using viruses, worms, trojan horses and many other malicious techniques. Once a device gets infected by any of the mentioned malicious technique, it becomes a part of the botnet and can be labelled as a bot. Bots can be any device as long as cybercriminals can infect them such as computers and smartphones. On the other hand, it is well known that botnet detection is an on-going problem. It is very challenging to detect botnets as they use small amounts of computing power and they can update their behaviours. They can be very dangerous as they are capable of carrying out distributed denial-of-service (DDoS) attacks, stealing sensitive data and performing a number of different malicious behaviours. They can cause a range of different and serious problems if they are not successfully detected and neutralized. To be more precise, leakage of sensitive data can lead to conflicts at different levels. If cybercriminals leak government secrets, this can cause a crisis at a national level. On the other hand, DDoS attacks can make important online services unavailable. For example, if cybercriminals decide to perform DDoS attacks on online banking system, this can lead to money transaction problems, money fraud and even more serious financial issues. These are only some of the few problems that botnets can cause. Therefore, it is important to detect and understand botnets. This chapter aims to increase the knowledge about botnets by giving information about different types of botnets with their uses and formation. Also, it aims to explain botnet's working principles, architecture, life-cycle, possible threats, infection and detection processes.

BACKGROUND

Many researches have been done in the areas of botnets and botnet detection in order to strengthen the domain knowledge about botnets and protect innocent users from possible attacks of botnets. Cooke et al. published a paper in order to draw attention to the current botnet problem and determine the origins and structure of bots and as well as botnets. The authors stated that, monitoring IRC communication or other command and control activity was not sufficient enough to detect botnets effectively. The authors concluded the paper by describing a system which was able to detect botnets with advanced command and control mechanisms by using secondary detection data from more than one sources (Cooke, Jahanian & McPherson, 2005). In 2014, Sebastián García presented three new botnet detection methods in his PHD thesis. These detection methods were SimDetect, BClus and CCDetector. SimDetect method focused on finding structural similarities, BClus focused on clustering network traffic based on connection patterns and CCDetector focused on training a Markov Chain to detect similar traffic in unknown networks. Also, he presented a new model for botnet behaviour analysis in the given network (Garcia, 2014). On the other hand, Muthumanickam K. et al. proposed a decentralized three phased botnet detection model for the detection of P2P based botnets. The first phase was the identification of P2P node, second phase was about collecting suspicious P2P nodes together and the final phase was the detection of botnets (Muthumanickam, Ilavarasan & Dwivedi, 2014). This is followed by a study in which the authors compared the outputs of three popular botnet detection methods by executing them over a range of different datasets (Garcia, Grill, Stiborek, Zunino, 2014). In another study, the authors proposed a new technique to detect botnet activity with the help of machine learning. The authors detected botnet activity based on traffic behavior analysis by identifying network traffic behavior. Also, the authors worked on the feasibility of locating botnet activity without having access to a complete network flow by identifying behavior based on time intervals (Zhao, Traore, Sayed, Lu, Saad, Ghorbani & Garant, 2013). In another paper, the authors presented an event-driven log analysis software that helped researchers to detect botnet activities and identify if an end-user's machine has become part of the botnet (Ersson & Moradian 2013). In another study, the researchers presented a method which used artificial fish swarm algorithm and a support vector machine together. The presented method was used to classify important features which determined the patterns of botnets (Lin, Chen & Hung, 2014).

On the other hand, for the early detection of botnets, the authors presented a new method for recreating botnet's port scanning patterns with the help of simple text classifier which illustrates these patterns like a matrix. Then, these patterns were used to train a hidden Markov model for early detection of botnets (Kim, Lee, Kang, Jeong & In, 2012). In another study, the authors proposed large scale and wide area botnet detection system which made use of a range of different techniques to eliminate the challenges imposed by the use of NetFlow data (Bilge, Balzarotti, Robertson, Kirda & Kruegel, 2012). In a recently published paper, the authors made a study about DDoS attacks which were launched by botnets. The authors stated that the geospatial distribution of attacking sources follows a similar pattern which enables prediction of future attacks. Also, the authors mentioned about an attacking trend where different botnets execute DDoS attacks on the same victim (Wang, Chang, Chen & Mohaisen, 2018). In a different research, the authors used machine learning algorithm to determine connections which belong to a botnet. In order to maximise detection rate of botnets, the authors found feature set according to the connections of botnets at their C&C (Alejandre, Cortés, & Anaya, 2017). On the other hand, a researcher invented a new national cyber-firewall called "Seddulbahir" against 21 different cyber-attacks (Sari, 2019). The researcher used artificial neural network radial basis function to set rules which can be used in the detection processes of these possible attacks (Sari, 2019). Lastly, the same author proposed a different study about the importance of context-aware intelligent systems of Fog Computing on analysing IoT data. The author stated that use of Fog Computing to analyse IoT data can help cybersecurity professionals to detect, mitigate and prevent possible attacks earlier (Sari, 2018).

BOTNET DEFINITION

A botnet is a collection of bots which usually communicate with a bot controller and other bots continuously. This is also known as a zombie army (Cooke, Jahanian & McPherson, 2005). The bot controller is also referred as botmaster. Botnets can be considered as networks of devices which are under control of malware (bot) code (Gu, Perdisci, Zhang & Lee, 2008). Generally, the term botnet itself means network of infected end hosts (bots) which are in control of botmaster (Rajab, Zarfoss, Monrose & Terzis, 2006). Usually, bots are not physically possessed by a botmaster and can be placed in several locations around the world. Botnets are capable of carrying out different types of malicious activity. In some cases, these activities can be very dangerous. They aim a range of different profiles changing from individual users to businesses. Therefore, they are considered to be one of the most serious cyber security problems.

BOTNET TYPES

Recently, the numbers of botnets have risen sharply, and new types of botnets have emerged. Botnets can be classified as IRC-Based, HTTP-based and Peer to Peer (P2P) botnets depending on Command and Control (C&C) architecture or communication protocol used.

Peer to Peer (P2P) Botnets

Peer to Peer (P2P) botnets have emerged recently as attackers noticed the weak points of using traditional centralised botnets (Wang, Aslam & Zou, 2010). P2P botnets make use of decentralized C&C structure. Mostly, usage of centralised servers resulted in a single point of failure for the network which makes it even easier to take down servers (Wang, Aslam & Zou, 2010). In P2P botnets, bots can act as C&C servers and as well as clients (Vormayr, Zseby, Fabini, 2017). Every bot is connected to each other, and the botmaster can only control the whole botnet when there is a flow of commands between connected bots. So, there is a potential for every bot to become a potential C&C server (Vormayr, Zseby, Fabini, 2017). Moreover, the communication between botnet elements would not be disrupted regardless of losing members of botnet (Wang, Aslam & Zou, 2010). Also, it is harder to detect, shutdown or monitor P2P botnets compared to other kinds of botnets. Another definition of P2P botnets was done by G. Gu, et al. (Gu, Perdisci, Zhang & Lee, 2008). The authors mentioned about commands which were transferred through push/pull mechanism. The bots use this mechanism to receive command files which were generated by botmaster. P2P bots stay in touch with adjacent bots to get commands and send "Keep Alive" messages to other members of the botnet in the network. Trojan.Peacomm botnet and Stormnet are examples of Peer to Peer botnets (Wang, Aslam & Zou, 2010).

The first known P2P botnet was Storm Worm and it appeared in 2007 (Van Ruitenbeek & Sanders, 2008). Attacks of this botnet mostly rely on social engineering techniques and it uses infected email attachments to trick users on opening them (Van Ruitenbeek & Sanders, 2008). These attachments contain Trojan horses which infect user's computers. After infecting the computers of users, the trojan horses try to establish a communication with others in the Storm Worm botnet and download the full payload (Van Ruitenbeek & Sanders, 2008). At the end, infected computers become a part of the botnet and start to receive commands and execute them consecutively.

IRC-Based Botnets

IRC protocol allows different kinds of communications such as point to point or point to multi-point to take place (Rajab, Zarfoss, Monrose & Terzis, 2006). The flexibility of this protocol and the presence of open-source implementations allow third parties to modify it for different uses. This is the reason why botmasters prefer IRC protocol as a botnet control mechanism (Rajab, Zarfoss, Monrose & Terzis, 2006). Internet Relay Chat (IRC) is a text-based messaging protocol between people who are connected with the internet (Liu, Xiao, Ghaboosi, Deng & Zhang, 2009). IRC servers are interconnected and transfer messages between each other. They are designed to set a communication between hundreds of clients by using more than one server (Liu, Xiao, Ghaboosi, Deng & Zhang, 2009). Multiple IRC (mIRC) is a situation of transferring communications between clients and a server to ones who established communication with the channel (Liu, Xiao, Ghaboosi, Deng & Zhang, 2009). IRC bots are capable of managing access lists, moving files, sharing clients and more (Liu, Xiao, Ghaboosi, Deng & Zhang, 2009).

HTTP-Based Botnets

Network-level signatures are easier to set up as existing network monitoring infrastructures can be used. These days, malwares use network connections to carry out their malicious activities such as getting malware updates or spamming. According to the findings, approximately 75% of malware samples produce HTTP traffic (Perdisci, Lee & Feamster, 2010). HTTP (hyper-text transfer protocol) botnets make use of HTTP protocol and do not pursue connection with a Command and Control (C&C) server (Lee, Jeong, Park, Kim & Noh, 2008). BlackEnergy is an example of HTTP-based botnets and mainly used for DDoS attacks. This botnet provides an easy control of web-based bots which are capable of carrying out different attacks (Lee, Jeong, Park, Kim & Noh, 2008).

ORIGINAL USE OF BOTNETS

Bots (IRC Bots) were originally used in Internet relay Chat (IRC) channel management (Oikarinen & Reed, 1993). Back in time, when Internet was a new piece of technology, Internet Relay Chat was used to communicate with new people all over the world. A typical Internet Relay Chat network allows users to communicate with each other and consists of different numbers of servers which are located at different geographical locations (Canavan, 2005). In 1993, a legitimate IRC bot known as Eggdrop was written by Robey Pointer to monitor a single channel (Canavan, 2005). It was written in C and used in execution of TCL scripts which were added by users to improve the functionality (Canavan, 2005). Eggdrop was considered as a non-malicious bot. It was used to coordinate legally transferred files, imposing channel admin commands and playing games (Grizzard, Sharma, Nunnery, Kang & Dagon, 2007). Also, early IRC bots were used to keep servers up and running by preventing them from shutting down due to inactivity in the servers. An expansion in the numbers of servers resulted in a term known as netsplit (Canavan, 2005). The term "Netsplit" is disconnection of a node from its previous connection. When the IRC Channel Operator loses its connection, another channel member was assigned as Channel Operator (Canavan, 2005). Some people took advantage of this and carried out attacks to cause netsplits in order to obtain Channel Operator status and use it for malicious purposes (Canavan, 2005). Those people modified server attack scripts to carry out malicious attacks on both individual users and other devices. These attacks include Denial of Service attacks (DDoS) and even more (Canavan, 2005).

HOW BOTNETS INFECT OTHER DEVICES?

Botnets are considered to be one of the most important threats to the internet community. They are capable of carrying out different types of attacks which are all very dangerous. Usually bots infect other vulnerable hosts by using exploitation tools in order to expand both their network and capabilities. Bots infect other vulnerable systems by taking advantage of software vulnerabilities, trojan insertion, use of different kinds of viruses and worms and use of social engineering skills to download malicious bot code (Feily, Shahrestani, & Ramadass, 2009). Also, recent studies showed that new bots have several exploit vectors to make exploitation process better and more efficient (Rajab, Zarfoss, Monrose & Terzis, 2006). In another research, the authors stated that the process of transferring malicious software to the victim's computers has changed a lot (Bailey, Cooke, Jahanian, Xu & Karir, 2009). These days, attackers prefer multiple automated propagation vectors instead of single propagation vector as single propagation vectors may need a manual installation (Bailey, Cooke, Jahanian, Xu & Karir, 2009). In addition, the authors mentioned about a movement away from using random scanning to robust "hitlists" such as list of hosts and email lists (Bailey, Cooke, Jahanian, Xu & Karir, 2009). Also, instead of looking for vulnerable services, attackers started to look at vulnerable applications and vulnerable users (Bailey, Cooke, Jahanian, Xu & Karir, 2009). In another study, the authors mentioned about attackers who made use of P2P networks to infect new computers as there was no centralised server which made exchange of malicious content easier (Wang, Aslam & Zou, 2010). Recently, the number of P2P malwares which have been used in this infection process has increased significantly (Wang, Aslam & Zou, 2010). These P2P malwares include active and passive P2P worms. Active P2P worms try to infect other computers in the network while passive worms stay in local file sharing directory and spread between other computers. After this infection process, the botnet is ready to be controlled by a botmaster as they are able to communicate through P2P protocol.

FORMATION OF BOTNETS

To explain this process in a simpler manner, the formation of botnets can be investigated in two phases. The first one is collection of bots. So, this phase involves infecting or tricking users. This can be achieved with the help of viruses, worms or other kinds of malwares. Increasing the number of infected devices will increase the capabilities of the botnet. The second phase is more about actions which are needed to be taken in order to form the botnet.

A botnet named *FrankenB.* can be used as an example to develop a better understanding on formation of botnets. In the formation process of *FrankenB.* botnet, a single web-based C&C server with an encryption is preferred. In order to build *FranklinB.* botnet, following steps are followed (Cho, 2003):

- A domain is taken and required environment is established.
- The host is connected to ADSL link with a static IP address.

- A web site which will act as front face to hide the C&C of the botnet is built on that host. The web site contains MySQL database and a directory found at the roof of the web server. There are two main files in this directory. One of them is the main script which bots connect to communicate with C&C and get further commands and the second one is another script which is used by botmaster to command *FrankenB*.

- Bots join to the C&C server with HTTP and send data inside a POST. Usually, HTML method is the most used one to submit data which is needed to be processed by a web server. Posts usually preferred when a user completes a form and submits it. Also, use of HTTP communication mechanism between bots and C&C makes the detection process even more difficult.

- As simple web site traffic is unencrypted the communication within botnet is visible. However, encryption can be used to overcome this problem. *FrankenB*. makes use of SSL certificate to protect transferred data.

- After that, bots find their C&C and they start to give reports and receive commands. It is important to make sure that this is done securely. This can be done by using encrypted POST. Also, the bots learn to build a trust to the SSL certificate of the C&C server.

- For security reasons it is important to make sure that only *FrankenB*. bots can communicate with the botnet. To address this issue, a simple authentication with a secret password can be used.

- After all of these steps, the botnet is ready for use. It can be used for many purposes such as email spamming.

LIFE CYCLE OF BOTNETS

Although there are many different types of botnets, it is possible to investigate their life-cycle in five main phases. The following paragraphs will examine these phases and their explanations (Feily, Shahrestani, & Ramadass, 2009):

1. Initial Infection
2. Secondary Injection
3. Connection
4. Malicious Command and Control
5. Update and Maintenance

Figure 1. Life cycle of botnets

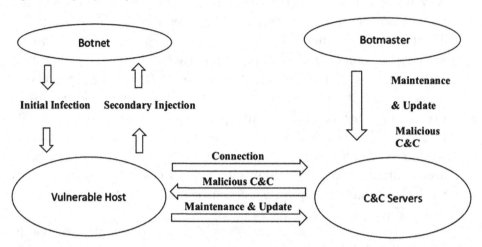

During the first phase, attackers try to find vulnerable points of machines and exploit them. This infection process can be achieved by using different types of malwares or exploitation techniques. In the second phase, infected hosts invoke a script which is also known as shell-code. With the help of FTP, HTTP or P2P, the shell code gets the bot binary from a predetermined location. Once the bot binary downloads itself on the infected machine, the computer starts to execute malicious code. This is followed by the connection phase. In this phase, command and control (C&C) channels are set up. This connects the infected computer which is also referred as zombie to the C&C server. As soon as C&C channels are set up successfully, the infected computers become part of the botnet. The malicious command and control phase is about botmaster commanding the botnet remotely. In this phase, infected computers receive commands from the botmaster and execute them. The last phase is about updating and maintaining the bots. It is important to keep botnets updated as the botmaster may be willing to add new functionality or new attacking techniques to overcome new detection mechanisms.

In another study, instead of five phases, the researchers examined the life-cycle of botnets under three phases (Hachem, Mustapha, Granadillo & Debar, 2011). These phases are (Hachem, Mustapha, Granadillo & Debar, 2011):

- Spreading and Injection: In this phase, the authors mentioned about the ability of botnets to spread, infect and inject themselves into new systems. They also mentioned about the how botnets spread between machines. Mostly, attackers make use of social engineering techniques and malicious email distribution to spread botnets between machines. According to the reports, there was an increase in spam and malware in 2010 on social networks compared to previous years. In addition, use of other botnets, software vulnerabilities and instant messaging which includes a computer worm that spreads by messaging are other ways of infecting and spreading between machines.

- Command and Control: The authors mentioned about the necessity of C&C for communication between botnet and botmaster. Also, the authors stated different models, and topologies for implementing C&C channel.
- Botnet Applications: This phase in about legitimate and illegitimate actions of botnets. The illegitimate actions include DDoS attack (Distributed Denial of Service), spamming and espionage.

ARCHITECTURE OF BOTNETS, CONTROL, AND COMMUNICATION

Botnets have certain characteristics which separates them from other malwares. One of these characteristics is the usage of Command and Control (C&C) channels to set a communication within botnet. This gives an opportunity to botmaster to take control of the botnet. Botnets have internal communication protocols which enable them to establish communication between bots and the botmaster. Simply, IRC (Internet Relay Chat) communication protocol, is created to establish a communication between clients and server by using communication channels (Hachem, Mustapha, Granadillo & Debar, 2011). It creates a connection for clients and agents. The flexibility of this protocol made itself a perfect choice for third parties as it can be customised for different purposes (Hachem, Mustapha, Granadillo & Debar, 2011). HTTP (Hypertext Transfer Protocol) communication protocol works on the basis of request-respond ideology. The bots create queries for the HTTP server and botmaster talks to them by giving commands (Hachem, Mustapha, Granadillo & Debar, 2011). Also, some of the botnets use P2P communication protocols. The idea is to create nodes which act both as client and server.

Moreover, the mentioned Command and Control channels can be updated and controlled for different purposes (Feily, Shahrestani, & Ramadass, 2009). Botmasters make use of a range of different Control and Command topologies and communication methods to overcome defence mechanisms and any legal shutdowns. These topologies have their own advantages and disadvantages. The following paragraphs will examine some of the communication topologies that botnets use.

Centralised Topology

Botnets which make use of centralised topology has a central point which transfers messages between clients. Usually, botmaster assigns a host to be the central point of all botnets (Hachem, Mustapha, Granadillo & Debar, 2011). This host can be either an infected machine or a legitimate public service provider (Hachem, Mustapha, Granadillo & Debar, 2011). As an advantage of using centralised topology, there is less delay in time taken to transfer messages between clients as messages only need to pass from a few hops (Bailey, Cooke, Jahanian, Xu & Karir, 2009). This is very useful topology to implement, as it is very easy to use and gives opportunity of customisation for different needs. However, centralised topologies come with some disadvantages. Firstly, centralised systems are easy to detect as most of the clients are connected to the same central point and secondly, discovery of this central point will result in detection of whole system (Bailey, Cooke, Jahanian, Xu & Karir, 2009).

Peer to Peer (P2P) Topology

P2P botnet communication has many advantages compared to other communication topologies. Firstly, it is hard to damage communication in P2P communication systems (Bailey, Cooke, Jahanian, Xu & Karir, 2009). Therefore, compromise of a single bot does not put whole botnet into a damage. Also, compared with other topologies, P2P topology is harder to get detected by detection mechanisms (Hachem, Mustapha, Granadillo & Debar, 2011). But, construction of P2P systems is complex and not easy. So, it may be time consuming to build it up and there may be some delays in message delivery (Bailey, Cooke, Jahanian, Xu & Karir, 2009).

Unstructured Topology

Unstructured botnet communication can take P2P communication concept and modify it in an extreme way that only a single bot is only aware of one other bot (Bailey, Cooke, Jahanian, Xu & Karir, 2009). In order to send a message, Internet is randomly scanned, and the message is passed along when another bot is detected (Bailey, Cooke, Jahanian, Xu & Karir, 2009). This communication type is very simple to design and loss of one bot would not damage the whole botnet (Bailey, Cooke, Jahanian, Xu & Karir, 2009). However, time taken to deliver a message would be very long and there is no guarantee of delivery of the message (Bailey, Cooke, Jahanian, Xu & Karir, 2009).

Star C&C Topology

Formation of centralised C&C topology has led to formation of star C&C topology and can be considered as an extension of centralised topology. The star topology makes use of a single centralised C&C resource to establish a communication with all bot agents and each bot receives commands from the central C&C point (Kavitha & Rani, 2015). Star topology will allow a direct communication between the C&C and the bot which results in a fast transfer of instructions (Ollmann, 2009). However, if the central C&C is damaged in some way, this will damage the whole botnet (Ollmann, 2009).

Multi-Server C&C Topology

Multi-Server C&C topology is considered as a logical extension of the star C&C topology. Multi-server C&C topology uses several servers to command bot agents (Kavitha & Rani, 2015). Using multiple servers for communication resulted in no single point of failure which is an advantage as a failure in one of the C&C servers would not prevent botmaster from controlling the whole botnet (Ollmann, 2009). Also, spreading servers wisely among different geographical regions will increase the speed of communication between botnet elements (Ollmann, 2009). However, building up multiple C&C servers is not easy and requires extra work.

Hierarchical C&C Topology

Hierarchical topology includes dynamics of principles used in compromise and subsequent propagation of bot agents themselves (Kavitha & Rani, 2015). In hierarchical C&C topology, some bots act as proxy servers for C&C servers (Hachem, Mustapha, Granadillo & Debar, 2011). One of the advantages of using this topology is that bots do not know the location of the whole botnet which makes evaluation of actual size of the botnet even harder (Ollmann, 2009). However, as commands pass from multiple communication branches, it becomes harder for botmaster to control the botnet simultaneously and this increases time latency issues (Ollmann, 2009).

Random C&C Topology

Random topology has no centralised C&C infrastructure and makes use of bot agents to transfer commands (Kavitha & Rani, 2015). Also, having no centralised C&C infrastructure makes it resistant against shutdowns. However, it is very easy to enumerate other members of the botnet by screening a single host (Ollmann, 2009).

POSSIBLE THREATS

These days, botnets are considered to be one of the most serious cyber security problems as they are capable of doing many illegal activities. These illegal activities can aim different profiles ranging from individual users to companies and even governments. Therefore, botnets have become favourite toy of hackers and other cybercriminals. Mostly, botnets are used for DDoS attacks (Distributed Denial of Service), password cracking, click fraud and email spamming, etc. According to the recent studies, DDoS attacks have started to become one of the leading disturbances of the global internet (Ioannidis & Bellovin, 2002). In a typical DDoS attack, a single system is flooded by massive amounts of traffic/request which are generated from different sources. This makes it even harder to stop incoming attacks. The aim is to overload the system and make it unavailable to its users. DDoS attacks include many compromised systems targeting a single system and usually these systems are infected by using Trojan horses or other malwares. In another research, the authors stated that botnets are the reason for approximately 70% to 90% of world's spam (Liu, Xiao, Ghaboosi, Deng & Zhang, 2009). Simply, a spam can be defined as a form of message which is sent to users who did not specifically asked for it. Usually, bots open the SOCKS v4/v5 proxy on infected hosts to be able to send spams (Liu, Xiao, Ghaboosi, Deng & Zhang, 2009). Botnets can also leak sensitive data from the infected machines as they are able to retrieve sensitive information in addition to normal traffic (Liu, Xiao, Ghaboosi, Deng & Zhang, 2009). So, user's passwords, usernames and other sensitive information are in danger. Not only that, botnets can also be used for keylogging. This is a process where bots record keystrokes and report them to their botmaster. According to the researches, botnets have started to develop more complex manner of finding and leaking important financial data (Pappas, 2008). This can result in loss of huge amounts of financial savings. Recently, botnets have started to play a role in identity theft with a process known as Phishing mail. These mails contain legitimate URLs which ask users to enter their personal information. Moreover, botnets can also be used for click-fraud. For example, they can be used to increase click through rate (CTR) artificially as they can be commanded to click on specific hyperlinks continuously. In some serious cases, these illegal activities of botnets may lead to government conflicts, shutdown of companies and other serious events. Furthermore, cybercriminals can use botnets to take control of some the most important public sectors and this can have very bad consequences. For example, taking control of health sector can affect hospitals and as a result, sick people who stay in these hospitals as cybercriminals are able to alter patient records and even affect machines which are used to treat sick people. On the other hand, performing an attack on education sector can have impact on students and as well as on the income of governments. Some governments mostly relay on tax generated from education sector as a source of income. If cybercriminals manage to perform attacks on the education sector of governments, this can discourage students from studying in these countries and therefore decrease the amount of income of these governments generated from education sector. For the companies, cybercriminals can use botnets to perform attacks and obtain confidential information which can be sold to other companies by these cybercriminals. To sum up, botnets are very dangerous. Cybercriminals can use them according to their needs. The only limit is their imagination. Therefore, new methods must be invented to detect, mitigate, traceback and neutralise these attacks before they start.

DETECTION OF BOTNETS

As botnets have become a huge problem in cyber security world, experts have started to invent new detection mechanisms to detect botnets before they launch a new attack and reduce the amount of damage they can give. Until now, many different methods have been proposed and tried. The following paragraphs will examine some of these methods:

Honeypots

Honeypots are recognised by their ability to detect threats, aggregate malwares and observe behaviours of attackers (Liu, Xiao, Ghaboosi, Deng & Zhang, 2009). Honeypots observe behaviours of attackers by letting subnets act as being infected by a Trojan which also allows identification of controlling hosts (Cooke, Jahanian & McPherson, 2005). As there are more honeynet tools on Linux, most of the researches are Linux-based researches (McCarty, 2003). Therefore, the number of tools which support honeypot deployment on Windows is very low which allowed attackers to dismantle the honeypot and take advantage of this (Liu, Xiao, Ghaboosi, Deng & Zhang, 2009). A honeynet consists of more than one honeypot working on a single network and is used to screen large networks. Some researchers conducted a study about producing a reactive firewall to protect compromises of honeypots (McCarty, 2003). The inbound attacks on compromised ports can be prevented as those ports are detected by such a firewall (McCarty, 2003). It is important to block incoming traffic carefully, as attackers download toolkits after an invasion (McCarty, 2003). These toolkits can be used as pioneer pieces of work in further researches. On the other hand, attackers have responded to this honeypot trap situation by finding new ways of avoiding them. They have invented new methods to detect these honeypots. A group of researchers have found a way of detecting honeypots with the help of intelligent probing on public report statistics (Bethencourt, Franklin & Vernon, 2005). In addition to this, another group of researchers have invented another way of detecting honeypots by using independent software and hardware (Zou & Cunningham, 2006). Also, they proposed a way of finding and removing infected honeypots with the help of peer to peer botnets (Zou & Cunningham, 2006).

Signature-Based Detection

Signature-based detection uses passive traffic monitoring to locate botnets. Behaviours and signatures retained from existing botnets are used in botnet detection. Simply, it is about gathering information from the traffic packets and comparing it with patterns found on database collected from existing bots (Liu, Xiao, Ghaboosi, Deng & Zhang, 2009). It can be really simple to compare every byte in the packet, but this comes with some disadvantages. These disadvantages are (Kugisaki, Kasahara, Hori & Sakurai, 2007):

- Detection of unknown botnets would not be possible.
- The database of signatures should be updated regularly which results in increase in management costs and decrease in performance.
- The database of signatures should be pathed with a pace or new bots may launch new attacks before that.

Another example of signature-based detection is Snort, which is an open source intrusion detection system (Snort - Network Intrusion Detection & Prevention System, n.d.). Snort is programmed with a set of behaviours or signatures to log traffic which is assumed to be suspicious (Snort - Network Intrusion Detection & Prevention System, n.d.).

Anomaly-Based Detection

Anomaly-based detection uses network traffic anomalies to locate botnets. These anomalies are high network latency, high volumes of traffic, traffic on unusual ports and any other unusual system behaviour which shows presence of bots (Feily, Shahrestani, & Ramadass, 2009). Unlike signature-based detection mechanisms, anomaly-based detection mechanisms can detect unknown botnets. However, it cannot detect IRC networks which may be a botnet but not active yet as there are no anomalies (Feily, Shahrestani, & Ramadass, 2009). In order to overcome this issue, an algorithm presented by a group of researchers. They used TCP-based anomaly detection with IRC tokenization and IRC message statistics to create a mechanism which can also locate client botnets (Binkley & Singh, 2006). Moreover, another algorithm which uses passive analysis of flow data located in transport layer for detection and characterisation of botnets was proposed by the researchers (Karasaridis, Rexroad & Hoeflin, 2007). On the other hand, Gu et al. presented a BotSniffer which makes use of network-based anomaly detection to determine C&C channels in a local area network (Gu, Zhang & Lee, 2008).

DNS-Based Detection

DNS-based detection is more like anomaly-based detection as same anomaly detection algorithms can be used on DNS traffic (Feily, Shahrestani, & Ramadass, 2009). Bots send DNS queries to be able to access the C&C server where they initiate communication and receive commands. Therefore, it is convenient to detect botnets by doing DNS monitoring on DNS traffic to detect anomalies (Feily, Shahrestani, & Ramadass, 2009). Choi et al. presented a study about anomaly-based detection where they screened group activities in DNS traffic (Choi, Lee, Lee & Kim, 2007). According to their findings, botnet queries can easily be differentiated from legitimate ones (Choi, Lee, Lee & Kim, 2007). The authors distinguished botnet queries from legitimate ones by looking at these features (Choi, Lee, Lee & Kim, 2007):

1. Only bots send DNS queries to the domain of C&C server.
2. Bots act and move around together simultaneously. This also includes their DNS queries.
3. Botnets make use of Dynamic DNS for their C&C servers whereas legitimate hosts do not use them frequently.

The researchers have used these features to propose a new algorithm which determines botnet DNS queries. They also invented an anomaly-based detection mechanism which detected C&C server migration and was more durable compared to other detection methods as it could detect any kind of bot or botnet by checking group activities on DNS traffic (Feily, Shahrestani, & Ramadass, 2009). In addition, it can also detect botnets with encrypted channels as it uses information from IP headers, however this approach requires high processing time (Feily, Shahrestani, & Ramadass, 2009). In 2005, a researcher presented a mechanism which detected domain names with high or temporally concentrated DDNS query rates in order to determine C&C servers of botnets (Dagon, 2005). However, this detection method can be fooled by using faked DNS queries (Feily, Shahrestani, & Ramadass, 2009). Also, in another research, it is proven that this method produces high false positive rate as it misclassifies legitimate domains which use DNS with short time-to-live (TTL) (Villamarín-Salomón, & Brustoloni, 2008).

Mining-Based Detection

Mining-based detection is more about detection of C&C traffic of botnets. As botnets communicate with their botmasters via C&C channels, it would be an intelligent move to detect C&C traffic. However, botnets use normal protocols for C&C communications which do not produce any anomalies such as high volume of traffic or high network latency (Feily, Shahrestani, & Ramadass, 2009). Therefore, it would be difficult to detect C&C traffic of botnets by using anomaly-based detection techniques. Here, mining-based detection comes into play which is a very effective way of detecting C&C traffic of botnets. In 2008, the authors proposed an approach to detect C&C traffic of botnets by using a technique known as multiple log-file mining which is a good example of flow-based botnet traffic detection (Masud, Al-Khateeb, Khan, Thuraisingham & Hamlen, 2008). In order to detect C&C traffic of botnets, the authors introduced multiple log correlation. The researchers correlated two host-based log files temporarily to detect botnet activity in a host machine (Masud, Al-Khateeb, Khan, Thuraisingham & Hamlen, 2008). Then, with the help of data mining techniques, the authors obtained relevant features from these log files and used them in C&C traffic detection of botnets (Masud, Al-Khateeb, Khan, Thuraisingham & Hamlen, 2008). As the mentioned approach does not need access to payload content, it works perfectly in situations where payload is encrypted or not available (Masud, Al-Khateeb, Khan, Thuraisingham & Hamlen, 2008). In another study, the authors proposed a detection mechanism known as Botminer which did not require any prior knowledge and still detect botnets regardless to C&C botnet protocol and structure (Gu, Perdisci, Zhang & Lee, 2008). Botminer groups similar communication and malicious traffic together and carries out cross cluster correlation to detect hosts with similar communication and attacking patterns (Gu, Perdisci, Zhang & Lee, 2008). Also, studies proved that Botminer has low false positive rates and can detect real world botnets such as IRC-based and P2P botnets etc (Gu, Perdisci, Zhang & Lee, 2008).

Detection With Machine Learning and AI

Detection mechanisms which employ machine learning or artificial intelligence aim for identification and classification of network traffic generated by botnets as they communicate with their botmaster and each other. Recently, many studies have been done in this area as capabilities of machine learning and artificial intelligence have realised by the researchers. Zhao et al. proposed a study in the area of botnet detection using machine learning where they analysed traffic behaviour of botnets by classifying network traffic behaviour (Zhao, Traore, Sayed, Luu, Saad, Ghorbani & Garant, 2013). The authors worked on the practicability of detecting botnet activity without seeing the complete network flow by grouping behaviour based on time intervals (Zhao, Traore, Sayed, Luu, Saad, Ghorbani & Garant, 2013). Also, they focused on behavioural analysis of Peer to Peer C&C channels (Zhao, Traore, Sayed, Luu, Saad, Ghorbani & Garant, 2013). As an advantage, the mentioned method can analyse encrypted network communication protocols as traffic analysis methods do not bound up with the payload of packets. On the other hand, Nogueira et al. used Artificial Neural Network to figure out licit and illicit traffic patterns (Nogueira, Salvador & Blessa, 2010). The authors trained multi-layer neural network with TCP connection-based features to detect HTTP-based botnet (Nogueira, Salvador & Blessa, 2010). Also, it is mentioned that the proposed method has low false positive detection rate and high accuracy of detecting HTTP botnets (Nogueira, Salvador & Blessa, 2010). Moreover, Venkatesh et al, proposed a new approach for botnet detection using Multilayer Feed-Forward Neural Network with an adaptive learning rate (Venkatesh & Nadarajan, 2012). The approach was based around extraction of TCP related features as HTTP-based botnets use TCP connections for communication purposes (Venkatesh & Nadarajan, 2012). The authors used bold driver back-propagation algorithm to optimise the learning rate coefficient during weight updating process (Venkatesh & Nadarajan, 2012). Studies have showed that, actively learned neural networks had better identification accuracy with less false positives (Venkatesh & Nadarajan, 2012). In another research, the authors proposed a new detection framework with three detection models where different machine learning classifiers are inspected for each model (Alenazi, Traore, Ganame & Woungang, 2017). The first model analyses applications and removes malicious ones while the second model controls regularity in timing of DNS queries of bots and uses this in the detection of botnets (Alenazi, Traore, Ganame & Woungang, 2017). The last model focuses on the characteristics of DNS domain names and determines algorithmically created domains and fast flux ones which are considered to be footprints of HTTP-based botnets (Alenazi, Traore, Ganame & Woungang, 2017).

CONCLUSION

Nowadays, building or purchasing botnets have become very easy. An individual person who knows how to use a computer and has no prior knowledge about botnets can purchase a botnet from black market with a very low price. Giving such a power to someone without required knowledge may result in a huge disaster. In addition, there publicly available support tools which let criminal people to build their own personal botnets for different purposes. This increases the number of botnets and threats in cyber security world. As botnets become more popular among cyber criminals, the use of botnets has peaked. They have started to build new kinds of botnets to overcome detection mechanisms created by experts. There is an invisible race between hackers and experts. Experts try to beat hackers by generating new ways of detecting and neutralising botnets while hackers try to build newer models of botnets to increase variety. Therefore, it is very important to increase awareness among individual users. Individual users need to know how botnets operate and how to protect themselves from possible threats. This is very important as botnets can target different profiles. They can aim big companies as well as individual users and even governments. The awareness of individual users can be increased with little training sessions. It will be useful to teach users how to protect themselves. Users should know the use of anti-virus software, anti-spyware or firewalls. Otherwise, they may become a part of botnet without them knowing. This will create a big threat against their identity, personal information or even financial data. This book chapter aims to increase knowledge about botnets and make individual users more familiar with the concepts related to botnets.

REFERENCES

Abu Rajab, M., Zarfoss, J., Monrose, F., & Terzis, A. (2006, October). A multifaceted approach to understanding the botnet phenomenon. In *Proceedings of the 6th ACM SIGCOMM conference on Internet measurement* (pp. 41-52). ACM. 10.1145/1177080.1177086

Alejandre, F. V., Cortés, N. C., & Anaya, E. A. (2017, February). Feature selection to detect botnets using machine learning algorithms. In *Electronics, Communications and Computers (CONIELECOMP), 2017 International Conference on* (pp. 1-7). IEEE. 10.1109/CONIELECOMP.2017.7891834

Alenazi, A., Traore, I., Ganame, K., & Woungang, I. (2017, October). Holistic Model for HTTP Botnet Detection Based on DNS Traffic Analysis. In *International Conference on Intelligent, Secure, and Dependable Systems in Distributed and Cloud Environments* (pp. 1-18). Springer. 10.1007/978-3-319-69155-8_1

Bailey, M., Cooke, E., Jahanian, F., Xu, Y., & Karir, M. (2009, March). A survey of botnet technology and defenses. In Conference For Homeland Security, 2009. CATCH'09. Cybersecurity Applications & Technology (pp. 299-304). IEEE doi:10.1109/CATCH.2009.40

Bethencourt, J., Franklin, J., & Vernon, M. K. (2005, August). Mapping Internet Sensors with Probe Response Attacks. In *USENIX Security Symposium* (pp. 193-208). USENIX.

Bilge, L., Balzarotti, D., Robertson, W., Kirda, E., & Kruegel, C. (2012, December). Disclosure: detecting botnet command and control servers through large-scale netflow analysis. In *Proceedings of the 28th Annual Computer Security Applications Conference* (pp. 129-138). ACM. 10.1145/2420950.2420969

Binkley, J. R., & Singh, S. (2006). An Algorithm for Anomaly-based Botnet Detection. *SRUTI, 6*, 7–7.

Botnet. (2018, September 22). Retrieved from https://en.wikipedia.org/wiki/Botnet

Canavan, J. (2005, October). The evolution of malicious IRC bots. In *Virus Bulletin Conference* (pp. 104-114). Academic Press.

Cho, M. (2003). *Mixing Technology and Business: The Roles and Responsibilities of the Chief Information Security Officer.* Retrieved from SANS Institute: SANS Institute: https://www.sans.org/reading-room/whitepapers/assurance/mixing-technology-business-roles-responsibilities-chief-information-security-of-1044

Choi, H., Lee, H., Lee, H., & Kim, H. (2007, October). Botnet detection by monitoring group activities in DNS traffic. In *Computer and Information Technology, 2007. CIT 2007. 7th IEEE International Conference on* (pp. 715-720). IEEE. 10.1109/CIT.2007.90

Cooke, E., Jahanian, F., & McPherson, D. (2005). The Zombie Roundup: Understanding, Detecting, and Disrupting Botnets. *SRUTI, 5*, 6–6.

Dagon, D. (2005, July). Botnet detection and response. In OARC workshop (Vol. 2005). Academic Press.

Ersson, J., & Moradian, E. (2013). Botnet Detection with Event-Driven Analysis. *Procedia Computer Science, 22*, 662–671. doi:10.1016/j.procs.2013.09.147

Feily, M., Shahrestani, A., & Ramadass, S. (2009, June). A survey of botnet and botnet detection. In *Emerging Security Information, Systems and Technologies, 2009. SECURWARE'09. Third International Conference on* (pp. 268-273). IEEE. 10.1109/SECURWARE.2009.48

Garcia, S. (2014). *Identifying, Modeling and Detecting Botnet Behaviors in the Network* (Unpublished doctoral dissertation). Universidad Nacional del Centro de la Provincia de Buenos Aires.

Garcia, S., Grill, M., Stiborek, J., & Zunino, A. (2014). An empirical comparison of botnet detection methods. *Computers & Security, 45*, 100-123.

Grizzard, J. B., Sharma, V., Nunnery, C., Kang, B. B., & Dagon, D. (2007). Peer-to-Peer Botnets: Overview and Case Study. *HotBots, 7*, 1–1.

Gu, G., Perdisci, R., Zhang, J., & Lee, W. (2008). *Botminer: Clustering analysis of network traffic for protocol-and structure-independent botnet detection*. Academic Press.

Gu, G., Zhang, J., & Lee, W. (2008). *BotSniffer: Detecting botnet command and control channels in network traffic*. Academic Press.

Hachem, N., Mustapha, Y. B., Granadillo, G. G., & Debar, H. (2011, May). Botnets: lifecycle and taxonomy. In *Network and Information Systems Security (SAR-SSI), 2011 Conference on* (pp. 1-8). IEEE. 10.1109/SAR-SSI.2011.5931395

Ioannidis, J., & Bellovin, S. M. (2002, February). Implementing Pushback: Router-Based Defense Against DDoS Attacks. In NDSS (Vol. 2). Academic Press.

Karasaridis, A., Rexroad, B., & Hoeflin, D. A. (2007). Wide-Scale Botnet Detection and Characterization. *HotBots, 7*, 7–7.

Kavitha, D., & Rani, S. K. (2015). Review of Botnet Attacks and its detection Mechanism. *International Journal of Innovative Research in Computer and Communication Engineering, 3*, 2377-2383.

Kim, D. H., Lee, T., Kang, J., Jeong, H., & In, H. P. (2012). Adaptive pattern mining model for early detection of botnet-propagation scale. *Security and Communication Networks, 5*(8), 917–927. doi:10.1002ec.366

Kugisaki, Y., Kasahara, Y., Hori, Y., & Sakurai, K. (2007, October). Bot detection based on traffic analysis. In *Intelligent Pervasive Computing, 2007. IPC. The 2007 International Conference on* (pp. 303-306). IEEE. 10.1109/IPC.2007.91

Lee, J. S., Jeong, H., Park, J. H., Kim, M., & Noh, B. N. (2008, December). The activity analysis of malicious http-based botnets using degree of periodic repeatability. In *Security Technology, 2008. SECTECH'08. International Conference on* (pp. 83-86). IEEE. 10.1109/SecTech.2008.52

Lin, K. C., Chen, S. Y., & Hung, J. C. (2014). Botnet detection using support vector machines with artificial fish swarm algorithm. *Journal of Applied Mathematics*.

Liu, J., Xiao, Y., Ghaboosi, K., Deng, H., & Zhang, J. (2009). Botnet: Classification, attacks, detection, tracing, and preventive measures. *EURASIP Journal on Wireless Communications and Networking*, *2009*(1), 692654. doi:10.1155/2009/692654

Masud, M. M., Al-Khateeb, T., Khan, L., Thuraisingham, B., & Hamlen, K. W. (2008, October). Flow-based identification of botnet traffic by mining multiple log files. In *Distributed Framework and Applications, 2008. DFmA 2008. First International Conference on* (pp. 200-206). IEEE. 10.1109/ICDFMA.2008.4784437

McCarty, B. (2003). Botnets: Big and bigger. *IEEE Security and Privacy*, *99*(4), 87–90. doi:10.1109/MSECP.2003.1219079

Muthumanickam, K., Ilavarasan, E., & Dwivedi, S. K. (2014). A Dynamic Botnet Detection Model based on Behavior Analysis. *International Journal on Recent Trends in Engineering & Technology*, *10*(1), 104.

Nogueira, A., Salvador, P., & Blessa, F. (2010, June). A botnet detection system based on neural networks. In *Digital Telecommunications (ICDT), 2010 Fifth International Conference on* (pp. 57-62). IEEE. 10.1109/ICDT.2010.19

Oikarinen, J., & Reed, D. (1993). *Internet relay chat protocol* (No. RFC 1459).

Ollmann, G. (2009). *Botnet communication topologies*. Academic Press.

Pappas, K. (2008). *Back to basics to fight botnets*. Academic Press.

Perdisci, R., Lee, W., & Feamster, N. (2010, April). *Behavioral Clustering of HTTP-Based Malware and Signature Generation Using Malicious Network Traces* (Vol. 10). NSDI.

Sari, A. (2018). Context-Aware Intelligent Systems for Fog Computing Environments for Cyber-Threat Intelligence. In *Fog Computing* (pp. 205–225). Cham: Springer. doi:10.1007/978-3-319-94890-4_10

Sari, A. (2019). Turkish national cyber-firewall to mitigate countrywide cyber-attacks. *Computers & Electrical Engineering*, *73*, 128–144. doi:10.1016/j.compeleceng.2018.11.008

Snort - Network Intrusion Detection & Prevention System. (n.d.). Retrieved from http://www.snort.org/

Van Ruitenbeek, E., & Sanders, W. H. (2008, September). Modeling peer-to-peer botnets. In *Quantitative Evaluation of Systems, 2008. QEST'08. Fifth International Conference on* (pp. 307-316). IEEE. 10.1109/QEST.2008.43

Venkatesh, G. K., & Nadarajan, R. A. (2012, June). HTTP botnet detection using adaptive learning rate multilayer feed-forward neural network. In *IFIP International Workshop on Information Security Theory and Practice* (pp. 38-48). Springer.

Villamarín-Salomón, R., & Brustoloni, J. C. (2008, January). Identifying botnets using anomaly detection techniques applied to DNS traffic. In *Consumer Communications and Networking Conference, 2008. CCNC 2008. 5th IEEE* (pp. 476-481). IEEE. 10.1109/ccnc08.2007.112

Vormayr, G., Zseby, T., & Fabini, J. (2017). Botnet communication patterns. *IEEE Communications Surveys and Tutorials*, *19*(4), 2768–2796. doi:10.1109/COMST.2017.2749442

Wang, A., Chang, W., Chen, S., & Mohaisen, A. (2018). Delving into internet DDoS attacks by botnets: Characterization and analysis. *IEEE/ACM Transactions on Networking*, *26*(6), 2843–2855. doi:10.1109/TNET.2018.2874896

Wang, P., Aslam, B., & Zou, C. C. (2010). Peer-to-peer botnets. In *Handbook of Information and Communication Security* (pp. 335–350). Berlin: Springer. doi:10.1007/978-3-642-04117-4_18

Xie, Y., Yu, F., Achan, K., Panigrahy, R., Hulten, G., & Osipkov, I. (2008). Spamming botnets: Signatures and characteristics. *Computer Communication Review*, *38*(4), 171–182. doi:10.1145/1402946.1402979

Zhao, D., Traore, I., Sayed, B., Lu, W., Saad, S., Ghorbani, A., & Garant, D. (2013). Botnet detection based on traffic behavior analysis and flow intervals. *Computers & Security*, *39*, 2–16. doi:10.1016/j.cose.2013.04.007

Zou, C. C., & Cunningham, R. (2006, June). Honeypot-aware advanced botnet construction and maintenance. In Null (pp. 199-208). IEEE. doi:10.1109/DSN.2006.38

ADDITIONAL READING

Al-Hammadi, Y., & Aickelin, U. (2010, January). Behavioural correlation for detecting P2P bots. In *Future Networks, 2010. ICFN'10. Second International Conference on* (pp. 323-327). IEEE. 10.1109/ICFN.2010.72

Chen, C. M., Ou, Y. H., & Tsai, Y. C. (2010, December). Web botnet detection based on flow information. In *Computer Symposium (ICS), 2010 International* (pp. 381-384). IEEE. 10.1109/COMPSYM.2010.5685482

García, S., Zunino, A., & Campo, M. (2012). Botnet behavior detection using network synchronism. In Privacy, Intrusion Detection and Response: Technologies for Protecting Networks (pp. 122-144). IGI Global. doi:10.4018/978-1-60960-836-1.ch005

Saad, S., Traore, I., Ghorbani, A., Sayed, B., Zhao, D., Lu, W., . . . Hakimian, P. (2011, July). Detecting P2P botnets through network behavior analysis and machine learning. In *Privacy, Security and Trust (PST), 2011 Ninth Annual International Conference on* (pp. 174-180). IEEE 10.1109/PST.2011.5971980

Strayer, W. T., Walsh, R., Livadas, C., & Lapsley, D. (2006, November). Detecting botnets with tight command and control. In *Local Computer Networks, Proceedings 2006 31st IEEE Conference on* (pp. 195-202). IEEE. 10.1109/LCN.2006.322100

Wang, B., Li, Z., Li, D., Liu, F., & Chen, H. (2010, May). Modeling connections behavior for web-based bots detection. In *e-Business and Information System Security (EBISS), 2010 2nd International Conference on* (pp. 1-4). IEEE. 10.1109/EBISS.2010.5473532

KEY TERMS AND DEFINITIONS

AI: AI stands for artificial intelligence. Artificial intelligence is a form of intelligence which is used by machines to carry out activities associated with humans. Learning new things or adapting to changes in an environment can be example to human associated activities.

Bot: A botnet consists of more than one bot working together in an accordance. If a botnet is considered as an army, then a bot can be considered as a single soldier in that army.

Botmaster: Botmaster is the cyber-criminal/attacker who owns the botnet and responsible for its actions. In other words, botmaster is a person who controls the botnet.

Command and Control (C&C) Server: Command and control (C&C) server is used to set communication with systems which are infected by malwares. C&C servers are controlled by cybercriminals who own those malwares. Botnets make use of these C&C servers, and botmasters use them as communication channels to be able to command their botnets.

Domain Name System (DNS): Domain name system (DNS) translates domain names into IP addresses so browsers can understand and load the required contents.

Honeypot: Honeypots let subnets act as being infected by a Trojan to be able to observe behaviors of attackers. This helps professionals to detect threats and aggregate malwares.

Markov Chain: Markov chain is a sequence of possible events and the probability of each event happening is determined by the state in the previous events.

Peer-to-Peer (P2P) Network: Peer-to-peer (P2P) networks consist of peers that are connected to each other with the internet. Files can be shared between systems and every computer has the probability of becoming a client and a file server.

Chapter 6
A Review of the Economic Benefits of Cyber Terrorism

Acheme Odeh
Girne American University, Cyprus

ABSTRACT

The internet technologies have made it even easier for terrorist activities to migrate smoothly to the internet. Nations are now benefiting from the act of cyberterrorism, making it more difficult to successfully fight this monster. This chapter aims to draw up a review on various published work addressing the financial benefits of cyberterrorism. The question is to know if economic benefits alone is significantly strong enough to encourage more cyberterrorism activities. Should this be the case, what can be done to curb this deadly cancer from spreading further? Scientific methods could prove to be a much efficient solution to the issue of cyber terrorism. But how is that going to happen and for how long should we wait to see this happen? Would it ever happen? Considering that the internet is an ever-growing technology with endless possibilities for both attackers and crime investigative specialist, do we forsee a cyber war between nations who can boost of better fighting and defending technologies? These questions and many more are discussed based on recent literature.

DOI: 10.4018/978-1-5225-8976-1.ch006

Copyright © 2019, IGI Global. Copying or distributing in print or electronic forms without written permission of IGI Global is prohibited.

INTRODUCTION

The google dictionary defines Terrorism as: "the unlawful use of violence and intimidation, especially against civilians, in the pursuit of political aims" (Terrorism, 2018). "Terrorism" has become a popular word in today's world, even surpassing common words such as "cyberspace". A google search of the word "terrorism" pulls out about 307,000,000 results as at December 2018, while "cyberspace" pulls out only 29,000,000 search results. This shows that terrorism is a major topic of discussion around the world till date. But the most worries should come from "cyberterrorism" – a growing area of concern which allows technology to be employed in lunching out deadly attacks on people, infrastructure and governments. More concerns are in areas where sophisticated devices are employed to carry out anonymous attacks on infrastructures using internet facilities. Cyberterrorism is simply defined as "the politically motivated use of computers and information technology to cause severe disruption or widespread fear." Considering the unlimited potentials that the internet technology presents to us these days, it is quite apt to wage a war against the deployment of terrorism on the internet. Reason being that it will pose a more devastating effect on the global community. Cyberterrorism could possibly pose an endless scenario of doomsday for the world (Giacomello, 2004).

Terrorist organizations would like to increase their global visibility and impact. This gives them an upper political hand across territories. The weapons used to achieve this is violence, including killing people and breaking things (Giacomello, 2004). They would want to show how powerful and deadly they can be. Bringing cyberterrorism into play would assist to increase their level of global awareness. They would take advantage of the media hype of today to get more publicity (Raymond, 1965). Yet another reason to worry about is the unwillingness of government officials to give relevant information on terrorism. The vulnerability of the possibilities offered by emerging technologies is also a huge concern in the fight against cyberterrorism. The public usually are not sure about the information that the media gives to them regarding terrorist activities. In all, terrorist organizations benefit from all these weaknesses in order to propagate their nefarious activates without control

Scholars in the past have proposed that cyberterrorism will not pose any tangible threats based on the cost of operation of such organization (Associated Press, 2004). Security experts also base their assumptions on the fact that after the September 11 terror attack, no other act of cyberterrorism has been recorded (Barnett, 2004). In response to this claim, (Biddle, 2004) is of the opinion that "*for terrorist to regard strikes at computer networks as a viable weapon, the attack should be sufficiently destructive or disruptive to generate fear comparable to that from physical acts of terrorism.*" (Park, Levy, Son, Park, & Hwang, 2018) clearly puts it here that a cyber attack on the US could take a lot of strategic planning by the terrorists, who possibly can attack an airport electronic system. Should this kind of attack happen by any means, it will be a great disaster for the US and the International community at large. Therefore, issues of cyberterrorism should be a major topic of consideration for the security of life and properties by any well-meaning government. It is therefore a necessary requirement that governments of nations collaborate to fight the insurgence cyberterrorism. There is a need for collaborative network for inter-governmental coordination to clamp down the activities of cyberterrorism.

One of the main areas of benefits that encourages Cyberterrorism is the economic benefit that is derived from such acts. A couple of research has been conducted by various researchers to address the benefits of cyberterrorism and other crimes. It is obviously clear that cyberterrorism is becoming a viable option to terrorist – reasons being that the internet offers a variety of sophisticated tools such as the deep web technology for attackers to conveniently carry out their activities without being exposed or caught. Our work wants to contribute to these debates by performing a review of some of the research done in this area with possible recommendations on how cyberterrorism can be clamped down even in the midst of all the uncertainties mentioned in this article. The structure of the article is as follows: We will do a brief review of published literature addressing the economic benefit of cyberterrorism to terrorist and supporting nations. We will also attempt to discuss on the possible solutions to curb the emergence of this dreadful enemy of humanity. Finally, we draw conclusions and recommendations at the end of the study.

ADVANCES IN CYBERSECURITY DESIGN: AN INTEGRATED FRAMEWORK TO QUANTIFY THE ECONOMIC IMPACTS OF CYBER-TERRORIST BEHAVIOR

Cybersecurity has seen great advances in design in the recent years. Organizations, multinational and governments needs to work hand in hand with security software designers to ensure the safety of their data, facilities and IT structures. This effort could be very helpful in challenging the emergence and growth of cyberterrorism. Once a terrorist organization can gain access into the major database of a nation, then we can smell doom for that nation. For this reason, governments spend huge amount of resources to secure sensitive data from unauthorized access. In this article titled above, the authors put forth an integrated framework to magnify what could likely be the economic impact of a cyber-attack on the United States airport security system (Park et al., 2018). No doubt a successful attack on the airport security system can curse unimaginable damage to the economy of the nation. But what is not covered in this article is the economic benefit that would instigate such an idea to attack a nation's major economic resources. They stated clearly that it would take a lot of calculated strategy by the terrorist groups to lunch such an attack. Not withstanding chances are that they might find a loop hole. The question that rises immediately from this article which should be given much more attention is "to what extend should a nation like the US go to protect the security of their airport system?" Even if it means placing embargo's on citizens or certain nationality which could be considered as treat from entering their territory? Definietly it would raise questions from the international community about discriminations as we have seen during the Trump administration in their attempt to clamp down on illegal immigrants into the United States. They identified the possibility for a simultaneous threat from attackers – making it even more challenging to predict and defend any attacks.

In a bid to offer a solution to the issue at hand, the authors suggested inter-governmental collaboration as a probable solution to hold down cyberterrorism against the United States. Their model was basically based on a strategic and deliberate effort to combine competitive and cooperate game scenarios in developing a strategy to curb cyberterrorism. Considering the negative effect of this kind of attack on a Nation's airport security system, any government would put forth at it can to ensure the security of her infrastructure. Hence, combining these two forces to fight cyberterrorism is not too much for a Nation like the united states. But what has not be discussed here is the motivation behind a terror attack such as this. The government also need to evaluate what could possible motivate a cyber attack on their airport security facilities. If this is political or based on economic gains. If it is political then the collaborative scheme is applicable. However, if a terrorist organization is planning an attack on the nation's airport security system to prove some points or for financial gain, then the government needs to investigate more realistic and deeper ways to handle such cases.

A terrorist group that is well motivated will use everything within their power include collaboration with enemy nations of the United State to lunch such a deadly attack such as the September eleven attack. A stronger alliance with other enemy nations will present a much more difficult situation for the United States. If the United States can identify such alliance and offer a competitive edge, then they stand a chance to win the battle against their enemy. In our opinion we suggest that this model can be modified to include two key factors: "the financial motivation for cyberterrorism and terrorist alliances with other rival nations." We believe that a more comprehensive model should consider these two factors for a balanced prediction and control of cyberterrorism.

CYBER TERRORISM: A CLEAR AND PRESENT DANGER, THE SUM OF ALL FEARS, BREAKING POINT, OR PATRIOT GAMES?

(Stohl, 2006) in their article examined the gap between known cyber characters and cyber-attack threats and other literatures that points out that cyberterrorism attacks are forthcoming. It is necessary to clearly define what cyberterrorism is, considering the dangers and threat that it presents for now and the future (Margaret, 2018). One of the challenges that makes it difficult to curb cybersecurity is the constant emergence of new technologies. The usual approach is to channel a greater portion of resources to protect system components that pose more threats than those with little risks. But to deal with the issue of cyberterrorism, advisory organizations are advocating for a more proactive and adaptive proposition.

The "National Institute of Standards and Technology (NIST)," recently modified the guidelines on their risk assessment structure to give room for more regular monitoring and real-time evaluation of security threats. This will help organizations to be apt in identifying possible threats of cyberterrorism attack and immediately device means to curb such insurgence. In April 2018, they released version 1.1 of their framework targeted towards improving the security of critical infrastructure. Again, in this case, we see the complete total omission of the possible motivation of cyberterrorism. It has not been put in consideration probably because the focus is more on defining cyberterrorism, it's scope and the chances of a cyberterrorism attack. It is still relevant that organizations such as the NIST that set standards and framework of this kind put in consideration the possible chances of investigating of economic benefits are some of the motivation behind cyberterrorism. Would terrorist make more money by using internet facilities to perpetrate their acts? Or is it just that they find it more affordable, easy to use or as an alternative to the conventional terrorist mechanism.

Cybersecurity frameworks have been developed for implementation in communication defense, banking and energy industries, which can also be deployed to other sectors including state and federal governments. In May 2017, the President of America, Trump issued the immediate adoption of the NIST cybersecurity framework. Seeing that this framework is very instrumental to the public, private and government agencies, we would like to also suggest that such framework should still be modified to give a wholistic evaluation of the cyberterrorism concept, including the economic benefits. This way, the root of cyberterrorism can be addressed with adequate measures before it escalates to an uncontrollable level. It has been reported that organizations are investing more into cybersecurity technologies and services since 2017. This report delivered by Gartner projected that expenditures on information systems security would reach about $84 billion and could possibly grow to around $93 in the current year (2018). With this kind of statistic, it is obvious that many people are making a fortune out of cybersecurity. If the economic benefits are not properly addressed, we would see more expenditures like this as the year progresses. The more we keep spending to defend, the more the threats will continue to advance. What we are saying here is that, if the economic benefits of cyberterrorism can be adequately cut down, many will be discouraged to go into such act. We completely understand the part of political motivation into cyberterrorism. But cutting down the economic benefits could also have a direct or indirect impact on the political motivations for carrying out cyberterrorism attacks.

THE STRATEGIES OF CYBERTERRORISM: IS CYBERTERRORISM AN EFFECTIVE MEANS TO ACHIEVING THE GOALS OF TERRORISTS?

For a successful cyberterrorism attack to be lunched on any organization, government or parastatals, a lot of energy, time and resources is put to strategically plan and execute such attack. The question (Chuipka, 2017) attempted to answer was to know if cyberterrorism is an effective tool for terrorist to achieve their goals. The question would be again: "what is/are these goals?" Are they politically motivated or financially motivated? In both cases, any viable means to achieve their goal is a welcome idea. Chuipka (2017), observed that the convergence of technologies and the physical world is at an exponential growth rate.

The convergence results from the increasing interconnectivity of various technologies. It has resulted in a growing concern among technocrats and stakeholders that, terrorist organization could possibly exploit the possibilities provided by this every growing technology to lunch a cyberattack, which could be dangerous and deadly. Considering the vulnerabilities in the cyberspace, the consequences of a major cyberterrorist attack could spell doom for any organization, government or individual.

Chuipka (2017) in their research article, argued that "the strategies of cyberterrorism may be limited to attrition in pursuit of policy change goals." They agreed that the threat of cyberterrorism is real but could also be over-hyped. They aligned to the possibility of a potential threat, but actual threat is lower. Their reasoning is that high level cyberterrorism attacks require huge resources, great skills, intelligence and time – invariably it is too risky to carry out a cyber-attack by a terrorist group because there are chances that many things can go wrong since technology is involved. The fact is that, their assumption is true, nevertheless, a well-motivated terrorist organization (which could be financial or political) will go out all in search of the best strategy to execute a smooth cyber-attack on major facilities. Internet facilities such as the deep web offers a variety of usable tools such as anonymity and other great hacking tools for a motivated attacker. It is quite understandable that develop and developing nations are working hard daily to close all possible chances of a terror attack on the cyberspace. That notwithstanding, nothing should be left to chances in the fight against terrorism.

The author also argued that kinetic weapons such as well-known machineries are more suitable to achieve the goals of terrorism. It will not be out of place to also state here that, the revolution that is currently being experienced in the information technology sphere could in the future present a surprise cyber-attack if care is not taking. For example, consider the advent of artificial intelligence and the future possibility of terrorist tapping into such technology in the coming future. This will be more disastrous than the physical weapons that we have seen been used to cause havoc. An attack on the information security system of a nation like the United State will not be a minor.

BANGS FOR THE BUCK: A COST-BENEFIT ANALYSIS OF CYBERTERRORISM

Bang for the buck is an idiom meaning the worth of one's money or exertion. The phrase originated from the slang usage of the words "bang" which means "excitement" and "buck" which means "money" (Wikipedia, 2018). Seth (2018) attempt to answer the question of a possible avoidance of a cyberterrorist attack. They mentioned that a strategic terrorist group that intends to employ the possibilities of internet facilities to lunch a cyber-attack would first consider the cost of such an attempt. With this hypothesis and attempting to answer the forgoing question, they concluded that cyberterrorism is not a very effective tool or substitute for the conventional tools. They added that information infrastructures could be a helpful tool for terrorist organizations to spread their idea and beliefs, but not for any form of physical attack.

This article of Seth (2018), was prepared in 2004, and looking from 2004 to date, there has been a lot of advancements in technologies. A quote from the article of Seth Harrison published by the Center for Strategic and International Studies stated thus: "Over the course of the 16-year War on Terror, experts have identified political and socioeconomic conditions as root causes of terrorism. The technological enablers that make terrorism possible are less studied, however. Innovations in computing and telecommunications—like widespread internet access,1 end-to-end encryption, and virtual private network (VPN) usage—have made new types of operations possible for a higher number of radicalized individuals" (Seth, 2018). Obviously, there is an impending danger of a major cyber terrorist attack if we completely ignore the possibility of a cyberterrorist attack in the coming years. It will therefore be safe for us to watch out and fight any trace of cyberterrorism with all the technology we have than ascertain fictitiously that it will never happen.

It's also been on record that the Islamic State group of terrorists capitalize on emerging technologies to remotely inspire and orchestrate their attacks (Rukmini, 2017). Seth (2018) mentioned in their article the necessity for policy makers to incorporate information technology conditions in their prediction of new ISIS hotspots. What more, in Malaysia for instant, the ISIS group takes advantage of the advancement in internet access to recruit youths into their army (Mohd Sani, 2016). Using the technology provide by twitter, the ISIS directed an operation to attack the Curtis Coldwell Center (Callimanchi, 2015). The use of VPN has also posed a greater threat, in the case of terrorist, the use of VPN prevents government agencies from tracking their location, movement and intentions (EUROPOL).

THE ECONOMIC IMPACT OF CYBER TERRORISM

Hau (2013) attempted to answer the question: "What is the economic impact of cyber terrorism? Can organizations achieve strategic advantage in the cyber terrorism game?" They proposed a general game theory to investigate the Information Systems' security investment vs the losses incurred due to cyber terrorists' attacks. The result of their experiment suggested that upcoming organizations, government and multinationals should invest more in information systems security to protect their information system infrastructure against any cyber terrorist attack with long term goals. Their result is a very welcome idea as to the emergence of improved technologies which can become a very useful instrument by terrorist organizations to lunch a major and massive cyber attack on any facility. Bearing this in mind, their recommendation is very apt to the idea that we share in our evaluation of the articles in the previous sections. To add to their research, we recommend that a more in-dept analysis of the motivation of terrorist attacks be carried out to investigate particularly on the economic benefits of cyberterrorism as a major motivation towards a cyber-attack. When this is done, more measures to guard against the encouragement of cyber terrorism can be put in place. The solution her is avoidance and not reacting to an incidence.

CONCLUSION AND RECOMMENDATIONS

The work of various researchers targeting cyberterrorism has been reviewed in this article. We have found out that many of these authors have expressed candid opinions that vary in ideology on the emergence and a possible cyber attack by terrorist. While some agree that there is a possibility, earlier researchers don't seem to be convinced of the possibility of a major cyber terrorism attack siting the sensitivity of such an attack. However, later researchers who have published articles dating 2016 to date, have shown some level of concern that a cyber terrorism attack is eminent of measures are not properly put in place to check the nefarious activities of terrorist groups and up coming gangsters. Reasons been the rate of emergence of new and more sophisticated internet technologies over the past years. The projection is that technology will continue to emerge, and the terrorist organizations will in the long run buy the idea of adopting sophisticated technologies to lunch even global terror attacks on information infrastructures that might cause major damages. One of the reasons we capitalize to evaluate in this article for cyber terrorism is the economic benefit. Many articles as we evaluated agreed to the fact that socio-economic factors are deeply responsible for terrorist activities.

Having said all of these, it is necessary for more definite approaches placing a renewed emphasis on defensive counterterrorism measures to be put in place to curb the emergence of cyberterrorism. While continuing to work to prevent attacks, law enforcement should also explore new ways to mitigate attacks' effectiveness. While the government's capacity to disrupt the promotion of terror is limited, it can evaluate the availability of these emerging technologies as a factor in identifying high-risk locations. "This increased awareness can be used to better target preventative efforts and assist officials in finetuning their threat assessments (Seth, 2013)."

REFERENCES

Aron, R. (1965). *Democratie et Totalitarisme*. Paris: Galliard.

Associated Press. (2004, June 11). U.S. Wrongly Reported Drop in World Terrorism in 2003. *The New York Times*, p. A9.

Bang for the buck. (n.d.). In *Wikipedia*. Available at: https://en.wikipedia.org/wiki/Bang_for_the_buck

Barnett, T. (2004). *The Pentagon's New Map: War and Peace in the Twentieth-First Century*. New York: Putnam and Sons.

Biddle, S. (2004). *Military Power: Explaining Victory and Defeat in Modern Battle*. Princeton, NJ: Princeton University Press.

Callimachi, R. (2015). Clues on Twitter Show Ties between Texas Gunman and ISIS Network. *New York Times*. Retrieved from https://www.nytimes.com/2015/05/12/us/twitter cluesshow-ties- between-isis-and-garland-texas-gunman.html

Callimachi, R. (2017). Not 'Lone Wolves' after All: How ISIS Guides World's Terror Plots from Afar. *New York Times*. Retrieved from https://www.nytimes.com/2017/02/04/ world/asia/isis-messaging-app-terror-plot.html?mtrref=t.co&gwh=EF42D2AC6FBB561

Chuipka, A. (2017). *The Strategies of Cyberterrorism: Is Cyberterrorism an effective means to Achieving the Goals of Terrorists?* Academic Press.

EUROPOL Public Information. (n.d.). *Changes in Modus Operandi of Islamic State Terrorist Attacks*. Academic Press.

Giacomello, G. (2003). Measuring 'digital wars': Learning from the experience of peace research and arms control. *Infocon Magazine, 1*.

Giacomello, G. (2004). Bangs for the buck: A cost-benefit analysis of cyberterrorism. *Studies in Conflict and Terrorism, 27*(5), 387–408. doi:10.1080/10576100490483660

Hua, J., & Bapna, S. (2013). The economic impact of cyber terrorism. *The Journal of Strategic Information Systems, 22*(2), 175–186. doi:10.1016/j.jsis.2012.10.004

Margaret, R. (n.d.). *Cybersecurity*. Retrieved 14th December 2018. Available at: https://searchsecurity.techtarget.com/definition/cybersecurity

Mohd Sani, M. (2016). *ISIS Recruitment of Malaysian Youth: Challenge and Response*. Middle East Institute. Retrieved from http://www.mei.edu/content/map/isis-recruitment-malaysianyouth-challenge-and-response

Park, J., Levy, J., Son, M., Park, C., & Hwang, H. (2018). Advances in Cybersecurity Design: An Integrated Framework to Quantify the Economic Impacts of Cyber-Terrorist Behavior. In *Security by Design* (pp. 317–339). Cham: Springer. doi:10.1007/978-3-319-78021-4_15

Seth, H. (2018). *Evolving Tech, Evolving Terror*. Center for Strategic & International Studies. Available at: https://www.csis.org/npfp/evolving-tech-evolving-terror

Stohl, M. (2006). Cyber terrorism: A clear and present danger, the sum of all fears, breaking point or patriot games? *Crime, Law, and Social Change*, *46*(4-5), 223–238. doi:10.100710611-007-9061-9

Terrorism. (n.d.). Available at: https://www.google.com/search?q=terror+meaning&rlz=1C1CHBF_enCY821CY821&o q=terror+meaning&aqs=c hrome.69i57j0l5.3245j1j9&sourceid=chrome&ie=UTF- 8#dobs=terrorism

Chapter 7

Guide for Modelling a Network Flow–Based Detection System for Malware Categorization:
A Review of Related Literature

Joshua Chibuike Sopuru
Girne American University, Cyprus

Murat Akkaya
Girne American University, Cyprus

ABSTRACT

Improved technology has led to significant changes in society over time. This has been accompanied by significant changes in the economy. The improvement in technology has also been accompanied by significant changes in the modeling of network-based systems. This is comprised of significant updates of computer and mobile operating systems. The development of mobile phones and operating systems have endangered essential individual and corporate data over time by making it vulnerable and prone to viruses, worms, and malware. This chapter focuses on reviewing literature that serves as guides for modeling a network flow-based detection system for malware categorization. The Author begins with an in-depth definition of mobile devices and how they have eased the spread of malicious software. Identifying Android OS as the most used operating system, Android OS operating system layer was explained, and the reason for user preferability unveiled. The chapter continued with a review of known malware and their behaviors as has been observed over time.

DOI: 10.4018/978-1-5225-8976-1.ch007

Copyright © 2019, IGI Global. Copying or distributing in print or electronic forms without written permission of IGI Global is prohibited.

INTRODUCTION

Improved technology has led to significant changes in the society over time. This has been accompanied by significant changes in the economy. The improvement in technology has also been accompanied by significant changes in the modeling of network-based systems. This is comprised of significant updates of computer and mobile operating systems. The development of mobile phones and Operating systems have endangered essential individual and corporate data over time, by making it vulnerable and prone to viruses, worms, and malware. This chapter focuses on reviewing literature that serves as guides for modeling a network flow-based detection system for malware categorization.

The development and continued innovations with regard to Operating systems have proofed to be very essential for making alternations in both the economy and the society over time. Mobile devices have increased the ease of transactions in the economy Wagener, & Dulaunoy, (2008). Transfer of liquid money has been made more effective and convenient for both mobile bankers and customers globally. This has been enabled through the development of improved Operating Systems. However, this has endangered individuals' and corporate financial information by making it prone to hackers and thieves overtime. This information is also prone to attack by malware which may lead to erroneous spreading of this data. This chapter, therefore, will be very crucial for the protection of customers' financial institution over time.

Marketing and advertisements have also been made easier through the development of certain mobile soft wares over time. Android operating systems allow the creation of applications and software, whereas iPhone operating system limits this. Through mobile phones, suppliers can connect with their potential customers globally. However, this has also laid a platform for hacking of data. It has also exposed these devices to dangerous malware attacks that resolve from utilizing erroneous links over time.

Learning has also been made convenient for both learners and tutors overtime. Through mobile devices, learning materials can easily be accessed in soft copies through online webs. This has contributed to the additional knowledge that learners have acquired over time. Also, different educational articles such as health and nutrition journals available online have been very crucial to different societies. Therefore, protection of mobile devices from attack by malware, viruses, and worms has been very crucial and essential in enhancing the extent to which learners and tutors can rely on this device for their learning activities and the extent to which they are convinced that their data is safeguarded from hackers and attack by malware and viruses.

This chapter, therefore, will focus on reviewing literature that will help guide developers on things to look into in developing Anti-malware programs. This will enable the convenience and effectiveness of such activities over time. Also, Operating system designer firms such as Google for Android Operating Systems, and Apple for IOS will receive more profits with the development of such programs. This will lead to economic development of nations due to the fact that the welfare of the citizens will be increased. Also, the gross domestic products will increase significantly due to increased transactions and reduced costs, therefore increasing savings of individuals and groups, which will be later converted into investments. Profitability of Operating Systems designing firms will also lead to economic development of their host countries. Therefore, this chapter proofs to be very crucial for the continued development of national economies.

DEFINITION OF TERMS

- **Malware:** A software developed with the intension of causing harm to computers or mobile devices.
- **Anti-Malware Programs:** Software/program designed precisely to protect devices against malware.
- **Operating Systems:** System software that enables computers or mobile phones to perform fundamental computing activities.
- **Malware Detection:** It is the ability to identify harmful pattern of malware before harm is caused on the target machine.
- **Malware Spreading:** the ability of malicious viruses or dangerous malware to multiply themselves and replicate to other devices.
- **Malware Evasion:** Different ways or methods through which invasion by malware can be essentially detected and handled.
- **Malware Categorization:** Ability to effectively define malware into groups based on some recognized characteristics.
- **Cybercrimes:** Illegal Activities intended to cause harm. It is usually associated with utilization of computer networks.

MOBILE OPERATING SYSTEMS

The operating system used on mobile devices are generally referred to as mobile operating systems. Devices such as phones, smartwatches, tablets, PDAs or other mobile devices make use of mobile operating systems to run programs and applications. Mobile operating systems are historically different from desktop OS as they were originally designed to support mobility of devices. However, this distinction is becoming obsolete as hybrid desktop operating systems are now revolutionized to accommodate mobility as seen in mobile devices. Features of traditional desktop operating system combined with features supporting mobility and handheld use are technically fussed to achieve a mobile operating system. For a system to be mobile, one should expect some basic features such as Global positioning system (GPS), Wi-Fi secured access, touchscreen, Bluetooth, Cellular, near field communication, speech recognition, infrared and mobile communication abilities. For mobile devices with mobile communication abilities (example smartphones), two mobile operating systems are contained in them, the main end-user platform supported by a low-level real time software which handles communication radio and other communication related hardware. According to research, the use of these two low-level systems may result to vulnerability of the mobile device allowing range of attacks from a malicious station. In checking security and other vulnerabilities, the design of a mobile OS is important as a mobile OS does not only determine the features and functions available for use on a mobile device but also determines third party software/applications permitted to run on the device.

Kushwaha, & Kushwaha, (2011) defines a mobile as a wireless gadget which enables users to have access to different types of information and data. Being mobile, individuals can easily carry these devices around and have access to data wherever they go. Mobile Operating Systems allow users to make different alternations to ensure that their everyday desires are met.

According to them, mobile phones were previously designed for voice calls alone, but in recent time this has changed with priority given to other aspects other than voice call. With this expansion, the structure of mobile OS has also changed over time to accommodate these advances.

A mobile OS (operating system) refers to software that is developed to control and power the hardware components of mobile devices.

The potentials of the hardware components of a mobile device is revealed by the operating system of that device. For example, Android OS has been observed to be preferable by users over its iPhone counterpart because the Android OS allows more applications to be developed on it than iPhone.

As confirmed by Silberschatz, Galvin & Gagne (2014), technological improvements have made it possible for mobile phones to meet the ever-growing needs of users. Mobile phones have affected positively currency transfers and exchange, fast and easy payment of liabilities and other bills, purchases and supplies have become easy and so many other essential tasks made easy. All these improvements and expansions are made possible when mobile OS are progressively transformed. There are distinguished "operating systems" for various phones, these include *"iPhone Operating systems"* for iPhone, Android OS, *"Window OS 7"* for windows phones etc. Blackberries, Nokia and Samsung phones also have distinguished and categorized operating systems which they utilize.

Mobile operating system plays vital role in determining several features/ characteristics of a mobile, therefore selecting a mobile OS is important.

According to Johansen, Van Renesse, & Schneider, (1995), the speed of connectivity and the ease of maintenance is determined by the type of "Mobile Operating systems" running on a mobile device. In other words, different mobiles with different OS have different speeds and maintenance techniques, with each mobile company competing to have the most improved Operating System for its phones. It is predicted that soon mobile phones will have better OS and would become more affordable.

Mobile OS are very important and cannot be overridden since they provide neccessary performance grounds for other platforms/software to operate. Android is recognized as the bestselling operating system ever developed. With regards to Sheikh & Dar, (2013), it is said that Android increased its market share to 81.3% in the third quarter of 2013 and has become the most successful smartphone OS company in the world. During the same period in 2013, the Android share of the global smartphone shipment market rose to over 270 million smart devices using android sold across the globe. Since smartphones and other mobile gadgets such as tablets have become common nowadays, their operating systems have also become more sophisticated with every new device being manufactured. Mobile devices using Android OS are often low powered and can function on rechargeable batteries. The devices also feature hardware features such as a camera, flashlight, Global Positioning System (GPS) receivers, Wi-Fi, touchscreen and UMTS (3G telephony) connectivity. What most have made Android OS more popular than other mobile OS? Is there an outstanding difference between Android and another OS?

Android OS was first introduced commercially in 2008 and in less than 2 years of introduction it had caused a revolution in the market. There are obvious reasons why users have preferred Android OS over its counterparts. One big question one must ask is, "is the popularity of the Android OS a security loophole?"

Feng & Aiken, (2014) argue that although the Android OS is similar to other mobile device Operating system, it is different from them all because of its kernel application framework which includes Java-compatible libraries that are powered by Apache Harmony. The Dalivk virtual machine attached to the Android OS offers just in time compilation of all java codes. This is important to note as it affects the speed of processes running in the Android OS environment. Because of Androids open source nature, a large team of developers and technicians work tirelessly developing applications that extend the functionality of the device. Relevant applications that seek to provide solutions to increasing demands from end users are constantly developed. Android OS continues to grow even as technological experts broaden their interest to other areas the Android OS can be utilized. Different sectors such as Mobile Attendance, Robot control from remote locations, Electric home appliances, internet of things and remote sensing are considered as sectors the Android OS can be of great impact. Figure 1 shows android OS dominating sales of other mobile phone OS in the US market.

Figure 1. Top smartphone operating systems in the US by market share

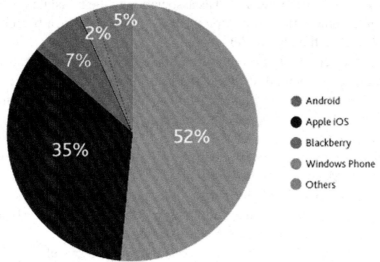

ANDROID OPERATING SYSTEM LAYER

Android is an operating system developed on the Linux kernel. Linux originally is an open source operating system with multi-user, multi-tasking functions, virtual memory and has a programmable shell. Being open source, it has enjoyed rapid improvement. Linux kernel was established by Linus Torvalds in 1991, written in C language the Linux kernel provides deep hardware manipulations and thus provides the Android OS great possibilities for improvement.

The Android OS system architecture can be broadly divided into 4 layers:

- Application layer
- Application framework layer
- Libraries
- Linux kernel

The Android OS Linux Kernel has a higher-level API that is written in C. The Linux API provides interfaces for user programs to run on the mobile devices. With a higher-level API application can easily be developed to interact with hardware components. Applications are programmed in Java and operated with the (DVM) Dalvik virtual machine. The Dalvik virtual machine is an open source software that executes applications developed for Android OS. Programs written for Android are compiled as bytecode and ran on Java VM. These programs are then translated to Dalvik bytecode. The. ".dex" and ".odex" files are stored as association to the translated programs. Just in time compilations are implement to to interpret Java bytecode and translate them to the Dalvik dex-code.

The Linux Kernel is important to a mobile operating system because it acts as its central processing unit. Being the heart of a mobile phone, it handles process management, file management, memory management, Unix user identifiers (UIDs), security settings and file authorization with the type-safe technique of Java.

A unique process and process identifier (UID) is created for each application running on an Android phone. Processes running on the Linux kernel do not have rights to access data belonging to other processes. This provides a top-notch security for applications as applications cannot modify data belonging to other applications with express permission from the OS.

One of the important technical responsibility of the kernel among others is sandboxing of each application. Sandboxing of applications ensures data belonging to the application are explicitly shared. The security level offered by Kernel when sharing data resources between applications is done statistically at the time the application is downloaded and installed to run. The Android operating system prompts users to accept at the time of installation using a technique that grants permission dynamically to boost the level of security.

Android applications have the topmost rank of the software stack. The application layer comprises of both Native and third-part applications. Third-party applications are applications written installed by programmers, developers while troubleshooting and the end-user after purchasing the mobile device, while native applications are primary applications offering basic functions like contact manager, short messages and dialler.

The basic role of the application framework layer is to provide several packages of higher-level services to the application that collectively form the environment within which they are constructed from replaceable, interchangeable, reusable components. The application layer also serves other functions such as data sharing, location management, and resource sharing. Among its sets of libraries, activities such as surface manager are used to compose windows on mobile screens, Free Type for Font Rendering, WebKit Browser Engine, SGL for 2D Graphics, Open GL&ES for 3D Library, Media Framework to record and play various audio, and SSL internet security library.

The Android operating system is similar to the iPhone operating system in some ways and can be totally different from the iPhone in many other ways. According to Maia, Nogueira, & Pinho, (2010), IOS is developed and marketed by Apple Company for the effectiveness, efficiency, and workability of Apple devices such as the iPhone. On the other hand, Android OS is built by Google, using *"Linux Kernel"* this OS is efficient in tablets and smartphones and can easily be expanded.

Tracy, (2012) postulated that different hardware and software components make up different Mobile phones, and also determine their workability overtime. Tablets and Smartphones are more efficient with the utilization of "Android OS," while "IPads and iPhone" utilize the IOS. There are certainly major differences between these two brands of operating systems which distinguishes them and their functionalities. The security, speed, and ease of use of these two Operating Systems differ significantly from each other. An individual will base his or her preference based on these characteristics.

Another major difference between IOS and Android is in its security, Gandhewar, & Sheikh, (2010) asserted that the security of IOS and Android OS varies over time. Smartphones are more convenient and efficient in usage as compared to iPhones. Mobiles enable users to hold essential and

Figure 2. Android OS architecture

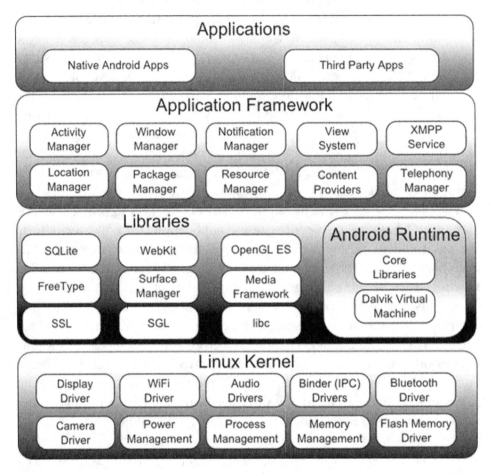

sensitive data and information easily. The extent to which this information is safeguarded has remained questionable over time. Invasion by viruses and instances of cyber crimes such as hacking are other security issues relating to storing essential data in smartphones or iPhone.

Despite IOS being more secured than Android, it has been observed by some researchers that more people utilize Android OS than IOS, this is because Android provides better flexibility and allows for better end user customization. According to Wei, Gomez, & Faloutsos, (2012), more people utilize android versions in their day to day activities due to the ease and convenience of the *"Android OS."* Smartphones are also more affordable and efficient. Despite this, Apple has continued to make more profits as compared to Google. This is essential because Apple keeps their focus on building more applications, while Google investments are mainly based on adverts. Also, employees at Apple are more highly motivated by higher incomes, which enhance their efficiency and productivity at work overtime.

Android has the power to run on different types of mobile devices. It is different from other operating systems in terms of size, functions of buttons, form and other technical operations. In order for different mobile phone companies to develop devices that have the possibility to conform to the standards set by Android, it is crucial for them to adjust the native user interface of the mobile operating system. The pitfall of having manufacturers to conform to standards set by Android is that they will need to customize mobile operating systems with regards to Android system updates that are available.

Since smartphones are similar to personal computers as they provide various related functions such as multitasking, expandable memory, social networking, and playing games. According to market share analysis and comparative analysis done towards the end of 2014, considering efficiency, windows and Android phones were found to be superior to other operating systems. According to findings, during the fourth quarter of 2014, about 80.7% of mobile phone users identified Android as the best smartphone operating system. Android was recognized as the best smartphone operating system ever developed. Considering Android as an open source OS, it allows for easy installation of third-party applications downloaded from play store and even unreliable sources. The openness of Android OS is sometimes a threat to its security as hackers can easily capitalize on it and create harmful programs intended to steal user's information. It is known that Android OS is exposed to a host of harmful malware attacks such as worms, spyware, viruses, adware, and Trojan horse. In the next section, the level of Android mobile OS malware security shall be explored to understand how they gain access and their spreading techniques, evasion ways and overview of known behaviour.

IOS AND ANDROID MOBILE MALWARE

Arora, Garg, & Peddoju, (2014) asserts that the continued use and reliance of mobile phones in day to day crucial activities have raised the alarm pertaining the security of data and information and the extent to which these devices are prone to viruses. Corporate and portfolio institutions require high security for their information. Mobile phone storage has raised numerous questions with regard to this. Misplacement or theft would resolve to exposure of such sensitive information.

According to Chan, & Song, (2014), Connections to internet, portability, and sharing of mobile phones make them vulnerable to invasion by viruses and cyber crimes such as hacking. Malware invasion can lead to malfunctioning, reduced speed or may collapse the Operating Systems. Crucial information can be oscillated or received without the user's insight. Installation of various applications can also dispose viruses to a mobile phone.

An example of android mobile malware software is DroidDream. The DroidDream malware is notorious for attacking and rendering over 65 legitimate applications useless in Play Store android market and was also blamed for harming the devices of 600,000 users across the world towards the end of June 2011. In addition to this, GG-Tracker is identified as a malware that lures users into downloading their malicious programs such as a phone battery saving app. The malicious software once installed sends messages that are charged after they are received by users. The cost of these premium charges may extend to $40 for every message.

Huang & Liang, (2014) A malware caused by Trojan can be identified when applications appear to run in a disguise to conceal the hidden intent of performing malicious acts in the background. The Trojan malware is very

Figure 3. Malware infection in the US by type in 2013

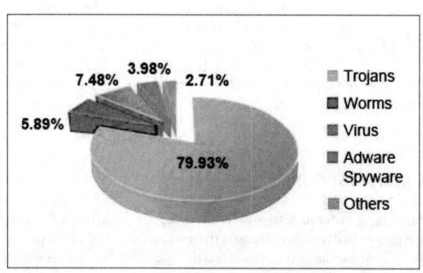

FIG.5. MALWARE INFECTIONS BY TYPE IN Q1 2013.

dangerous because it assists attackers to gain unauthorized entry into a system by performing functions that might expose the system to security breaches. Ransomware is identified as a type of malware that is used by cybercriminals to block users from gaining entry to their device as well as encrypt their data files until they make payments for ransom. A *"bot"* is a popular malware that is recognized for its ability to infiltrate machines and give attackers control over the affected mobile device. In other instances, *"Web Robot"* is used by cybercriminals as a way of gaining access into a device remotely through network channel and could also be described as *"botnet."*

Spywares are spying software used to stalk a user's device activities. Unlike the others, spy wares operate unnoticed because they run in the background while they collect information and allow cyber intruders to have a peek when they gain access remotely. In tandem with Macafe LABs, it is stated that the number of malware in the US from 2007 has been increasing dramatically every two years. Recently, the antivirus and operation system security company identified that the number of malware in the first quarter of 2017 had exceeded 16 million. Figure 4 shows a table of Macafe LABs world stats of malware infection rate during the first quarter of 2017.

Kaur & Sharma, (2014) postulate that mobile malware is the most dangerous threat to devices security because they comprise a host of software programs

Figure 4. Global malware infection rate

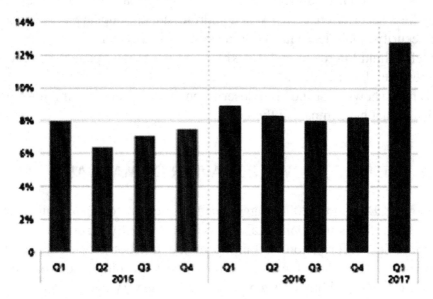

that are designed to intrude and damage personal files and the operating systems of a user's computer, mobile phone device, and tablet. The impact of having these viruses on a device is that it can disrupt mobile operations and also delete some of the files and directory within the operating system. Kaur & Sharma identify that the world is riddled with software programmers with malicious intents and it is important for every user to know what malware is and how they attack their effects and how to avoid them to protect their devices.

Several mobile malware is designed to incapacitate a device in one way or another so that weakness is created allowing malicious users to control the mobile device or steal a user's personal information. The personal information is stolen from the user's mobile device. Among the most common malware programs notorious for attacking mobile devices are such as DroidDream and kung fu. The two malware are accused of causing problems such as creating loopholes where the user's personal information can be stolen and changing how user's mobile devices to function.

Alazab et al., (2010) claim that there are unique features that make every mobile operating system unique. Mobile phones have become open sources with the highest degree of customization, especially in phones using the Android operating system. Since mobile phones have become common, they have also become more susceptible to malware and bugs. Unlike the iPhone operating system that uses proprietary software and provides a little option for customization, Android can automatically or manually launch updates to address security concerns. When android launches updates, it does so to seal security loopholes in its operating system. It is evident that the company has left behind Microsoft and Blackberry because their updates are scanned and resolved less frequent.

Table 1 shows a list and brief description of the 12 most common Android malware that have impacted the US

OVERVIEW OF KNOWN BEHAVIOR OF MALWARE

Wagener, & Dulaunoy, (2008) suggested that various actions can be undertaken by different forms of mobile malware overtime. Firstly, viruses and worms attain critical information pertaining to the functionality of the mobile operating systems. This, therefore, makes these files vulnerable to dangerous malware attacks. Hiding files would, therefore, be very essential in ensuring that essential files remain hidden from such attacks.

Table 1. Summary of the 12 most common Android Malware

Malware	Description	First observed
Acecard	It is a trojan designed specifically for banking. It hides behind android applications to steal users banking information. This malware is usually distributed through infected apps.	The first case was noticed in 2015
AdDown	This adware came in 3 different variants, Joymobile, Nativemob, and Xavier. It secretly installs the app (if the device is rooted), shows unwanted adverts and steals user information without any form of encryption.	It was first discovered in January 2015
ExpensiveWall	This malware specializes in sending fraudulent messages and charging users for fake transactions. It also keeps track of user location and IP address secretly	It was first notified to Google on August 2017
Fakeapp	A trojan that downloads configuration files. It checks for compromised Facebook accounts, attempt to retrieve login details and if successful, it steals personal information from its victims Facebook account	It was first discovered in 2012
FakeBank	This Android trojan clones banking apps installed on a user mobile. By deleting the original banking app, Fakebank creates an exact copy of the deleted bank app with a sole purpose of stealing user information. FakeBank also included call-barring functions making it impossible for its victims to call their bank.	It was first discovered in 2013
Marcher	This Trojan was designed to steal credit card information from Google Play. It simply displays a fake payment portal with the intention of copying the payment details of its victim	It was first discovered in 2013
Morder.A	This is an Android Trojan which disguises itself as a .pdf application. It immediately gains administrative rights when installing in other for it not to be deleted. Its main duty is to steal user contact information, reveal user location, it also records audio and takes pictures secretly.	It was first observed on 12th January 2016
Pawost	This Android malware embeds itself into mobile applications and initiates calls using Google talk. During calls, it disables keyboard and other functions capable of ending the call.	It was first discovered in June 2016
KevDroid	It is a remote access trojan posing as an antivirus application with the aim of stealing data. KevDroid monitors its victim's location every 10 seconds, steals information regarding the victims' calls, emails, SMS etc. and sends it to a C2 server	First discovered by ESET on Apr 03, 2018
LightsOut	It is an adware used to generate ad revenue for its developers. LightsOut hijacks a victim's phone forcing its victims to click on pop-up adverts.	The first application with this virus booted in Sept. 2017
MilkyDoor	They are believed to be legitimate applications redesigned by attackers to enter secured networks. This Malware makes use of SOCKS to gain unsuspicious access into secured networks affected devices connect to	Its first variant "NotCompatible" was observed in 2012
MysteryBot	The MysteryBot contains three components: ransomware, keylogger, and banking trojan. It uses its keylogger feature to still inputted information from its victims. MysteryBot also takes files ransom by adding passwords to files in a ZIP folder.	First discovered by Threatfabric probably in June 2018

Alazab et al., (2010) postulated that malware also is known to carry out various networking activities. This gives insight into the various ways through which such malware are propagated from one device to a wide range of others. Also, it gives a valid explanation to the various reasons as to why various codes and links lead to device invasion by viruses.

According to Santos, Devesa, & Bringas, (2009), Viruses are also known to replicate themselves. Through replication, these viruses have the capability of building an entirely "new system." This, therefore, explains how viruses and mobile worms spread and increase on the same device over time, and their ability to be propagated to other devices over time. Ability to create new systems also enables viruses to corrupt existing files and affect effective functioning of existing files.

Tracy, (2012) identifies that a worm has a specific method of manifesting itself. Unlike viruses that require a host to propagate themselves, but malware such as worms operate automatically without the need of a host. With regards to how worms autonomously work within programs, they routinely replicate themselves on computers and transfer to others making it difficult to contain it. There are also those which take advantage of the weakened security of a computer network to intrude their victim's devices. Malware is distributed unevenly using different channels as illustrated in Figure 5.

Figure 5. Chart of malware distribution methods

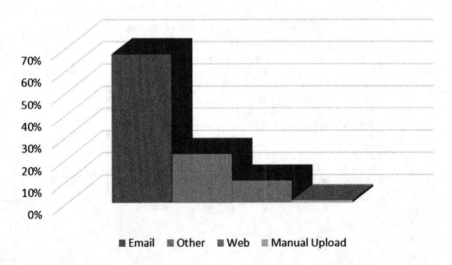

Kushwaha, & Kushwaha, (2011) on the other hand suggest that a virus works in such a way that it infects files by gaining access in them. Software such as Trojan horse appears to be useful in a computer system but actually act as windows that compromise the system. When one opens them, they act as loopholes that allow originators to override the users' system and compromise the security of their computer so that they can abuse its resources.

Gandhewar, & Sheikh, (2010) recognize that internet users are often bombarded by a wave of hoaxes that try to gain access to their computers. The hoaxes usually present themselves as jokes or warning emails that inform users their device is infected and they need to scan and fix them urgently. It is crucial to note that a user could use just a simple technique to recognize whether the emails are not legitimate is that the warning emails are often hoaxed.

Chan, & Song, (2014) cites that another indicator of the hoax is the request by anonymous users to forward the email to family members and friends. This is particularly is done when renowned companies such as Nokia, Windows, and AOL pretend to warn users that they should scan their personal computers using virus warning messages.

Table 2 illustrates the data that was gathered over a span of two years at Anubis from over 120 countries in the world. The study by Anubis was conducted on the number of submitters who were grouped into four different categories, which are; single, small, medium and large. A single submitter on the table is an entity that submits lets than 10 samples, while a small submitter is one that submits 10 to 100 various samples to the study. A medium submitter is referred to any individual or organization that submits between 100 and 1000 different types of samples. However, a large submitter is denoted as one that submits more than a thousand samples to the study.

The table describes in detail the findings of the submitters. It is worth noting that there were 20 large submitters with more than one thousand different samples submitted and it accounted for about 90% of all the submissions got by Anubis. In the study, it was noted that the number of single submitters was high although they accounted for 5% of the aggregate submissions made, it was learned that 75% of the submissions were marked as being malicious and harmful to the systems. It is evident that about 50% of the samples collected from single submitters were malicious and this led to the conclusion that single individuals are likely to become victims of malicious malware than their counterparts.

Table 2. Observed malware behaviour

Observed Behaviour	Samples in %	Clusterin %
Installation of a windows kernel driver:	3.34%	4.26%
Installation of a windows service:	12.12%	7.96%
Modifying the hosts' file:	1.97%	2.47%
Creating a file:	70.78%	69.90%
Deleting a file:	42.57%	43.43%
Modifying a file:	79.87%	75.62%
Installation of an IEBHO:	1.72%	1.75%
Installation of an IE Toolbar:	0.07%	0.18%
Display a GUI window display a GUI window:	33.26%	42.54%
Network Traffic:	55.18%	45.12%
Writing to Stderr:	0.78%	0.37%
Writing to Stdout:	1.09%	1.04%
Modifying a registry value:	74.50%	69.90%
Creating a registry:	64.71%	52.52%
Creating a process:	52.19%	50.64%

It can be seen that a large number of malware samples represented as binary account for 70.8% and they have the ability to introduce changes on the file system. The binary samples suggest that new files are created and existing files are modified. When those new files are assessed in depth, it can be identified that they all belong to two main groups which are executable files and non-executable files. The binary copies are the new polymorphic variant and often total up to 37.2% as executable files. About 23.2% of all the malware pick windows directory as their target. It is evident that a large fraction of 15.1% of malware creates the executable in the user's folder under settings and documents. The statistics represent how harmful software is developed to operate successfully with the permission of their primary user and therefore, cannot modify the system folder.

The second group of files consists of a non-executable group of files. These type of file represents 63.8% of all the samples that contain a host of a various mix of temporary data files, batch scripts, and necessary libraries (DLLs). Several of these files are either stored in the user folder or windows directory. One of the most outstanding features that make the non-executable group be unique is that they contain temporary internet files that are created by internet explorer. Furthermore, the execution of 21.3% of the samples used in the table was got from such files. With regards to how the files are created, they come into existent when the Internet Explorer is used to download content from the internet.

The internet is prone to malware and serves as a channel in which it is transferred to a computer when the user downloads content. The malware that attacks a computer often comes loaded with additional components that are dropped into the windows system folder. The additional components are what are used by cybercriminals to establish their malicious activities on the computer and target specific data. A majority of system activities are because of windows recording events in the system audit system.

In a number of reported cyber malware cases, the programs attacked are often utilities in the system folder or popular programs such as windows media player or internet explorer. It often found by web developers that the files formatted from the computer are mostly deleted operations that target files that the malware code had created previously. Windows malware does not take action in clearing any records from the log data; this is because it assumes that users will not check these logs.

Nosrati & Hasanvand, (2012) contend that malware is one of the most important problems on the internet because it exposes users to a host of attacks from cybercriminals and hackers. Despite the fact that much research needs to be done on the various aspects of malicious coding, little has been done on the host-based activity of malicious programs. In the years to come, it will be crucial to do some study on host-based activities of malicious software that often infect computer systems.

EXAMPLES OF MALWARE SPREADING TECHNIQUES

Malware has different means of spreading. As Mobile devices move from place to place connecting to different networks, the chances of spread of malicious applications increase. The aim of the malicious application can sometimes define the best spreading technique.

Garetto, Gong, & Towsley, (2003) postulated that the installation of various applications and programs in defective mobile devices would lead to the formation of malware. Sharing this applications and programs with other users will lead to a quantitative spreading of these viruses over time. Spreading spam and defective information by the use of messages or emails also leads to a substantial invasion by viruses.

According to Firdausi, Erwin, & Nugroho, (2010), internet connectivity also motivates the spreading of mobile viruses. Various adverts and links open erroneously, and this can be termed as viruses. Therefore, a strategy can be formulated to ensure a reduction of internet-based viruses. Various codes also risk mobile phones by making them prone to malware. Scanning to search for essential information from mobile devices also makes them vulnerable to viruses. There should be relatively fewer scans to reduce the risk of malware invasions for mobile devices.

Because of the coverage limits of the internet, a single Internet service provider (ISP) sometimes needs to be hopped wirelessly to increase coverage. This form of an extension of ISP is referred to as multi-hop broadcast. Using a multi-hop broadcast tool can also increase the spread of Malware.

Willems, Holz, & Freiling, (2007) postulated that although the *"multi-hop broadcast tools"* which includes "deluge," "MNP" and "trickle" has ensured an effective large-scale sharing of data, this wireless broadcasting technique has also served as a means of propagating viruses. Usually, this mobile connectivity allows viruses to circulate and oscillate among the connected devices. It is therefore essential to come up with protection strategies for devices utilizing this form of a broadcast. "Conficker" is also another form of newly widespread techniques in which malware is propagated over time. This network-based malware spreading development proposes new protection developments for mobile phones, as a means of securing essential data and information stored on mobiles.

Network intrusion is a method used by cybercriminals to gain access to user's machines and initiate communication with the remote host, network intrusion attacks are initiated by the attacker. Mathur, & Hiranwal, (2013) argue that victims hosts run programs that process incoming data on several layers of the protocol stack. It is evident that manipulated data packages can exploit vulnerabilities and take over control of a host. The harms that can be caused by network intruders are unimaginable because they gain unauthorized access to a user's data and documents.

In Wagener, & Dulaunoy, (2008) social engineering attacks are said to take advantage of human's weakness rather than that found on software. Social engineering works in a way that tries to trick users into running malicious binaries. On the other hand, users are manipulated into believing that there is a malware on their computer so that they can buy into their idea of downloading their free antivirus software to assess and sanitize their device systems. The Koobface attack is recognized as a classic example of social engineering. The malware leverages on social relationships and trust built between users. It specifically operates its malicious activities on Facebook where an account is accessed from the infected computer and post messages on their messenger using the very accounts. After the antivirus has accessed the social media platform, it then spreads out to their trusted friends who view those messages.

During the beginning of 2003, the internet came to a standstill when it was infiltrated by a new web-server worm. The malware contributed to a breakdown of a number of important system services such as that of Bank of America ATM services. Willems, Holz, & Freiling, (2007) identify that the malware attack during that period targeted financial systems of banks. The worm was later identified as SQL Slammer. Contrary to popular beliefs concerning the worm's title, the malware did not use SQL language to manifest itself but operated by exploiting a buffer overflow bug in Microsoft's desktop engine database and SQL server products. The dangerous worm was designed to use code functions that generate random IP addresses which assist it to distribute itself by running Microsoft SQL server's unpatched copy. During the incident, many hosts became affected by the worm and began to spread it to other vulnerable victims. Before the developers created a technique to thwart SQL slammer, it had already infected a number of victims with the rate of one victim in every 15 seconds. It is claimed that after fifteen minutes had passed after its detection, SQL slammer had already infected half of the servers that support internet activities around the globe.

Crowdsourcing platform known as micro job sites is often used by cybercriminals to post an assignment like (Download and Install the file) with an explanation you are then expected to test the software on different platforms, which pretty much explains why one needs to launch it. Garetto, Gong, & Towsley, (2003) explains that when the user has completed downloading the malicious software and installed the file, their gadget and machines get infected by a malware. This technique is commonly used by cybercriminals to target a large number of individuals. Since the file is in zip format the malware easily escapes from the radar of antivirus applications and virus scanning sites. It is because of this loophole that it is estimated about 10 users of the internet get hooked.

The social network has become a favorite playing platform for cybercriminals to disseminate malicious software in the form of spam to unsuspecting users. Gandhewar, & Sheikh, (2010) recognizes that this is done by sending inappropriate messages in bulk using fake accounts as the avenues of social spamming. The cybercriminals spread malicious links, post fraudulent reviews to build trust, share inappropriate content such as pornography. Social network spamming is one of the leading techniques. Users usually fall for such tricks because they simply click on the link given in the post to get more details, without even realizing that they are installing a malware.

Chan, & Song, (2014) claims that fake websites are the leading cause of spreading malware. They are simple to create using blogging sites such as WordPress and to download or buy a malicious script. Once the website is created, the malicious attackers purchase advertisement from some channels and then target the right audience to get most installs to spread their harmful code. The only drawback is the need for the advertising, but it is nothing in front of the download made.

Online games allow cybercriminals to spread infections via games that are often played by kids. Wei, Gomez, & Faloutsos, (2012) recognizes that when users search for a game to play online, a small file is provided that needs to be downloaded to play a game. The file is usually coded with malware, when it is successfully downloaded and installed, the machine being used gets infected and all the user data is compromised. Personal information could be stolen for financial benefits or maliciously used to harm individuals.

GameoverZeus (GoZ) is described by Wagener, & Dulaunoy, (2008) as a very complex type of banking Trojan that is known for causing the most damage to botnet across the US. The malware is used by cybercriminals to intercept and seize information needed to gain access to online bank accounts and lost millions of pounds of relevant data from users. The malware is dangerous because it can blend with other harmful software variants to increase the effectiveness and scope of activities to introduce blended threats. In Chan, & Song, (2014) GameoverZeus is identified as an infection used by most hackers to hijack computers by hacking sessions and mint personal information with the aim of financial gain.

MALWARE EVASION TECHNIQUES

Before late 1980 malware did not defend themselves from anti-malware programs. DOS virus cascade was the first malware which attempted to defend itself by encrypting its own code. Previously anti-virus programs work by analyzing file codes, this method has become obsolete as malware try to evade detection as much as possible. Self-defence techniques employed by malware can be categorized into 3:

- Anti-SecTools
- Anti-Sandbox and
- Anti-Analyst

Marpaung, Sain, & Lee, (2012) suggests that There are majorly two methods used to detect worms and viruses on mobile phones. *"Signature-based techniques"* are among these methods. The functionality of these techniques incorporates critical analysis of various codes. Analysis of malware characteristics can be detected and evaluated using the *"behavior-based techniques."*

According to Rastogi, Chen, & Jiang, (2013), static evaluation of mobile worms and viruses fails in enabling the detection of unrecognized worms and viruses effectively and conveniently. However, it offers an advantage in the exposition and revelation of the form of malware overtime. It also enables convenient and effective evaluation of *"multipath"* worms and malware. This is as opposed to the *"dynamic evaluation,"* which enables evaluation of anonymous worms and viruses. However, it is slower in the evaluation of *"multi-path malware."*

Petsas et al., (2014) postulated that there are various ways in which viruses can be avoided. Mobile phones can be protected from viruses through *"code obfuscation,"* which enables users to secret codes from access to others. This makes these codes difficult to understand and allows decryption for encrypted files. Packing is also another means through which mobile Operating Systems can be protected from worms and viruses. This allows secretion of the initial codes, hence offering protection to compressed files.

Cavallaro, Saxena, & Sekar, (2008) asserts that antimalware programs are very effective in offering protection against mobile malfunctioning caused by worms and viruses. It works effectively by blocking or preventing corrupt files and malware from attaining access to mobile operating Systems and important files. Antivirus programs incorporate various detection methods with the aim of preventing or cleaning files. The *"signature-based techniques"* adds *"bytes"* to files hence makes them corrupt. The efficiency of detecting this form of malware enables blocking of mobile worms and viruses before their development.

According to Chen, Andersen, Mao, Bailey, & Nazario, (2008), *"Cloud-based detection"* is convenient and effective for protecting files. This is enabled through critical data recording and analysis of files free from malware. This, therefore, enables the offering of protection to files before they are invaded by viruses. *"heuristics-based detection"* is an effective method of protecting mobile Operating Systems from invasion by malware and viruses over time. Antivirus and antimalware programs form therefore a convenient and effective platform for detection of malware and offer protection against the corresponding viruses.

According to Kushwaha, & Kushwaha, (2011), antimalware programs are very essential in analyzing files and discovering if they have actually been affected. There are various methods through which antiviruses among other antimalware programs are able to discover malware and viruses in mobile phone devices and computers over time. Although the functionality of these programs is not readily comprehensive, it is very essential to understand how these programs function with the aim of developing such new programs and developing diverse ways through which malware threats can be curbed.

Gandhewar, & Sheikh, (2010) postulated that *"Heuristic Based Techniques"* are among the common methods used by antiviruses in the detection of viruses and worms. *"Signature-based techniques"* function through effective and efficient *"heuristic-based methods."* This methods mainly functions through critical analysis of information and data in stored files. To increase the convenience of these methods, *"artificial knowledge"* is utilized.

According to Chan & Song, (2014), use of mutation, combination, traits inheritance and other biological methods that majorly explain the process of replication are very essential in discovering viruses, worms and other forms of malware overtime. This is majorly through *"genetic algorithm."* This method is very effective in the suggestion of prompt answers to malware attacks.

Garetto, Gong, & Towsley, (2003) asserted that over time, the use of statistics and mathematics analytical models has proofed to be very effective in prompt detection and discovering of viruses, worms, scams and other forms of malware overtime. The ability to detect these malware has enabled the provision of effective responses and hence answers over time.

Santos, Devesa, & Bringas, (2009) suggests that artificial immune technology could be used to withstand and destroy technological viruses. The system is known to combine evolutionary logarithms and agents in order to identify new types of malware, and an immune associative memory based that combine's immune first reaction for known malware. The second approach is able to detect unknown malware, new variants, and similar malware. However, Chan, & Song, (2014) contends that due to associative memory and real-time calculation capacity, researchers have considered the use of activation networks to provide computer security in terms of paralleled process, self-organization, self-learning, and information classification.

Sandboxing is a mechanism recognized by Kushwaha, & Kushwaha, (2011) as a process that consists running programs in a separate environment by controlling all the resources allocated in case of damage or attack by harmful malware software. The method is commended by Mathur, & Hiranwal, (2013) for its ability to imitate malware interaction as well as catching and documenting changes made to an infected system. Once a malware has been identified, it is recommended that a lot of information should be gathered concerning it so as to catch and document changes made to an infected system. It is evident that in order to determine changes performed in the system, one should identify patterns and understand their behavior. Sandboxing, however, has been in recent time not so efficient as many malware has implemented an adaptive mechanism to hide their behavior when running on a sandbox environment.

Fragmentation and session splicing is a technique of malware evasion which takes advantage of a feature of IP protocol called packet fragmentation, that allows handling packets of different sizes. Wagener, & Dulaunoy, (2008) holds the evasion technique affects security devices as they have to wait for the whole package to arrive and assess it. File-less malware technique is another evasion technique that was discovered by Kaspersky Labs. The technique contains some sort of obfuscation to increase complexity. The method does not leave digital traces on permanent storage so that malware is locked out.

Gandhewar, & Sheikh, (2010) argue that ways of evading malware attacks are becoming more refined with each passing day and this has made malware inconspicuous and hard to detect. Traditional techniques such as code reuse technique are a good example of how code injection security measures have been rendered useless defense because they are easily bypassed by a number of modern malware and hackers. Security can only be boosted by adding other layers of security to make it formidable to withstand attacks. Among the combinations that can be used to provide layers of security are Packed, Polymorphic, and Printable ReturnOriented programming (malware execute codes in a security defense environment). In the years to come, malware evasions methods will continue to become technical because it will also become trickier to detect malware. In order to evade an attack, security software will have to strive to expose camouflaged malware and identify other harmful system behaviors.

Nosrati & Hasanvand, (2012) argue that malware programs have the ability to hijack existing processes and use running programs that they find available. It is evident that in the modern times, malware can be analogized with cancer in the human body; this is because it is difficult to separate healthy tissues from those that are infected. According to the table below, there are various malware evasion techniques that could be used to provide value, detect difficulty, the level of sophistication, and impact. In the table, impact shall be used to denote the effort that shall be required by vendors to promote their systems and address threats. Apparently, it can be seen that code reuse attacks are identified as the most profound, this is because they are difficult to detect, prevent its spread and control.

When attacks are labeled as sophisticated, there is difficulty in implementing malware override because the probability of attack is reduced significantly. There is going to be significant changes in malware evasion in the near future because there are several documented ways that are currently being shared on public hacker joints. Among the classical techniques being used to evade malware infections are fragmentation and obfuscation. It is evident that these attempts of masking malware attack payloads often need payloads that require a form of decryption or reassembly to be launched inside the memory of the user's device so that the signature is detected in the resulting payload.

CONCLUSION

The classification of malware has overtime proofed to be very beneficial since it has aided in the formulation of various ways through which devices can be protected from such malware and related threats. Ability to detect such malware through various methods such as statistical and signature-based methods has enabled programmers to formulate various was through which devices can be protected from such threats.

Table 3. Comparison of malware evasion techniques

Evasion Technique	Metric		
	Sophistication	Detection Difficulty	Impact
Obfuscation	Low	Low	Medium
	Low	Low	Low
Application Violations	Medium	Low	Medium
Protocol	Medium	Low	High
Insertion	Medium	Medium	Medium
Dos	Medium	High	Medium
Code Reuse	Very High	Very High	Very High

This chapter articulated the numerous means through which malware spreads to other devices. The ability of malware to replicate themselves and spread to other devices poses an underlying threat to the functionality of these devices over time. This raises the alarm for the formulation of procedures through which the replication process of malware can be halted.

Traffics created by users, applications among other network agents are very crucial, as they determine the speed of connectivity and the extent to which devices are able to store power.

In summary, due to the increased use of technology and mobile devices, it is very essential that the security of user information is ensured overtime through the development of dynamic malware detection systems. A detection system that will withstand the ever-increasing malware evasion techniques.

REFERENCES

Alazab, M., Layton, R., Venkataraman, S., & Watters, P. (2010). *Malware detection based on structural and behavioral features of API calls*. Academic Press.

Cavallaro, L., Saxena, P., & Sekar, R. (2008, July). On the limits of information flow techniques for malware analysis and containment. In *International Conference on Detection of Intrusions and Malware, and Vulnerability Assessment* (pp. 143-163). Springer. 10.1007/978-3-540-70542-0_8

Chan, P. P., & Song, W. K. (2014, July). Static detection of Android malware by using permissions and API calls. In *Machine Learning and Cybernetics (ICMLC), 2014 International Conference on* (Vol. 1, pp. 82-87). IEEE. 10.1109/ICMLC.2014.7009096

Chen, X., Andersen, J., Mao, Z. M., Bailey, M., & Nazario, J. (2008, June). Towards an understanding of anti-virtualization and anti-debugging behavior in modern malware. In *2008 IEEE International Conference on Dependable Systems and Networks With FTCS and DCC (DSN)* (pp. 177-186). IEEE. 10.1109/DSN.2008.4630086

Feng, Y., Anand, S., Dillig, I., & Aiken, A. (2014, November). Apposcopy: Semantics-based detection of Android malware through static analysis. In *Proceedings of the 22nd ACM SIGSOFT International Symposium on Foundations of Software Engineering* (pp. 576-587). ACM. 10.1145/2635868.2635869

Firdausi, I., Erwin, A., & Nugroho, A. S. (2010, December). Analysis of machine learning techniques used in behavior-based malware detection. In *Advances in Computing, Control and Telecommunication Technologies (ACT), 2010 Second International Conference on* (pp. 201-203). IEEE. 10.1109/ACT.2010.33

Gandhewar, N., & Sheikh, R. (2010). Google Android: An emerging software platform for mobile devices. *International Journal on Computer Science and Engineering, 1*(1), 12–17.

Garetto, M., Gong, W., & Towsley, D. (2003, March). Modeling malware spreading dynamics. In *INFOCOM 2003. Twenty-Second Annual Joint Conference of the IEEE Computer and Communications. IEEE Societies* (Vol. 3, pp. 1869-1879). IEEE. 10.1109/INFCOM.2003.1209209

Huang, J., Zhang, X., Tan, L., Wang, P., & Liang, B. (2014, May). Android: Detecting stealthy behaviors in android applications by a user interface and program behavior contradiction. In *Proceedings of the 36th International Conference on Software Engineering* (pp. 1036-1046). ACM. 10.1145/2568225.2568301

Johansen, D., Van Renesse, R., & Schneider, F. B. (1995, May). Operating system support for mobile agents. In *Hot Topics in Operating Systems, 1995. (HotOS-V), Proceedings., Fifth Workshop on* (pp. 42-45). IEEE. 10.1109/HOTOS.1995.513452

Kaur, P., & Sharma, S. (2014, March). Google Android a mobile platform: A review. In Engineering and Computational Sciences (RAECS), 2014 Recent Advances in (pp. 1-5). IEEE. doi:10.1109/RAECS.2014.6799598

Kushwaha, A., & Kushwaha, V. (2011). Location-based services using the Android mobile operating system. *International Journal of Advances in Engineering and Technology, 1*(1), 14.

Maia, C., Nogueira, L. M., & Pinho, L. M. (2010, July). Evaluating android os for embedded real-time systems. In *6th international workshop on operating systems platforms for embedded real-time applications* (pp. 63-70). Academic Press.

Marpaung, J. A., Sain, M., & Lee, H. J. (2012, February). Survey on malware evasion techniques: State of the art and challenges. In *Advanced Communication Technology (ICACT), 2012 14th International Conference on* (pp. 744-749). IEEE.

Mathur, K., & Hiranwal, S. (2013). A survey of techniques in detection and analyzing malware executables. *International Journal of Advanced Research in Computer Science and Software Engineering*, *3*(4).

Moser, A., Kruegel, C., & Kirda, E. (2007, December). Limits of static analysis for malware detection. In Computer security applications conference, 2007. ACSAC 2007. Twenty-third annual (pp. 421-430). IEEE. doi:10.1109/ACSAC.2007.21

Nosrati, M., Karimi, R., & Hasanvand, H. A. (2012). Mobile computing: Principles, devices, and operating systems. *World Applied Programming*, *2*(7), 399–408.

Petsas, T., Voyatzis, G., Athanasopoulos, E., Polychronakis, M., & Ioannidis, S. (2014, April). Rage against the virtual machine: hindering dynamic analysis of Android malware. In *Proceedings of the Seventh European Workshop on System Security* (p. 5). ACM. 10.1145/2592791.2592796

Santos, I., Penya, Y. K., Devesa, J., & Bringas, P. G. (2009). N-grams-based File Signatures for Malware Detection. *ICEIS*, *9*(2), 317–320.

Sela, Y. (2016). *U.S. Patent No. 9,521,705*. Washington, DC: U.S. Patent and Trademark Office.

Sheikh, A. A., Ganai, P. T., Malik, N. A., & Dar, K. A. (2013). Smartphone: Android Vs IOS. *The SIJ Transactions on Computer Science Engineering & its Applications (CSEA)*, *1*(4), 141-148.

Silberschatz, A., Galvin, P. B., & Gagne, G. (2014). *Operating system concepts essentials*. John Wiley & Sons, Inc.

Tanenbaum, A. S. (2009). *Modern operating system*. Pearson Education, Inc.

Tracy, K. W. (2012). Mobile Application Development Experiences on Apple¿ s iOS and Android OS. *IEEE Potentials*, *31*(4), 30–34. doi:10.1109/MPOT.2011.2182571

Wagener, G., & Dulaunoy, A. (2008). Malware behavior analysis. *Journal in Computer Virology, 4*(4), 279-287.

Wei, X., Gomez, L., Neamtiu, I., & Faloutsos, M. (2012, August). ProfileDroid: multi-layer profiling of android applications. In *Proceedings of the 18th annual international conference on Mobile computing and networking* (pp. 137-148). ACM.

Willems, C., Holz, T., & Freiling, F. (2007). Toward automated dynamic malware analysis using cwsandbox. *IEEE Security and Privacy*, *5*(2), 32–39. doi:10.1109/MSP.2007.45

Chapter 8
A Review of Research Studies on Cyber Terror

Esra Söğüt
Gazi University, Turkey

O. Ayhan Erdem
Gazi University, Turkey

ABSTRACT

Thanks to the internet, the distances between the countries are easily overcome and the communication network rapidly expands. This situation also affects the cyber security of the countries to a great extent. Attacks on critical infrastructures, companies, and public institutions can be magnitude that make great harms. These developments in cyber space bring new problems. One of them is cyber terror. Cyber terror does not have a certain and well-known definition. Cyber terror is the realization of terrorist acts in the field of cyber war. In addition, cyber space is a place of display for terrorist acts. The effects of cyber terror attacks have reached a level to scare all countries. There is not enough information about the definition, characteristics, methods used in cyber terror attacks and cyber terror groups. It is important for national administrators and staff to become conscious and to become informed about cyber terror. In this chapter, information will be presented, endeavors on awareness-creation will be made, and a role of guiding the future studies will be taken.

DOI: 10.4018/978-1-5225-8976-1.ch008

Copyright © 2019, IGI Global. Copying or distributing in print or electronic forms without written permission of IGI Global is prohibited.

INTRODUCTION

Nowadays, the fields in which internet and computers are not used are gradually decreasing. Many processes are carried out quickly and easily thanks to the internet, which has also become a big part of life. However, as the amount of information used, updated and stored during these processes has increased, their safe storage has become a major problem as well. To illustrate, cyber attacks are carried out against public institutions and organizations, critical infrastructures, commercial companies and states, or against people. Depending on the significance of the information, attacks may also change and become complex.

Information technologies are becoming more important and rapid developments in the field force the systems of private or state institutions to change. This situation makes the large institutions dependent to the internet and internet-based systems as much as it does the individual users. The attackers or attack groups, who are aware of this, conduct the terrorist activities via the internet. Cyber terror is formed by the combination of terror and cyber space. Cyber terror attacks to be carried out at critical infrastructures and places where the important information such as health, education, election, communication and security are kept and processed, can be effective enough to cause chaos throughout the country.

According to Dr Jones, the countries most affected by cyber terror will be the most developed ones (Jones, 2005). Considering countries such as Afghanistan, the rate of dependence on high technology is extremely low. In this case, countries in general will not be affected by the abuse of cyber technologies as much as developed countries. Although, the effects of cyber terror attacks are discussed the definition, framework, scope and effects of cyber terror attacks are not fully clear. For these reasons, it is very difficult to be prevented and stopped. The studies conducted by governmental institutions and concerning this issue are too few. Most of the existing studies relate to verbal expressions and making framework identifications. In a small number of studies, the framework and decision mechanisms are proposed to ensure security. The 9/11 attacks, some attacks of terrorist organizations such as ISIS, Al-Qaeda or PKK can be given as an example of cyber terrorist acts. In particular, the 9/11 attack is considered as an awareness point for cyber terror attacks (Temizel, 2011).

The number of studies conducted in the field of cyber terror is not much. The majority of existing studies have the purpose of ensuring the explanation of the concept of cyber terror and determination of its framework. Part of the literature provides information about the relationship between cyber warfare, traditional terrorism and cyber terror. Some sources recommend a draft of framework to ensure security. Very few of these offer suggestions for decision support mechanism. Some techniques have been proposed to prevent cyber terror attacks. These are decision support systems, expert systems, risk models and different methods. Analysis of the terrorist groups' websites has also been made.

The aim of this study is to give information about cyber terror attacks, their characteristics, components and methods. In this study, the scope of cyber terror will be determined. The relationship between traditional terrorism, cyber warfare and classical crime will be explained. Previous studies and used methods will be grouped and examined in detail. Thus, personnel and system administrators will be informed about cyber attacks that may occur in Central SCADA (Supervisory Control and Data Acquisition Systems) or ICS (Industrial Control Systems) or at institutions. Awareness will be provided for system administrators and users by means of making predictions on attacks that may happen in the future. Comments and suggestions will be made about cyber terror. It is aimed to introduce new anti-terrorism security models that will help to evaluate new cyber security threats such as cyber terror.

THE PLACE OF CYBER TERROR IN CYBER ATTACKS

The word cyber (kubernesis) means to manage, to rule, in Greek. The term Cybernetique was used by American mathematician Nobert Wiener and then continued to be used in informatics.

Figure 1 presents the groups of cyber attack types and the place of cyber terror in cyber attacks (Uma & Padmavathi, 2013).

According to this diagram, attacks are divided into 5 main groups. These are: Based on Purpose, Legal Classification, Based on Severity of Involvement, Based on Scope, Based on Network Types. These main groups are examined in sub-headings.

Figure 1. Diagram of cyber attack classification

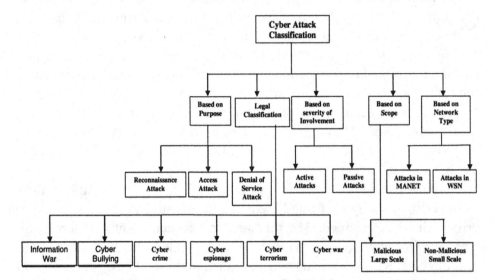

BASED ON PURPOSE

When the attacks are divided into groups according to their purposes, Reconnaissance, Access and Denial of Service attacks appear.

Reconnaissance Attack

The discoveries for unauthorized areas and services include system mapping studies. Packet sniffing and port scanning attacks are among the examples of reconnaissance attacks (Uma & Padmavathi, 2013).

Access Attack

An attacker who does not have access privileges is able to exploit the vulnerability of the system or infiltrate the system and gain data. Man in the middle attack, social engineering, phishing can be given as examples (Ranum, 1997).

Denial of Service

It is defined as slowing down the system or disrupting the system. It is also possible to corrupt or delete data with this attack (Mishra & Saini, 2009).

LEGAL CLASSIFICATION

Cyber terror is in this group. The sub-groups of the legal classifications for cyber attacks are as follows: Information War, Cyber Bullying, Cyber Crime, Cyber Espionage, Cyber Terror and Cyber War.

Information War

It can be defined as "to carry out an action that will affect the information-based processors, information systems and information-based network systems belonging to the other side and to protect their own systems" (Güntay, 2017).

Cyber Bullying

Individually or as a group, it is designed to support repetitive hostile behavior or to harm others. It is realized by using information and communication technologies such as sending e-mails, using mobile phone applications, using instant messaging applications or publishing humiliating websites (Keith & Martin, 2005).

Cyber Crime

It can be defined as the "the use of an information technology to facilitate the handling of illegal acts or crimes". The term computer crime refers to all crimes involving the use of computers and/or information technologies in the broadest sense. Computer crimes, cybercrime, information technology crime, high technology crimes, and internet crimes are often used interchangeably (Hatipoğlu, 2017). Viruses, logic bombs, botnets, worms are examples of this group.

Cyber Espionage or Cyber Spying

This group includes malicious software such as trojan horses and spyware, and methods of capturing the target system. Cyber espionage or spying is the illegal use of software or methods and the capture of important information from unauthorized or confidential areas. Such operations can be performed by specially trained spies, malicious hackers or programmers (Uma & Padmavathi, 2013).

Cyber Terror

Cyber terror is another dimension of the terror that emerged and mutated in the 21st century. Such terrorist attacks are both easy to accomplish and the damage that would be created is beyond imagination. It is a form of terror that is quite difficult to fight against (Yılmaz, 2012). According to the definition of the FBI, cyber terror is the actions carried out in a way that can lead to chaos by destroying the functioning of institutions and critical infrastructures (Kurnaz, 2017).

Cyber War or Cyber Warfare

It is possible to define this concept of cyber warfare as "Intrusion activities of a state conducted to damage or suspend the computer systems or networks of another state" (Güntay, 2017).

BASED ON SEVERITY OF INVOLVEMENT

Cyber attacks can be classified according to the severity of attacks and their interest. Active and Passive Attacks can be examined in two parts.

Active Attacks

Attacks that allow an attacker to transmit data to all parties or block data transmission in a unidirectional / bidirectional manner (Uma & Padmavathi, 2013).

Passive Attacks

Passive Attack: The attacker is secretly listening to the communication between the two parties in order to play the information stored in a system by phone listening or the like. Moreover, unlike the active attack, the database cannot be accessed, but a crime crime might have still been committed (Uma & Padmavathi, 2013).

BASED ON SCOPE

Cyber attacks can also be grouped according to their fields of activity. These are: Malicious Large Scale and Non-Malicious Small Scale.

Malicious Large Scale

The attacks in this group are aimed at gaining personal or group benefits or threatening system reliability. Such software is involved in attacks that disrupt the target system or cause chaos in society (Uma & Padmavathi, 2013).

Non-Malicious Small Scale

These are the attacks that affect a small section in the target system, cause low property damage or cause recoverable data loss. It is performed by novice attackers or novice employees (Uma & Padmavathi, 2013).

BASED ON NETWORK TYPE

Attacks by network types are classified as Mobile Adhoc Networks (MANET) and Wireless Sensor Networks (WSN) (Simmons & Ellis & Shiva & Dasgupta & Wu, 2009).

Attacks in MANET

There are many attacks in this group (Rai & Tevvari & Upadhyay, 2010). These include: Byzantine Attack, The Black Hole Attack, Flood Rushing

Attack, Byzantine Wormhole Attacks and Byzantine Overlay Network Wormhole Attacks.

Attacks on WSN

There are two attacks in this group (Lupu, 2009). These are: Cryptography and Non-cryptography Related Attacks and Attacks Based on Network Layers.

With the international dimension of these cyber threats, philosophical and ideological approaches are addressed together with international security issues. At this point, cyber security data and studies reveal a conceptual phenomenon regarding the development of cyber terror. Increased dependence on cyber space creates different ratings in the dimension of terror. This rating of cyber threat and terror brings about a cyber warfare phenomenon (Güntay, 2017).

STUDIES CONDUCTED

There are very few studies conducted on cyber terror. Some of them propose a framework to provide security. Very few offer recommendations for the decision support mechanism. The studies in the literature are grouped and given in Table 1.

The studies conducted in the literature are summarized in sub-headings.

Table 1. Literature

Literature No	Related Studies in Literature
1,2,3	Methods of prevention from cyber terror attacks
4,5,6,7,8,9,10,11,12	Creating a framework for cyber terror
13,14	New approaches to cyber terror
15,16,17,18	Solution proposals for cyber security of critical infrastructures (SCADA, ICS)
19,20,21,22,23	Solution proposals for protection from cyber attacks
24,25	Investigation of internet usage of terrorists

METHODS OF PREVENTION FROM CYBER TERROR ATTACKS

Literature: In these studies, fuzzy logic based decision support system was developed in order to act more consciously in the face of cyber terror attacks and to see what can be done against cyber attacks to be carried out on critical systems. The developed model evaluates different criteria with a fuzzy logic. In addition, it reveals how to act against cyber terror attacks. These criteria were determined according to the opinions of cyber security experts (Javed & Pandey, 2014) (Dell, 2015) (Mohammed & Kankale 2016).

CREATING A FRAMEWORK FOR CYBER TERROR

Literature: This article deals with cyber terror and its logic in an asymmetrical context. The methods that cyber attackers can use to plan and execute an attack, the effects and consequences of cyber terror are described in an actor-target-impact chain (Heickero, 2008).

Literature: A conceptual framework for the fundamental aspects of cyber terror is proposed. This study focuses on the field of cyber terror, the techniques, objectives, effects, characteristics and capabilities required and focus on clarifying cyber terror in a conceptual framework (Veerasamy, 2009).

Literature: In this study, an overview of the concept and basic elements of cyber terror is presented. The policy framework of cyber security initiatives is also developed here (Yunos et al, 2010).

Literature: This study confirmed the previous studies of the Author. The conceptual framework of previously proposed cyber terror was analysed with a group of 30 in this study. It was said that more research could be done to test or verify the conceptual framework (Ahmad et al, 2012).

Literature: Qualitative methodology has become an increasingly popular approach in the social science discipline. The aim of this paper is to describe the implementation of a qualitative method in the development of a cyber terror framework. In this research, interviews were conducted to collect data. The analysis demonstrated that the framework describing cyber terror consists of six different components. These are motivation, target, attack method, domain of effect, action or the affect carried out by the attacker (Yunos & Ahmad, 2014).

Literature: In this study, application of a mixed method in the development of cyber terror framework is suggested. There are two main objectives of this study. The first one is to explore the theory and then to develop a conceptual framework that defines cyber terror. The second one is to validate the conceptual framework. A mixed method research is suggested to obtain the final findings of the study. Qualitative and quantitative data are collected and analysed at a separate stage, respectively. The main source of data collection is interviews/meetings conducted with the participants. Questions were asked to the participants and statistics were obtained from the responses. No definite and clear results were obtained in the study (Yunos & Ahmad & Yusoof, 2014).

Literature: These studies propose a framework that defines the basic components of cyber terror. The framework defines cyber terror in six aspects. These are motivation, target, attack method, domain of effect, action carried out by the attacker and the affect. To propose this framework and to define cyber terror; a dynamic path (Ahmad & Yunos, 2012), grounded theory (Ahmad & Yunos & Sahib, 2012), a qualitative method (Yunos & Ahmad, 2014) and a qualitative method for Malaysia (Yunos & Ahmad & Sahib, 2015) is presented. All of these methods propose the same framework.

NEW APPROACHES TO CYBER TERRORISM

Literature: The "M.U.D" (Monitoring, Using, Disrupting) approach is a well-organized approach. According to this approach, the Monitoring step provides information on forums, blogs and frequently updated terrorist websites, the aims, mentalities, viewers, attack plans, potential target groups and possible attack targets of terrorist organizations. In Using step, data can be obtained to identify the links between propagandists, members, people and organizations. This approach also helps identify countries supporting terrorists through finance and politics. The Disrupting step may be the destruction or alteration of terrorist websites and their contents by viruses and worms (Knop, 2008).

Literature: According to this study, defences of companies in the field of cyber security is not always sufficient to reduce cyber threats. Therefore, there is a need for a wider cooperation. This cooperation consists of two steps. The first is to group organizations that use similar systems or face similar threats. The best example is the cooperation between Internet Service Providers (ISPs). Considering Distributed Denial of Service attacks, it will be easier to intervene in these attacks by working together on ISPs. The second step is to organize national and international laws. Generally, if cyber-attacks are strictly prohibited in every country, the number of these attacks in the whole world will surely decrease (Colarik & Janczewski, 2008).

SOLUTION PROPOSALS FOR CYBER SECURITY OF CRITICAL INFRASTRUCTURES (SCADA, ICS)

Literature: A cyber-terror SCADA risk framework approved by a group consisting of SCADA industry experts is presented. The framework consists of three stages: risk assessment, qualification assessment model and control model (Beggs & Warren, 2009).

Literature: This study examines ongoing research and provides information on threats, risks and blocking strategies in the field of SCADA security. Attackers are classified according to their motivation, abilities and objectives. Based on the historical analysis of (reported) attacks against critical infrastructures, it is emphasized that these attacks are related to cyber warfare (Nicholson et al, 2012).

Literature: After the profile of the attacker was modelled, the authors of the study proposed a fuzzy model for the success rate of attack. The attack success rate defines the attacker's ability to interrupt the functioning of the target system. This ratio is mostly affected by four parameters. These are the previously established profile score of attacker, system protection level, system weaknesses and the cost of restoration. Recommended input parameters are classified as small, medium and large (Pricop & Mihalache, 2015).

Literature: In this study, the basic 3-dimensional approach is proposed to ensure cyber security of critical infrastructures. These dimensions are the technical dimension concerning the technical infrastructure of corporate systems, the technical dimension concerning the management of critical infrastructures and the national and international cooperation dimension, which is an important issue in the provision of cyber security. With this study, it is aimed to propose the necessary measures to ensure the cyber security of critical infrastructures and to create a structure where the systems can be more easily controlled (Roldan-Molina et al, 2017).

SOLUTION PROPOSALS FOR PROTECTION
FROM CYBER ATTACKS

Literature: In this study, a system has been developed in order to calculate the uncertain risk faced by an institution under cyber attack. A decision support system has been proposed for uncertain threat rates, countermeasure costs and impacts on assets. The system uses the genetic algorithm to analyse the best precautionary methods. The data collected from manufacturing companies present a result sample under realistic input conditions (Rees et al, 2011).

Literature: In this study, it is aimed to create a knowledge-based expert system and its general framework for more effective intervention of cyber-attacks to be carried out on the Ministry of Transport, Maritime Affairs and Communications (MTMAC). An expert system was designed with an aim for detecting the attacks on MTMAC systems, keeping records and finding system failures with the help of expert personnel who are specialised in their fields. It is planned to apply the knowledge and experience of the authorized personnel on MTMAC systems when creating the knowledge base of the system. The system aims to make faster and more effective decisions against cyber-attacks (Göztepe & Boran & Yazgan, 2012).

Literature: The purpose of this study is to develop a fuzzy rule based technical indicator for cyber security by means of an expert system called Fuzzy Rule Based Cyber Expert System. Rule-based systems can use the fuzzy rule to automate complex processes. In this paper, cyber threats for cyber experts are used as linguistic variables (Göztepe, 2012).

Literature: In this study, a cyber-security risk model based on Bayesian Networks was proposed to integrate cyber security in nuclear facilities. Two models were utilised for this. The first one, activity-quality analysis model, was developed to assess how well people or organizations comply with the regulatory guidelines on cyber security. The second one, however, is an architectural analysis model and was designed to assess the effects of security vulnerabilities and measures for cyber security. These two models are integrated into a single model as a cyber-security risk model. Thus, cyber security can be evaluated simultaneously with procedural and technical perspectives (Shin & Son & Heo, 2015).

Literature: This book proposes a cyber-strategy lifecycle model. The authors propose a 5-stage life cycle approach for cyber security. These are assessing, protecting, verifying, educating and monitoring/management.

The framework is designed to protect critical cyber security assets with 5 effective stages in this method. Each of these stages is the continuation of the previous one (Richet, 2015).

INVESTIGATION OF INTERNET USAGE OF TERRORISTS

Literature: In this research, with reference to the cyber-terrorism approach expressed as a global problem, the official and unofficial 25 websites of 12 terrorist organisations that continue terrorist activities against Turkey were examined. The websites were subjected to content analysis for 33 criteria in total, including basic, visual and contextual criterion in three main categories (Özkan, 2006).

Literature: This study focuses on websites classified as Foreign Terrorist Organizations by the United States. Terrorist groups' misuse of the internet, web site content and media is the points that this study emphasizes. Based on the research, the terrorist groups used the internet to communicate between the groups and grouping via the Internet (Conway, 2007).

RELATIONSHIP BETWEEN TRADITIONAL TERROR AND CYBER TERROR

There is no generally accepted definition of terror or terrorism. Similarly, there is no general definition of cyber terror or cyber terrorism. In order to qualify a cyber attack as a cyber terror attack, information about the identity, purpose, intention and motivation of the attacker should be given. It is quite difficult to say that a cyber terror attack has been carried out without sufficient information.

Differences between traditional terrorism and cyber terror are given in Table 2 (Kara& Aydın & Oğuz, 2013) (Bayraktar, 2015) (Güntay, 2017). The tools and domains used to determine the differences between the two terrors differ significantly. Due to cyber terror attacks, computers, software or hardware can be physically affected. Assuming that cyber terror attacks are not life-threatening, the desired goal can be reached more quickly than traditional terrorist attacks. The detection of terrorists is easier for traditional terror. Finding the guilty person in the cyber space is more complex and

Table 2. Differences between traditional terror and cyber terror

	Traditional Terror	**Cyber Terror**
Tools used	Weapons, bombs	Chips, computers, hardware, software
Objective	Terrorism, to deliver messages to the political regime and society	Terrorism, in order to harm society or the state, and to influence it politically and socially
Domain	Limited by region or area of attack	Effective at national or international level
Encountered Risk	The persons or groups attacks carried out on are at risk	Effective attack without any risk of life
Supervision	It is partially possible to control, monitor and destroy terrorists	It is impossible to detect or destroy cyber terrorists
Penalty Given	The penalty to be applied according to the nature of the offense is certain	The penalty will be applied according to the nature of the crime

time consuming than the physical world. It is unclear which laws or articles will be applied when cyber terror attacks take place. States work to organize policies and guidelines on this issue.

There are several studies conducted to define cyber terror. According to The Federal Emergency Management Agency, cyber terror is the attack on computers and computer-related systems to force or coerce the government or the public on political or social issues. According to expert Dorothy Denning, it is the operations that are carried out to cause people to die or experience economic losses (Wilson, 2005).

The concepts of traditional terror and cyber terror can be confused. The effects and forms of attack play an important role in the separation of the two terrors. The attacks on the Internet without physically interacting with the critical infrastructures are also called cyber terror attacks. The deliberate targeting, attack of computers and computer systems by terror groups indicates the dangerous direction of cyber terror (Wilson, 2005) (Yılmaz, 2012).

CYBER TERROR ATTACKS AND METHODS USED

In Denning's book, the Kosovo War is described as the first war on the internet. In the war zone, banned photos and videos are shared on the Internet and the fear and tension were spread around the world (Denning, 2001). Another example is the attack on the electrical systems in the US in 1998, which killed 11 people. This attack is clearly regarded as a cyber-terrorist attack (Kurnaz, 2017). Another example of such cyber terror attacks in which hundreds of people are killed is the 9/11 attacks. It was detected that air pirates who organized the 9/11 attacks had used libraries and internet cafes. Hence, it was also confirmed that pirates purchased their airfare tickets online and sent e-mails to many addresses. In the investigations and the intelligence information acquired, it was revealed that the terrorists used music and photo files (mp3, jpeg, bim, tiff, doc. Files) to hide their messages. Maps, target charts to be hit and notes that are normally not seen by naked eye are attached to these files. Along with the developing technology, terrorism methods are also changing extensively and this new type of terrorism, namely cyber terror attacks, threaten all countries in the world (Temizel, 2011).

Table 3 shows the levels and capacity values of cyber terror that threatens security both individually and internationally (Bayraktar, 2015). Cyber terror levels were grouped in a simple, advanced and complex manner, and the capacity values of cyber terror groups were evaluated based on these groups. Simple and unstructured, cyber terror organizations have basic skills and act with the help of others. Pakistani and Palestinian hacker groups are examples of this group. Advanced, structured groups have the skills to perform systematic attacks. The most dangerous groups have complex, coordinated levels. The 9/11 attacks of Al-Qaeda can be given as an example for such attacks (Sökmen, 2015).

With the psychological warfare, the power of the Internet to reach hundreds of thousands in a short time increases the propaganda of terrorist organizations. In fact, a message in the cyber space reaches millions in a message. The asymmetrical war actions of the terrorist organizations that have entered the horizontal hierarchy are noteworthy. The cyber space facilitates coordination

Table 3. Levels of cyber terror acts

Cyber Terror Levels	Simple-Unstructured	Advanced-Structured	Complex-Coordinated
Target	Single system or network	Multiple systems or networks	Multiple networks
Target Analysis	Beginner's level	Intermediate level	Detailed
Organizational Capacity	Low Level	Intermediate Level	Very Advanced
Impact Control	Non-focused	Focused	Controllable
Potential Benefit	Propaganda	Tactical actions	Strategic actions

and planning between terror cells. This stage emerges in two different ways: steganography and dead dropping methods. The steganography method is used to store the message in the photo with the special coding technique and the other party works in the same way to reveal the message or instruction through a special program. With dead dropping, shared mail account is created and a message is written but it will not be sent but saved in drafts, and then another member of the organization logs into this account, and reads the draft message and writes the answer. Thus, a channel is opened between them in the cyber area (Özalp & Asker, 2017).

Cyber terror groups and sympathizers try to provide financial support for groups with these methods. For example, the terrorist Samudra, who was involved in the Al-Qaeda group, called for all the Muslim pirates in the book he wrote in prison, calling them to seize the websites of Western countries and tried to be a guide. 007 Code Younis Tsouli AQ established funds for the Irish Republican Army (IRA), shared materials and provided support for the organization (Sökmen, 2015) (Wilson, 2008).

It is known that cyber terrorists communicate with encrypted e-mails and satellite telephones and plan their actions. In addition, it is seen that information about bomb building, bombing, police interrogation was given on the internet. (Kara & Aydın & Oğuz, 2013)

CYBER TERROR GROUPS

Terrorism and the Internet are related in two ways. First, the Internet has become a forum for the members of terrorist organizations to communicate with each other, to convey their messages of violence and hatred to the masses and their sympathizers. Second, members of the terrorist organization can attack computer networks individually or in groups, via the Internet, and perform actions that are considered cyber terror (Özcan, 2018).

As seen in Turkey, terrorist organizations use the Internet as more of a propaganda tool and communication tool. Sometimes it is seen that terrorist organizations that are planning terrorist acts by communicating between their members through encrypted e-mails use the internet as a propaganda tool in a political and ideological sense. With the help of communication tools, satellites, and the Internet, terrorist groups are better at communication and command than most states (Reeve & Koca, 2001).

For example, in 1996, the sympathizers of a terrorist organization called Tubac Amaru, who attacked the Japanese embassy in the city of Lima of Peru, and held the diplomatic, military and political staff, in the US and Canada set up many sites supporting the organization's activities. They also published plans to attack the Japanese Embassy building along with support for propaganda and action. Another example is Zapatista, which operates in Mexico. Since 1994 they have been engaged in intensive propaganda activities on the internet (Sökmen, 2015) (Özcan, 2018). The Revolutionary Armed Forces of Colombia organization in Colombia and the Shining Path organization in Peru are terrorist organizations that use the Internet effectively as a propaganda tool. Terrorist organizations in Latin America are generally terrorist organizations that use the Internet environment effectively. These organizations and others train their sympathizers on terror education by giving addresses on their web pages. On these sites, the construction of a bomb is described in the finest details from the works of terrorists such as the Handbook of the Terrorist and the Terrorist's Cookbook.

Organizations such as Hamas, Hizb-ut-Tahrir, Harkat-ul-Ansar can be given as examples of cyber terror groups (Özcan, 2018). A well-known example is that in 1995, Had Shoko Asahara and Aum Shinrikyo group carried out a Sarin gas attack and caused death. The reason why this attack was so effective was that the group was able to hack the Tokyo power system, stopped the subway trains, and held the passengers captive on the trains and carried out the attack (Jane's Information Group, 1999). The Pakistani group with the name of G-Force and Doctor Nuker caused damages on the websites of the Indian Parliament, the Zee TV Channel, the Indian Institute of Sciences and the Bhabha Atomic Research Center. Pakistan Hackers Club had shown how sensitive the critical infrastructure was by damaging the Indian Air Force and the Ministry of Energy (Vatis, 2001).

According to Yıldız, there are many terrorist organizations that continue to exist on the internet. Some of these are as follows: Hezbollah in the Middle East, Hamas, Al-Aqsa Martyrs Brigade, Islamic Jihad Organization, People's Mujahedeen Organization, PKK / Kongra-Gel, DHKP/C, IBDA-C, ISIS; ETA in Europe, Armata Corsa, IRA; National Liberation Army, ELN in Latin America, Armed Revolution Forces, Tupac Amaru; Al Qaeda in Asia, Ensan al Islam, Japanese Red Army, Tamil Guerrillas, Hizbul Idin. Out of these organizations, there are the ones that use the technology very well and thus make money. For example, in Japan, the Aum Shinrikyo Terrorist Organization did not reveal its identity, owned a computer firm and software company, and worked in different states and sectors. It is well known that Al-Qaeda used the technology very well and made computer experts in countries such as Pakistan, Iran, Egypt and Indonesia their sympathizers. It is also known that it used these sympathizers to infiltrate computer systems of countries such as the Vatican and the US (Yıldız, 2017).

CONCLUSION

In this article, the studies conducted on cyber terror and cyber terror attacks are mentioned to be insufficient. In order to eliminate this deficiency, existing studies are evaluated in this study.

Working in the field of cyber terror and making recommendations for security measures on a corporate basis is of great importance for every state using technology. It is an important issue that concerns not only one country but also all the states. Therefore, studies to be carried out on this issue will be effective at universal level.

There are also adverse effects together with the improved efficiencies that the information technology brings out. The significantly increased trust in information technologies and the Internet increases the complexity of information systems and infrastructures. It also increases their dependence on each other. This level of trust leads to a reduction of the safe zone in many infrastructures. It also increases the access of terrorists to our telecommunications, defense, banking and financial institutions and other critical infrastructures.

In case of information-based supervision and the operation of the equipment being affected by terrorist acts; the performance of infrastructures that can trigger critical and different systems such as railways, electricity, power networks, oil and gas pipelines is greatly affected. This includes information technology, SCADA or ICSs, Global Positioning Systems and satellites. For these systems, it is necessary to re-evaluate the changes between efficiency, reliability, usability and safety. Appropriate risk assessment and management strategies should be developed. Emergency action plans should also be prepared.

The fight against cyber terror by states is important for the efficient functioning of all institutions and organizations, especially for critical infrastructures. New and hybrid solutions should be produced to minimize the damage caused by cyber terror attacks and to prevent these attacks. For this purpose, a database about past attacks should be created. When a new attack occurs, the database should be updated and information should be shared with relevant institutions. Commercial sectors and government institutions should also work in cooperation. Cyber terror attack information should be shared not only as corporate but also as universal. The systems, software and hardware used must be up-to-date and the vulnerability scan should be performed frequently. Patches published by developers and manufacturers should be applied to the systems as soon as possible.

As dependence on the cyber space increases gradually, prospective plans should be made and cyber awareness trainings should be given from primary school. In addition, national and universal awareness studies should be conducted to reduce the participation of individuals in cyber terror groups. Employees, children and parents should be encouraged to use the Internet technology in a good and beneficial way.

The perspectives of states to cyber terror may be different. The attacks may not be considered as terror according to different states. National policies and guidelines should be prepared and cooperated internationally in such cases.

The issue of cyber terror has to be addressed in a universal dimension and there are some restrictions. These can be listed as follows:

- There are different interpretations of the definition, scope and characteristics of cyber terror, but not a single structure has yet been set forth.
- The characteristics of cyber terrorists or cyber terror groups cannot be precisely determined, and it is not clear whether the actions carried out are cyber terror attacks.
- As States are concerned, perspectives of the states on terror differ and other states' calls for cooperation are not answered. International cooperation for cyber terror is important.
- As the difference between the cyber warfare and cyber terror attacks has not been fully set forth, there are also a limited number of studies involving security practices against cyber terror attacks. Many of them also propose a framework structure for the security draft.
- Cyber terror attacks, shown as examples in some sources, are not shown as cyber terror attacks in other sources.
- The developments and changes experienced in the field of cyber security are advancing very rapidly and this speed causes terrorist acts to diversify.

Cyber terror seems to be a major problem, especially for technology-critical institutions and countries that use it extensively. As the level of development and Internet dependency increases, terrorist attacks via the internet will be able to come to a level that could stop life. It is aimed that this study will be useful and guiding for future studies to be conducted on cyber terror.

REFERENCES

Ahmad, R., & Yunos, Z. (2012). A dynamic cyber terrorism framework. *International Journal of Computer Science and Information Security*, *10*(2), 149.

Ahmad, R., Yunos, Z., & Sahib, S. (2012). Understanding cyber terrorism: The grounded theory method applied. In *Cyber Security, Cyber Warfare and Digital Forensic (CyberSec), 2012 International Conference on* (pp. 323-328). IEEE.

Ahmad, R., Yunos, Z., Sahib, S., & Yusoff, M. (2012). Perception on cyber terrorism: A focus group discussion approach. J. *Information Security*, *3*(3), 231–237. doi:10.4236/jis.2012.33029

Bayraktar, G. (2015). *Siber Savaş ve Ulusal Güvenlik Stratejisi*. İstanbul: Yeniyüzyıl Yayınları.

Beggs, C., & Warren, M. (2009). Safeguarding Australia from cyber-terrorism: a proposed cyber-terrorism SCADA risk framework for industry adoption. In *Australian information warfare and security conference* (p. 5). Academic Press.

Colarik, A. M., & Janczewski, L. (2007). *Cyber warfare and cyber terrorism*. Yurchak Printing Inc.

Conway, M. (2007). *Reality Bites: Cyberterrorism and Terrorist 'Use' of the Internet*. Retrieved from http://firstmonday.org/article/view/1001/922

Dell Security Annual Threat Report. (2015). *Boom: A Journal of California*, *5*(1), 12-13.

Denning, D. E. (2001). Activism, hacktivism, and cyberterrorism: The Internet as a tool for influencing foreign policy. *Networks and netwars: The future of terror, crime, and militancy, 239*, 288.

Goztepe, K. (2012). Designing fuzzy rule based expert system for cyber security. *International Journal of Information Security Science, 1*(1), 13–19.

Göztepe, K., Boran, S., & Yazgan, H. R. (2012). *Siber Saldırıların Tespiti ve Engellenmesi İçin Uzman Sistem (US) Tasarımı: Siber Savunma Uzman Sistemi (SİSU). Yöneylem Araştırması ve Endüstri Mühendisliği 32.* İstanbul: Ulusal Kongresi.

Güntay, V. (2017). Uluslararası Sistem ve Güvenlik Açısından Değişen Savaş Kurgusu; Siber Savaş Örneği. *Güvenlik Bilimleri Dergisi, 6*(2), 81–108. doi:10.28956/gbd.354150

Hatipoğlu, C. (2017). Teknolojik Savaşlar: Siber Terörizm Tehditleri. *ICPESS 2017 Proceedings Volume 1: Political Studies.*

Heickero, R. (2008). *Terrorism online and the change of modus operandi. In Proceedings of 13th International Command And Control Research and Technology Symposium* (pp. 1–13). Seattle, WA: ICCRTS.

Jane's Information Group. (1999). *Cyberterrorism hype.* Retrieved from http://www.iwar.org.uk/cyberterror/resources/janes/jir0525.htm

Javed, A., & Pandey, M. K. (2014). Advance Cyber Security System Using Fuzzy Logic. *ACME: Journal of Management &IT, 10*(1), 17–27.

Jones, A. (2005). Cyber terrorism: Fact or fiction. *Computer Fraud & Security, 2005*(6), 4–7. doi:10.1016/S1361-3723(05)70220-7

Kara, O., Aydın, Ü., & Oğuz, A. (2013). *Ağ Ekonomisinin Karanlık Yüzü: Siber Terör.* Retrieved from http://kisi.deu.edu.tr/oguz.kara/Ag%20 Ekonomisinin%20karanlik%20yuzu%20siber%20teror.pdf

Knop, K. V. (2008). Institutionalization of a Web-Focused, Multinational Counter-Terrorism Campaign-Building a Collective Open Source Intelligent System. A Discussion Paper. *NATO Security Through Science Series E Human and Societal Dynamics, 34*, 8.

Kurnaz, İ. (2017). Siber Güvenlik ve İlintili Kavramsal Çerçeve. *Cyberpolitik Journal,* (1), 62-83.

Merrick, K., Hardhienata, M., Shafi, K., & Hu, J. (2016). A survey of game theoretic approaches to modelling decision-making in information warfare scenarios. *Future Internet, 8*(3), 34. doi:10.3390/fi8030034

Mohammad, M., & Kankale, A. P. (2016). Designing Forward Chaining Inference Engine For Fuzzy Rule Based Expert System For Cyber Security. *International Journal of Pure and Applied Research in Engineering and Technology*, *4*(9), 725–730.

Nicholson, A., Webber, S., Dyer, S., Patel, T., & Janicke, H. (2012). SCADA security in the light of Cyber-Warfare. *Computers & Security*, *31*(4), 418–436. doi:10.1016/j.cose.2012.02.009

Özalp, A. N., & Asker, A. (2017). *Devletin Güvenlik Politikalarında Siber İstihbaratın Rolü ve Önemi, Akademik Bilişim Konferansları, 2017*. Aksaray Üniversitesi.

Özcan, M. (2018). *Siber Terörizm ve Ulusal Güvenliğe Tehdit Boyutu*. Retrieved from http://www.turkishweekly.net/turkce/makale.php?id=87

Özkan, T. (2006). *Siber Terörizm Bağlamında Türkiye'ye Yönelik Faaliyet Yürüten Terör Örgütlerinin İnternet Sitelerine Yönelik Bir İçerik Analizi*. Yüksek Lisans Tezi, Anadolu Üniversitesi Sosyal Bilimler Enstitüsü.

Pricop, E., & Mihalache, S. F. (2015). Fuzzy approach on modelling cyber-attacks patterns on data transfer in industrial control systems. In *Electronics, Computers and Artificial Intelligence (ECAI), 2015 7th International Conference on*. IEEE. 10.1109/ECAI.2015.7301200

Rees, L. P., Deane, J. K., Rakes, T. R., & Baker, W. H. (2011). Decision support for cybersecurity risk planning. *Decision Support Systems*, *51*(3), 493–505. doi:10.1016/j.dss.2011.02.013

Reeve, S., & Koca, G. (2001). *Yeni çakal'lar: Remzi Yusuf, Usame Bin Ladin ve terörizmin geleceği*. Everest.

Richet, J. L. (Ed.). (2015). Cybersecurity Policies and Strategies for Cyberwarfare Prevention. IGI Global. doi:10.4018/978-1-4666-8456-0

Roldán-Molina, G., Almache-Cueva, M., Silva-Rabadão, C., Yevseyeva, I., & Basto-Fernandes, V. (2017). A Decision Support System for Corporations Cybersecurity Management. *Proceedings of 2017 12th Iberian Conference on Information Systems and Technologies (CISTI)*, 1-6. 10.23919/CISTI.2017.7975826

Shin, J., Son, H., & Heo, G. (2015). Development of a cyber security risk model using Bayesian networks. *Reliability Engineering & System Safety*, *134*, 208–217. doi:10.1016/j.ress.2014.10.006

Sökmen, A. İ. (2015). *Dünya'da Siber Terör Örnekleri.* Retrieved from http://www.academia.edu/20041386/D%C3%BCnyadaki_Siber_Ter%C3%B6r_%C3%96rnekleri

Temizel, M. (2011). Terörizmde Yeni Milad: 11 Eylül 2001. *Selçuk Üniversitesi Sosyal Bilimler MYO Dergisi*, *14*(1-2), 311–348.

Vatis, M. A. (2001). *Cyber attacks during the war on terrorism: A predictive analysis.* Dartmouth Coll Hanover Nh Inst For Security. doi:10.21236/ADA386280

Veerasamy, N. (2009). *Towards a Conceptual Framework for Cyber-terrorism.* *4th International Conference on Information Warfare and Security*, Pretoria, South Africa.

Wilson, C. (2005). *Computer Attack and Cyberterrorism: Vulnerabilities and Policy Issues for Congress.* Library of Congress. Washington, DC: Congressional Research Service.

Wilson, C. (2008). *Botnets, cybercrime, and cyberterrorism: Vulnerabilities and policy issues for congress.* Library of Congress. Washington, DC: Congressional Research Service.

Yıldız, S. Ö. (n.d.). Makarenko'nun "Kara Delik Sendromu" Teorisi ve Terörizmin Finansmanında Sınıraşan Organize Suçlar. *Güvenlik Stratejileri Dergisi*, *13*(25), 27-64.

Yılmaz, S. (2012). Türkiye'nin İç Güvenlik Yapılanmasında Değişim İhtiyacı. *Çukurova Üniversitesi Sosyal Bilimler Enstitüsü Dergisi*, *21*(3).

Yunos, Z., & Ahmad, R. (2014). Evaluating cyber terrorism components in Malaysia. In *Information and Communication Technology for The Muslim World (ICT4M), 2014 The 5th International Conference on* (pp. 1-6). IEEE. 10.1109/ICT4M.2014.7020582

Yunos, Z., Ahmad, R., & Mohd Sabri, N. A. (2015). A qualitative analysis for evaluating a cyber terrorism framework in Malaysia. *Information Security Journal: A Global Perspective*, *24*(1-3), 15-23.

Yunos, Z., Ahmad, R., Suid, S. H., & Ismail, Z. (2010). Safeguarding malaysia's Critical National Information Infrastructure (CNII) against cyber terrorism: Towards development of a policy framework. In *Information Assurance and Security (IAS), 2010 Sixth International Conference on* (pp. 21-27). IEEE.

Yunos, Z., Ahmad, R., & Yusoff, M. (2014). Grounding the component of cyber terrorism framework using the grounded theory. In *Science and Information Conference (SAI)*, 2014 (pp. 523-529). IEEE. 10.1109/SAI.2014.6918237

Chapter 9

From Conventional to Sophisticated:
A Cyber Guise to Terrorism in the Middle East

Mustafa Küçük Firat
Lund University, Sweden

ABSTRACT

Improvements in the technology unequivocally aids everyday life. These advancements lead states to save time and money. The crucial point is the facilitation that the internet and cyber services offer. Internet can be used for providing services to the citizens and can be benefitted while storing massive amounts of data. Nevertheless, cyberspace comes with serious problems too. The security of the data that have been transferred to the digital space ought to be protected in absolute terms. In cases of lack of securitization, cyberspace becomes vulnerable to attacks and, obviously, terrorist organizations can benefit from this. The Middle East, too, is an arena for such actions. But, the particular importance of the region reveals itself via its affiliation with the most widespread and dangerous terrorist organizations. Their ability to use the internet for propaganda and organizing attacks should not be disdained. Referencing these, this chapter will focus on the transfer of conventional terrorism to cyberspace in the Middle East.

DOI: 10.4018/978-1-5225-8976-1.ch009

Copyright © 2019, IGI Global. Copying or distributing in print or electronic forms without written permission of IGI Global is prohibited.

INTRODUCTION

If something is for sure, the technology is changing and evolving day by day. It is incumbent upon the states to catch up to the trends and new developments that are shaping the international relations. In cases where the state achieves to catch these epochs or the periods, this renders it possible for a nation to utilize its benefits. But if the scenario is the vice versa, then both the state and, its citizens have to face the consequences. It has always been said that history repeats itself and, the motion remains the same. The most prominent example of winners and losers of this process are the countries that were able to catch the industrial revolution and the ones which could not. The exact motif or the pattern is again visible in the cyberspace and the classification or the categorization of the states will be determined by regarding their ability on the issue. Nevertheless, before elaborating the subject and its vivid examples in the Middle East, it is of utmost importance to know, what cyberspace stands for. The term encompasses all of the human activities that direct the information in a virtual space; which is infinite and, based on computers and the internet infrastructure (Benedickt, 1991). Looking at the aspects that create enormous amounts of possibilities and opportunities, doubtlessly cyberspace has been facilitating and, will facilitate the lives of both states and citizens. However, by regarding the fact that innovations cannot be contained, these newly emerged areas and its services might fall into the wrong hands if, the necessary measures are not taken. The concern here is the terrorist organizations and their activities. The action is based on the use of violence in a systematized manner to create fear and ignite a social decline in the society for the sake of a political objective or to express the grievances of a particular group (Jenkins, 2018). The pattern is the same for the cyber terrorism as well, but this time the scope is much broader. Bogdanski and Petreski define the concept as "the use of information technology by terrorist groups or individuals to achieve their goals. This may include the use of information technology to organize and execute attacks against networks, computer systems, and telecommunications infrastructure, and to exchange information and perform electronic threat" (Bogdanoski & Petreski, 2013). This definition is also applicable for the terrorists and their activities in the Middle East that are using cyberspace and its opportunities to terrorize the West and its allies, in an attempt to make their complaints recognized. However, it would be a mistake to assess and evaluate the region and these organizations in the same manner as it is done for Europe or Northern America.

The dynamics of the Middle East are completely different and alien to the West. First and foremost, there are cultural barriers that prevent a full-scale comprehension of the realities of the region. The point here cannot be limited only to religious differences; concrete cultural differences should be the discourse (Ourfali, 2015). Secondly, the involvement of the Imperial powers during the colonization era formed an antipathy towards the West and its allies. Thirdly, the existence of a Judea state Israel and biased Western attitudes towards its existence merged and enhanced grudge with a response. A combination of these reasons and many more triggered a reaction and, this reaction was framed around the cyberspace by utilizing the technology. However, regardless of their rightfulness, terrorizing innocent people should not be the way to solve problems. Rather, diplomacy and its tools should be utilized to provide a firm conclusion to the issues on the ground. Unfortunately, none of the sides are eager to solve these problems via negotiation. Thus, this pushes the capable countries to take the necessary measures in order to prevent cyber terrorism and cyber warfare. Even though the threat is still blurred for some states and their leaders, it is vivid and much more serious compared to the previous terrorist attacks. As an instance for cyber terrorism, the attacks towards Israel by Palestinian hackers can be given. Throughout these attacks DoS (Denial of Service); which aims to disturb the function of the web by slowing the flow of information (Gurkaynak & İren, 2011) and, DDoS (Distributed Denial of Service); which targets an online web service and makes it unavailable via excess amounts of traffic from various sources strategies were used (Digital Attack Map, 2013). Starting from September 2000, these attacks are known as Inter-Fada and commenced at the same time with the Second *Intifada* (Gurkaynak & İren, 2011). There was no change in the motivation of the attacks, which were against the Israeli occupation of the West Bank and Gaza Strip (Intifada, 2018). As the chapter suggests, a transformation is evident from the conventional struggle to cyber warfare and terrorism, from *Intifada* to the cyber version, *Inter-Fada*. Therefore, to prevent such activities, the transformation process must be examined and analysed in greater detail. By doing this, further attacks may be foreseen and avoided. The term, which must be emphasized is cybersecurity. It is the activity of preventing attacks to servers, computers, electronic systems, mobile devices and, networks from malevolent actions (Kaspersky, 2018). Nevertheless, this is a race. A race that has been going on at a great pace and it is of utmost importance to not be left behind. As it is touched upon before, the scope of the cyber terrorism and the warfare is directly proportional to the services and the data that have been transferred to the digital arena. The greater amount of dependency brings about greater risks. Even though there are efforts to stand against this sort of terrorism, both nationally by the states themselves and multilaterally via international organizations, an ultimate end still seems far away. The Organization for Economic Co-operation and Development (OECD), North Atlantic Treaty Organization (NATO) and the International Telecommunication Union (ITU) are the main international organizations that have been adjusting their agendas for the concern (Choucri, Madnick, & Ferwerda2014). Nonetheless, due to their polarization by regarding their policies and ideologies, the vulnerability increases. Obviously, this paves the way for these attacks to become more widespread and, severe. Although the United Nations (UN), the biggest international organization, takes part; the outcomes were limited, the reason being the excess number of organizations. Thus, reaching a final solution with the current separated structure will be hard and, losing time can only benefit the terrorist organizations. In order to boost cooperation and, encourage integration to fight against cyber terrorism, new plans should be contemplated and a central organization has to be formed. The UN doubtlessly must play a major role to provide necessary common ground for the states to meet and determine the rules and also the processes that will be used against these kinds of activities. If the current situation is to be continued, terrorist organizations such as Hamas, al-Qaeda, ISIS, Hezbollah, PKK, and, YPG also other umbrella organizations like Muslim Brotherhood will enhace their power and not only realize their actions in the Middle East, but also in the West. Through the suggested integration, the process of transformation from conventional (traditional) to cyber terror may be analysed and prevented before it creates world-wide problems. The main idea here is cyber intelligence or counterintelligence. The term can be defined as "Information gathered and activities conducted to protect against espionage, other intelligence activities, sabotage, or assassinations conducted by or on behalf of foreign governments or elements thereof, foreign organizations, or foreign persons, or international terrorist activities" (United States Government The Secretary of Air Force, 2014). Thus, the goal of this chapter is to provide a wide range of analysis of thereto organisations for combating against cyber terrorism in the Middle East via analysing the process of transformation from traditional (conventional) to cyber terrorism.

All things considered, cyberterrorism is a serious threat to humanity in many ways. Hence, it has to be eradicated. The enhanced scope that it has acquired due to the cyberspace, renders it possible for terrorists to reach an incredible amount of audience and, realize many severe strikes against the government authorities. In order to prevent these scenarios, governments should embark upon to collaborate with international organizations to prevent further attacks by sharing intelligence. As a result of this process, the wider picture of the transformation can be realized and thus, be prevented. Even though the existent agencies strive to fight against cyber terrorism, they are not sufficient to eradicate it, but rather postpone it. The polarization or the excess amount of organizations that are dealing with the issue is creating a puzzling situation, where the pieces are strewn all around. Thus, these pieces, the information, must be integrated and the puzzle should be finished. To reveal the transformation process of terrorism from conventional, or in other words ordinary to more sophisticated and cyber base methods, this chapter will obtain the following outline; The First section will elaborate the conventional war and, terrorism in the Middle East by describing the concepts under sub-titles that are related to the issue and, the general reasons which have a stake to ignite the conflict and pave the way for parties to engage in conflict with each other. The second section will shed light to terrorist groups namely; al-Qaeda, ISIS, Hezbollah, the umbrella organization group Muslim Brotherhood with its affiliate Hamas, PKK, YPG and, their conventional activities within the region under sub-headings. The section will focus on their emergence, analysing their history and, detailing the grievances that agitate them to be on guard to against the legitimate authorities. The third section will address the cyber war and, the cyber capacity of terrorism in the Middle East by elucidating the important concepts, analysing the cyber-terrorist groups in the region and their activities. In the last section, the outcome of the mutation in terrorism from conventional to cyberspace will be examined and, necessary proofs will be unveiled via exemplifying the subject by cyber-attacks. In the last section, findings and conclusions & future suggestions will be provided.

CONVENTIONAL WAR AND TERRORISM IN THE MIDDLE EAST

The Perception of The Middle East

In order to comprehend the realities of the Middle East, it is necessary to understand the facts and also the dilemmas that the term has in itself. The Middle East has different locational definitions that create controversy. It can be described as the area that involves the territories of Morocco to Afghanistan and, somehow the area that was conquered by the first Islamic conquests during the Rashidun Empire and too the Anatolia (Keddie, 1973). However, some accounts tend to limit their scope to the region that is between Caucuses in the north, Arabian Peninsula in the south, Iran in the east and Turkey in the west by excluding North Africa (The World Factbook, 2018). George W. Bush administration of the US after the 9/11 attacks has broadened the scope and put a new concept, the Greater Middle East that includes countries in West Africa and, West and Central Asia besides declaring that these regions are the places that lack democracy (Steward, 2005). By referencing these, it is quite hard for one to have a concrete definition of the Middle East since the term was fabricated to serve the imperial interests of the European powers at the end of the 19th Century too. Merging both Near and the Middle East as a combination of aforementioned accounts, with the common semi-arid and desert climate, the population is overwhelmingly formed by Muslim communities that are divided into sects and, more deeply into Islamic Jurisprudence (*Fiqh*) (Keddie, 1973). The term, Middle East was first used by an American Captain Adm. Alfred Thayer Mahan in 1901 to stress on the commercial, meanwhile military importance of the area that is between the Mediterranean and, Indian Oceans (Koppes, 1976). Later, this term reached a common usage indeed and, started to be used by British parliamentarians and, later a member of a parliament, Sir Mark Sykes in 1916. Unequivocally, his intention was not the literature or etymology, but, to introduce a new phase of exploitation under the flag of imperialism. In the 19th century, it was crystal-clear that once magnificent and invincible Ottoman empire was weakening. The heavy burdens of the long-standing Turko-Russo wars led both economy by heavy taxes and, military by huge defeats to seek help from the flourishing European powers namely; Great Britain and France. Even though they were keen on to help, their real intention was to carve the Middle East for their own interest and exploit the vast amount of oil reserves. Their aim turned to a more realistic project during the WW1, when the Ottomans have aligned themselves with Germans and Austria-Hungary empire. This project was the Sykes-Picot Agreement. The compromise was foreseeing to give the control of the Syrian coast and majority of Lebanon to France, southern parts of Mesopotamia, Basra and Baghdad provinces to Great Britain, while Palestine would be given to the International administration (History, 2018). It is utmost important to acknowledge that their aim was to exploit, thus they introduced divide and conquer strategies, where they supported the minorities via religious sects to subjugate the majority and, this exacerbated the already existing Sunni-Shia conflict (Tibi, 1990). The tendency of subjugating the majority continued and led the creation of tyrants as it can be seen in most of the Levant in Post-1945 (independence period) era and today. In addition to this, both Turkish and Persian states break their centuries-long relations and, also the guardian role of the Arab people and their land. Mustafa Kemal Ataturk in Turkey and Pahlavi dynasty in Iran started to move away from the Arabs and strived to form a firm, meanwhile long-lasting relationships with Europe (Keddie, 1973). It is this reason that the term the Middle East cannot go beyond a geographical term to form a unity. By all means, their efforts could not lead them to elude from the Oriental etiquette or the stigma that has been attached to them by the Europeans as it was stated by Arthur James Balfour "It designated Asia or the East, geographically, morally, culturally. One could speak in Europe of an Oriental personality, an Oriental atmosphere, an Oriental tale, Oriental despotism, or an Oriental mode of production, and be understood" (Said, 1995).

Conventional War and Its Outcomes in the Middle East

For sure the war should not be a way of solving issues between communities, states or blocks or if, and the conditions are dragged into a conflict, then it should be the last resort. Although human beings are endowed with the ability to think, assess and solve their problems via interaction, there is nearly no era in history, where peace prevailed and, conflicts are adjourned. Throughout the time the tools and the strategies of the war have transformed and, evolved to suit the requirements of the period. Even there is a scientific definition of the war between states. The interstate war should has 1000 deaths during the conflict and, a state to be acknowledged as a war participant or a belligerent state, must have 100 deaths or 1000 armed personnel that are actively engaging in combat (Small & Singer, 1982). The history is full of such events and the most significant ones are the World Wars that have cost millions of lives and, a myriad amount of wounded. All of the wars, up until the 21st century were the conventional wars, where battle tanks, attack helicopters, warships, artillery jet fighters, missiles and small arms such as rifles were used. It is surely beyond doubt that, the conventional war has outdistanced in terms mortality compared to other types of war, including; chemical, biological and, even nuclear (Henderson, 2010). For sure the Middle East has been experiencing the fatal outcomes of the conventional war, as well. USA`s total arms export have surpassed 25 billion dollars in 2017 to the region and, this fact illustrates the terrifying outcomes of a war scenario (Armstrong, 2017). Contradictorily, conventional war has affected the winner side of the combat too in terms of lives and also, economics due to the lavish use of resources. The Iran-Iraq war of 1980-1988 is an instance, where thousands died and, a vast amount of resources were spent for a stalemate. Hence, if the discourse is to determine a winner in the conventional war, the answer should be exhausted and lost, not won and lost. Nevertheless, the new developments are on their way to alter the concept of war that a commoner has to another dimension. A level that will cost less and kill more, meantime designating an absolute winner.

Grievances What Terrorists Are Motivated From

It is obvious that every choice comes with a trade-off. Renouncing from something, in an endeavour to achieve another task, primary as one conceive. This is a process that all men face in their lives, so as their states. As a result of making a choice or valuing something more than the other, states form their agendas and array the things by regarding their importance and, then, there are the others, which are excluded from the list. The last group is the factors that motivate the terrorists to act against the legitimate authority. Terrorism can be described as "The unlawful use of violence and intimidation, especially against civilians, in the pursuit of political aims" (Oxford Dictionaries, 2018). Nearly all terrorist groups possess mutual grievances. These people are the minorities that are lost in a Majority and, rather than being a part of the mosaic that represents a country as a whole, they are excluded. Most of the time there is a subjugation process, which their language, religion, economic independence and, autonomy are under the threat of extinction. The risk of degeneration and also assimilation lead them to take extensive measures at their expense. The most prominent examples of this are the insurgencies against the government. Being unable to have a standing army, these groups mostly use guerrilla warfare tactics that foresee, "the use of hit-and-run tactics by small, mobile groups of irregular forces operating in territory controlled by a hostile, regular force" (Dictionary.com, 2018). By using these asymmetric methods, terrorists focus on the weaknesses of a standard army, which is designed for battlefield or front (trench) warfare. It is utmost important for the state to dispatch the necessary forces such as gendarmeries or task force teams to prevent the casualties (Sudhir, 2008). Nonetheless, it should not be forgotten that these people are the freedom fighters of a community, who are striving for autonomy. Thus, rather than crashing them violently, alternative ways ought to be found.

THE ACTIVE TERRORIST GROUPS, THEIR IDEOLOGIES AND, CONVENTIONAL ACTIVITIES IN THE MIDDLE EAST

Salafi Ideology

Unequivocally, Islam has an almighty and indisputable position for a Muslim, if, it is to be compared with other monotheistic religions and, their worshippers. The reason lies beneath the scope of the religion. It can be seen as a package that encompasses all aspects of human life. By referencing this, Islam has emanated in politics, science, philosophy and also in law (Lewis, 2004). One can talk about political Islam and Islamic philosophy deeply and, analyse the impacts of it to the modern day, while both Peace of Westphalia and French Revolution has diminished the power of the Catholic church centuries ago on. It is the same for the Sharia Law too, which is still practiced by theocracies like Iran and, several Muslim states such as Saudi Arabia and Sudan. Since the connection of the religion and the everyday life of a Muslim is blended and interwoven, the interpretation of life takes its stake as well. Salafi – Jihadism can be taken as a way to define the life and, alter the mistakes as the ideology comprehends. To understand the Salafi-Jihadist Ideology, it is necessary to know the Salafi creed. To a considerable extent, Salafis share a common precept that ties them together and, helps them to apply the teachings of Islam to the modern-day problems. Their motto frames around the *Tawhid*, which is the oneness of the God or *Allah* and adaptation of *Sharia* law meantime implementation of human reasoning *Ijtihad*, remains controversial (Wiktorowicz, 2006). The only way to practice the commands of the God passes through following the rules and wisdom of the Qur`an and the Sunna that is the collection of examples, words, and acts of the Prophet Muhammad. By regarding this principle, there should be one and sole religious interpretation and thus, the existence of Islamic pluralism is quite out of the question (Wiktorowicz, 2006). As it was mentioned before, they are very adamant about following the path of the Prophet Muhammad and, if, there is an ambiguity in the Qur`anic verses, particularly applying it to contemporary issues, Hadiths, the words and deeds of the Prophet and his companions (*Salafs*) seen as crucial (Oxford Islamic Studies, 2018a). Because of this, they are mostly known as *Ahl al-Hadith*, the people of Hadith (Wagenmakers, 2016). Salafis are also divided into fractions within themselves. The first group is the Purists that that takes the Meccan period of the Prophet's life. Their main tenet is protecting the purity of the Islam that is provided by the Qur`an, consensus or *Ijma* of the Prophet`s companions and, Sunna. The action at their expense will lead to injustice and corruption if, it is promoted before Islam is purified and understood by the people (Wiktorowicz, 2006). The right way to implement the religion can only be via *Tarbiya* that is education, *Tazkiyya*, the purification and, *da`wa* with the propaganda. They are mostly found in Saudi Arabian clerics as scholars (Wiktorowicz, 2006). The second group is the Politicos. Between the years of 1980-1990, the authority of the Purist scholars has challenged by a relatively young and active group of Salafis. They were the Politicos. Their main concern was the lack of ability that Purists perform to grasp the modern day issues. Politicos share the same creed as Purists put forward, but rather than isolating themselves, they see the remedy in politics. By engaging in modern issues, they believe that rulers can be contained from destroying the *Tawhid* and Islam. The movement achieved to spread its politicized Islam with the help of a Salafi, Sayyid Qutb, who was heavily influenced by well well-known Salafis like, Abd al-Wahhab and Ibn Taymiyyah (Wiktorowicz, 2006). Qutb's` books were crucial for the creation of the al-Qaeda and, the second man later the leader of the organization, Ayman al-Zawahiri used to be one of his students. The main criticism towards the Purist scholars that can affect Saudi politics was their approval of US soldiers to use the land of Islam to invade another Islamic country. From the Politico account this was a clear invitation for colonization. Hence, this led them to use their will and power on education to spread the politico belief among the young Salafis and Muhammad Qutb, the brother of Sayyid Qutb and other Politicos became the prominent figures in this project (Wiktorowicz, 2006). The last group is the Jihadis, who are responsible for the majority of the terrorism in the Middle East today. The faction emerged as a response to the Soviet invasion of Afghanistan. Rather than isolating themselves as Purists do or strive to use politics as a tool as politicos, Jihadists use violence to establish Islamic states (Wiktorowicz, 2006). Compare to other fractions they acquire their political training in the conflicts, this is why they see politics as warfare. Moreover, Purists are accepted as quite knowledgeable at their account, even they refer them as *al-ulama al-sultan*, the scholars of power (Wiktorowicz, 2006). However, they share the common ground with politicos and oppose Purists isolationist manner or apathy towards the contemporary world. As it was touched upon before, Purist scholars, especially in Saudi Arabia have close ties with the Ministry of the Interior Affairs. This creates a shadow on the eyes of Jihadists as well. The most prominent, Usama Bin Laden, although acknowledging the Purist knowledge, criticized them as being "adjacent to the royal palace" (Wiktorowicz, 2006). By referencing their criticisms towards the first two fractions, they see Jihad as a tool or a belief that will lead them to their ultimate aim. At this point, it is crucial to know the meaning of the *Jihad*. As an act of misconception or misrepresentation *Jihad* creates anxiety for the Westerners. The term *Jihad* stands for struggle or effort. Rather than as it was conceived by the people that are alien to the term, it has much more meaning than the holy war. It stands for the strive of a Muslim to live the religion to all means. Another aim of it to build a prosperous, meanwhile fair Muslim Society. Without any doubt, it also means holy war too, but, there are rules or *Kaide* for it (Oxford Islamic Studies, 2018b). First, the call for *Jihad* should be made by a legitimate authority or simply by the Islamic state or the caliphate. It is stemming from this that Jihadist are so keen on to establish a caliphate. Second, it should be made after a call to convert to Islam or if a treaty is violated. Third, non-combatants, women, and children should be unharmed (Oxford Islamic Studies, 2018b).

Al-Qaeda

Although it was mentioned before, comprehension of Salafi-Jihadism is essential for understanding the mental background of groups like al-Qaeda. The breakdown of the thought is two-phased. Firstly, Salafi-Jihadists claim that there are serious problems in the contemporary understanding of Islam. Thus, in order to fix it the past and particularly *al-salah*, the first followers of the Prophet Muhammad must be taken as models. Secondly, to realize this mission, a struggle, *Jihad* emerges as a necessary step to take. In other words, Salafism is the ideology and *Jihad* is the path to achieve this ideal. Al-Qaeda, the Base emerged as a response to the Soviet Invasion of Afghanistan in 1979 (Burke, 2004). By recruiting soldiers via utilizing Jihad, al-Qaeda led the Soviets to retreat from Afghanistan in 1989 (Burke, 2004). Of course, USA`s aids should not be disdained to the *Mujahidin* (Afghan Jihadist Fighters) as being one of the proxy wars that should be won. After 1989, the group experienced a dispersion, however, continued to oppugn the corrupt leaders as they perceived under the Taliban regime (Burke, 2004). To achieve this, they continued their recruitments from all around the world to realize attacks towards their aims. The most distinct of these attacks was the September 11, 2001, or as it is more commonly referred to as 9/11 attacks. Under the Usama Bin Laden`s leadership al-Qaeda hijacked 4 passenger planes and attacked different targets in the US. 2 of them achieved to hit the Twin Towers (World

Trade Centre), one of them to the Pentagon and another one crashed into a field in Pennsylvania (History, 2018). There are also claims that al-Qaeda bases these attacks on the Sword Verse, *ayat as-sayf* in the Qur`an. The verse states that "fight and slay the Pagans wherever ye find them". However, they only take these words of the verse and do not regard the rest which says "if any of the idolaters seeks of thee protection, grant him protection till he hears the words of God; then do thou convey him to his place of security -- that, because they are a people who do not know". As a result, these terrorist attacks led intense US responses and also the formation of the *Bush Doctrine* that aimed to fight terrorism with pre-emptive strikes (Constitutional Rights Foundation, 2018). By referencing this doctrine, US invaded Afghanistan and Iraq in an attempt to eradicate terrorism. In the same year on the 2nd of May Usama Bin Laden was killed by a navy seal in Pakistan and, this led to the rise of a new leader in the organization, Ayman Muḥammad Rabī` aẓ-Ẓawāhirī (Burke, 2004).

ISIS

The emergence of the ISIS or Islamic State of Iraq and al-Sham cannot only be contained to the Salafi-Jihadism, in spite of this, an amalgamation of causes should be discussed. The leadership struggle that happened after the death of Osama bin Laden and Ayman Muḥammad Rabī` aẓ-Ẓawāhirī`s, incapableness to fill his position and lack of charisma led cracks in the al-Qaeda. One of these fractions was the al-Qaeda in Iraq (AQI). In the previous decade the group was loyal to his pledge to al-Qaeda leadership but, in 2004 Abū Bakr al-Baghdadi a former fighter of the Iraq war against the US invasion had an opportunity to realize his plan to merge AQI with Jabhat al-Nusra Front, another Salafi-Jihadist organisation (Byman, 2016). Nevertheless, al-Qaeda leadership was not so keen to this idea. Thus, they have rejected Baghdadis idea and even threatened him with an annulment from the organization. However, this has not affected Baghdadi much and, what is more, he has consolidated his place further (Zelin, 2014). By all means, there are other external factors that aided ISIS to rise. The destruction of the Iraqi army, overthrown of Saddam Hussein and the *de-Ba`athification* of the society following the US invasion ignited a response and facilitated Salafi-Jihadists to portray themselves as the savers for the society. The destruction of the Iraqi army and not creating a force that will supersede the strong divisions like Republican Guards and a working state structure led Salafi-Jihadists to be unrivalled (Brown, 2018). Although there were initiatives to prevent the spread of these groups such as the Anwar Awakening, a long-lasting solution could not be reached. Unequivocally, Saddam was a dictator and his regime was very brutal but, the Ba`athist ideology was secular and Hussein was oppressing these groups both for the ideals of the party and also with credits to his survival. The similar scenario has happened in Syria as well and this underlines an important fact. Frankly, the lack of effective government control in the Middle East invites these groups to emanate into the region and, by all means, events like Arab Spring have exacerbated the situation and diminished the government control. By utilizing the vast amount of resources that they have controlled, ISIS became able to fund itself and also the lack of effective government control as it was touched upon, led Baghdadi to organize attacks not only within the *Levant* but also to the other countries easily, both Europe and closer countries such as Turkey. The 2015 Ankara bombings that have cost 90 people`s lives and many more wounded as a result of a suicide bomb in Kizilay is one of the most fatal attacks of ISIS (Letsch & Khomami, 2015). From the theological view of point, as the discourses suggest ISIS too as al-Qaeda, bases its attacks on the Sword Verse in the Quran. In addition to this, ISIS also uses al-Anfal Surah, *Sūrat al-Anfāl* for to justify the plunders that they did in the territories they have controlled. The point here is the *Ijtihad*, which they do in order to justify their acts. Most of the time they take the *Surah* which fits their situation and merges it with an *Ayat* to justify both their claims and actions.

Muslim Brotherhood (Islamic Fundamentalist)

Even though the Muslim Brotherhood or as it's better known as *al-Ikhwān al-Muslimūn* did not mention above as a terrorist group, it has an important role in the creation of the Islamic Fundamentalist terrorist organizations. The main argument or the discourse of the movement is their combination of Islamic charity work with political activism and this has inspired terrorist groups like Hamas to invest in social services. The Muslim Brotherhood was founded by Hassan al-Banna in 1928 in Ismailia, Egypt, who was intensely inspired by Rashid Rida about establishing the Islamic state to achieve universal Islamic order by encouraging Islamic morals and law by integrating with the society via providing social services (Harvard Divinity School The Religious Literacy Project, 2018). By creating benefits as it was touched upon before, the group targets the lower income populations and utilize them to reform the existing political regimes in the Arab world. However, rather than doing it by force, of course excluding some exceptions, the main path has passed through the politics (Munson, 2016). To broaden the issue of exceptions the actions of the Brotherhood can be given in Egypt. The group was very anti-colonialist and joined the struggle against the British domination of Egypt. In addition to this, they were side by side with the *Free Officers* movement to overthrow the monarchy in the country and, they achieved their common aim (Munson, 2016). However, this was a strange bedfellows case, the reason being the Free Officers Movement led by Gamal Abdel Nasser was coming from a secular background, while the Brotherhood`s main aim was to achieve the universal Islamic order. The tension between the seculars on one hand and the Islamists on the other reached a peak when an assassination attempt was made from a young Brotherhood member to Nasser in 1950. As a result of this, a leading member of the Islamists, Sayyid Qutb were sentenced and even executed in 1966 (Munson, 2016). Between the given time frame of 16 years, many members of the organization were jailed. Nevertheless, this policy has changed by Anwar Sadat, the next president after Nasser and an amnesty was came into force and, Islamic front grew and consolidated. However, Sadat`s policy turned against himself, when he signed a treaty with Israel and recognised its existence, in return of the Sinai Peninsula in 1973 aftermath of the Yom Kippur War (Finklestone, 2013). Egyptian Jihadists saw the Egypt first policy of Sadat as a weakness and, assassinate him in 1981. Nonetheless, regardless of the efforts to eradicate the organization in Egypt throughout the following decades, Brotherhood achieved to win the elections in the post-Arab-Spring era. Mohamed Morsi, the Brotherhood candidate, later the president stayed in charge for a year, before a coup replaced him with Abdel Fatah al-Sisi. Apart from their stronghold in Egypt, the Muslim Brotherhood as a movement achieved to spread other Arab countries (Al Jazeera, 2018). Hamas in Palestine and, Ennahda in Tunisia are the cases, which the organizations` affiliates accepted and Russia, Saudi Arabia, and the United Arab Emirates are the failed cases, where it was proclaimed as a terrorist organization.

Hamas (Islamic Fundamentalist Perspective)

It is obvious that the Middle East is one of the most problematic regions in the world. Because of the colonization and its legacy, already existed majority-minority problems have ignited such as, in Iraq and Syria. However, the most tragic of these conflicts is the Palestinian-Israeli conflict. To understand the conflict, it is crucial to have a background on the issue. As it was mentioned in the holy books of Jewish people, the God promised the people of the Prophet Moses to settle, (Jewish People) in the area that is remaining between the Nile river on the West and Tigris and Euphrates rivers on the East and, the *Canaan* is a land bridge that situates at the cross point of the great centre of ancient civilisations (Noll, 2012). Nevertheless, throughout the time these areas were heavily populated by the Muslim Arabs, who have been living there for centuries. Thus, this creates the problem of "whose, land is it?". By regarding the changes in the world, Jewish people who have suffered a lot achieved to have lobbies and pressure groups all around the globe. The biggest of them were in the UK and USA. In 1917, their efforts to turn back to *Canaan* reached a conclusion and, *Balfour Declaration* led a Jewish homeland or a Jewish state to be more concrete, to be established in the Palestine province of Ottoman Middle East (Johnson 2013). However, this newly created state also encompassed one of the holy sites of Islam that was Jerusalem or *al-Quds*. As it was expected, this newly established state did not welcome by its neighbours and also faced serious revolts by the local Palestinians. The Israeli Independence War, the Six Day War, and the Yom Kippur Wars are the main instances and of course with the Palestinian uprisings are the refusal of Arabs to acknowledge a Jewish state in the heart of the Islam. The main Palestinian response to the Israeli occupations were the establishments of PLO and later Hamas and, also other radical Islamic groups like Palestinian Islamic Jihad (Beauchamp, 2018). From the religious point of view, these organizations can be nominated as Islamic fundamentalists and their common ground is the Jerusalem issue. This is why the religious dimension of the conflict renders it possible to utilize Jihad to boost struggle against the Israeli state. One of the most prominent events that have escalated the religious aspect of the issue was the 1993 Philadelphia Conference, where George H. Bush mentioned about the Muslim Brotherhood in the US and, directed Hamas as being irreconcilable due to its rejection of the Oslo Accords. Hamas leadership perceived this not only a threat to them, but also the Islam itself since, they had the fear that the Western culture will dominate them (Lefkowitz, 2007). However, Hamas and other Salafi-Jihadist organizations should not be considered as same since it engages in skirmishes especially with ISIS. To start with, Hamas or *Ḥarakat al-Muqawamah al-Islamiyyah* is an Islamist political organization that was founded in 1987 soon after the First *Intifada*, the shake off or uprising. It was a response to Israeli occupation of Westbank and Gaza strip in December 1987.

Another analyst, Mazin Qumsiyeh argues that it was due to demonstrations that happened one month before the invasions. The period ended with the series of agreements in the Madrid Conference and, later in the Oslo accords in 1993 (Middle East Monitor, 2017). After 7 years of mildness, the Second *Intifada* or as it is better known as *Intifadat al-Aqsa* started in September 2000. The main motivation of the Palestinian uprising was the speech of the opposition (Likud) leader of the Israeli parliament member Ariel Sharon in his visit to the Temple Mount (Pressman, 2006). Sharon stated that "The Temple Mount is still in our hands", and this was seen as a provocation by the Palestinians who have been seeing the *al-Aqsa* mosque as the third holy place of Islam, thus a new phase of *Intifada* was commenced (Greenberg, 2000). Besides it is getting its sketch from the Muslim Brotherhood as making charity works to help the needy people or providing benefits and services, the group responses Israel organizing attacks towards Israel via rockets and suicide bombers. Their main aim is to replace Israel with the Palestinian state (Beauchamp, 2018).

Hezbollah

Hezbollah or *Ḥizbu 'llāh*, the Party of Allah is a powerful Shia organization in terms of both militarily and, also politically in Lebanon (Norton, 2014). Their ideology frames around Shia Jihadism, which takes its roots from the guidelines of the establishers of the *Jaf-ari* jurisprudence, Ja'far al-Sadiq. The perception of the *Jihad* is relatively different compared to the Sunni Tradition that sees it as a requirement. Shia thought differently, takes it into another level and, promote the concept of *Jihad* as a pillar or foundation of the Muslim faith stemming from the importance of the soul of *Karbala* catastrophe (Ayoub, 1978). In addition to this, Hezbollah also follows the ideas of the first Supreme Leader of the Iran, Ruhollah Khomeini, that are collected under the ideology of the Khomeinism. Due to possessing a Shi`ite population, having Lebanon on its side has always been conspicuous for Iran and, the 1982 Israeli Invasion of Lebanon was an epic opportunity to extend its sphere of influence against Israel and other Sunni states in the Middle East. Thus, to achieve this task Hezbollah was established in 1982 soon after the invasion by the funding and also the training that were given by the Iranian Revolutionary Guards (IRG) (Harik, 2005). However, the main concern of Israel was the relocation of the Palestine Liberation Organizations` (PLO) to Lebanon from Jordan. After a decades-long struggle against the Israeli occupation, 2000 became the year that Israel ended its occupation. Ironically, both Hamas, a Sunni group and Hezbollah a Shi`ite group have commonalities and this is not only their anti-Zionist ideology but, also their strategy to emanate into the society. Both organizations provide social services and benefits to poor people to win their support and they are also active in politics. Thus, from a macro view, it ought not to be assessed as a wrong statement if, one says they are using the same strategy that the Muslim Brotherhood was utilizing decades ago. For the Hezbollah, it is almost a state in a state case, where the group can act separately from the state of Lebanon and even boycott the elections. This was the situation at the end of the 2000s and a compromise has only reached when Hezbollah gained its right to veto in the parliament (BBC, 2010). Of course, the place of the organization is different compared to the other political parties in the parliament. The paramilitary branch of the organisation incumbents upon to intervene the politics, since it had the major role to strive against the Israeli occupation. The role of the Hezbollah was also decisive in the Syrian Civil War. By aligning itself with Iran and also Bashar al-Assad, it helped the regime to control the regions that were captured by ISIS and other fractions (Sullivan, 2014). Since the death of the spiritual leader Abbas al-Musavi, the leadership has owned by the secretary-general who is the current leader of the organization, Hassan Nasrallah (Haaretz, 2018).

Nationalism as a Triggering Force

The history is full of ideologies that have changed the structure of the earth. Each of these, remained their marks on the history and also, more importantly, on the contemporary order of the world. The most epic of these ideologies is the nationalism. The definition of the term is twofold. First, it encompasses the demeanour of an individual or a group when, the issue is their national identity and secondly, the actions of that specified group in an attempt to achieve their self-determination and gain independence (Stanford Encyclopaedia of Philosophy, 2014). The results of this idea can be exemplified via the Peace of Westphalia (1648) that ended the Thirty Years War between the European powers. This was a sectarian war between Catholics that were on the side of the Holy Roman Empire and the Protestant nobles of Europe. As a result of the war, Holy Roman Empire was defeated and acknowledged the right of Germanic people to determine their religion. However, this was also the end of the Catholic church's sphere of influence (History, 2018). The power vacuum led the emergence of a new ideal and this was the notion of nation, where the church will remain at a minimal level, while the idea of a nation will unite the ethnically same people together (Collins, 2018). In addition, the treaty is also accepted as the emergence of the sovereign state concept. Another epic instance, where nationalism was consolidated is the French Revolution of 1789. Beside of the ideals that the revolution promoted that were liberty, equality and, fraternity (*liberté, égalité, fraternité*), it diminished the role of Catholic Church in France and, even a de-Christianisation process was commenced (Virtual Museum of Protestantism, 2018). Without any doubt, the gap of the religion was filled by the ideals of the revolution and, the nationalism to consolidate the idea of a nation state. The impacts of the revolution were echoing all around Europe and, the Ottoman Empire was the one that has been affected the most. The reason for this lies beneath the elements that were creating the Empire. The Ottoman Empire has formed by *Millet* system, which stands for nations or religious communities. The French Revolution inspired these groups to rebel against the Ottomans to gain their independence. Even though the ruling class and Sultans tried to solve this phenomenon by introducing different ideas such as Ottomanism, Islamism, and Pan-Turkism, the disintegration was inevitable (Gürsoy, 2007). Arabs and Kurds in the Middle East were the main instances that the idea of being a nation-state has fascinated.

Hamas (Nationalist Perspective)

In order to understand the soul of the Palestinian nationalism, it is necessary to analyse the roots. The most organized revolt that has promoted the idea of Palestinian nationalism was the Peasant`s Revolt of 1834. Muhammad Ali of Egypt enforced policies that have pushed away dominant factions in the region and increased taxes led Palestinians to revolt against the authority. Even though Palestinians have defeated, the idea of a being a nation was formed (Rood, 2006). However, the main event that has ignited the Palestinian identity was definitely the *Nakba*, catastrophe. It is the day that Israel gained its independence after the ethnic cleansing of a hundred thousand Palestinians by the Zionist paramilitaries. This was an expected outcome, the reason being the British, who were controlling the area has already aligned themselves with the Zionists several decades ago via the

Balfour Declaration. Although the Palestinian efforts to overcome this project, they were not effective. Decades-long strives reached a conclusion when a more ordered insurgency was established in 1987. Hamas define itself as "a national Palestinian movement that works with the rest of the Palestinian people and with all national and Islamic factions and bodies and people of conscience all over the world on resisting the Israeli occupation as well as liberating the Palestinian land, Jerusalem, and Islamic and Christian holy places, securing the right of Palestinian refugees to return to their homeland and establishing a sovereign Palestinian State" (Hamas.ps, 2017). From the nationalistic point of view, their struggle is against the Israeli occupation of their land. In addition to this, the frustration that triggers them to struggle against their opponents stems from, the rejection of their sovereignty, while the Israeli state is recognized as a sovereign state.

PKK

The Idea of Kurdish nationalism that foresees a sovereign state to be given the Kurds in the territories of Turkey, Northern Iraq, and Syria dates back to the *Treaty of Sevres* that was imposed to Ottomans at the end of the WW1 (Danford, 2015). The treaty was contemplating a Kurdish state to be established in the regions that became the dominations of the British, once the treaty was signed. A separate state was proclaimed to be granted to Kurdish people via the articles of 62, 63 and, 64 The (Treaty of Sevres, 1920). However, Kurds find this problematic and sided with Mustafa Kemal Ataturk to fight against the imperial powers in the Turkish Independence War (*Kurtulus Savasi*) (Danford, 2015). By the fact that the *Sevres Treaty* was not recognised by the Ankara Government that represents the Turkish people, the proclaimed promises could not be realized. After the Turkish Independence War in 1923, the Ankara Government that represents the people against the imperial powers emerged as the victor by expelling the Allied powers from the Anatolia and, achieve to capture the majority of the planned territory in the *Misak-i Milli* decisions. The Kurdish nationalism and autonomy remained at the hearths of Kurdish people that triggered rebellions such as *Sheikh Said* in 1925 and *Kocgiri Rebellion* that its impact is still vivid today. It was in late 1970`s that the Kurdistan Workers` Party or *Partiya Karkerên Kurdistanê*, a Marxist political party established by Abdullah Öcalan to achieve the dream of the sovereign Kurdish state in the territories of Turkey and Northern Iraq. The organisation reached its peak after the coup of September 12, 1980, by the

General Staff of the Republic o Turkey, Kenan Evren (Bacık 2011). The cases such as the *Diyarbakir Prison* persuaded the organization to intensify the asymmetric warfare that they were continuing with the Turkish state since 1978. The group is active today as well. Apart from the seasonal peace talks, terrorism is almost the part of the daily news of the Turkish media. One of the most tragic actions of the PKK was their terrorist attack on the 50 soldiers in 17th of December 2016. By using a bombed track, an ambush was set up and this has cost 50 deaths and many more wounded (Sozcu, 2016). Kurdish groups in the Middle East cannot only be contained to PKK, rather all of them such as, YPG that will be elaborated in the following section are the components of a bigger organization. Kurdistan Communities Union or *Koma Civakên Kurdistan* (KCK) was established in 2005 by Abdullah Öcalan and, it can be nominated as an ethnic nationalist umbrella organization that has 4 components. These are PKK in Turkey, YPG in Syria, PJAK in Iran and, PCDK in Iraq (dw.com, 2018).

YPG

Peoples Protection Units or *Yekîneyên Parastina Gel* is an organization of units that was formed by the group, who suffered from the Syrians` Ba`ath regimes' attacks in 2011. Their aim, as it was stated by them is to defend their territory, which is the North Rojova region (Gunes, 2015) Even though their relation was relatively better compared to PKK with Turkey, especially on Ankara`s attitude towards the siege of Kobani, this momentum has lost in the case of Afrin. In order to prevent the formation of the *Kurdish Corridor*, which involves the regions of Iraqi Kurdistan, Northern Syria until the Hatay border of Turkey, Ankara had to make the right move (Tanış, 2016). Turkish state commenced the *Firat Shield Operation* and later the *Afrin Operation* (Olive Branch) and, YPG became the target of the Turkish Forces (Micallef, 2017). Turkeys` claims were concrete about these regions and government had to prevent the formation of a core, in an attempt to create a future Kurdish state. Such a state will create serious problems for Turkey even it will exist beyond its boundaries. In addition to the position of YPG in Afrin towards Turkey, the co-chairman of the organization, Salih Muslim (2018) stated that "the victory will be Kurds in this war", for the Afrin operation and this escalated the hostility between Turkey on one hand and YPG on the other. As a result of the war, Turkish forces were victorious although the Kurds prepared by digging trenches and, holding sufficient amount of artillery and weaponry. Without any doubt, this was due to the excess US support to them (Middle East Monitor, 2018). There were also other claims that the weaponry that YPG was using against the Turkish Forces was even newer and better compared with the Turkish equipment. One of the epic proof of this is the pictures that were taken in the *Raqqa Operation*. The Kurdish militias were using *FGM-148 anti-tank missile*. Although it is very hard for a militia to use such a missile, YPG fighters were using them without any problem (Yeni Akit, 2017). This creates another question, "from where these militias got their training ?". The same scenario was experienced in *Afrin Operation* as well. Even though US officials refuse the claims of their extensive support to these militias, Analysts such as Mete Yarar points that weapons like *Milan*, *TOW* and, *AT4* cannot be found on the black market (Sputnik News, 2017).

THE ACTIVE TERRORIST GROUPS AND THEIR ENGAGEMENT WITH CYBER-TERRORISM IN THE MIDDLE EAST

Unequivocally, every action invokes a response and in this case cyber threat should be prevented by the cybersecurity. There are certain steps that are needed to be taken by the authorities such as, investing more on the security of the SCADA systems, building firewalls but, the utmost importance should be given to the military. The confidentiality and the security of the systems should be kept in absolute terms. There are states who have been heavily investing in mass destruction weapons of all kinds that are controlled via electronically. If the necessary measures are not to be taken, these weapons may fall into the hands of the terrorist organizations. Unfortunately, then, states need to exhume the scenarios that have been prepared and laid aside by the end of the Cold War. No doubt that ruthless terror organizations are quite keen on to use these vulnerabilities for their so-called purposes without considering the civilian dimension of the issue. In order to understand the link between cyberspace and terrorism in a more meaningful manner, the factors which have pushed these groups to follow the alternative path must be elaborated. In the 21st century, there is no change in the aim or the motivation of the terrorist groups. The changing variable is the way that they express their grievances. The differentiation includes a clear calculation of the financial means and the risk factors. The financial reasons include the cost-effectiveness of the attack both in terms of material and human resources. To elucidate it differently, the terrorists will spend no money to purchase conventional arms but, just need a few experts compared to hundreds of guerrilla fighters. Moreover, it is less risky due to none of the attackers have a chance to be killed immediately by the authorities and it is very hard to track in comparison with a conventional attack. This kind of change is a result of a logical assessment in which the pros and cons of an attack are determined and, where the most pragmatic way is chosen. In other words, these are non-emotional reasons that persuade the terrorist groups to adopt the cyber-space as an arena to express themselves. The emotional motivations are embedded into the terrorist's character. These are frame around political and religious reasons. The discourse here is nationalism or has a religious base. Thus, the following section will analyse the cyber activities of the terrorist organisations under two groups; religiously motivated, which will involve ISIS and al-Qaeda and, politically motivated that will encompass, PKK-YPG, Hamas and Hezbollah.

Religiously Motivated

Nearly all of the terrorist activities are the expressions of groups that have been ignored for a long time. These actions are their efforts to led others to know about their grievances. In other terms, grab the attention of the public in an attempt to recognise their claims. The same process is also valid for groups, which are religiously motivated. Their perception of the contemporary world led them to perceive it as a threat to the very nucleus of their faith. They see the world and thus its powers as are in an assault against the religion. Thus, this led them to protect their faith and repel all of its enemies.

Al-Qaeda

For sure, the hallmark of the Salafi-Jihadism is al-Qaeda. By regarding their strikes against the authorities, which they have perceived as threats against their ideology, their aim is to rescue the religion from the encroachments. Nevertheless, by the engagement of Salafi-Jihadist groups with the cyber-space, a new term emerged to describe their acts, the *Electronic Jihad*. The term stands for, the alteration of the strategies or the need for alternative ways to follow the developments in the world and, make their steps by referencing the changing world structure. To make it simple, they are aware of the advantages that cyberspace is providing and do not refrain to use them against their targets. The issue here is *Ijtihad*. It requires religious authorities questioning of a practice to be compatible with Islam by not merely looking the Qur'an and Sunnah but also reliance to their own understanding and the interpretation of the texts (Bar, 2004) In other words, it is the self-reasoning to commit an act or not. Therefore, Salafi-Jihadists amply usage of the cyber-space is a product of their *Ijtihad*. They are doing this because they have interpreted it as being more pragmatic and cost-effective compared to other means. Nevertheless, the "Achilles Heel" of this paradigm is the existence of *bid'ah*. The term basically stands for the religious innovation and stipulates that any of such attempts are against Islam (Peters, 1980). Nonetheless, regardless of this irony, the Salafi-Jihadist organisations like al-Qaeda prefer to ground the preceding thought by claiming that it is for the *da`wa* and they are doing this to reach the ultimate goal, to purify the Islam and struggle against the encroachments of the West and its allies. To exemplify the issue, the cyber-attacks against Israel can be given. Al-Qaeda used Denial of Service attacks to overload the websites by making them temporarily disable. The aim, in this case, was the computer server of the Israeli Prime Minister, which was also available in the court records of the one captured al-Qaeda member Mohamedou Ould Slahi's confessions (Kingsbury, 2010). Another action of al -Qaeda is the anti-American Operation Black Summer. With the partnership of Tunisian Cyber Army (TCA), al-Qaeda in Egypt (AQE) targeted prominent websites of US government agencies with multinational companies. The attacks panned to commenced on 31 May 2013 and continue through the summer (Liu, 2015). However, the group could not be effective as much as they did in their conventional strikes.

ISIS

It is a fact that the Islamic State of Iraq and Syria has superseded al-Qaeda if the discourse is terrorism. Nevertheless, both organisations share the same creed although each of them wants to own the legitimacy of the Salafi-Jihadism. Although it was well mentioned before, ISIS born within the Al-Qaeda but, throughout the time they have split and the latter, dismissed the future founding members of the ISIS from the Al-Qaeda reason being, non-compliance of the orders. There are still infights between these groups as well. None of them confirms the actions of each other and claim the absurdity of the other's albeit, being ironic. As they share the same creed to some extent, ISIS too uses *Ijtihad* a lot while justifying its actions. Apart from the justification, they also seek acceptance by providing an explanation of their adaptation of new strategies. The most significant feature of ISIS is their immense and amply use of social media for propaganda and if one, accepts al-Qaeda as the initial point of *Global Jihad*, then ISIS should be the hallmark of the *E-Jihad*. There are many areas that the organisation uses social media such as a battleground for enemies, recruiting sympathizers, all-encompassing propaganda and undermining rivals (Afifi, Majid et al 2018). Although ISIS does not recognize officially, the group United Cyber Caliphate, are fighting against the enemies of the Islamic State, undermining its rivals and also engaging with espionage activities. In addition to this, this is the group that spreads brutal killings of hostages that have been withheld by ISIS (Knox, 2017). It is also known that South East Asia has affected highly from these cyber attacks. ISIS's attacks to the IRC servers which, led them to be down for extended periods via DDos and flooding the same server via Jihadi propaganda can be given as examples to their cyber activities (Sulin, 2018). There are also groups that directly belong to the ISIS for propaganda purposes. Al-Furqan is the group that is responsible to deliver the messages of the leadership to the audience and also retweeting the important materials from the other ISIS internet sites to the Tweeter (Liang, 2015). Al-Hayat is another group of ISIS which is responsible to produce impressive video contents to attract followers all around the world. The group owns the recruitment process of Jihadist from various countries by "*Mujatweets*", which they portray the lives of the fighters in Iraq and Syria in an epic way to encourage other fundamentalist and pro-Jihadist individuals to join the ISIS (Liang, 2015). For sure ISIS's monthly journal *Dabiq* that was publishing by al-Hayat media centre was quite effective as well. With an appealing style and amply reliance on Hadiths, the journal has been published online and not only in English but also other languages too. By the so-called advices and the proclamation of the "right way", *Dabiq* used by ISIS to reach its audience all around the world as a propaganda machine and the *Lumpenproletariat* of the Western societies has become the major hotbed where ISIS propaganda reached and worked. Indeed, via a detailed analyse, a considerable extent of Jihadis who has either joined ISIS or realized attack to the Western society and morals come from that strata of the society.

Hezbollah

Although it was touched upon, it is beneficial to remind that Hezbollah has strong links with Iran both financially and ideologically. For the ideological discourse, this can be seen through their targets. As Iran, Hezbollah has a long-running hostility against Israel for two reasons. First, because of Israel's invasion of Lebanon. Second, which is the ideological side of the argument, Hezbollah has a religious affiliation due to being a Shia terrorist organization and Israel's attitudes towards Islam and Muslims are seen inciting by them. To keep pace with the changing conditions of the world and to adopt new ways of surprising its enemies, Hezbollah embarked to the Cyber arena as well. There were previous attacks as well, which have been used as a propaganda tool for convincing people to the limits of their power. Rising their flag in an Israeli military compound and filming it on *al-Manar* a satellite TV in 1991 that was broadcasting in Beirut, shows their tendency to use alternative ways to mystify their enemies meanwhile boosting their self-esteem (Clarke, 2017). For sure, Iran's support has a decisive stake on Hezbollah's cyber capabilities. Stemming from the confrontations with the US and the *Stuxnet Virus Attack* towards its nuclear facilities by Israel, Iran invested heavily on the Cyber-warfare and, Hezbollah is relying on both the experiences and the financial support of the Iranians (Schaefer, 2018). The group has proved its capacities by the attack named as *Volatile Cedar*, which they have infiltrated into the Israeli Defence Sector via vulnerabilities and caused damage (Schaefer, 2018). However, their attacks are not only limited to the Israeli authorities but to other countries beginning with the targets in the US as well (Schaefer, 2018). Another action of them is basing on the "Catfishing" technique where, they use fake attractive women profiles to invite people, partcularly soldiers to downland a "more secure and private" application to obtain useful information for the organisation such as contacts and, photographs (Emerson, 2018).

Politically Motivated

The groups that are politically motivated find their inspirations in nationalism, which trigger their need for autonomy and this leads them to fight for independence. In another saying, these groups are the voices of the communities that are wanting to be seen as equals of other nations and, their actions are the responses of others disdain. Prominently, there is a gradual shift from the conventional ways of indicating this complaint to the cyberspace.

PKK-YPG

The Kurdish terrorist organizations prefer to reach the cyberspace via using already existing groups andits own branch PKK hack Team. They have no acquaintance, they form affiliations and drag other hacker groups to their fight against the authorities and in the Kurdish case, this is mostly against Turkey because, Iran has already possessed the capability to tackle against these attacks due to their long-lasting cyber-war with the US (Anderson & Sadjadpour, 2018). For the other Middle Eastern states such as Iraq and Syria, they do not see it as a vital step to take, the reason being they are able to rely on conventional tactics since both of them are weak states and barely or in some regions has no control in their territories. PKK Hack Team is the cyber branch of PKK and, although there is no amply information about them, their actions dates back to 2006 to infiltrate government websites (Çalikpala, n.d.). In addition to this, Antagonist Kurdish groups in Turkey rely on other two hacking groups as well; the Redhack and the Cold Hackers (CMG). The majority of their activities are espionage and for the Redhack damage to SCADA systems too. Sharing stolen data with PKK and emanating into the ministry servers were the most recognisable actions that have remained in the minds of the Turkish People. However, Turkey has started to take some measures to prevent these cyber attacks or respond them in the same manner. Turkish hackers are collaborating with the government to prevent these attacks to affect the larger population (Eren, 2017). PKK and its cyber affiliates can orchestrate attacks co-ordinately to damage the critical infrastructure. Their hybrid usage of kinetic and cyber attacks make them extra dangerous (Çelikpala, n.d.).

Hamas

Hamas has a long lasting struggle against the Israeli authorities for the sake of the Palestinian people's independence. Throughout the decades, the organization has struggled against the Zionism via conventional strikes, however, they could not achieve to realize their goals besides spending huge amounts of human and material resources. By referencing this, Hamas has been seeking alternative ways to reach its audience and convey its grievances so as other terrorist organizations such as PKK. Obviously, the new path passes through the cyberspace. Thus, this is another indicator that shows there is a transformation in terrorist activities from conventional to the cyber arena (Akdağ 2009). This switch is also visible in the actions of Hamas. The Gaza Strip is the most known place, where Israeli Defence Forces (IDF) and Hamas are clashing each other. 2014 Gaza War is crucial to investigate because a two-dimensional warfare was conducted between the belligerents. Apart from the guerrilla warfare, there were cyber-attacks towards IDF and, Hamas in collaboration with Hezbollah and Iran was seen as responsible. Most of these attacks were DDOS based, which aims to slow the operation systems (Shamah,2015). There were other strikes as well that can be classified as the espionage activities. The Gaza Cybergang is a group that is an affiliation of Hamas. Being active since 2012, their main way is using pieces of Malware that are attached into a malicious mail to stole the all possible information (Kovacs, 2017). Hence, this put forward the change from *Intifada* to *Interfada*. To mention more about espionage activities, Hamas uses the same tactics as Hezbollah uses. By aiming IDF soldiers through seductive profiles on Facebook, they invite them to download an application from the official store and try to reach classified information (idf.il, 2018). Thus along with Kurdish groups, Hamas is able to use both kinetic and cyber means to atack Israel.

FINDINGS

Throughout the research and in the writing phase various amount of materials and sources have been analyzed. By regarding this endeavour, certain findings have been obtained. There are clear proofs that illustrate, the major use of cyberspace to reach an audience and let other people hear about their grievances are done by Salafi-Jihadists (religiously motivated). By opening the gates of the *Ijtihad*, prominently ISIS, highly relied on social media to recruit soldiers and deliver messages through various social media services. As it was touched upon before, al-Furqan and al-Hayat are the groups under the ISIS to realize these actions. Al-Qaeda too, relies on cyberspace for their action as well but to a major extent the name E-Jihad has been owned by ISIS and they somehow missed the epoch of cyberspace. Nationalist (politically motivated) organisations differently, use cyberspace for attacking their enemies beside their usage of propaganda too. PKK's attacks toward the SCADA systems via groups like Redhack are the main instances of these actions. Another finding is that Hamas, Hezbollah and Kurdish groups too engage with espionage and intelligence activities to obtain information from the authorities that they are fighting. Hamas's infiltration to Israeli soldiers phone and Hezbollah's *Volatile Cedar Operation* can be seen as the cases, where this kind of activities have been conducted. At that point, a distinction should be made between two types of groups, who are using cyberspace for their activities. In the first group, there are teams like Anonymous, Cyber-Warriors and Türk Hack Team that have the means and wherewithal to realize fatal actions towards not only organisations but, also to the states. However, if the acts of the aforementioned groups are to be examined, they have never been targeted the lives of the masses directly. However, if the same opportunities are to be held by the both religiously and the politically motivated terror organizations that were the topic of the chapter, they could have already done it. This is stemming from their perception of the actions. To put differently, they have accepted the conventional tactics, which they have been using as a warning to their rivals and aware that it is not working efficiently. Thus, they are planning to change their tactics and damage more to the authorities, who are disdaining their grievances for too long.

CONCLUSION AND FUTURE RECOMMENDATIONS

Without any doubt, every choice comes with a trade-off that creates two sides and it is almost impossible to reach a complete satisfaction of all parties if the concern is the governance. The displeased group all the time seeks a way to reverse the situation or at least reach a balanced position. The dissatisfied group has always been named as terrorists, be that as it may, they are the freedom fighters of the other people. Although diplomacy and interaction should be the way to solve these issues, all parties prefer to solve conflicts via violence. However, the distinction between the terrorists and the legitimate government are their target group. In an attempt to push governments to recognise their claims, terrorists do not refrain from enlarging their scope to encompass civilians to their target group too. This is the main point that creates the antipathy and hate in spite of empathy and convergence. In the 21st century, a differentiation should be noticed by referencing their actions. As it has mentioned early in the very beginning of the chapter, there is a move from conventional tactics from the cyberspace and this comes with the advantages that the latter provides. It's cost-effectiveness, hard to be chased and, being able to impact on a larger scale with severe harming capacities render the cyberspace to be more attractive to the terrorists. With these being said and all of the changes with mutations, the aim remained same, to push authorities to recognise their claims. This is same for the all groups that this chapter has focused from religiously to politically motivated. At that point, both governments and societies should take the necessary measures to prevent these actions to happen. For the account of the authorities, it is utmost important to establish institutions to commence research and develop counter-tactics to prevent terrorists to reach the vulnerabilities of the SCADA systems, which renders it possible to them to affect on a major scale. However, more importantly, international establishments should be gathered under a roof organisation like the United Nations in a more organised manner to intervene in the issue collectively by intelligence sharing. There are other measures that states individually must take. There are reasons that push the qualified people of the minorities into the hands of terror organizations, to name one; isolation. Rather than using them for the benefit of the state, authorities prefer to ignore by regarding their ethnic and social background. Instead of this, mutually beneficial policies ought to be followed both for the state and the disdained people. By offering at least the same opportunities that the majority members of the society hold, qualified people who are eligible to commit cyber activities should be embraced. This can be done either by an all encompassing education system to integrate these people, as a long run-solution or via proposing offers that they cannot refuse easily such amnesty for previous crimes or privileges (passport & money). For the societies which are the target of these actions, they should know more about terrorism and especially the cyberspace to take the necessary measures that they can such as the safe usage of social media. The issue is education, to invoke an awareness of the approaching threat. If the conscious for the cyber world is to be instilled at a very young age, then it will be much harder for terrorists to infiltrate not only personal data but also classified state documents.

REFERENCES

Akdag, P. (2009). *Siber Suçlar ve Türkiye'nin Ulusal Politikasi* (Master's thesis). Retrieved from file:///F:/email/2009-TEZ-Siber%20Su%C3%A7lar%20ve%20T%C3%BCrkiye'nin%20Ulusal%20Politikas%C4%B1-Polis%20Akademisi.pdf

Al Jazeera. (2018). *What is the Muslim Brotherhood?* Retrieved from https://www.aljazeera.com/indepth/features/2017/06/muslim-brotherhood-explained-170608091709865.html

Alfifi, M., Kaghazgaran, P., Caverlee, J., & Morstatter, F. (2018). *Measuring the Impact of ISIS Social Media Strategy.* Retrieved from http://faculty.cs.tamu.edu/caverlee/pubs/alfifi2018mis2.pdf

Anderson, C., & Sadjadpour. (2018). *Iran`s cyber threat espionage, sabotage and revenge.* Washington, DC: Carnegie Endowment for International Peace.

Armstrong, M. (2017). *The USA's Biggest Arms Export Partners.* Retrieved from https://www.statista.com/chart/12205/the-usas-biggest-arms-export-partners/

Ayoub, M. M. (2011). *Redemptive suffering in islam: A study of the devotional aspects of ashura in twelver shi'ism* (Vol. 10). Walter de Gruyter.

Bacik, G., & Coskun, B. B. (2011). The PKK problem: Explaining Turkey's failure to develop a political solution. *Studies in Conflict and Terrorism, 34*(3), 248–265. doi:10.1080/1057610X.2011.545938

Bar, S. (2004, June/July). The religious sources of Islamic terrorism. *Policy Review, 125,* 27–37.

BBC. (2010). *Who are Hezbollah?* Retrieved from http://news.bbc.co.uk/2/hi/middle_east/4314423.stm

Beauchamp, Z. (2018). *What is Hamas?* Retrieved from https://www.vox.com/cards/israel-palestine/hamas

Benedickt, M. (1991). *Cyberspace: first steps.* Cambridge, MA: MIT Press.

Bogdanoski, M., & Petreski, D. (2013). Cyber terrorism–global security threat. Contemporary Macedonian Defense-International Scientific Defense. *Security and Peace Journal*, *13*(24), 59–73.

Brown, D. (2018). *15 years ago, the US invaded Iraq – here`s how it changed the Middle East country*. Retrieved from https://www.businessinsider.com/us-invasion-iraq-anniversary-how-it-changed-middle-east-country-2018-3#in-march-2004-a-few-months-after-saddam-hussein-was-captured-near-tikrit-four-blackwater-contractors-were-killed-and-hung-by-insurgents-from-a-bridge-in-fallujah-5

Burke, J. (2004). Al Qaeda. *Foreign Policy*, (142), 18–26. doi:10.2307/4147572

Byman, D. (2016). ISIS Goes Global: Fight the Islamic State by Targeting Its Affiliates. *Foreign Affairs*, *95*, 76.

Çelikpala, M. (n.d.). *Cyber security and nuclear power plants: International framework* (Doctoral dissertation).

Choucri, N., Madnick, S., & Ferwerda, J. (2014). Institutions for cyber security: International responses and global imperatives. *Information Technology for Development*, *20*(2), 96–121. doi:10.1080/02681102.2013.836699

Clarke, C. P. (2017). *How Hezbollah came to dominate information warfare*. Retrieved from https://www.jpost.com/Opinion/How-Hezbollah-came-to-dominate-information-warfare-505354

Collins. (2018). *Definition of 'nation-state'*. Retrieved from https://www.collinsdictionary.com/dictionary/english/nation-state

Constitutional Rights Foundation. (2018). *The Bush Doctrine*. Retrieved from http://www.crf-usa.org/war-in-iraq/bush-doctrine.html

Danford, N. (2015). *Forget Sykes-Picot. It's the Treaty of Sèvres That Explains the Modern Middle East*. Retrieved from https://foreignpolicy.com/2015/08/10/sykes-picot-treaty-of-sevres-modern-turkey-middle-east-borders-turkey/

Dictionary.com. (2018). *Guerrilla Warfare*. Retrieved from https://www.dictionary.com/browse/guerrilla-warfare

Digital Attack Map. (2013). *What is a DDoS Attack?* Retrieved from https://www.digitalattackmap.com/understanding-ddos/

Dw.com. (2018). *The Middle East's complex Kurdish landscape.* Retrieved from https://www.dw.com/en/the-middle-easts-complex-kurdish-landscape/a-38863844

Emerson, S. (2018). *Hezbollah Hacked Into Mobile Devices Globally.* Retrieved from https://www.newsmax.com/emerson/catfishing-checkpoint-mares-masrayk/2018/10/11/id/885922/

Eren, V. (2017). *Türk Korsan Gruplarının Siber Terörizmle Mücadelede Etkileri.* Retrieved from file:///F:/email/VahapEren.pdf

Finklestone, J., & Obe, J. F. (2013). *Anwar Sadat: visionary who dared.* Routledge. doi:10.4324/9781315035864

Greenberg, J. (2000). *Sharon Touches a Nerve, and Jerusalem Explodes.* Retrieved from https://www.nytimes.com/2000/09/29/world/sharon-touches-a-nerve-and-jerusalem-explodes.html

Gunes, C., & Lowe, R. (2015). *The impact of the Syrian War on Kurdish politics across the Middle East.* Chatham House.

Gurkaynak, M., & İren, A. A. (2011). Reel dünyada sanal açmaz: Siber alanda uluslararasi ilişkiler. *Suleyman Demirel University Journal of Faculty of Economics & Administrative Sciences, 16*(2), 264–276.

Gürsoy, A. K. Ç. A. (2007). Osmanli millet sisteminin dönüşümü. *Doğu Anadolu Bölgesi Araştırmaları,* 57-68.

Haaretz. (2018). *Hezbollah.* Retrieved from https://www.haaretz.com/misc/tags/TAG-hezbollah-1.5598890

Hamas.ps. (2017). *About Hamas.* Retrieved from http://hamas.ps/en/page/2/

Harik, J. P. (2005). *Hezbollah: The changing face of terrorism.* Ib Tauris.

Harvard Divinity School, The Religious Literacy Project. (2018). *Hassan al-Banna.* Retrieved from https://rlp.hds.harvard.edu/faq/hassan-al-banna

Henderson, C. W. (2010). *Understanding International Law*. Blackwell.

History. (2018a). *Britain and France conclude Sykes-Picot agreement.* Retrieved from https://www.history.com/this-day-in-history/britain-and-france-conclude-sykes-picot-agreement

History. (2018b). *9/11 Attacks*. Retrieved from https://www.history.com/topics/9-11-attacks

History. (2018c). *Thirty Years War ends*. Retrieved from https://www.history.com/this-day-in-history/thirty-years-war-ends

IDF. (2018). *Hamas' online terrorism*. Retrieved from https://www.idf.il/en/minisites/hamas/hamas-online-terrorism

Jenkins, J. P. (2018). *Terrorism*. Retrieved from https://www.britannica.com/topic/terrorism

Johnson, P. (2013). *History of the Jews*. Hachette, UK.

Kaspersky. (2018). *What is Cyber-Security?* Retrieved from https://www.kaspersky.com/resource-center/definitions/what-is-cyber-security

Keddie, N. R. (1973). Is There a Middle East? *International Journal of Middle East Studies*, *4*(3), 255–271. doi:10.1017/S0020743800031457

Kingsbury, A. (2010). *Documents Reveal Al Qaeda Cyberattacks*. Retrieved from https://www.usnews.com/news/articles/2010/04/14/documents-reveal-al-qaeda-cyberattacks

Knox, P. (2017). *Cyber Jihadis Who are the United Cyber Caliphate and what do the pro-Isis hacking group believe in?* Retrieved from https://www.thesun.co.uk/news/3242477/united-cyber-caliphate-isis-hacking/

Koppes, C. R. (1976). Captain Mahan, General Gordon, and the origins of the term 'Middle East'. *Middle Eastern Studies*, *12*(1), 95–98. doi:10.1080/00263207608700307

Kovacs, E. (2017). *Hamas-Linked 'Gaza Cybergang' Has New Tools, Targets*. Retrieved from https://www.securityweek.com/hamas-linked-gaza-cybergang-has-new-tools-targets

Lefkowitz, J. (2007). *The 1993 Philadelphia Meeting: A Roadmap for Future Muslim Brotherhood Actions in the US*. NEFA Foundation.

Letsch, C., & Khomami, N. (2015). *Turkey terror attack: mourning after scores killed in Ankara blasts*. Retrieved from https://www.theguardian.com/world/2015/oct/10/turkey-suicide-bomb-killed-in-ankara

Lewis, B. (2004). *The crisis of Islam: Holy war and unholy terror*. Random House Incorporated.

Liang, C. S. (2015). Cyber Jihad: Understanding and Countering Islamic State Propaganda. *GSCP Policy Paper*, (2), 4.

Liu, E. (2015). *Al Qaeda Electronic: A Sleeping Dog*. Academic Press.

Michallef, J. V. (2017). *Turkey and the Kurdish Corridor: Why the Islamic State Survives*. Retrieved from https://www.huffingtonpost.com/joseph-v-micallef/turkey-and-the-kurdish-co_b_7994540.html

Middle East Monitor. (2017). *Remembering the First Intifada*. Retrieved from https://www.middleeastmonitor.com/20171209-remembering-the-first-intifada-2

Middle East Monitor. (2018). *What is behind the US' support of the YPG?* Retrieved from https://www.middleeastmonitor.com/20180130-what-is-behind-the-us-support-of-the-ypg/

Munson, Z. (2001). Islamic mobilization: Social movement theory and the Egyptian Muslim Brotherhood. *The Sociological Quarterly*, *42*(4), 487–510. doi:10.1111/j.1533-8525.2001.tb01777.x

Noll, K. L. (2012). *Canaan and Israel in antiquity: A textbook on history and religion*. A&C Black.

Norton, A. R. (2014). *Hezbollah: A Short History-Updated Edition* (Vol. 53). Princeton University Press. doi:10.1515/9781400851447

Ourfali, E. (2015). Comparison between Western and Middle Eastern Cultures: Research on Why American Expatriates Struggle in the Middle East. *Otago Management Graduate*, 33-40. Retrieved from https://www.otago.ac.nz/management/otago632081.pdf

Oxford Dictionaries. (2018a). *Terrorism*. Retrieved from https://en.oxforddictionaries.com/definition/terrorism

Oxford Dictionaries. (2018b). *Intifada*. Retrieved from https://en.oxforddictionaries.com/definition/intifada

Oxford Islamic Studies. (2018a). *Hadith*. Retrieved from http://www.oxfordislamicstudies.com/article/opr/t125/e758

Oxford Islamic Studies. (2018b). *Jihad*. Retrieved from http://www.oxfordislamicstudies.com/article/opr/t125/e1199

Peters, R. (1980). Idjtihād and taqlīd in 18th and 19th Century Islam. *Die welt des Islams*, *20*(3-4), 131-145.

Pressman, J. (2006). The second intifada: Background and causes of the Israeli-Palestinian conflict. *Journal of Conflict Studies*, *23*(2).

Rood, J. M. (2006). The Time the Peasants Entered Jerusalem: The revolt against Ibrahim Pasha in the Islamic court sources. *The Jerusalem Quarterly*, 27.

Said, E. W. (1995). Orientalism: Western conceptions of the Orient. Harmondsworth, UK: Penguin.

Schaefer, B. (2018). *The Cyber Party of God: How Hezbollah Could Transform Cyberterrorism*. Retrieved from http://georgetownsecuritystudiesreview.org/2018/03/11/the-cyber-party-of-god-how-hezbollah-could-transform-cyberterrorism/#_edn11

Shamah, D. (2015). *Official: Iran, Hamas conduct cyber-attacks against Israel*. Retrieved from https://www.timesofisrael.com/official-iran-hamas-conduct-cyber-attacks-against-israel/

Small, W., & Singer, D. J. (1982). *Resort to arms: international and civil wars, 1816-1980*. Sage Publications.

Sozcu. (2016). *Son dakika: Kayseri'de hain saldırı*. Retrieved from https://www.sozcu.com.tr/2016/gundem/son-dakika-kayseride-patlama-1570850/

Sputnik News. (2018). *A Kurdish fighter from the People's Protection Units (YPG) looks at a smoke after an coalition airstrike in Raqqa, Syria June 16, 2017 Kurdish Forces Use NATO Weapons Against Turkey – Military Analysts.* Retrieved from https://sputniknews.com/analysis/201802021061298505-kurds-nato-weapons-turkey-afrin/

Stanford Encyclopedia of Philosophy. (2014). *Nationalism.* Retrieved from https://plato.stanford.edu/entries/nationalism/

Stewart, D. J. (2005). The greater Middle East and reform in the Bush administration's ideological imagination. *Geographical Review*, *95*(3), 400–424. doi:10.1111/j.1931-0846.2005.tb00373.x

Sudhir, M. R. (2008). Asymmetric War: A Conceptual Understanding. *CLAWS Journal*, 58-66.

Sulin, O. (2018). *Cyber Attack Campaigns in Political Conflicts: A case study of Anonymous hacktivists' campaign against ISIS* (Master's thesis).

Sullivan, M. (2014). *Middle East Security Report 19-Hezbollah in Syria.* Academic Press.

Tanış, T. (2016). US-Turkey relations at a breaking point over the Kurds. *Turkish Policy Quarterly*, *14*(4), 67–75.

The Treaty of Sevres. (1920). *The allied and associated powers and turkey.* Retrieved from http://sam.baskent.edu.tr/belge/Sevres_ENG.pdf

The World Factbook. (2018). *Middle East.* Retrieved from https://www.cia.gov/library/publications/the-world-factbook/wfbExt/region_mde.html

Tibi, B. (1990). The simultaneity of the unsimultaneous: Old tribes and imposed nation-states in the modern Middle East. *Tribes and State Formation in the Middle East*, 127-152.

United States Government. The Secretary of Air Force. (2014). *Air Force Policy Directive 10-7, Information Operations* (Operation No: OPR: AF/A3O-QI). Retrieved from http://static.e-publishing.af.mil/production/1/af_a3_5/publication/afpd10-7/afpd10-7.pdf

Virtual Museum of Protestantism. (2018). *Dechristianisation during the Reign of Terror (1793-1794).* Retrieved from https://www.museeprotestant.org/en/notice/dechristianisation-during-the-reign-of-terror-1793-1794/

Wagemakers, J. (2016). Religion. *Oxford Research Encyclopedias*.

Wiktorowicz, Q. (2006). Anatomy of the Salafi movement. *Studies in Conflict and Terrorism*, *29*(3), 207–239. doi:10.1080/10576100500497004

Yeni Akit. (2017). *YPG'nin kullandığı silah şoke etti!* Retrieved from https://www.yeniakit.com.tr/haber/ypgnin-kullandigi-silah-soke-etti-275642.html

Zelin, A. Y. (2014). The war between ISIS and al-Qaeda for supremacy of the global jihadist movement. The Washington Institute for Near East Policy, 20(1), 1-11.

Chapter 10
Dark Web and Its Research Scopes

Athira U.
Kerala University, India

Sabu M. Thampi
Indian Institute of Information Technology and Management Kerala, India

ABSTRACT

Internet has become the most unavoidable phenomenon in our daily life. Together with it has risen the most unfathomable aftermath of anonymity exploitation. The internet available for the normal users are limited to the sites that are directly indexed by common search engines. But apart from these contents, a major portion of the internet lies hidden from regular search engines and is not available to users resorting to ordinary browsers. This part forms the deep web and within it lies the darkest part also known as dark web. Several illegal activities take place in this darkest part, including child pornography, financial fraudulence, drug deployment, and many others. Thus, countermeasures to put a curb on these activities are very much required. The chapter focuses on the most relevant research areas and possible research scopes in the area of the dark web.

DOI: 10.4018/978-1-5225-8976-1.ch010

Copyright © 2019, IGI Global. Copying or distributing in print or electronic forms without written permission of IGI Global is prohibited.

INTRODUCTION

Ross William Ulbricht was a physicist and at the age of 28 he intended to make a bundle out of his endeavor named "The silk road": an online market place set up in 2011 by assuming the name "Dread Pirate Roberts" (DPR). The venture opened up platforms for several vendors to sell their products. The luxury offered by the market was that, the entire process of buying and selling took place under the veil of anonymity. The buyers and sellers traded without being tracked or identified by means of IP address or any other forms of identity. This resulted in sudden influx of vendors selling products including drugs, poisons, weapons and even hitmen on request. The anonymity accelerated the secret trading business and eased the access of illegal products at one's finger tips. It is assumed that DPR reaped a commission of over $13 Million from the vendors. But the story of success did not last long as it was seized by Federal Bureau of Investigation (FBI) in the year 2013. By 2015 DPR was sentenced to life imprisonment. Though FBI furnished an attempt to counter the threat of anonymity, it was far from perfect in putting an end to the precarious after math of unfathomable internet. There emerged several versions of Silk route and many similar kinds of anonymous internet businesses that thrive on online anonymity. These activities take place in the deeply buried part of the internet named as dark web. The contents of this part of the web remain inaccessible to ordinary users and are obtained only via special browsers named as the Onion Router (TOR). The requests to the contents, via TOR, remain intractable and are aided by several relay machines that add encryption to the node address of a user request thereby preventing the origin from being traced. The transactions pertaining to these activities online are carried out by means of digital currency named as Bitcoins. This money gets mixed up in the network without leaving any trace of the origin as well as preventing the exposure of the identity of the recipient.

The dark web was not originally designed to breed illegal cyber activities. It was a step by step evolution to guarantee privacy in online environment. The Tor browser was implemented to establish a secure channel for conveying military communications across the globe. The motive was to legitimately serve good to the nations and its security. The purpose of Bitcoins was also to facilitate safe and secure anonymous transactions pertaining to crucial applications. The inventors of these advances were advocates of privacy. But the good intentional innovations were irrationally exploited for individual benefits that strew mayhem to the innocent users of internet. The consequences of the maltreatment include the identity theft, unnecessary exaltation of illegal and lethal products, child abuse and improper harnessing of youth intelligence.

There exists a need for a planned strategy to lay balance between the privacy guaranteed and the exploitations in darkweb. The explorations in this regard open the door to scopes of researchers in cybersecurity to lay hands on means to guarantee security (secure privacy) and identifying ways to break open the security (identifying vulnerabilities). The area holds a flimsy test environment for a researcher to contribute to the darkweb threat counter measures by asserting the privacy aspects of the internet users. Thus one need to adopt proficient methods to prevent the illegal cyber activities contaminating the web. The area of darkweb forensics offers a wider scope of research that demands more scrutiny and exhibits numerous challenges.

This chapter devotes to the identification of research scopes in the dark web. The article emphasizes the real dark web scenario, complex problems in dark web that are unaddressed, research challenges, existing research developments and possible research directions in connection with dark web.

DARK WEB AND DEEP WEB

The existence of the dark web scenario is actuated by the structure of internet which provides access to the surface of the web via the search engines. The structure of internet can be visualized in terms of an "ice berg analogy" as depicted in Figure 1. The Figure 1 details the structure of internet by dividing it into three layers namely surface web, deep web and dark web.

The static web pages can be easily obtained by search engines like Google, Yahoo, Bing, Ask, AOL etc. The search engines make use of crawlers to crawl through a static web page by traversing the links in the page. The daily web searches, emails, shopping sites and social networking sites are accessed in this way and are part of the surface internet. Such information forms only 4% of total web contents and is referred to as surface web or visible web. But this is not the complete picture as stated by Bergman (Bergman, 2001)

Searching on the Internet today can be compared to dragging a net across the surface of the ocean. While a great deal may be caught in the net, there is still a wealth of information that is deep, and therefore, missed.

Figure 1. The structure of Internet

Thus the rich source of information ingrained in the web finds place in the deepest part of the internet where databases, research articles, private websites which require login credentials, web archives, newspaper contents, medical records, subscription information, organizational repositories, corporate intranets, legal documents, confidential information and so on reside. This is called the deep web. These are pages that are not indexed by search engines and hence do not appear in the search result. The ordinary search engine strategy of traversing the links is not possible here, as many times it requires human interventions like filling forms and providing with login credentials. These sites can be accessed by the specific address. They remain protected mainly at the discretion of the owner who provides permission for authorized users or invited guests to gain access to the contents.

The data obtained by the search results comprising of static web pages indexed by traditional search engines do not suffice the modern day user specifications. Harnessing the treasure chest deep hidden in the deep web can contribute to topic specific search with intelligence added to the information extraction process. For example a person searching for treatment related to a particular disease obtain links of important blogs and sites containing the keywords that are contextually and semantically related to search query. But the engines cannot give access to the required site contents that are accessible only via the main website link which is not publicly available. They are intended towards providing suitable links to search query rather than search contents. Harnessing this information from deep web can contribute in a better way to improve the search experience of users who are dealing with unstructured big data.

Harvesting suitable topic based search results that are rich in contents is an area of high demand in deep web research. Several attempts by pioneering groups aim at garnering the contents pertinent to the user query (Pederson, 2013). These efforts aim at retaining maximum information in addition to metadata, keywords, title and url of the page. This enables the search to be flexible in term of its analytical capability as well as versioning of the dynamic pages that undergo frequent refurbishments. Thus fine tuning the data from deep web and converting it into intelligence is a promising area for cyber security researchers to lay focus on.

Going further deep down the internet is the menacing contents of the dark web comprising of black markets and other fraudulences. The terms deep web and dark web are often used inter-changeably, which is a common misconception. The dark web can be visualized as the deepest and a smaller portion of deep web which has been kept anonymous purposefully and thus the users are denied access via ordinary web browsers. These contents can be accessed via random anonymous nodes in the network of decentralized nature (Finklea, 2015). The most common networks of this type are Tor, I2P (Invisible Internet Project) and Freenet.

THE ONION ROUTER

Tor is a decentralized network and is a protocol that encrypts the data and sends the traffic through random intermediate nodes that serve as the relay machines. In this way the IP address of the sender remains undisclosed to the destined recipient. Tor Browser opens up the way to Tor network. Tor was established initially by US Naval Research Laboratory in the year 2002 as a part of The Onion Routing Project, the purpose of which was to make naval communications in a confidential manner across the internet. Since the purpose was meant for secret naval communications, the network also incorporated other users so that the original conversations go inconspicuous amidst other public discussions (Tor Project, 2018).

Tor attains its objective of anonymity by adding encryption to the web traffic in different layers analogous to the layers of an onion. The messages within the tor network that originates from the source are encapsulated by adding different layers of encryption. This is attained by encrypting the message using the public key associated with the intermediate nodes. The encrypted message is then passed through different intermediate machines that voluntarily serve as relay machines across the world. Each of these machines remove single layer of encryption before transmitting it to the next node. The decryption is carried out by using the private key of the concerned node. The decrypted message holds the address of the next location to which it is to be sent. Finally, the message arrives at the exit node which when decrypts the message using its private key receives the intended secret message which is sent to the destination. The whole process makes it theoretically impossible to identify the ip address of the originator. This because, each node is aware only about the previous node that transmitted its message and the next node to which it has to send the message. The Figure 2 gives a brief insight into the tor routing strategy.

Tor has been created for the purpose of anonymous and private communications. Though it serves well its purpose, the fraudulent use of Tor has caused havoc to the users. The anonymous nature of the network has allured numerous illicit activities taking toll on the internet. Dark web and tor has become so intertwined that it is almost impossible to find a means to track illegal activities in the veil of anonymity and at the same time to preserve privacy of legitimate users. The recent statistics depicts very high usage of

Figure 2. Tor routing strategy

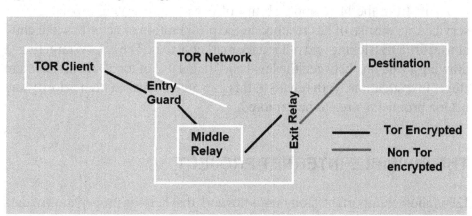

tor especially in United States followed by Russia, Germany and United Arab Emirates (Finklea, 2017). The usage of tor enables a vast majority to gain free access to the net (Going Dark, 2014). Further it enjoys the benefit the decentralized storage strategy guarantees enriched durability of data by preventing it from permanent damage or loss. The legal use of tor enables the users the provision to access huge collection of informative resources including e-books.

The usage of TOR in conjunction with VPN(Virtual Private Network) is yet another important way of gaining access to network with additional layer of protection form VPN in such a way that no TOR node can ever get to know the home IP address of the user. At the same time the traffic influx to the VPN server of the user remains encrypted to the home network thus ruling out the chance of being identified by Internet Service Provider (ISP) for using TOR network. This proves to be an added advantage of VPN users who rely upon VPN providers and assumes privacy. The combination of TOR and VPN enable overcoming the challenges incurred in employing the technique exclusively. The combination of TOR and VPN provides enhanced privacy. Apart from its advantages, the combination results in a much slower connectivity.

TOR can be combined with VPN using two strategies:

- TOR through VPN
- VPN through TOR

VPN through Tor is preferred to the other way round. It offers advantages in terms of privacy by hiding the user's IP address and also reduces the chance of being infected with the bigs from malicious tor nodes.

Apart from the huge applicability of privacy preserving aspects of Tor services, its misuse of has resulted in the proliferation of activities like child abuse, drug trafficking and other dark market places. The efforts targeting at drawing a fine line between the legal and illegal use of tor is still at the infant stage. Investigations with regard to this gap area are worth high priority and offer a promising area to be explored.

THE INVISIBLE INTERNET PROJECT

I2P is another important anonymous network that helps in propagation of data packets without third party monitoring. Unlike tor which intends to provide anonymous access to internet contents, I2P aims to host anonymous websites hence calling itself internet within internet. One need to install special software to gain access to I2P network that provides anonymous communications. A message from source to destination traverses via several intermediate tunnels which ultimately reaches the intended recipient. Just like Tor network, each data packet is encrypted in multiple layers, allowing each tunnel to decrypt the message once thereby gaining details of the next tunnel to which the message is to be forwarded. The encryption followed is AES encryption (Daemen, 1999) and the authentication is done using El-Gamal (ElGamal, 1985). This happens multiple times until the message reaches the intended recipient. The message follows a random path through several intermediate tunnels (virtual paths) before reaching the destination thus making it difficult for a third party to determine the exact route and the recipient. Each machine is provided with several messages which can either be messages originated from itself or the message to be relayed from someone, or message to be received by itself. Thus, it is difficult to monitor a node and identify to whom exactly is it delivering a message or receiving a message from.

The added benefit of I2P in comparison with Tor is that it allows adding more than one message to an encrypted block that making it even more difficult to be tracked. This type of routing strategy is referred to as garlic routing. The alteration of the hop path in random intervals makes it even more difficult to trace the message path and the communicating nodes. The entire process has been explained by Taher ElGamal in his journal (El Gamal, 1985).

The features of I2P includes email and chat services that promote secure and anonymous exchange of messages and anonymous chats. It also provides options in form of Eepsites to host anonymous websites with operators remaining anonymous. It provides the users with added benefit of torrenting thereby offering enhanced anonymity.

I2P is a most promising way of anonymous communications and with its delayed garlic routed mechanism and tunneling to support pooling and mixing messages, it guarantees sufficient anonymity to the users. But delay in the routing has induced some sort of disadvantage in its applicability. The future releases of the new versions of I2P aim at reduced or no delay in routing and has also designed First in First Out strategy associated with tunneling. (A gentle introduction to how i2p works, 2018). The effective impact of I2P is debated by its limitation in terms of the scalability attained. The challenging aspect of I2P investigations points to the need for the users to login to gain access to the contents. The tunneling architecture makes it impossible to monitor the contents in I2P.

The I2P acts like a new abode to cybercrime ventures like silk road. All the traffic being equipped with end to end encryption, the network is difficult to be tracked. It is a network that is decentralized in its entirety. Despite its strong anonymity, the chances for tracking individuals browsing outside I2P are more. But the severe challenge faced by the researchers is that they are unable to automate the process of gaining access to the .i2p sites as they demand the apprehension of Base 32 or Base 64 address, in unison with a string of number and characters which is very difficult to be harnessed. Yet the investigations with regard to this area offer a huge platform that attracts cyber security and privacy advocates.

BIT COINS

The anonymous transactions find their way out using world-wide decentralized payment furnished by crypto-currency known as bit coin. Crypto-currencies are those digital payment means where the currency is generated as encrypted entities. All the transactions and transfer of funds are managed in a decentralized environment devoid of a central bank. (Olivia, 2018). The transactions using bit coins involve only the owner and the receiver party and the transactions are broadcasted via P2P network. The transactions are recorded and stored in digital ledger books referred to as transaction blocks. Each block forms the part of a chain of block where every single block stores the information regarding the block preceding it and all the transactions involving bit coins. These public nodes are anonymous in nature. The transactions using bit coin are conducted by digitally signing the hash of the transaction preceding it and at the same time maintaining the details of the public key associated with the recipient (or succeeding owner) of the coin. In this way the path of the digital coin is maintained and verified in a public ledger there by making the duplication or double spending, impossible without manipulating the entire transaction history (proof-of-work) associated with the single bit coin. (Nakamoto, S, 2008). The proof-of-work is a piece of data that is required to prevent the manipulation as it involves certain conditions to be satisfied. The Hashcash (Back, A, 2002) proof-of-work employed by the bitcoin checks the legitimacy of a newly formed block by performing a hashing on the miner's block and checking its compatibility with the next block. The Figure 3 provides a detailed visual representation of bitcoin transaction system.

Unlike traditional banking system that involves a trusted third party to maintain element of privacy, here the participating entities publish their

Figure 3. The BitCoin transaction system

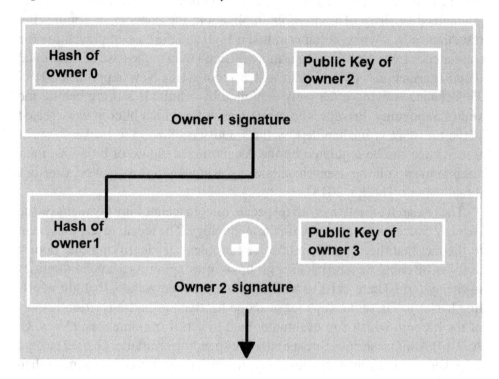

transactions with the general information being shared with other being the occurrence of transfer of amount between two parties, without leaking the information regarding the details of the parties indulged in the transactions. Bit coins have been chosen as effective transaction method in Silk Road. Here the constituent parties remain hidden from each other by adapting to a strategy that every sending party sends the money to the Silk Road which in turn sends the money to the recipient once an acknowledgement has been received from the sender of money regarding the product delivery.

The bitcoin and block chain technology has several positive implications in social and economic front. The block chain technology that backs the crypto-currency concept overcomes the security loop holes associated with existing systems like being tracked and engulfed by hackers. The bitcoin is a technology that is inherently organized and will be undermined by inept government intervention (Tapscott, D, 2017). But without proper stewardship the bitcoin technology would witness an emergence of invisible powers. The users who attain around 40% of computing power can manipulate a reverse transactions to exercise forgery (Malhotra, Y, 2013). Even with the guaranteed security of impossible duplication, the chances of committing fraudulence by a white-collar criminal is high and the ease of preventing the fraudulence from proliferating is more difficult than in the case of traditional wired transactions. (Blockchain and Bitcoin Offer New Approach,2018). This chance is being effectively exploited by criminals lurking behind the veil of anonymity. Privacy: the prime reason for which bitcoin was created is the tool that is mishandled by the fraudsters. Since the hackers' act of fraudulence can be regulated by the decentralized nature of bit coins, their attempt to exploit the users' machines by using keyloggers can be a serious threat (Monic Thudja, 2018).

The research initiatives with respect to bitcoin technology lay focus on the security concerns associated with the technology. The recent researches point to the fact that there exists an unsolved problem of identifying the 'honest users' of bit coins. Several hacking groups aim at exploiting the vulnerabilities of the system. There exist several attacks on online wallets that allow off-line back up. These backups leave scope for tracing the transaction history of the bit coin which can eventually lead to act of fraudulences. (Vyas, C. A,2014) Another serious threat of double spending (Karame, G,2012) where a hacker successfully manages to spend illegally a bit coin on more than one transactions. This can be made possible by altering the time counters associated with the network.

The proof of work based block chain mechanism triggers the enormous consumption of computational power which is yet another important matter of concern that requires serious research consideration (Mosakheil, 2018). Bit coin faces a major challenge with respect to the amount of power consumed to attain its consensus mechanism using proof-of work that verifies the accountability of a newly added block. Another security challenge where computational power concerns become a factor is that, many a times honest users are tricked by 'Selfish miners' (Eyal, I, 2018) into putting in their computing powers for cycles that go wasted while the hackers bifurcate the block chain network for their blocks that are kept private.

Counter measures for several attacks (Kwon, Y, 2017), (Narayanan, 2016) remain to be unaddressed areas that demand effective solutions. Thus the gap in the literature exhibits a clear requirement of strategy that dedicate itself to identify honest users from fraudsters and offer a sound, scalable and secure platform to use the crypto-currencies.

WHY WE NEED DEEP WEB?

From the above sections we can clearly conclude that deep web is a tool, the scope of which when effectively leveraged can contribute to a better social scenario. The original reason for its emergence being privacy, the appropriate usage of it can result in numerous benefits. The true highlights can be listed as follows. All Tor users cannot be tormented for illegal use as there exists numerous benefits of dark web which can serve general good to the legitimate users.

Freedom of Expression

Whistle blowing plays a major role in imparting democracy among citizens. But people across the globe face severe threats in expressing their voices freely bypassing government censorship. There have been attempts from government authorities to suppress the public views in social forums by banning online social networks. For social activists and others who raise their voice for the general public can use deep web as a platform to whistle blow at the oppressive establishments. The deepest part of the web can be an encouraging part for the like-minded individuals to persuade or express their valid views. Since deep web cannot be brought under single point of control, the chances of it being suppressed by capitalist government policies that curb public social forums that might go against the government policies, are less. There have been examples of using dark web as a platform to expose the pitfalls and secret businesses in the government levels which would have otherwise been impossible to execute via government approved legal channels (Sui. D, 2015). This can prevent the tyrannical endeavors from the ruling party to oppress the citizens of a nation and can impart protection from capitalist acts.

Hacktivism

Hacktivism is the process of computer aided propagation of political or social agenda. A hacktivist may use tools similar to that of a hacker, but the purpose of hacking might involve a socially relevant cause. The hacktivism can be termed as an electronic civil disobedience as reported in the article (Stefany.Wray, 2018). Earlier the protest against a controversial government or organizational stand could be expressed by physical 'blockades' imposed on the organizations. The hacktivism aims at 'virtual' blockades on the capitalistic firms by enabling citizen to contribute from their home or work place. The concept can be used for the purpose of general good as well as to tweak the real fact. The process of hacktivism gains its full freedom in the dark web spaces. A case of hactivist group who collected and published the details of users involved in online child abuse proved to be a blameless initiative that serves a social good (Finklea, K.M, 2015).

Critical Information Sharing

The dark web forms an important and secure platform for sharing private files, Medias and information without the hazard of information breach. The dark web sites serve as the most appropriate venue for journalist and news reporters who can share crucial and important files without being monitored by the parties involved in the news. They have the freedom to share and store the valid proof against corruptions and malpractices of officials without being spied on. Similar is the case of privacy associated with personal information. All online digital repositories on the surface web are prone to information leakages and spying eyes. The suitable means to evade the scrutiny of tricksters is to be safe behind the dark web.

Privacy Preservation

The dark web proves to be the most relevant solution for the advocates of privacy. All confidential transactions, conversations, information and details remain to be anonymous and intractable in this environment. The transactions are difficult to be manipulated and hence the chance of financial fraudulences is less.

Free Internet

The dark web enables people to enjoy free net on daily basis, though it exhibits a sort of infringement upon several organizations aiming at monopolizing the academic and relevant information repositories. The access to dark net enables one to gain access into wide range of research journals and articles. Important information which otherwise was not reachable to the individuals can be effectively harnessed from the deepest corners of internet. The effective harvesting of the resources in the dark web can prove to be an excellent source of information trove.

Government Use

The Deep Web technology is adopted by government to contribute to military intelligence and enforcement of law. The anonymity offered in the environment enables secure online surveillance and enforcement methods that are difficult to be bypassed. Just as the motive of the technology, the networks can be effectively utilized for sharing military communications and crucial information. (Finklea, K.M, 2017)

Why Should We Fear Dark Web?

Apart from the above-mentioned highlights and the promising mobilization of dark web, it suffers from serious threats of improper exploitation of dark web capabilities. The major problems arise from ill treatment of the privacy information and its trading. The following are the most dreadful aftermath of dark web exploitation.

Nefarious Usage

The propagators of privacy never expected TOR networks, deep web and crypto-currency to impose troubles onto the innocent users of anonymous networks. But the anonymity for which it was created turned out to be a huge reason for which it has been used by cyber criminals looming at large in online realm. The anonymity offers the dark web space, the luxury to trade illicit products including drug, weapons and everything hazardous. The comfort of being unnoticed promotes the criminal instincts within an individual which would otherwise have been over powered by the fear of being watched. This can harm the safety of other innocent victims falling prey to the evil intentions of criminals.

Identity Thefts

The dark web forums form important venues where confidential information once leaked remain a trading piece. The forums which are difficult to be traced and monitored offer platforms where stolen credentials are sold. As per the report of Javelin Strategy and Research (Javelin,2018), around 16.7 million Americans fell prey to the identity theft in 2017. The corporate organizations find it a challenging task to protect the customer information from being stolen and traded in dark web forums.

Data Piracy

The information breach arising out of the security flaws in existing security mechanisms result in lost confidential information that are publicized in dark web forums. The recent data breach targeting Equifax (Daily Dot,2017) is an example of how the personal details including social security numbers, driving licenses and other crucial details of several Americans have been compromised when the hackers exploited the vulnerability prevailing in the application. The tactics of trading the trade secrets of flourishing organizations are serious threats to corporate organizations. The digital repositories are prone to be hacked by cyber criminals who immediately trade these details in dark web sites. The stolen data faces the challenge of being rapidly spread via the dark web sites resulting in less time to deal with the adverse effects.

Sexual Abuse of Children

The scariest implications of dark web exploitations point to the online sexual abuse of kids and child pornography. The recent research initiatives inferred a rigorous rate of child abuse using the dark web sites. The traffic to these sites dominates the traffic to any other sites. The chances can be that, child pornography being an important issue that requires attention; the investigating officers are constantly monitoring the activities within these sites. Thus hit made by the officials in terms of monitoring also adds to the regular traffic reported to these sites.

Improper Harnessing of Youth Intelligence

The activities within the dark web including the evolution of Silk Road and many dark market places cast light on the fact that many young intelligent people find it as an easy place to reap benefit by unethical means. The youth intelligence which could have otherwise properly channeled is being diverted towards gaining benefits from illegal means. This can cause serious social trauma that restrains the effective nurturing of young mind for the benefit of the society.

CHALLENGES

The investigations in dark web and deep web security are marked by several challenges. The dark web which refer to the deepest part of the internet are comprised of sites that are not indexed by search engines. Thus the challenges involved can be enlisted as follows:

Hidden Sites

The earlier researches in the dark web are delimited by the fact that the proper security measures could not be imparted due to the fact that they are not easy to find. There exists no external link to these hidden sites. The access of dark web sites demands tor browsers to gain access into its contents. Further the access to most of these sites requires login credentials that impose the need for manual activities like form filling. These intuitive activities cannot be simulated by ordinary crawlers. Thus most of these sites can be monitored only by means of manual intervention. Further it burdens the investigators to find criminals lurking behind in a difficult to find place.

Content Richness

The contents in the dark web are impregnated with high sized media files the size of which surpasses the indexable file size. Thus even if once access has been gained, the proper monitoring is possible only if the files are tracked efficiently. Most of these sites stipulate session time outs thus resulting in log out every now and then that hinders the extraction of huge sized files.

Collection Recall

Important issue faced by dark web investigators and monitoring mechanism is that, once a specially designed crawler has been detected, the sites make move to block this crawler and evade its detection. This becomes cumbersome as the investigation phase requires creating the crawler accordingly based on the modified site strategy.

Difficult to Crawl

The extraction of content from dark web is different from the mining of surface web sites as these sites are not indexable. The ordinary search engines return as search results the pages that are indexed. Thus the scarcity of crawlers capable of directly accessing dark web contents makes it impossible to mine content of dark web. Content paucity can be a serious problem in investigations as tracking and monitoring the sites become difficult.

Inseparable Honest and Suspicious TOR Users

The TOR has been created with the aim of guaranteed privacy in transactions and interactions. But now it has become the popular spot for the cyber criminals whose activities remain anonymous and mixed up in the crowd without being noticed. Any impositions on the TOR usage would affect the genuine users of the network. Thus drawing up a fine strategy that guards the privacy concern of honest users and the one that prevents dubious users is difficult to attain.

Segregating Regular and Investigative TOR Traffic

The recent malpractices in TOR networks have resulted in rigorous investigations aiming at identifying the network traffics and TOR user activities. Thus majority of objectionable sites are under the scrutiny of law enforcement officials. The traffic arising out of inquisition hinders the comprehension of regular TOR traffic thus giving deceiving statistics on network traffic to certain sites. For example the traffic to child pornography sites exhibit a higher rate of traffic in comparison with other sites. This can be attributed to the fact that since this is the most crucial problem that requires official attention; more resources are dedicated towards its monitoring thus resulting in increased traffic.

Regulation of Dark Web Policies

Impositions on Dark web are challenging to be incorporated as it involves the regular and legitimate routine of surface web users, deep web users and dark web users. The global acceptance with regard to the general policies of dark web is difficult to be put into practice. A sustainable action plan requires an efficient global consensus.

STATE OF THE ART METHODS FOCUSING DARK WEB

The research focusing in the area of dark net is committed towards lessening the impact of the impairments invoked by the impertinent utilization of dark web resources. The three parallel streams of research pertaining to dark net research are user-based mechanisms, content based mechanisms and dark net forensics. The methods can be illustrated as shown in Figure 4.

Figure 4. State of the art methods focusing on dark web classification

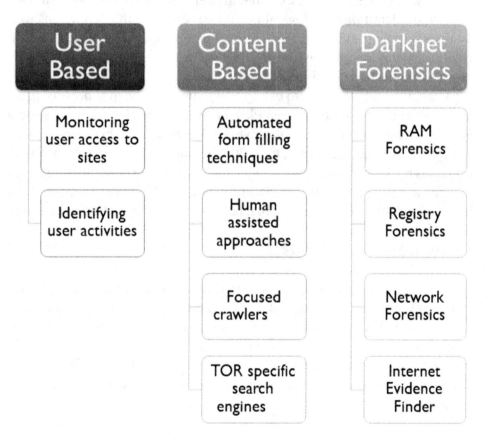

User Centric Methods

The user centric methods mainly aim at identifying the malicious users without compromising on the user anonymity. These attempts are useful in tracking individuals who are frequent visitors of sites that are identified to be proliferating illicit activities. Computer and internet protocol address verifier is a tool that has been employed by FBI to track down individuals who operate by choosing proxies to access objectionable sites (Poulsen, K, 2007). This favors the investigators by segregating the access to the ordinary sites and access to the tor networks and hence enhances the law enforcement schemes.

Another tool called Memex has been developed by Department of Defense Advanced Research Projects Agency to track the user activities by identifying the specific pattern of requests that hold malicious purpose. The patterns for evil –intended user requests are learned and the patterns followed by the users that are in match with such patterns are identified. (Davies, S, 2011)

Another method has been explored in (Pinheiro, M, 2017)) which attains the task of identifying the logical profile associated with a suspicious user by assessing their attack pattern and modus operandi. The basic effective solutions to this mission have been described by the author in terms of crowd sourcing (collective intelligence).

A hacking tool was put into use by FBI to uncover the ip address of users accessing child abuse sites named Playpen. The appraoch tracked only users gaining access to child abuse sites, while other users remain anonymous.

A work by (Van Hardeveld, G. J.,2017) explores the tools that the cyber criminals resort to in putting their plots into actions. The paper also describes how the activity pattern of the criminal can be used in unison with the loop holes in the tools to track the criminal behind the illicit activities in dark web.

Content Based Methods

Content based research initiatives in dark web scenario face the challenge of content paucity. Most of the dark web sites require user logins and have session time-outs that prevent automation of content extraction from dark web sites. Thus the demand for methods that are capable of extracting dark web contents effectively are problems that remain unaddressed. The attempts to develop crawlers to mine hidden web contents are research initiative that gained much attention.

Ahmia is a research initiative aimed at crawling tor websites. It provides an indexing mechanism by identifying the onion addresses and providing it to the users on request. But the search engine that is of centralized nature in the current scenario of Ahmia ehich faces several security challenges in the anonymity network. Attempts are targeting towards a decentralized solution to crawl tor contents. The article (Tor Project, 2018) provides a comprehensive overview of different tools available to monitor dark web. Cyber monitoring has become an important aspect of dark web security researches. There are several initiatives and products available to monitor the dark we to check for the information breach of an organization or individuals. These tools aim at executing checks in dark web to monitor the presence of our information in dark web and alert us with regard to the illegal mention of our details in dark web sites.

There are advanced research initiatives that aim at developing focused dark web crawlers that perform automated crawling by adopting different strategies. The earlier approaches of dark web content acquisitions involved semi-automated approaches that thrived on human interventions that assisted accurate retrieval from dark websites. Here the certain parts of the process that require intuitive human elements are indeed performed manually. A human aided crawler has been explained in (Fu, T., 2010) where the contents of dark web forums are collected by making use of URL ordering features.

Human aided crawling is not a time efficient mechanism as majority of the dark web sites are equipped with form filling and submission. To take human intuition into consideration, several automated query generation engines aim at extracting dynamic contents based on auto generated search queries. The work by (Ntoulas, 2005) describes an engine that automatically generates search queries to retrieve deep web sites that do not have static links that are indexed. But majority of the sites involve form filling that often require human intervention. But simulating the human method of form filling to result in successful submission is a challenging task that requires careful consideration. A method has been proposed by (Spencer, B., 2017) which aims to analyze sites that require form submission. The method aims at learning the actions of human mediated form fillings to result in successful submission. The method takes into consideration the constraints of client side java script code.

Another type of crawler termed focused crawler pursue the extraction of contents from dark web based on the topic of interest. The approach takes into consideration a classification method that learns, local and global context of the source and destination hyperlink so as to gain insight into the topic relevance. (Iliou, C., 2017)

The survey on deep web crawlers provided in ((Hernández, I, 2018) concludes by pronouncing a need for a bench mark to evaluate the performance and scalability issues associated with crawling.

Dark Net Forensics

Another stream of research focuses on identifying the culprit behind the scene of crime and it involves careful analysis of all possible clues left behind by the fraudsters (Rathod.D, 2017). The general strategies adopted as the part of dark web forensics can be investigating the memory dump of the computer to learn about the traces of information that can be crucial in detecting the criminal. There are several tools available for performing RAM forensics. Belkasoft (Belkasoft, 2018) is an example of such kind of forensic tool.

Registry forensics is a type of forensic strategy that aims to identify the recent updates in registry key by inspecting the time stamps. GUI based, command line based and remote live analysis of registry is possible along with a chance for offline analysis. The regshot analysis reveals the history of Tor access of the suspicious user.

Network forensics involves analyzing the network traffic to garner evidence in the event of a security attack. Either the packets in the traffic are saved in its entirety for inspection or only relevant details are saves for future speculation. The storage requirement is more in case of network traffic analysis.

Bitcoin transaction forensics aim at the collection of information regarding the bitcoin usage history by examining the digital wallet application installed in the machine. Internet evidence finder provides option for accessing bit coin details.

Research Scopes of Dark Web

Having discussed about the different aspects of dark web and the challenges involved in it, we explore the applicability and research directions that find relevance in dark web scenario. The area attains high significance in current day scenario of increased popularity of internet and digital resources. The main sectors that can be the potential beneficiaries of the research activities can be explained as follows:

Corporate Sectors

The improper usage of dark web results in trading of stolen credentials. The stolen information includes credit card details, and other financial credentials. Thus it serves as a threat to the corporate organizations dealing with sensitive user data. The reputation of the organizations depends on the defense or recovery strategy adopted by it in dealing with these disastrous activities. This shows the importance of dark web research in corporate sectors that finds its application in two levels. The research initiatives that aim at preventing the secure information from being leaked are very important. But the security loop holes in existing mechanism can result in information gain by malicious party. To maintain the reputation of the organization, one needs to adopt suitable methods to prevent proliferation of stolen details. The recovery mechanism should be in such a way so as to reduce the impact of the stolen information.

Sexual Abuse

Another important issue that requires the attention of researchers is the online sexual abuse. The advantage offered by the online anonymity favors the sexual perverts who engross themselves in the illicit acts of eve teasing and child abuse. Several cases have been reported regarding the dark web activities that procreate cyber bullying over dark web sites. The child abuse issue is the most crucial problem that remains unaddressed. The research orientations with regard to identification of sites that spreads this activities, or research initiatives aiming at identification of users that subscribe to these sites are worth considerations in this realm. Also research initiatives to alert an individual regarding the online activities that can eventually lead to their abuse in dark web frame of reference based on previous history, also gain prevalence.

Crawlers

Developing crawlers that can mine the data from dark web forms an important area that requires attention. Developing intelligent crawlers that can work without human intervention is the area of research that has attained the stage of its infancy. The content based monitoring is the best way to identify security breaches and can be the best way to track illegal activities. Thus developing a crawler can be an efficient means to contribute to the curbing of illegal cyber activities in dark web space.

Contributing to a Standard Test Bed

The experiments and investigations in the area of dark web lack a performance evaluation benchmark in terms of data and approach. Thus contributing to a standard test bed that can serve as the performance measure can be a fruitful line of research.

Imposing a Consensus Mechanism

Since dark web does not have a single point of control, the imposition of policies becomes unregulated without proper consensus from nations. An adaptable, scalable and secure protocol can be a promising way to impart security regulation globally.

Reputation Management

The area of dark web forensics exhibits the need for a reputation management system that can determine the credibility of the dark web user based on his activities. The reputation management system that is capable of assessing how trustworthy an individual is and how much truthful his activities, can act as a measure of genuineness associated with him. This score can be used as a mark of credibility for all interactions with him.

Deanonymising Tool

Implementation of deanonymising tool capable of revealing the identity of users who earn bad reputation can be yet another promising area of research in dark web scenario. The blind guarantee of anonymity is the reason for propagation of objectionable activities in dark web. The warning act of deanonymisig the bad reputed individual can lessen the severity of illegal activities. But this should not be at the cost of hindrance caused to the honest users.

Thus inspecting the various aspects of the dark web researches, it is clear that the area opens door to innumerable scopes that demand serious explorations.

CONCLUSION

The chapter evinces a comprehensive overview of dark web and its potential implications. The discussion delineates the important components of dark web and elucidates the important research requirements with regard to these components. Thus in conclusion we can infer that the scope of research in the area of dark web span across diverse open challenges that require careful research considerations. They can be listed as follows.

Effective Employment of Dark Web Capabilities to Ensure Privacy

Deep web being an advancement aimed at guaranteeing privacy to a legitimate user, is to be recognized as an area that require much of concern from the part of researchers. The capabilities of deep web can be leveraged to ensure desired privacy to the user. Several privacy demanding solutions can be exported to the platform of deep web to ensure privacy and relevant usage. But exploiting it in a manner to reap benefits out of the anonymity that eventuates from it need to be put into control to establish a safe cyber realm.

Identifying the Illegal Activities Within Dark Web

Intelligent monitoring of dark web contents is very important in identifying the underlying illicit activities in the dark web sphere. This opens door for the researchers to explore on the possibilities to track the inappropriate employment of the technology. Several of these illegal activities can be controlled to an extent by operating at the user level, content level or network level. Thus user-based reputation management systems and content based identification and darkweb forensics are emerging hot areas of research.

Overcoming Dark Web Challenges

The state of the art methods to deal with dark web data mining point to the urgent need for mechanism capable of monitoring the dark web contents. The need for a mechanism to crawl dark web data without human intervention can be a promising solution to get away with the security risks associated with dark web. The current methods employed are even more constrained by the facts that intelligent automation of the procedure to gain entry is seldom possible due to the change in strategy to login, as well as the challenge associated with rich multi-media contents. Thus the research aspects need to be broadened to incorporate the effective handling of the challenges.

Immediate Recovery From the Fraudulent Acts

As important as identification of fraudulence is the recovery from fraudulence. Explorations in the area of identification of the occurrence of fraudulences and ingenious methods to decelerate severity of the aftermath attains importance in the research possibilities of dark web.

Distinguishing the Legitimate and Illegitimate Users

The efforts targeting at bringing in credibility of dark nets in turn prove to be vex to the innocent users. The policies aimed at preventing illegal exploitation, unintentionally tampers the user's privacy. Thus tracking legitimate users or the user credibility and reputation emerges as an important area to be explored.

The research initiatives in the area of dark web are at initial stage that require much consideration and efforts from researchers. The future directions of the research call for the need of unequal anonymity based on the online reputation of the users. Though the computer mediated research finds its significance in the well-being of proper deep web browsing, the need for a general consensus among the policy makers round the globe is the most essential factor that underpins the successful existence of deep web.

REFERENCES

A gentle introduction to how i2p works. (n.d.). Accessed on July 2018 https://geti2p.net/en/docs/how/intro

Back, A. (2002). Hashcash-a denial of service counter-measure. *Belkasoft*. Retrieved from https://belkasoft.com/

Bergman, M. K. (2001). White Paper: The Deep Web: Surfacing Hidden Value. *The Journal of Electronic Publishing: JEP*, 7(1). doi:10.3998/3336451.0007.104

Blockchain and Bitcoin Offer New Approach, Risks to Cyber Security. (n.d.). Accessed on July 2018, https://online.maryville.edu/blog/blockchain-and-bitcoin-offer-new-approach-risks-to-cyber-security/

Daemen, J., & Rijmen, V. (1999). *AES proposal: Rijndael*. Taher ElGamal.

Daily Dot. (n.d.). *Huge Equifax data breach affects almost 148 million Americans*. Retrieved from https://www.dailydot.com/debug/equifax-data-breach/

Davies, S. (2011). Still building the memex. *Communications of the ACM, 54*(2), 80–88. doi:10.1145/1897816.1897840

ElGamal, T. (1985). A public key cryptosystem and a signature scheme based on discrete logarithms. *IEEE Transactions on Information Theory, 31*(4), 469–472. doi:10.1109/TIT.1985.1057074

Eyal, I., & Sirer, E. G. (2018). Majority is not enough: Bitcoin mining is vulnerable. *Communications of the ACM, 61*(7), 95–102. doi:10.1145/3212998

Finklea, K. M. (2015). *Dark web*. Congressional Research Service. Accessed on July 2018 https://www.fas.org/sgp/crs/misc/R44101.pdf

Finklea, K. M. (2017). *Dark web*. Congressional Research Service.

Fu, T., Abbasi, A., & Chen, H. (2010). A focused crawler for Dark Web forums. *Journal of the American Society for Information Science and Technology, 61*(6), 1213–1231.

Going Dark. The Internet behind the Internet. (2014). Accessed August 30, 2016. http://www.npr.org/ sections/alltechconsidered/2014/05/25/315821415/going-dark-the-internet-behind-the-internet

Hernández, I., Rivero, C. R., & Ruiz, D. (2018). *World Wide Web (Bussum)*. doi:10.100711280-018-0602-1

Iliou, C., Kalpakis, G., Tsikrika, T., Vrochidis, S., & Kompatsiaris, I. (2017). Hybrid focused crawling on the Surface and the Dark Web. *EURASIP Journal on Information Security, 2017*(1), 11

Internet- deep web darknet. (n.d.). Accessed on July 2018, https://darkwebnews.com/wp-content/uploads/2017/11/internet-deep-web-darknet.png

Javelin, Identity Fraud Hits All Time High With 16.7 Million U.S. Victims in 2017, According to New Javelin Strategy & Research Study. (n.d.). Accessed on December 12 2018, https://www.javelinstrategy.com/press-release/identity-fraud-hits-all-time-high-167-million-us-victims-2017-according-new-javelin

Karame, G., Androulaki, E., & Capkun, S. (2012). Two Bitcoins at the Price of One? Double-Spending Attacks on Fast Payments in Bitcoin. *IACR Cryptology ePrint Archive, 2012*(248).

Kwon, Y., Kim, D., Son, Y., Vasserman, E., & Kim, Y. (2017, October). Be selfish and avoid dilemmas: Fork after withholding (faw) attacks on bitcoin. In *Proceedings of the 2017 ACM SIGSAC Conference on Computer and Communications Security* (pp. 195-209). ACM. 10.1145/3133956.3134019

Malhotra, Y. (2013). *Bitcoin Protocol: Model of 'Cryptographic Proof' Based Global Crypto-Currency & Electronic Payments System. Monic Thudja, The Impact of Blockchain (and Bitcoin) on Cybersecurity*. Accessed on July 2018, https://www.incapsula.com/blog/impact-of-blockchain-bitcoin-on-cybersecurity.html

Mosakheil, J. H. (2018). *Security Threats Classification in Blockchains*. Academic Press.

Nakamoto, S. (2008). *Bitcoin: A peer-to-peer electronic cash system*. Academic Press.

Narayanan, A., Bonneau, J., Felten, E., Miller, A., & Goldfeder, S. (2016). *Bitcoin and cryptocurrency technologies: a comprehensive introduction*. Princeton University Press.

Ntoulas, A., Zerfos, P., & Cho, J. (2005, June). Downloading textual hidden web content through keyword queries. In *Proceedings of the 5th ACM/IEEE-CS joint conference on Digital libraries* (pp. 100-109). ACM. 10.1145/1065385.1065407

Olivia. (2018). *Bitcoin and Cyber Security: Digital Frenemies*. Accessed on July 2018, https://www.cybrary.it/2018/01/bitcoin-cyber-security-digital-frenemies/

Pederson, S. (2013). *White Paper: Understanding the deep Web in 10 MinUtes*. Birghtplanet.

Pinheiro, M. (2017). Know Thy Enemies. *IOSR Journal Of Humanities And Social Science, 22*(10), 39–44.

Poulsen, K. (2007). FBI's secret spyware tracks down teen who made bomb threats. *Priv. Secur. Crime Online, 1*, 40–44.

Rathod, D. (2017). Darknet Forensics. *International Journal of Emerging Trends and Technology in Computer Science, 4*(6).

Spencer, B., Benedikt, M., & Senellart, P. (2018, June). Form filling based on constraint solving. In *International Conference on Web Engineering* (pp. 95-113). Springer. 10.1007/978-3-319-91662-0_7

Stefany. (n.d.). *Electronic Civil Disobedience and the World Wide Web of Hacktivism: A Mapping of Extraparliamentarian.* Retrieved from https://www.webpagefx.com/research/electronic-civil-disobedience-hacktivism.html

Sui, D., Caverlee, J., & Rudesill, D. (2015). T*he deep web and the darknet: a look inside the internet's massive black box.* Google Scholar.

Tapscott, D., & Tapscott, A. (2017, June). *Realizing the Potential of Blockchain. A Multistakeholder Approach to the Stewardship of Blockchain and Cryptocurrencies.* World Economic Forum White Paper. Tor Project. Accessed on July 2018 https://www.torproject.org/about/overview.html

Tor Project. (n.d.). *Tor at the Heart: The Ahmia project| The Tor Blog.* Retrieved June 12, 2018, from https://blog.torproject.org/tor-heart-ahmia-project

van Hardeveld, G. J., Webber, C., & O'Hara, K. (2017). Deviating From the Cybercriminal Script: Exploring Tools of Anonymity (Mis) Used by Carders on Cryptomarkets. *The American Behavioral Scientist, 61*(11), 1244–1266. doi:10.1177/0002764217734271

Vyas, C. A., & Lunagaria, M. (2014). Security concerns and issues for bitcoin. *Proceedings of National Conference cum Workshop on Bioinformatics and Computational Biology.*

KEY TERMS AND DEFINITIONS

Bit Coins: Bit coins are cryptocurrencies that enable transactions that involve only the owner and the receiver party, and the transactions are broadcast via P2P network.

Dark Web: It is regarded as the subset of deep web and is accessible only via special browsers known as onion routers. Thus, the sites within it are those with URLs ending in .onion. This part of the internet offers the user the highest level of anonymity. This in turn has proven to be a reason for proliferation of illegal activities in dark web.

Darknet Forensics: The fraudulent activities taking place in the veil of darknet need to be addressed by considering the frameworks capable of identifying and countering the illegal activities. The field of study aimed at identifying the fraudulences in dark web can be categorized into darknet forensics.

Deanonymisation: It is a datamining technique that aims at the identification of source of data that is anonymous in nature by utilizing information capable of differentiating one source form other.

Deep Web: The part of internet that contains sites that are not indexed by search engines and are not available to users by ordinary browsers. This includes account specific details like social network account profile page which is accessible only via password protected login procedure.

Invisible Internet Project: This is a network within network that guarantees privacy in transmitting crucial information without the risk of external surveillance. A message from source to destination traverses via several intermediate tunnels which ultimately reaches the intended recipient and these data packets are encrypted.

Onion Router: TOR is a decentralized network and is a protocol that encrypts the data and sends the traffic through random intermediate nodes that serve as the relay machines. In this way the IP address of the sender remains undisclosed to the destined recipient.

Chapter 11
Enhanced Security for Network Communication With Proposed IS–IS Protocol

Onder Onursal
Girne American University, Cyprus

Arif Sari
iD https://orcid.org/0000-0003-0902-9988
Girne American University Canterbury, UK

ABSTRACT

This chapter is a literature review of intermediate system to intermediate system (IS-IS) routing protocol to provide basic security mechanisms against cyber-attacks and enhance network security. IS-IS was originally developed by the International Organization for Standardization (ISO) as a link state routing protocol. It was first built with the ability to route CLNPs or connectionless network protocols according to the OSI standard equal to IP. IS-IS is also developed so that it can accommodate routing for any layer three-based protocol. Internet Engineering Task Force (IETF) in 1990 specified the support for IP and introduced IPv6 extensions in 2000. IS-IS protocol implementation was written as modules in order for it to be distributed freely and easily installed on the GNU routing software. SourceForge.net supported the project and gave access for developers to easily contribute to the project. The chapter elaborates the ISIS routing protocol for network security and proposes a critical survey on security routing protocols.

DOI: 10.4018/978-1-5225-8976-1.ch011

Copyright © 2019, IGI Global. Copying or distributing in print or electronic forms without written permission of IGI Global is prohibited.

INTRODUCTION

Describe The IS-IS is an interior Gateway Protocol (IGPP) licensed by the IETF. It is commonly used for large network service provider. IS-IS provides rapid scalability and convergence based on a link-state routing protocol. It makes use of network bandwidth which makes it very efficient.

Cisco is one of the active IS-IS member group under IETF, they make most of the updates and enhancements in the protocol (Medhi & Ramasamy, 2018a). IS-IS was initially developed following the Digital Equipment Corporation DECNET phase 5 Network Technology.

In naming its protocol, IS-IS utilizes a terminology slightly different from the OSPF naming terminology. Packets sent to describe network topologies are termed link-state protocol data units. IP routes checksums and other information make up the PDUs.

All received information recorded in the received link-stated PDU are placed in their respective link state database just as in OSPF. IS-IS run the SPF algorithm contained in the link-state database. The shortest destination path on the network is determined and next destination placed depending on the outcome of calculations on the routing database (Cisco, n.d.a).

IS-IS functions on Layer 2 of OIS which separates it from other IP routing protocols. Large routing domains are supported using two-level hierarchy. Large domains can administratively be divided into different areas. Each system resides in one area in this form of routing. Level 1 routing refers to routing within same location while level 2 routing involves routing in different areas. Tracks of destination area path is recorded by a level 2 system while level 1 intermediate system records routing tracks in its area. Packets are sent by a level 1 IS to the closest level 2 IS not considering the destination of the packets for packets destined to another area. Packets move from routing level 2 to the targeted destination area, where it otherwise would have moved from routing level 1 to the target destination. Note, selecting an end destination from routing level 1 to the closest level 2 system might lead to a suboptimal packet routing.

As a control plane for IEEE 802.1aq SPB, IS-IS is usually applied. SPB allows forwarding based on shortest-path on a mesh network. Many paths with equal cost paths are used to make it possible. SPM provides support for large layer 2 topologies thereby improving the utilization of mesh topology and fast convergence. Small number of sub-TLVs and TLVs are used to augment IS-IS. The 802.lah and 802.lad providers are supported by IS-IS. No state machines and other substantive changes to IS-IS are required by SPB.

IS-IS operates from a high level as follows:

- Hello packets are sent out from routers running IS-IS to all interfaces with enabled IS-IS. This is done to identify neighbors and subsequently establish adjacencies.
- If a hello packet bears information meeting stated requirement and is sent from routers having common data link, an IS-IS neighborhood can then be created if all requirements for adjacency is met. Depending on the kind of media used, requirements for forming adjacency differs. The most important requirements considered are the MTU size, matching authentication and IS-type.
- Based on local interfaces of routers configured for IS-IS and prefixes information gotten from other routers, routers develop a link-state packet (LSP).
- Link-state databases are constructed by routers from LSPs.
- The shortest path routing table is created by computing the shortest-path tree (SPT) (Goralski, Gadecki, & Bushong, 2011).

INTERIOR GATEWAY ROUTING PROTOCOL

Protocols used for routing can be classified based of the purpose, operation and behavior.

Exterior Gateway Protocol (EGP) and Interior Gateway Protocol are classification based on purpose, Link-state protocol, distance vector protocol and path-vector protocol are classification based on operation while classless or classful protocol are classification based on operation.

Group of routers within a known administration is called autonomous system (AS). Example of such common administration includes an organization or a company. An ISP's network or the internal networks of a company are examples of an AS.

Internet is built on the basic concept of an AS. As a result, two routing protocols of IGP and EGP are considered:

IGP which refers to the interior gateway protocol are implemented for routing in AS. This concept is referred to as intra-AS routing. Some forms of intra-AS routing include OSPF, RIP, EIGRP and IS-IS. Organizations and service providers utilize these protocols.

EGP which refers to Exterior Gateway protocols are on the other hand used for autonomous system routing. This form of routing is also known as inter-AS routing. EGP can be used as an interconnection for companies and service providers in this case. In this case, the EGP which is the official internet routing protocol is the Border Gateway Protocol (BGP) (Cisco, n.d.).

IGRP which refers to Interior Gateway Routing Protocol allows communication in a host.

IGRP was created by Cisco to handle the limitations observed in Routing Information Protocol (RIP). With this improvement IGRP can handle a maximum hop count of 255 compared to the initial 15 count handled by RIP. IGRP achieves two main goals:

1. Relate routing information to routers connected within its autonomous system or boundary.
2. Update continuously if a change occurs in the network path.

Every 90 seconds, IGRP updates all connected routers on changes within the network.

A routing table with records of optimal paths to nodes and sub networks within a parent network is effectively managed by IGRP. As a distance vector protocol, it utilizes distant parameters to determine metric for best path to destinations. Bandwidth, load, delay, reliability and MTU are some of the parameters used by IGRP.

For bandwidth, reliability, internetwork delay and load, IGRP utilizes a composite metric derived based on the factoring of weighted values. The weighting factor can be defined by administrators for each metrics. Guidelines should be strictly adhered to before adjusting any value. Reliability and load bear values somewhere in the range of 1 and 255; data transfer capacity can take values that are reflecting speed from 1200 bps to 10 Gbps, while lags can take on any incentive from 1 to 224. These wide measurement ranges are additionally supplemented by a progression of user perceptible constants.

"The constants are hashed against the metrics in an algorithm that yields a single, composite metric. The network administrator can influence route selection by giving higher or lower weighting to a specific metric".

The IGRP permits several gateways to manage their routing for some reasons (Medhi & 2018b).

1. Stable routing complex systems.
2. No routing circles ought to happen.

3. Rapid reaction to changes in system structure.
4. Low overhead. IGRP ought not to utilize more data transfer capacity than required for its assignment.
5. Dividing traffic among a few routes with equal attractive quality.
6. Taking into record mistake rates and dimension of traffic on various ways.

Present application of IGRP manages routing for TCP/IP. However, different protocols are handled by the normal structure.

"A single tool cannot handle routing problems. Usually routing problems are divided into multiple parts. IGRPs are referred to as "Internal Gateway Protocols". IGPs are applied within sets of individual networks and managed singularly or coordinately. For coordinated networks, External Gateway Protocols (EGPs) are used. IGPs are designed for keeping record of the network topology. Main objective of developing an IGP is to produce respond quickly to change while establishing optimal routes.

EGPs serve to save guide a single system of networks from intentional misrepresentation by other systems or against errors. An example of protocol used is BGP. EGP is designed with administrative controls and stability as priority. EGP usually produce reasonable routes rather than optimal routes"

The Xerox's protocol which is an older routing protocol has some of its characteristics found in IGRP, other protocols with similarities include Dave Mills' Hello and Berkeley's RIP. The major difference IGPR has from these older protocols is that IGPR are developed specifically for more complex and large networks.

Just as older protocols, IGPR is based on adjacent gateways. Routing information contains summaries regarding the entire network. Using distributed algorithm, all gateways can be represented mathematically as solving same problem. Each gateway solves a portion of the task and receives only part of the data.

A compliment to IGRP is Enhanced IGRP (EIGRP) and SPF (shortest-path first) algorithms. OSPF technique is based on flooding, every gateway is updated about the status of every interface on other gateways. Using data from the entire network, each gateway optimizes a solution from its own point of view. Each approach has some advantages. In some cases, SPF responds quickly to changes. To avoid routing loops, new data are ignored for some minutes after changes have been implemented. SPF gets information straight from each gateway. This helps to overcome routing loops. New information can be addressed immediately. Nevertheless, in messages between gateway and in internal data structures, SPF handles higher volume of data when compared to IGRP.

IGRP offers a wide range of features designated for stability enhancement such as split horizons and holddowns.

- **Holddowns**: They are utilized to keep frequently updated messages from improperly reestablishing a dead route. At the point router is down, other routers recognize this by not getting the normal scheduled messages. New routes are then computed by the routers and messages dispersed informing neighbors of the change of route. This starts an influx of activated updates that passes through the system. These activated updates don't arrive instantly to every connected device. Subsequently, a network device yet to be informed about the failure can attempt to sending an update message announcing a failed route as active to a device which was previously informed about the system failure. In this case inaccurate routing data will be contained by the device. Holddowns instructs routers to delay any change that may influence routes for some timeframe. The holddown period is generally determined to be more noteworthy than the timeframe important to update the whole system with a route change.
- **Split horizons:** It takes note of the reason of which data regarding a route cannot be sent back to its source. R1 pitches a route to network A. No reason behind R2 consolidating back to R1 since route R1 has more proximity to Network A. This principle stipulates that route R2 strikes this available route from subsequent updates sent to R1. The split-horizontal standard maintains a strategic distance from the superfluous reiteration of routing. Holddowns should keep this, split-horizons helps in maintaining the algorithm (Medhi & Ramasamy, 2018a).

DVR or Distance Vector Routing Protocols

Distance vector routing (DVR) is a routing protocol that is distributed. It permits automatic discovery of reachable destination by routers in a network. Shortest paths to each destination are also determined by the DVR protocol. Considering associated costs or metrics, the DVR records shortest paths (Riley et al., 2003).

The distance vector protocol is intended to work with smaller networks. Instances of such protocols incorporate IGRP and RIP. They are easy to design and do not require more support than connection-state protocols.

High CPU and transfer speed usage are required. Therefore, they make use of more combination time than the link state protocol.

Hop counts are used by distance vector protocol to identify the best path possible within an internetwork. The sum of routers a packet will access to from a host A to another host B is referred to as the hop count. For example, if A sends a "telnet" request to another host, and packet must pass three switches to reach B, at that point the hop count is 3 (Cisco, 2005).

Distance vector protocol dependably picks the shortest hop count as the best choice. An issue can however arise when the path with the shortest hop count does not represent the best path available. "For example, supposes host A is trying to connect to host B and there are two paths available: Router A is using a T-3 connection and Router B is using a dial-up 28.8 Kbps connection. If Router B is one hop away, but Router A is two hops away, Router B will be chosen as the best route, even though it's not the fastest alternative".

Routing Information Protocol (RIP)

RIP is an IGP. It was developed to manage smaller networks. RIP is based on distance-vector algorithm. It has many limitations and is not suitable for every TCP/IP environment.

The best possible route is determined in RIP using hop count. In RIP, when a hop count equals 16 it means the destination is unreachable. This limits the longest path in the network that can be managed by RIP to 15 gateways.

"An RIP router broadcasts routing information to its directly connected networks every 30 seconds. It receives updates from neighboring RIP routers every 30 seconds and uses the information contained in these updates to maintain the routing table. If an update has not been received from a neighboring RIP router in 180 seconds, a RIP router assumes that the neighboring RIP router is down, sets all routes through that router to a metric of 16 (infinity), and stops using those routes when routing IP packets. If an update has still not been received from the neighboring RIP router after another 120 seconds, the RIP router deletes from the routing table all of the routes through that neighboring RIP router".

Route Tags

The Route tags are utilized to isolate inward RIP Routes from outside routes that may have been gotten from another IGP or an EGP.

Variable Subnetting Support

Variable length subnet is incorporated into routing data with the goal of reaching dynamically added routes outside a system.

Immediate Next Hop for Shorter Paths

Next hop addresses are incorporated into routing data to dispense with packets being routed through additional hops in the system.

Authentication for Routing Update Security

Authentication keys can be configured for inclusion in outgoing RIP Version 2 packets. Incoming RIP Version 2 packets are checked against the configured keys.

Super Netting Support

The super netting highlight is a part of Classless Interdomain Routing (CIDR). Super netting gives an approach to consolidate different system routes into fewer routes, along these lines diminishing the quantity of courses in the directing table and in advertisements.

Enhanced Interior Gateway Routing Protocol (EIGRP)

In Open system interconnection (OSI) and TCP/IP GRP is used. This technology excludes the need for individual routers to learn link relationships of the entire network. Using a corresponding distance, destinations are advertised by individual routers. Distances are adjusted and propagated by each sending and receiving router.

"The distance information in IGRP is represented as a composite of available bandwidth, delay, load utilization, and link reliability. This allows fine tuning of link characteristics to achieve optimal paths".

EIGRP is an improved version of IGRP. Distance vector technology is also used in IGRP, and the underlying distance information does not change. It retains existing IGRP investment as it supports improved architecture.

Loop-freedom throughout a route is achieved using Diffusing Update Algorithm (DUAL). Synchronization of routers in a topology becomes possible with loop-freedom. Routers immune from the effect of topology are excluded in this recompilation.

EIGRP has expanded to be and independent network-layer protocol, hence it allows DUAL support for other protocol suites.

EIGRP consists of Four fundamental elements: Discovery/recovery of Neighbor, Reliable Transport Protocol (RTP), DUAL Finite State Machine, and Protocol Dependent Modules.

- **Neighbor Discovery/Recovery:** It refers to the ability of a router to learn dynamically about routers attached to its network. Routers also can learn when a router is reachable or not. This is achieved by sending "hello" packets to learn the state of connected neighbors. inasmuch as a received notification for the sent package is gotten, a neighbor can be identified as active. On determining that the neighbor is active, communication can now take place.
- Reliable transport ensures that ordered EIGRP packets are delivered successfully to neighbors. Intermixed transmission of unicast or multicast packets is supported by EIGRP. It is an essential requirement for some EIGRP packets to be reliably transferred whereas other packets may be transmitted without the reliability check. On a multi-access network with multicast abilities for example reliability is not necessary. A single hello is multicast to receivers with indications informing receivers the packets do not need to be recognized. Packets such as updates need acknowledgment. Such need for acknowledgement is also noted in the packets. When there are no unacknowledged packets, reliable transport can send multicast packets quickly. This feature ensures a low convergence time amidst different speed links.
- DUAL finite state machines incorporate decision making for every route and monitors advertised routes. Metrics are used to select the best loops of free paths. Based on possible successors, routes are selected to be included on a routing table. Successors is a router within the neighborhood used to forward a packet having at least cost path to a destination not part of the routing loop. A recompilation must take place when there exist neighbors advertising a destination but no possible successors. During recompilation a new successor is assigned. Convergence time is affected by the duration of recompilation. Though recompilation is not processor-intensive, it is recommended it is avoided if possible (Aboelela, 2003).
- The protocol-dependent modules are responsible for network layer, protocol-specific requirements. For example, the IP-EIGRP module

is responsible for sending and receiving EIGRP packets that are encapsulated in IP. IP-EIGRP is responsible for parsing EIGRP packets and informing DUAL of the new information received. IP-EIGRP asks DUAL to make routing decisions and the results of which are stored in the IP routing table. IP-EIGRP is responsible for redistributing routes learned by other IP routing protocols.

Link State Routing Protocol

This protocol is intended to work in enterprise-level systems. They are exceptionally complex and are substantially harder to install, manage, and investigate when compared to distance vector protocols. Nevertheless, link state protocols conquer lots of observable weaknesses of vector protocols.

"Link state protocols use a different algorithm than distance vector protocols for calculating the best path to a destination. This algorithm takes into account bandwidth as well as other factors when calculating the best path for a packet to traverse the network. Additionally, link state convergence occurs faster than distance vector convergence. This is because link state establishes a neighbor relationship with directly connected peers and shares routing information with its neighbors only when there are changes in the network topology" (Aboelela, 2003).

Open Shortest Path First

In distributing routing information amidst a unit autonomous system, the open Shortest Path First protocol (OSPF) is used. Resulting in other to introduce a functional internal Gateway Protocol (IGP) the OSPF protocol was introduced.

The OSPF protocol is based on link-state technology, which is a departure from the Bellman-Ford vector-based algorithms used in traditional Internet routing protocols such as RIP. OSPF has introduced new concepts such as authentication of routing updates, Variable Length Subnet Masks (VLSM), route summarization, and so forth."

OSPF has preferable convergence over RIP. Because routing changes are proliferated quickly and not occasionally. It likewise takes into consideration better load balancing. It takes into consideration a legitimate meaning of systems with possibilities of routers to be isolated. This additionally gives a technique to accumulating routes and eliminating superfluous engendering of subnet data.

OSPF considers directing confirmation by utilizing diverse techniques for secret word verification. OSPF considers the exchange and labeling of outside routes infused into an Autonomous System. This monitors outer routes infused by outside conventions, for example, BGP.

Intermediate System to Intermediate System (IS-IS)

Intermediate systems allude to a router referring to a node. ES-IS protocols enable routers and hubs to recognize one each other; IS-IS performs a similar role between nodes used in routing purposes in the same manner as other routing protocols, for example, OSPF (Open Shortest Path First) (Rouse & Ward, 2007).

IS-IS stores data about the condition of links and utilizations that information to choose paths. IS-IS is utilized to irregularly convey link state data over the network, so every router can keep up a present picture of system topology. Discretionary measurements are utilized to distinguish organize deferral, cost, and error triggered with the utilization of a specific connection.

ISPs possess the potential of forming several VRF-aware IS-IS instances running on a single router, instead of the need of more than one router. ISPs use this feature to separate client information whereas adding the data to applicable providers (Cisco, n.d.b).

Link-state is more advantageous than distance-vector protocols. It conveys data faster, accommodates larger internetworks, and is also less susceptible to unnecessary routing loops (Cisco, 2007).

IS-IS features include:

- Hierarchical routing
- Classless behavior
- Rapid flooding of new information
- Fast Convergence
- Very scalable
- Flexible timer tuning

Similarities and Differences of OSPF and IS-IS

One major difference between OSPF and IS-IS is the way they operate. Unlike OSPF, IS-IS can send the routing information of any routable protocol without restriction of IP. Below are some of the comparisons of the protocols (Cisco, 2007).

Comparing Basic Characteristics (Similarities)

- Both protocols are widely used
- They both work on link-state protocols
- IP environment are supported by both
- Hierarchical design and area division are adopted on both protocols

Comparing Basic Characteristics (Differences)

- CLNP environment is supported by IS-IS
- Only PPP and broadcast network are supported by IS-IS; PPP is supported by OSPF, it also supports P2MP, broadcast and NBMA network.
- Virtual link can be applied to OSPF
- There are differences in encapsulation format of packets
- Attachment of OSPF routers to multiple areas having different interfaces is possible. However, it is possible to attach IS-IS routers to only one area. Comparison of Adjacency Relationship

Comparison of Adjacency Relationship (Similarities)

- Comparison of adjacency relationship (Similarities)
- Neighbors discovery and formation of adjacencies via Hello Protocol
- DR election is on multi-access networks

Comparison of Adjacency Relationship (Differences)

- Adjacencies formation conditions are not the same in OSPF, formations on PPP links are more reliable.
- Nodes form adjacencies with BDR and DR only in OSPF but not with one another. However, in IS-IS every node form adjacency with one another.
- DIS and DR elections process are different.

Comparison of the Link-State Database Synchronization Process (Similarities)

- Basic mechanism of LSDB synchronization is followed by both protocols.
- Comparison of the link-state database synchronization process (Differences):
- IS-IS utilizes only LSP routers and pseudo node LSP whereas OSPF utilizes several different LSA.
- Process of synchronization is totally different in the two protocols
- Time remaining is counted from 0 to 15 minutes in the LSP in other to clear existing LSP whereas time remaining is goes up to 60 minutes in the OSPF.

Comparison of Route Calculation Process (Similarities)

- SPF algorithm is used in both protocols for route calculation.

Comparison of Route Calculation Process (Differences)

- IP prefixes are treated as belonging to the SPT node in OSPF whereas IS-IS treats them as leaves of SPT
- In comparison to OSPF, IS-IS has more complex matric type.

Comparison of Performance (Similarities)

- The protocols are fast convergence, loop-free and support large-scale networks

Comparison of Performance (Differences)

- Dial on demand links are supported by OSPF whereas it is not supported in IS-IS (Cameron, Cantrell, Killion, Russel, & Tam, 2005).

IS-IS ROUTING DOMAIN

Routers run Integrated IS-IS protocol via IS-IS domains and oblige intradomain transfers of routing information. IP-only can be used, ISO CLNP-only, or both. The IS-IS protocol was at first developed for CLNP only. RFC 1195 adjusts the first IS-IS detail (ISO 10589) to accommodate IP, which is now known as integrated IS-IS.

Designing dual domains such that selected areas only route IP and others CLNP, or a combination of IP and CLNP is possible. However, restrictions have been imposed by RFC 1195 on the way CLNP and IP can be combined in an area. The main objective of IS-IS routing is achieving the steady routing information occurring inside an area by assigning unique link-state databases on routers in same location. Subsequently, routers designated within an area are expected to be designed following the same protocol of IP only or CLNP alone or both. Routers in the same designated area cannot have two different configurations. However, no such restriction exists in the domain level. Same protocols or different combination of protocols can be maintained by routers on this level. Connections to a backbone can have routers connected in different ways. However, links connecting areas must have the same configuration (Magnani, Carvalho, & Noronha, 2016).

The CLNP addresses comprises of the following 3 components:

1.   Area identifier prefix
2.   System Identifier
3.   N-selector.

N-selector represents users of network services, example is routing layer or transport protocol. N-selector can be considered like the IP transmission control protocol (TCP) or the application port number in use (Boukerche et al., 2011).

IS-IS AREAS AND ROUTING HIERARCHIES

Group or routers are considered from same area if they have same area identifier (ID). It is important to remember that IS-IS routers relate to a physical geographical area. This area is determined based on the identifier of the area contained in NSAP. Using multiple NSAPs routers can be programmed such that each have different area identifiers but the same system identifiers (sysID) in locations with need of routers connecting to multiple areas. Utilizing multiple connections however, all areas are merged into one physical area. Such routers participating in a common location and are involved level 1 routing are known as level 1 routers (D'Arienzo & Romano, 2016). Collection of adjacency information and SysID are features of CLNP routing for routers involved in level 1 routing. Information are exchanged among routers located in different places utilizing level 2 routing. This form of routers is known as backbone or level 2 routers. Location prefix information are exchanged with routers in Level 2 routing. In IP routing, exchange of prefixes within an area is done in level 1 routing (Vallet & Brun, 2014).

A routing domain is divided into zones and L1 routers bear information regarding their very own zone won't know the data of routers or locations outside of their region. Level 1-only routers look at the appended bit in level 1 LSPs to locate the nearest L1/L2 router in the area and utilize the nearest L1/L2 router to leave the area.

Between territories routing may have neighbors around and will know the level 2 topology and which addresses reachable by means of each level 2 routes. They don't have to know the topology inside any level 1 area, but to the degree that a dimension 2 switch may likewise be a level 1 router inside a solitary area. They can pass information packets or routing information straightforwardly with external routers situated outside of its area (Medhi & Ramasamy 2018b).

Cisco routers running IS-IS can be configured to be either Level 1-only, Level 2-only, or both. By default, they are both Level 1 and Level 2, and special configuration is required to disable Level 1 or Level 2 capability. Caution must be taken when disabling either capability because this might introduce disruptive inconsistencies into the routing environment. Routers RTA-1, RTA-2, RTA-3, and RTX must be Level 2-capable to participate in routing between the areas. RTX can be in its own dedicated area and because it doesn't connect to any Level 1 routers, it can be configured to be Level 2-only. However, the others must be Level 1-2 and each identified with a specific area for which it provides interarea connectivity. RTB-n, RTC-n (n = 1,2,3) can be configured to be Level 1-only if they don't need to connect to the backbone. (Martey, 2002a).

IS-IS PACKETS AND PACKET FORMAT

It is important to understand the basics of packet formats and IS-IS packets before delving to more advance notion in IS-IS protocol. With this knowledge, we will have better understanding of the protocol and its application. Data is transmitted as packets in connectionless oriented protocols of which IP and CLNP are examples. According to ISO 10589 standards, packets are described as PDUs (protocol data units). In a connectionless environment more than one packet types are utilized (Goralski, 2017).

The IS-IS packets consist of three different categories of:

- "Hello Packets"
- Link-state packets and
- Sequence number packets.

The hello packets trigger and make sure IS-IS neighbors are adjacently placed. The distribution of routing information from one node to another is done by the sequence number packets and link-state packets control the distribution of nodes (i.e. link-state packets), also implementing synchronization of databases in a routing area (Lv, Wang, Zhang, & Huang, 2018).

A common header is shared by each IS-IS. The following PDUs are used by IS-IS for information exchange.

The IS-IS Hello (IIH) PDUs is sent to neighboring system in other to discover the active state of the neighbors. The PDU also determines the level of the system. Adjacencies are established with other routers based on three unique formats.

Preset lengths are assigned to Hello PDUs. PDUs are not resized by the IS-IS router in other to match the maximum transmission unit (MTU). A maximum IS-IS PDU size of 1492 bytes is supported by each interface. The hello PDUs are padded to fit to the maximum IS-IS byte.

Link-state PDUs: Information regarding the state of adjacencies are contained in the link-state PDUs. Periodical flooding occurs to the Link-state PDUs within an area. PDUs need to be refreshed periodically and acknowledgement sent inform of information within a few PDU.

A partial sequence number is used to identify each link-state on a point-to-point. On broadcast however, complete sequence number (CSN) is sent to the entire network.

Complete sequence number PDUs (CSNPs): The complete sequence number PDUs contains complete lists of link-state PDUs. CSNPs are periodically sent to all links. The recepient system utilize information contained in the CSNP to update their link-state PDU storage. Routers send multicasts on CSNPs via broadcast.

Partial sequence number PDUs (PSNPs): Multicast messages are sent by receivers when a missing link-state PDU is detected. A PSNP is sent by the receiver to the system transmitting CSNP, this PSNP requests the missing link-state PDU be retransmitted. The routing devices subsequently forwards missing link-state PDU to the router requesting a transmission.

"A PSNP is used by an IS-IS router to request link-state PDU information from a neighboring router. A PSNP can also explicitly acknowledge the receipt of a link-state PDU on a point-to-point link. On a broadcast link, a CSNP is used as implicit knowledge. Like hello PDUs and CSNPs, the PSNP also has two types: Level 1 and Level 2" (Juniper Networks, 2018).

When the link-state PDU is missing by a device comparing its local database to a CSNP, a PSNP is issued by the router for the lost link-state PDU. The PDU is then returned to a link-state PDU by the router releasing the CSNP. Upon completion, the link-state PDU is saved on a local database with an acknowledgment sent to the sending router.

Reachability information contained in IS-IS link-state PDUs are preserved for IPv4 and IPv6 configurations. During link-state PDU regeneration, IP prefixes and their original packet are preserved (Liu, Barber, & DiGrande, 2009).

Table 1 shows IS-IS packet types.

IS-IS PROTOCOL FUNCTIONS

The routing layer limits given by the IS-IS convention are consistently orchestrated into 2 central classes: subnetwork-dependent capacities and subnetwork-independent capacities. In IS-IS, subnetwork implies the data interface layer. This differentiation from IP language where a subnetwork

Table 1. ISIS packet types

Category	Packet Type	Type Number
Hello	LAN Level-1 Hello	15
	LAN Level-2 Hello	16
	Point-to-point Hello	17
LSP	Level-1 LSP	18
	Level-2 LSP	20
PSNP	Level-1 Complete SNP	24
	Level-2 Complete SNP	25
	Level-1 Partial SNP	26
	Level-2 Partial SNP	27

relates to IP address subnet. Exclusively 2 sorts of IS-IS subnetworks are of reasonable noteworthiness in current uses of the IS-IS convention: point-to-point and communication links.

The subnetwork-dependent functions identify with abilities for interfacing with the data-link layer. It essentially includes tasks for sleuthing, shaping, and keeping up routing adjacencies with neighboring switches over differed sorts of interconnecting system media or connections. The ES-IS protocol and beyond any doubt segments of CLNP are critical to the task of the subnetwork-subordinate capacities.

"The subnetwork-independent functions provide the capabilities for exchange and processing of routing information and related control information between adjacent routers as validated by the subnetwork-dependent functions" (Martey, 2002b).

The IS-IS routing engine expounds on the connection between subsystems (procedures and databases) that give the subnetwork-free capacities inside the structure of a regular router.

General Topology Subnetworks

General topology subnetworks are for all time built upon point-to-point links. A previous case is Packet over SONET/SDH. Asynchronous Transfer Mode (ATM) point-to-point switched virtual circuit (SVC) is a case of the last mentioned.

Broadcast Subnetworks

They are local-area network media having communication capacities. Dynamic Packet Transport Technology (DPT) and Ethernet are an example of broadcast subnetworks (Medhi & Ramasamy, 2018c).

Security Issues in IS-IS

The IS-IS protocol is one of a family of IP Routing protocols. IS-IS does not run over Internet Protocol (IP) Each ISIS router diffuse information about its local state. This is done by specifying the best route for the information through a packet-switched network and operating by reliably flooding link state information throughout a network of routers.

The main disadvantages of Intermediate System – Intermediate System is that totally one system has only one network service access point (NASP) address (Goralski, 2009).

CONCLUSION

IS-IS is one of a kind among the present routing protocols, due to its multiprotocol structure. Incorporated routing of CLNS and IPv4 probably won't intrigue many yet IS-IS utilized as single routing protocol for both IPv4 and IPv6 is entirely attainable.

The contrasts among OSPFv3 and IS-IS are not major, and the previous is in reality nearer to IS-IS than OSPFv2. Also, introduction of IPv6 support in IS-IS was anything but difficult to accomplish, IS-IS was the first link state routing protocol that includes support for IPv6 inside the routers of most vendors.

The execution ISIS was done as an open source project and had an immense number of developers from everywhere throughout the world. Starting at 2002 ISIS has been dealing with IPv6 routing on a FreeBSD workstation that goes about as a router between production and a test organize at the Institute of Communications Engineering of Tampere University of Technology.

REFERENCES

Aboelela, E. (2003). Laboratory 7 - OSPF: Open Shortest Path First: A Routing Protocol Based on the Link-State Algorithm. In *Network Simulation Experiments Manual*. Morgan Kaufmann. doi:10.1016/B978-012042171-8/50022-

Andrés, S., Kenyon, B., & Birkholz, E. P. (2004). *Routing Devices and Protocols, Security Sage's Guide to Hardening the Network Infrastructure*. Syngress. doi:10.1016/B978-193183601-2/50010-5

Boukerche, A., Turgut, B., Aydin, N., Ahmad, M. Z., Bölöni, L., & Turgut, D. (2011). Routing protocols in ad hoc networks: A survey. *Computer Networks, 55*(13), 3032-3080. doi:10.1016/j.comnet.2011.05.010

Cameron, R., Cantrell, C., Killion, D., Russell, K., & Tam, K. (2005). Routing. In Configuring NetScreen Firewalls. Syngress. doi:10.1016/B978-193226639-9/50011-6

Cisco. (2005). *Cisco Networking Academy, Introduction to EIGRP, 2005.* Retrieved from: https://www.cisco.com/c/en/us/support/docs/ip/enhanced-interior-gateway-routing-protocol-eigrp/13669-1.html#intro

Cisco. (2007). *Cisco Networking Academy, Intermediate System-to-Intermediate System Protocol, White Paper, 2007.* Retrieved from: https://www.cisco.com/en/US/tech/tk365/technologies_white_paper09186a00800a3e6f.shtml

Cisco. (n.d.a). *Cisco Datasheets, Intermediate System-to-Intermediate System (IS-IS).* Retrieved from https://www.cisco.com/c/en/us/products/ios-nx-os-software/intermediate-system-to-intermediate-system-is-is/index.html

Cisco. (n.d.b). *Cisco Networking Academy, IS-IS Protocol and IP-Route and Configurations.* Retrieved from: https://content.cisco.com/chapter.sjs?uri=/searchable/chapter/content/en/us/td/docs/ios-xml/ios/iproute_isis/configuration/xe-16-6/irs-xe-16-6-book/

Cisco Networking Academy. (2014). *Cisco Networking Academy's Introduction to Routing Dynamically.* Available at: http://www.ciscopress.com/articles/article.asp?p=2180210&seqNum=7

D'Arienzo, M., & Romano, S. P. (2016). GOSPF: An energy efficient implementation of the OSPF routing protocol. *Journal of Network and Computer Applications, 75,* 110-127. doi:10.1016/j.jnca.2016.07.011

Goralski, W. (2009). IGPs: RIP, OSPF, and IS—IS. In The Illustrated Network. Morgan Kaufmann. doi:10.1016/B978-0-12-374541-5.50021-3

Goralski, W. (2017). IGPs: RIP, OSPF, and IS-IS. In The Illustrated Network (2nd ed.). Morgan Kaufmann. doi:10.1016/B978-0-12-811027-0.00015-1

Goralski, W. J., Gadecki, C., & Bushong, M. (2011). *JUNOS OS For Dummies: The IS-IS Protocol functionalities* (2nd ed.). Retrieved from https://www.dummies.com/store/product/JUNOS-OS-For-Dummies-2nd-Edition.productCd-0470891890.html

Juniper Networks. (2018). *IS-IS overview*. Retrieved from https://www.juniper. net/documentation/en_us/junos/topics/concept/is-is-routing-overview.html

Liu, D., Barber, B., & DiGrande, L. (2009). Routing Protocols: RIP, RIPv2, IGRP, EIGRP, OSPF. In Cisco CCNA/CCENT Exam 640-802, 640-822, 640-816 Preparation Kit. Syngress. doi:10.1016/B978-1-59749-306-2.00009-9

Lv, J., Wang, X., Zhang, Q., & Huang, M. (2018). LAPGN: Accomplishing information consistency under OSPF in General Networks (an extension). *Journal of Network and Computer Applications, 119*, 57-69. doi:10.1016/j. jnca.2018.06.014

Magnani, D. B., Carvalho, I. A., & Noronha, T. F. (2016). Robust Optimization for OSPF Routing. *IFAC-PapersOnLine, 49*(12), 461-466. doi:10.1016/j. ifacol.2016.07.654

Martey, A. (2002a). *IS-IS Network Design Solutions*. Indianapolis, IN: Cisco Press.

Martey, A. (2002b). *Integrated IS-IS Routing Protocol Concepts*. Retrieved from http://www.ciscopress.com/articles/article.asp?p=26850&seqnum=5

Medhi, D., & Ramasamy, K. (2018a). IP Routing and Distance Vector Protocol Family. In Network Routing (2nd ed.). Morgan Kaufmann. doi:10.1016/ B978-0-12-800737-2.00007-7

Medhi, D., & Ramasamy, K. (2018b). Routing Protocols: Framework and Principles. In Network Routing (2nd ed.). Morgan Kaufmann. doi:10.1016/ B978-0-12-800737-2.00004-1

Medhi, D., & Ramasamy, K. (2018c). OSPF and Integrated IS–IS, Editor(s): Deep Medhi, Karthik Ramasamy. In Network Routing (2nd ed.). Morgan Kaufmann. doi:10.1016/B978-0-12-800737-2.00008-9

Riley, C., Flannagan, M. E., Fuller, R., Khan, U., Lawson, W. A., O'Brien, K., & Walshaw, M. (2003). IP Routing. In The Best Damn Cisco Internetworking Book Period. Syngress.

Rouse, M., & Ward, M. (2007). *IS-IS (Intermediate System-to-Intermediate System protocol)*. TechTarget. Retrieved from: https://searchnetworking. techtarget.com/definition/IS-IS

Vallet, J., & Brun, O. (2014). Online OSPF weights optimization in IP networks. *Computer Networks, 60,* 1-12. doi:10.1016/j.bjp.2013.12.014

Warren, H. (2000). Should you use distance vector or link state routing protocols? *Networking.* Available at: https://www.techrepublic.com/article/should-you-use-distance-vector-or-link-state-routing-protocols/

KEY TERMS AND DEFINITIONS

BGP: Border gateway protocol.
CIDR: Classless interdomain routing.
EIGRP: Enhanced interior gateway routing protocol.
IGRP: Interior gateway routing protocol.
IS-IS: Intermediate system to intermediate system.
LSP: Link state packet.
OSI: Open system interconnection.
OSPF: Open shortest path first.
RIP: Routing information protocol.
SPT: Shortest-path tree (SPT).
VLSM: Variable length subnet masks.

Chapter 12
Economic Impact of Cyber Attacks on Critical Infrastructures

Merve Şener
Girne American University, Cyprus

ABSTRACT

Critical infrastructures ensure that activities that are vital and important for individuals can be safely delivered to the society uninterruptedly. The damage on these critical infrastructures caused by cyber-attacks whose control is carried out through computers and network systems is very large. Cyber-attacks directly or indirectly affect companies, institutions, and organizations economically and cause great financial losses. In this chapter, two different categories, energy and finance sector, which are described as critical infrastructure, are discussed; cyber-attacks carried out on these sectors, cyber-attack weapons, and economic losses caused by these attacks are examined.

DOI: 10.4018/978-1-5225-8976-1.ch012

Copyright © 2019, IGI Global. Copying or distributing in print or electronic forms without written permission of IGI Global is prohibited.

INTRODUCTION

Cyber space, which is called as the fifth war zone following land, air, sea and space, is consisting of physical layer –comprised of all kinds of hardware, and users-, software layer – enabling the functioning of hardware in virtual sense-, content layer –comprised of messages, data, information etc. being in circulation over the previous two layers-, and regulatory layer – comprised of national and international legal regulations relevant to cyber space- (Meral, 2015). And the concept of cyber attack means causation of interruption by seizing the control through accessing the governments' or corporations' computer systems or networks, prevention of access to the systems, stealing and amending of information, and misguidance by the attackers. In cyber-attacks, it is quite difficult to identify the identity details of the attackers. Moreover, damage occurring as the result of attack is immense. In this context, the critical infrastructures of the countries are the focus of the attackers. Critical infrastructures are defense technologies, finance services, air traffic control systems, health services, telecommunication infrastructures, energy production and distribution systems, power plants, water production and distribution networks.

Capturing and managing the critical infrastructures by cyber attackers whose control is carried out through computers and network systems feeds the economy of the crime by causing great economic losses. The crime economy, which is included in the informal (unrecorded) economy, is defined as the economic income obtained as a result of the activities considered as a crime legally. The earnings obtained as a result of the activities defined as crime by law regardless of whether it is traditional or virtual constitute the crime economy (Pekkaya, Temli,Ozturk,2017).

For instance, the WannaCry virus, which affected numerous countries in 2017, and which was Ransomware type malware targeting Microsoft Windows, had caused the cessation of patient admissions except operations and emergencies by enabling collapse of the National Health Service (NHS) of England as well as causing great losses in economic aspect. Ransomware is a malware which is preventing access to data in different formats (.doc,. xls,.jpeg,.avi) in the computers by encrypting the data of computer users in 1024 bit format via Gpcode, and which is requesting ransom for opening them to access (Sarı, Biricik, Keser, Gündoğdu, 2014). As per the result of

"2017 Internet Crime Report", published by Internet Crime Complaint Center, Ransomware had caused a loss of more than 2.3 million dollars in 2017.

As another example, in 2018, Github and an anonymous USA based company had incurred a great Distributed Denial of Service (DDoS) attack. DDos attack is occupying the bandwidth of the target by sending request from many different points to the determined target(s), and as a result deactivating the target (Çetin, Gundak, Çetin, 2015). While the anonymous USA based company had incurred a data flow of 1.7 terabits per second, Github had incurred a data flow of 1.3 terabits per second, and the attack had been able to be prevented after about 10 minutes. Moreover, the attackers had also attached ransom notes to those DDoS attacks, and had requested more than 50 Monero virtual monies from the companies for ceasing the attack. Ponemon Institute, in its report of "Cyber Security on the Offense: A Study of IT Security Experts", has disclosed that the cost of interruption period of 1 minute -caused by DDoS attacks- is varying in between 1 dollar and 100 thousand dollars Along with the presence of many known examples of cyber attacks such as these, there are many cyber attacks that are not noticed yet by the governments, companies, institutions and organizations, or that are not being disclosed due to reasons such loss of prestige.

According to the report of "Net Losses: Estimating the Global Cost of Cybercrime", published in 2014 by The Center for Strategic and International Studies (CSIS) and McAfee, it is being observed that the cost of cyber attacks on global economy was about 400 billion dollars in 2013. Again according to the report of "The Economic Impact of Cybercrime—No Slowing Down", published by CSIS and McAfee in 2018, it is being found out that this figure had reached to about 600 billion dollars in 2017. According to the report of 2017, the losses, that the countries incurred as the result of cyber attacks, are being shown in Table 1.

According to the report, it is being observed that the economically developed and developing countries' losses based on cyber attacks are much more compared to underdeveloped countries. And it is being determined that the countries suffering the most in proportion to national income are the middle income counties. The reason of this is the possibility of causing greater economic loss in developed and developing countries compared to countries which couldn't make economic progress, and insufficiency of medium scaled countries in the domain of cyber security despite being digitalized.

Table 1. Losses incurred by the countries as the result of cyber attacks

Region (World Bank)	Region GDP (USD, Trillions)	Cybercrime Cost (USD, Billions)	Cybercrime Loss (% GDP)
North America	20.2	140 to 175	0.69 to 0.87%
Europe and Central Asia	20.3	160 to 180	0.79 to 0.89%
East Asia & the Pacific	22.5	120 to 200	0.53 to 0.89%
South Asia	2.9	7 to 15	0.24 to 0.52%
Latin America and the Caribbean	5.3	15 to 30	0.28 to 0.57%
Sub-Saharan Africa	1.5	1 to 3	0.07 to 0.20%
MENA	3.1	2 to 5	0.06 to 0.16%
World	**$75.8**	**$445 to $608**	**0.59 to 0.80%**

It has been urged upon two different categories in this study as being Energy Sector and Finance Sector –from among critical infrastructures-, and the cyber attacks made on these sectors, weapons of cyber attacks, and economic losses caused by such attacks have been examined.

CYBER ATTACKS ON CRITICAL INFRASTRUCTURES, AND THEIR ECONOMIC EFFECTS

The infrastructure systems, ensuring communication to society of activities –having vital value and significance for the individuals- as continuously in a secure manner, are being referred as "critical". Critical infrastructures are comprising of systems and physical infrastructures such as defense technologies, finance services, air traffic control systems, health services, telecommunication infrastructures, energy production and distribution systems, power plants, water production and distribution networks. The definition, scope and priority order of critical infrastructures are changing depending on the threats that the countries encounter, and on the geography (Acer et. al, 2012). But when the protection of critical infrastructures is in subject, even if the primarily taken security measures are changing as per the factors such as natural disasters and terrorist attacks that the countries incur depending on their geography, the measures to be taken against the threat of 'cyber attack' have to rank first for all the countries. Because the critical infrastructures –formed over controlled computers and network systems- have a distributed and complex system. Sectors, such as energy generation, processing of petroleum and natural gas, chemical processing, are controlled, monitored and reported by the industrial control systems (ICS). Moreover, by SCADA (Supervisory Control and Data Acquisition) –being one of the industrial control systems-, the facilities are able to controlled remotely. Thus, when the SCADA system incurs any attack, this attack may cause immense physical and economic losses and even death by affecting the whole system (Karakuş, 2011). For this reason, full protection of the critical infrastructures is nearly impossible. Due to this vulnerability and the possibility of occurrence of immense losses, the critical infrastructures are the initial target points of cyber attacks. In other words, the critical infrastructures are the most fundamental building blocks of countries in terms of their ability to fulfill the vital functions and being sustainable, and we can say that 'cyber attacks' have the character of a dynamite enabling the deterioration of these building blocks.

By the research of "Kaspersky Lab Discovers Vulnerable Industrial Control Systems Likely Belonging to Large Organizations", performed by Kaspersky in 2016, it had been determined that there were 188.019 systems in total -in 170 countries- which are compatible with the parts of ICS, and that there was gap against threats in 92% of these ICS, and while 87% of these systems had medium level weak points, 7% of them had high level of gaps.

In the following part of the study, cyber attacks made on Energy Sector and Finance Sector – from among critical infrastructures-, cyber attack weapons, and economic losses caused by these attacks have been examined.

Cyber Attacks Targeting Energy Sector and Their Economic Effects

1. Stuxnet Attack

In 2009, Stuxnet attack had been carried out on Iran's Natanz Nuclear Fuel Enrichment Facility, and the presence of Stuxnet virus in the facility had been able to be determined after a year. By the researches performed, it had been determined that the virus had targeted the SCADA system in the critical infrastructure facilities. Stuxnet virus had seized the control of SCADA system at Natanz Nuclear Fuel Enrichment Facility in two stages. In the first stage, it had seized the control circuits of Programmable Logic Controller (PLC)

–which is determining the speed of centrifuge machines used at the facility in enriching uranium-, and then it had caused the breaking up of machines by decreasing and increasing with an extraordinary speed and continuously the electrical current frequency which were being generated by the PLC and which were feeding the centrifuges (Çelik, 2013). About 1.000 centrifuge machines at the facility had fallen to pieces. Moreover, as Iran is subject to international embargoes, it is unable to access to international markets in order to purchase materials relevant to nuclear such as centrifuge machines (CSS Cyber Defense Project, 2017). It is being known that replacing the broken machines, removing the viruses from other machines, and making the installations again had brought Iran's nuclear operations to a standstill for 2 years (Kara,2013).

2. Black Energy Trojan Horse and Kill Disk Trojan Horse

Black Energy trojan horse had first been observed in 2007 in simple DDoS attacks, and then it had been used for sending spams and bank fraud, and in 2004 it had become a very harmful malware used as a back door for making network discovery on computers, collecting data from hard drives, and enabling the remote control of computers . And Kill Disk trojan horse is a type of malware designed for closing and sabotaging the critical systems in ICS, and deleting the system files allowing the restarting of the system (Çeliktaş, 2016).

On December 23, 2015, three regional power companies in Ukraine had simultaneously incurred great cyber attacks by this malware (ICS-CERT, 2016). The attack had been realized by accessing the companies' computers and SCADA systems through collective use of Black Energy and Kill Disk trojan horse malware (SANS and E-ISAC, 2016). As the result of the attack, about 225.000 individuals (SANS and E-ISAC, 2016) had incurred power failure for 3 to 6 hours (Assante,2016).

In the report of "Analysis of the Cyber Attack on the Ukrainian Power Grid", published by SANS (Escal Institute of Advanced Technologies) institute, E-ISAC (Electricity Information Sharing and Analysis Center) in 2016, it has been specified that 7 transformer stations of 110 kV, and 23 transformer stations of 35 kV of Kyivoblenergo –among the regional electric distribution companies of Ukraine- were disconnected during the attack. In the report, it has been specified that primarily the spear phishing e-mails of Black Energy malware were used for making network discovery. By these spear phishing e-mails, Microsoft Office documents (Word and Excel) –in which Black Energy malware was inserted- were sent to the company's employees. Thus, by these Word and Excel files –which were including malware-, which the employees saw no harm in opening as they were familiar, network discovery and data collection processes had been initiated. By this way, the attackers had seized the IT network of al the units, and had realized the power failure by accessing the SCADA which was the main target. And by the Kill Disk malware, the system files had been deleted in order to prevent the restarting of the system. In addition, the attackers had deactivated the uninterruptable power supply (UPS) of one of the power companies, and had also enabled the company's building and information center to remain without power during the failure (SANS and E-ISAC, 2016). And as the result of this, interference to the system and remote control of transformer stations couldn't be ensured, and it had been required for the employees to interfere physically by going to the transformer stations (Zetter,2016). Moreover, one of the power companies had incurred TDoS (Telephony Denial of Service) attacks (SANS and E-ISAC, 2016). TDoS is preventing the users from making call by attacking the target phone services (Dantas, Lemos, Fonseca, Nigam, 2016). Thus, by sending thousands of fake calls to the company's call center through the TDoS attack, the making call of individuals –incurring failure- had been prevented (SANS and E-ISAC, 2016).

Bringing the functioning of the systems to a standstill through power failure by affecting all the sectors from banking and finance sector to electronic communication sector, from transportation sector to public and private sectors, from fuel oil sector to automotive sector is causing great losses in economic aspect.

3. Shamoon Attack

Shamoon is an harmful critical infrastructure weapon used against to corporation in energy sector in Middle East (Zhioua, 2013). The business network of Aramco –the national oil company of Saudi Arabia-, which incurred one of these attacks on August 15, 2012, had been severely damaged due to Shamoon malware (Dehlawi, Abokhodair, 2013). In the attack, 30.000 computers had been damaged and had become unusable in a few hours (Kara, 2013). Shamoon is making the computers inaccessible by deleting data from

Windows computers, and by making attacks to MBR (Master Boot Record) (Zhioua, 2013). By the Shamoon attack, Aramco Oil Company had incurred great economic loss (Kara, 2013). Moreover, it is clear that it had played a significant role in terms of global economy considering that Kingdom of Saudi Arabia is one of the significant energy suppliers of the world by its extensive petroleum and gas reserves (Dehlawi, Abokhodair, 2013)

Cyber Attacks Targeting Finance Sector and Their Economic Effects

All kinds of specific information such as an individual's ID information, passport information, driving license information, profession information, contact information, personal income, financial assets, tax payments, account numbers, account balance, credit card data, loan information, shares, e-mail addresses or passwords, genetic information such as fingerprint, hospital records, shopping information, and where s/he is and with whom is personal data. Along with the integration of human life to technology, the protection of such personal data is a critical issue for the sectors and internet users. Because the seizure and use of personal data by cyber attackers is able to become a dangerous weapon in all aspects for the humanity. When it comes to the economic aspects of cyber-attacks, theft or destruction of personal data by cyber attackers not only causes serious financial losses by institutions, organizations or companies, but also damages their reputations and thus decreasing the trust and loyalty of individuals. In particular, the protection of trust and stability in the financial sector is of great importance in terms of ensuring the continuity of investments in the country and as a result of this, the realization of economic growth. Because the financial system is the structure where the fund transfer is made between the people or institutions having the excess funds required for economic growth and those who have a funding gap . The transfer of funds by the financial system is carried out by means of investment and financing instruments through financial institutions. Thus, funds are transferred to the right channels and contribute to economic growth. Achieving financial deepening, that is, the ones who have fund surpluses and the ones who have a funding gap that the financial system has, the investment instruments and the expansion and increasing and the investment instruments is very important for the economic growth. In this context, trust in financial services such as banks and insurance companies must be fully provided in order to achieve financial deepening in the country. Otherwise, unrecorded financing comes into play and savings cannot be turned into investment.

For instance, Heartland Payment Systems –located in USA- had incurred a great data hack in 2008. The cyber attackers had stole credit card information of 134 million individuals by uploading spyware to data systems of Heartland through SQL injection attacks. Among this information, there are all the information along with name of the card holder, card number and data coded on the magnetic tape of the card required by the attackers in order to produce fake ID cards. In the period of attack, Heartland was realizing 100 million transactions a month for 175.000 business administrators. And as the result of the attack, Heartland had temporarily lost its conformity with Payment Card Industry Data Security Standard (PCI DSS), and also it had been obliged to make payment of 145 million dollars as indemnity for the fraudulent payments made (Ritchey, 2015).

And JPMorgan Chase -among the oldest financial institutions of USA- had incurred a cyber attack in 2014, and the contact information of about 76 million individuals from among its customers, and the contact information of 7 million small enterprises had been stolen by the attackers (Glazer, 2014). JPMorgan Chase had not disclosed the cost of attacks. But in a study performed by Ponemon Institute, the average cost of data breach per record had been calculated as 154$. In this context, it is being estimated that JPMorgan Chase had incurred a loss of about 12,782 billion dollars through the stealing of 83 million data (Howden, 2015).

Equifax –the credit rating agency of USA- had incurred a cyber attack in 2017, and dates of birth, addresses, social security numbers, driving license information of its customers, and credit card information of 209 thousand customers, and ID information of 182 thousand customers included in credit report conflicts had been stolen by the cyber attackers. The attack had not just affected the customers in USA, and also the limited personal information of some customers in England and Canada had been seized by the attackers. Following the disclosure of attack by Equifax, the value of its share certificates had decreased by more than 20%, and according to Wall Street, that attack had caused a cost of 4 billion dollars against Equifax (CHIP Online, 2017).

As the result of cyber attack incurred by Uber in October 2016, the names, e-mail addresses, phone numbers, data of travel routes of about 57 million drivers and passengers in the whole world, and also driving license numbers of about 600 thousand drivers working in USA had been stolen.

As the result of that, Uber's offer of making a payment of 100,000$ to the computer hackers for preventing the news from getting out had drew great reaction, had caused the security managers to lose their jobs, and thus the company had incurred a great damage of reputation as the result of the attack. In addition, following the attack, the company had offered free credit monitoring and ID theft protection service to the drivers who were affected by the incident (STM, 2017).

The "MyFitnessPal" named application and internet site of Under Armour –sport wear and shoe producer located in USA- had incurred a cyber attack in 2018, and the data of about 150 million of its users had been stolen. By the disclosure of Under Armour regarding that the e- mail addresses and passwords of its users were stolen due to data leakage, the company's shares had showed a decrease down to 4.6% (Turner, 2018).

Yahoo, being one of the largest technology companies of USA, had incurred a cyber attack in 2014, and the information of its 500 million users had been stolen. Names, e-mail addresses, phone numbers, dates of birth, security questions required for verifying accounts had been among this information. Moreover, Yahoo had incurred a cyber attack also in 2013, and e- mail addresses, phone numbers, dates of birth and account verification records of its 1 million users had been stolen (STM, 2016).

America's JobLink (AJL), a multi-state web-based system that links job seekers with employers, had incurred a cyber attack in 2014, and the information of its 5.5 million users had been stolen. Names, dates of birth and social security numbers had been among this information (Kaspersky Lab, 2017).

eBay, being one of the largest online shopping sites of USA, had incurred a cyber attack in 2014, and the information of its 145 million users had been stolen. Names, encrypted passwords, e-mail addresses, phone numbers and dates of birth had been among this information (Roman,2014).

The Zomato Company, which was established in India, and which is serving as restaurant search service in the whole world, had announced that e-mail addresses and passwords of its 17 million users were stolen by the cyber attack it had incurred (Thomas, 2017). In addition, it had been specified in many open sources that this data was put up for sale by the attackers for 1,001.43$ over Dark Web.

According to the report of "2018 Cost of a Data Breach Study: Global Overview", published by IBM Security Business Unit and Ponemon Institute, numeric dimension per person of direct cost losses and indirect cost losses arising due to data leakage has been shown in Figure 1 on the basis of countries.

Figure 1. Direct and indirect costs (Measured in US$)

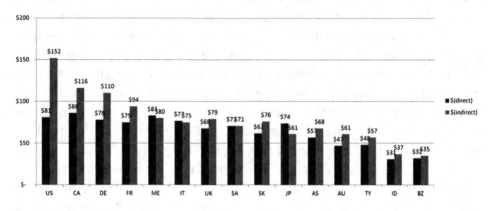

In Figure 1, directs costs have been determined as funds spent to accomplish a given activity such as engaging forensic experts, hiring a law firm, or offering victims identity protection services, and indirect costs have been determined as the allocation of resources, such as employees' time and effort to notify victims and investigate the breach, the loss of goodwill and customer churn.

Moreover, one of the most significant examples of data leakage was leaking to the internet of NSA's (National Security Agency) cyber tools (WannaCry, Notpetya ransom viruses) by the Shadows Brokers hacker group in 2016, and determining the price of each of the tools in between 1 and 100 bitcoins (about 930$ and 93,000$ by the end of December 2016) on Dark Web, and putting up all the tools for sale for about 930,000$ in total. And in 2017, Shadow Brokers had revealed the Windows vulnerability referred as EternalBlue –which is a part of the exploitations developed again by NSA, and which would be used later on in WannaCry and Notpetya ransom software attacks-, and had put up for sale on Dark Web. (STM, 2016, 2017).

Cyber Attacks Against SWIFT System in Banking Sector and Their Economic Results

SWIFT (the Society for Worldwide Interbank Financial Telecommunication) is a cooperative company whose headquarter is in Brussels, and in which about 11,000 financial institutions and banks are members in more than 200 countries. The speed, low cost and reliability of SWIFT are causing a large part of the international transactions and payments in the world -in other words 2.5 billion payment orders each year and billions of dollars of transactions each day- to be realized over this network (Katasonov, 2016). For this reason, SWIFT is playing a significant role in the world's finance ecosystem.

While the financial institutions and banks –being members of SWIFT- are making money transfer to each other, not the transfer itself but only its information is being transmitted. And the target of cyber attackers is the content of the message covering the payment information. In other words, the location where the money will be transferred, the amount or other information are being changed by the cyber attackers, and the transfer is being realized to the location and in the manner they want (STM, 2016).

As from 2013 until 2018, it is being observed that numerous SWIFT attacks had been realized. By the report of "Threat Analysis SWIFT Systems and the SWIFT Customer Security Program", published by MWR InfoSecurity, it has been disclosed that banks in Bangladesh, Equator, Philippines, Ukraine, Taiwan and Nepal had incurred immense losses by the SWIFT attacks. And then, it had been disclosed that also the banks in Russia and Turkey had incurred these attacks (STM, 2016).

According to the report of MRW InfoSecurity, first the Sonali Bank in Bangladesh had incurred a SWIFT attack in 2013, and the attackers had stolen 250,000$ from the bank. And then The Bank of Bangladesh had also incurred an attack in 2016, and the attackers had stole 81 million $ from the bank. Not much is being known about the attack incurred by Sonali Bank in 2013. And then, by the attack of The Bank of Bangladesh -which was realized in 2016-, the court file was opened again, and as the result of the inspections, it had been revealed that the attack to the SWIFT system had been realized by stealing of the ID information of employees and then by realizing the attack with this information. In the attacks of The Bank of Bangladesh, 35 SWIFT transactions with a value of 951,000,000$ had been realized, but only 81,000,000$ of it could be stolen as being transferred to bank accounts in Philippines. The remaining transactions had been saved by the typing errors determined in the SWIFT messages. Again according to the report, The Far Eastern International Bank in

Taiwan had incurred an attack in October 2017, and fraudulent transaction of 60,100,000$ had been made, and consequently 160,000$ had been stolen from the bank by the attackers. Moreover, Financial Regulator of Taiwan had imposed a fine of 266,524$ to the bank on the grounds that the bank's security standing was not in the manner determined by Banking Law of Taiwan. Thus, the total financial loss of The Far Eastern International Bank had been 426,524$. In 2015, Tien Phong Bank in Vietnam had realized suspicious SWIFT messages, and had prevented the stealing of 1,130,000$ by the attackers.

As another example, Central Bank of Russia had incurred an attack in 2016, and had incurred a loss of 31,3 million $, and then 3 Turkish Banks had incurred SWIFT attacks on December 08, 2016. Along with knowing that the attack had occurred in banks where there were high numbers of SWIFT transactions such as 15.000 – 20.000, only Akbank had disclosed its exposure to attacks. In the disclosure made by Akbank, it had been specified that the maximum risk amount was 4,000,000$ (Nebil, 2016).

In 2018, Banco de Chile in Chile had incurred a SWIFT attack, and Eduardo Ebensperger Orrego –CEO of the Bank- had specified in his press statement that 10,000,000$ was stolen from the bank. In addition, the bank had disclosed that it had deactivated its workstations in order to elude the attack (Kirk, 2018).

The SWIFT attacks and financial losses, which occurred in between 2013 and 2018, are being shown in Table 2.

Ransomware

Ransomware is all kinds of malware by which the data on computers, mobile phones and other connected devices are being seized by the cyber attackers, and by which the attackers request ransom from the owner of the data for allowing access to the data (Çelik, Çeliktaş, 2018). First, the attackers are accessing the programs and files of the users by sending message through a pop-up window or e-mail which seems to be reliable. And then, they are encrypting the seized data in 1024 bit format by Gpcode, and preventing the user from accessing to such data. And in the next step, the attackers are informing their ransom requests by preparing messages in formats such s .txt, .jpeg in the parts of the systems most frequently used by the user in order to indicate that the data had been seized. In these messages, the attackers are informing that password for access to data will be provided to the user only against the payment of requested ransom amount (Sarı, Biricik, Keser, Gündoğdu, 2014). In addition, the attackers are giving a specific period for the payment of ransom, and the victims' attempts to recover the data are being prevented by decreasing such period by each incorrect password tried by the user in order to recover the data (Çelik, Çeliktaş, 2018). Worse

Table 2. SWIFT attacks which occurred in between 2013 and 2018

Date	Bank / Country	Amount	Stolen / Prevented	Reference
2013	Sonali Bank / Bangladesh	$250,000	stolen	MWR INFOSECURITY REPORT
2015	Banco del Austroz / Ecuador	$12,000,000	stolen	MWR INFOSECURITY REPORT
2015	an unknown Philippines bank	$Unknown	stolen	MWR INFOSECURITY REPORT
2015	Tien Phong Bank / Vietnam	$1,130,000	prevented	MWR INFOSECURITY REPORT
2016	The Bank of Bangladesh / Bangladesh	$951,000,000	$81,000,000 (of $951,000,000) stolen	MWR INFOSECURITY REPORT
2016	Unnamed Ukrainian Bank / Ukraine	$10,000,000	stolen	MWR INFOSECURITY REPORT
2016	Russian Central Bank / Russia	$31,100,000	stolen	Nebil, 2016
2016	Akbank / Turkey	$4,000,000	stolen	Nebil, 2016
2017	The Far Eastern International / Taiwan	$60,100,000	$160,000 (of $60,100,000) stolen	MWR INFOSECURITY REPORT
2017	NIC Asia Bank / Nepal	$4,400,000	$580,000 (of $4,400,000) stolen	MWR INFOSECURITY REPORT
2018	Banco de Chile / Chile	$10,000,000	stolen	Kirk, 2018

than it, according to the data of "Must-Know Ransomware Statistics 2017", published by Barkly Company, 20% of the companies –in other words 1 of 5 companies- paying the amount of ransom requested by the attackers couldn't get the right of access to their data. Moreover, in some cases, the attackers had also requested a second ransom. Again according to the report, Rhode Island Law Office had paid 25,000$ for numerous ransom requests it had incurred, and it had incurred a loss of 700,000$ due to interruption and due to inability to access its files.

Moreover, according to the data of "Must-Know Ransomware Statistics 2018" of Barkly, in the attack incurred in November 2017 by Spring Hill – located at State of Tennessee of USA- during the Ransomware attacks carried out against local governments, the ransom amount of 250,000$ requested by the attackers had not been paid, but the cost of removal of malware had been 100,000$. In the attack incurred in December 2017 by Mecklenburg County – located at State of North Carolina-, the ransom amount of 23,000$ requested by the attackers had not been paid, but the cost of removal of malware had been estimated as more than 2 million dollars. And Rockport –located at State of Maine- had incurred an attack in April 2018, and the ransom amount of 1,200$ requested by the attackers had not been paid, but the cost of removal of malware had been in between 38,000$ and 48,000$. As another example, the Hollywood Presbyterian Medical Center –located in Los Angeles-, which incurred a Ransomware attack in February 2016, had made a ransom payment of 17,000$ in bitcoins (Mattei, 2017).

According to the data of "Internet Security Threat Report", published by Symantec Company in March 2018, the average ransom amounts requested by the attackers as per years are as in Figure 2.

According to the data published by Cybersecurity Ventures in 2018, the damage caused on global economy by the Ransomware attacks had reached to 5 million dollars in 2017 while it was 325 million dollars in 2015. Moreover, it is being estimated that this figure will reach to

11.5 billion dollars per year until 2019. In the report, it had been specified that the reality lying behind this cost was not just the requested ransom

Figure 2. 2014-2017 amounts of ransom requests

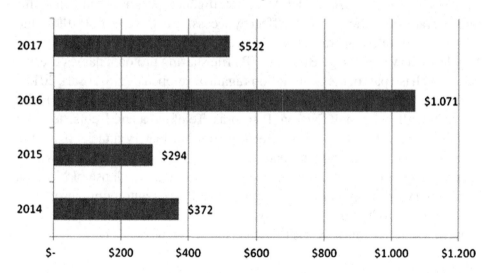

amount, but also reasons such as waiting periods passing due to not being able to access the data, damage or destruction of data, loss of productivity, judicial inquiries and loss of reputation were also effective.

Attacks Carried Out in Finance Sector by Derivatives of Ransomware and Resultant Economic Losses

The becoming of ransomware an income source for the attackers is also causing the increase of derivatives of ransomware. These ransomware derivatives are able to cause significant damages especially in the domains of finance, health, telecommunication and transportation which are qualified as critical infrastructures. In the following part of the study, WannaCry, Petya/Notpetya and Samsam ransomware derivatives –which had caused significant economic losses in recent years- have been examined.

WannaCry

It is being known that WannaCry ransomware derivative had appeared on May 12, 2017, had affected 150 countries such as USA, England, Spain, Russia, Taiwan, France and Japan in the direction of the information obtained from numerous open sources, and had made 300 ransom requests by operating in 27 different languages in the systems it had penetrated. It is being observed that the tools used in WannaCry attacks are weapons developed by National Security Agency (NSA) of USA for intelligence purposes, and that this ransomware created an extensive effect by accessing to more than 300 thousand Windows derivative operating systems as benefiting from the vulnerability of Windows Server Message Block (SMB) file sharing protocol names Eternal Blue which is a part of the exploitations again developed by NSA (Sarı, 2017).

Russian Central Bank, Russian Interior Ministry, UK's National Health Service, FedEx, Renault, Nissan, Petrobras, Telefonica and Deutsche Bahn are also among the ones being affected from WannaCry attacks (Castillo, Falzon, 2018). WannaCry attack had caused the cessation of patient admissions except the operations and emergencies by enabling the collapse of National Health Service of England, and Renault –the French automobile producer- had stopped production at its factories in France and Slovenia in order to prevent the spread of the virus (Norton Rose Fulbright, 2017).

Risk-modeling firm Cyence and Lloyd is estimating that the WannaCry attacks had caused an economic damage of 8 billion dollars in the whole world along with business interruption and incident interference costs (JLT, 2017).

Petya/Notpetya

Right after the WannaCry ransomwire derivative, Petya ransomware had appeared on June 27, 2017. Petya ransomware is also benefiting from the SMB vulnerability of Windows operating systems just line WannaCry, and as different from WannaCry, it is scanning many systems on the network and accessing the same by using more than one tools (Sarı, 2017).

Banks of Ukrain, state power utilities, airport and metro system of Kiev (Solon, Hern, 2017), Merck –from pharmaceuticals industry sector based in USA-, Maersk –cargo company based in Denmark-, Rosneft –oil giant of Russia- are among the ones affected from the Petya/Notpetya attacks (STM, 2017). The cost of Petya/Notpetya ransom attack had been 135 million dollars for Merck (Davis,2017), and the logistics company FedEx Corp had incurred a decrease of 3.4% in its share prices as the result of the attack, and the company had announced in its statement that the losses had increased due to improvement of systems affected from the attack, and also that the company didn't have cyber insurance for covering these damages (JLT, 2017).

Risk-modeling firm Cyence and Lloyd is estimating that the Notpetya attacks had caused an economic damage of 850 million dollars in the whole world along with business interruption and incident interference costs (JLT, 2017).

SamSam

According to the report of "SamSam: The (Almost) Six Million Dollar Ransomware", published by SOPHOS, the cost of attacks of SamSam ransomware –which penetrates the network as targeting the web servers, which is also encrypting the configurations and data files required to operate the applications as different from many ransomware, and which requests bitcoins as ransom payment- on global economy is about 6 million dollars. (NOTE: This figure has been obtained by considering the dollar value on the date of request of ransom in Bitcoins.) Moreover, it had been specified in the report that 74% of the targets of these attacks was USA, and that Canada, Middle East and England were among the other affected regions. Again according to the report, Atlanta –the capital of State of Georgia of USA-, and Colorado Department of Transportation had incurred a great SamSam attack. According to

"Must-Know Ransomware Statistics 2018" data of Barkly Company, Atlanta had not paid the ransom amount of 51,000$ requested by the attackers, but the costs of recovery had been about 17 million $. And Colorado Department of Transportation had not paid the requested ransom amount that it keeps confidential, but had spent about 1.5 million $ for recovery. As another example, Hancock Health Hospital –located in State of Indiana of USA- had incurred a SamSam attack on January 11, 2018, and as a consequence, it had paid a ransom of 55,000$ (Trend Micro, 2018).

In Figure 3, the ransom amounts paid as the result of SamSam attacks in between January 12, 2016 and July 21, 2018 according to the report of "SamSam: The (Almost) Six Million Dollar Ransomware" published by SOPHOS are being shown.

CONCLUSION

Critical infrastructures are ones that ensure the presentation of systems – required by the individuals in order to fulfill their vital functions- to the service of society in a secure and uninterrupted manner. The stealing and changing

Figure 3. Amounts of ransoms paid in between January 12, 2016 and July 21, 2018

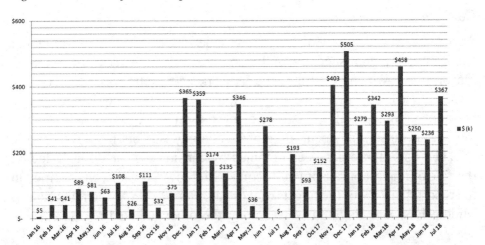

of data, misguidance and interruption through prevention of access to the system by the attackers as the result of exposure of these critical infrastructure systems to cyber attacks are causing significant economic losses. As the result of attacks carried out in Energy Sector as benefiting from the vulnerability of industrial control systems, power companies, oil companies and nuclear fuel enrichment plants had incurred damages which could be compensated by high costs, and along with the interruption of these infrastructures, various companies, institutions, organization and individuals had also incurred financial losses successively. And the cyber attacks in finance sector had decreased the trust of individuals in companies, institutions and organizations incurring attack. The protection of trust and stability in the financial sector is of great importance in terms of ensuring the continuity of investments in the country and as a result of this, the realization of economic growth. In this study, the economic dimension of the losses occurring as the result of cyber attacks targeting SCADA –being one of the industrial control systems in energy sector-, and cyber attacks targeting the finance sector has been examined, and the magnitude of the occurring financial losses has been observed. In this context, Energy Sector –which is important in terms of operating of nearly all the systems-, and Finance Sector –which is important in terms of ensuring the sustainability of investments in the country- should be assessed as critical infrastructure systems which are required to be primarily addressed.

REFERENCES

Acer, Y., Aydınlı, E., Demirkan, O., Çelikpala, M., Ekinci, A. C., İpek, P., . . . Yüksel, H. (2012). *Final Report of Critical Energy Infrastructure Security Project*. Available at: https://books.google.com.cy/books?id=oY r4AgAAQBAJ&pg=PT14&lpg= PT14&dq=co%C4%9Frafyaya+g%C3% B6re+de%C4%9Fi%C5%9Fiklik+ g%C3%B6stermektedir&source=bl& ots=p054yN3UaZ&sig=g1JN0Ztr9FcqTWa9f2DNT5yf6jI&hl= tr&sa=X&ved=2ahUKEwiRjJ yIirvdAhXSl4sKHclVB0oQ6AEwAHo ECAAQAQ#v= onepage&q=co%C4%9Frafyaya%20g %C3%B6re%20 de%C4%9Fi%C5%9Fiklik%20g%C3%B6stermektedir&f=false

Arif, S. (2017). *Analysis of Ransomware and Recent Derivatives WannaCry & Petya*. Available at: https://www.slideshare.net/CezeriSGACezeriSiber/ ransomware-ve-son-varyantlar-analizi-wannacry-petya

Assante, M. J. (2016). *Confirmation of a Coordinated Attack on the Ukrainian Power Grid*. Available at: https://ics.sans.org/blog/2016/01/09/confirmation-of-a-coordinated-attack-on-the-ukrainian-power-grid

Barkly. (2017). *Must-Know Ransomware Statistics 2017*. Available at: https://blog.barkly.com/ransomware-statistics-2017

Barkly. (2018). *Must-Know Ransomware Statistics 2018*. Available at: https://blog.barkly.com/ransomware-statistics-2018

Castillo, D., & Falzon, J. (2018). *An Analysis of the Impact of WannaCry Cyberattack on Cybersecurity Stock Returns*. Available at: http://www.bapress.ca/ref/ref-article/1923-7529-2018-03-93-08.pdf

Çelik, S., & Çeliktaş, B. (2018). *Current Cyber Security Threats: Ransomware.* Available at: http://dergipark.gov.tr/cyberj/issue/39157/460303

Çeliktaş. (2016). *Siber güvenlik kavraminin gelişimi ve türkiye özelinde bir değerlendirme.* Available at: file:///C:/Users/DEO/Desktop/data/ SBERGVENLKKAVRAMININGELM VETRKYEZELNDEBRDEERLENDRME.pdf

Çetin, H., Çetin, H. H., & Gündak, İ. (2015). A Research on E-Business Security and Cyber Attacks. *Çankırı Karatekin University Journal of Institute of Social Sciences, 6*(2), 229. Available at: http://dergipark.gov.tr/download/article-file/253880

CSS Cyber Defense Project. (2017). *Hotspot Analysis: Stuxnet*. Available at: http://www.css.ethz.ch/content/dam/ethz/special-interest/gess/cis/center-for-securities-studies/pdfs/Cyber-Reports-2017-04.pdf

Dantas, Y. G., Lemos, M. O. O., Fonseca, I. E., & Nigam, V. (2016). *Formal Specification and Verification of a Selective Defense for TDoS Attacks.* Available at: https://link.springer.com/chapter/10.1007/978-3-319-44802-2_5

Davis, J. (2017). *Petya cyberattack cost Merck $135 million in revenue.* Available at: https://www.healthcareitnews.com/news/petya-cyberattack-cost-merck-135-million-revenue

Dehlawi, Z., & Abokhodair, N. (2013). *Saudi Arabia's response to cyber conflict: A case study of the Shamoon malware incident*. Available at: https://ieeexplore.ieee.org/abstract/document/6578789/authors

Fulbright, N. R. (2017). *WannaCry Ransomware Attack Summary*. Available at: https://www.dataprotectionreport.com/2017/05/wannacry-ransomware-attack-summary/

Glazer, E. (2014). *J.P. Morgan Says About 76 Million Households Affected By Cyber Breach*. Available at: https://www.marketwatch.com/story/jp-morgan-says-about-76-million-households-affected-by-cyber-breach-2014-10-02-17103316

Howden, S. (2015). *What was the cost of the JP Morgan Chase data breach?* Available at: https://www.morganmckinley.co.jp/en/article/what-was-cost-jp-morgan-chase-data-breach

IBM 7 Ponemon Institute. (2018). *2018 Cost of a Data Breach Study: Global Overview*. Available at: https://databreachcalculator.mybluemix.net/assets/2018_Global_Cost_of_a_Data_Breac h_Report.pdf

ICS-CERT. (2016). *Cyber-attack against Ukrainian critical infrastructure*. Available at: https://ics-cert.us-cert.gov/alerts/IR-ALERT-H-16-056-01

Internet Crime Complaint Center. (2017). *2017 Internet Crime Report*. Available at: https://pdf.ic3.gov/2017_IC3Report.pdf

JLT. (2017). *Notpetya attack disrupts infrastructure and business*. Available at: https://www.jltspecialty.com/our-insights/publications/cyber-decoder/notpetya-attack-disrupts-infrastructure-and-business

Kara, M. (2013). *Cyber Attacks-Cyber Wars and their effects*. Available at: https://core.ac.uk/download/pdf/51099850.pdf

Karakuş, C. (2011). *Cyber Attacks Against Critical Infrastructures*. Available at: http://ckk.com.tr/bilimsel/siber.pdf

Kaspersky Lab. (2017). *2017 yılında simdiye kadar yasanan en büyük 5 veri sızıntısı*. Available at: https://www.kaspersky.com.tr/blog/data-leaks-2017/4261/

Kaspersky Lab. (2016). *Kaspersky Lab Discovers Vulnerable Industrial Control Systems Likely Belonging to Large Organizations*. Available at: https://usa.kaspersky.com/about/press-releases/2016_kaspersky-lab-discovers-vulnerable-industrial-control-systems-likely-belonging-to-large-organizations

Katasonov, V. (2016). *The SWIFT System: A Potential Weapon in the Hybrid War*. Available at: http://www.voltairenet.org/article191715.html

Kirk, J. (2018). *Banco de Chile Loses $10 Million in SWIFT-Related Attack*. Available at: https://www.bankinfosecurity.com/banco-de-chile-loses-10-million-in-swift-related-attack-a-11075

Mattei, T. A. (2017). *Privacy, Confidentiality, and Security of Health Care Information: Lessons from the Recent WannaCry Cyberattack*. Available at: https://www.worldneurosurgery.org/article/S1878-8750(17)30996-8/abstract

Meral, M. (2015). *Importance of protection of critical infrastructures within the scope of cyber security*. Available at: http://afyonluoglu.org/PublicWebFiles/Reports-TR/Akademi/2015-Siber%20g%C3%BCvenlik%20kapsam%C4%B1nda%20kritik%20altyap%C4%B1lar%C4%B1n%20korunmas%C4%B1n%C4%B1n%20%C3%B6nemi.pdf

Micro, T. (2018). *SAMSAM Ransomware Hits US Hospital, Management Pays $55K Ransom*. Available at: https://www.trendmicro.com/vinfo/my/security/news/cyber-attacks/samsam-ransomware-hits-us-hospital-management-pays-55k-ransom

MwrInfosecurity. (n.d.). *Threat Analysis SWIFT Systems and the SWIFT Customer Security Program*. Available at: https://www.mwrinfosecurity.com/assets/swift-whitepaper/mwr-swift-payment-systems-v2.pdf

Nebil, F. S. (2016). *Swift attack had occurred in 3 Turkish banks, BDDK warned the banks*. Available at: http://t24.com.tr/yazarlar/fusun-sarp-nebil/swift-saldirisi-3-turk-bankasinda-yasanmis-bddk-bankalari-uyardi,16136

Pekkaya, M., Temli, M., & Ozturk, Z. (2017). *Siber Saldırıların Firmalara etkileri: Zonguldak Ornegi*. Available at: https://www.researchgate.net/publication/322250063_SIBER_SALDIRILARIN_FIRMALARA_ETKILERI_ZONGULDAK_ORNEGI

Ponemon Institute. (2012). *Cyber Security on the Offense: A Study of IT Security Experts*. Available at: https://security.radware.com/uploadedfiles/resources_and_content/attack_tools/cybersecurityo ntheoffense.pdf

Ritchey, D. (2015). *Data Breach Directions: What to Do After an Attack*. Available at: https://www.securitymagazine.com/articles/86071-data-breach-directions-what-to-do-after-an-attack

Roman, J. (2014). *eBay Breach: 145 Million Users Notified*. Available at: https://www.bankinfosecurity.com/ebay-a-6858

SANS & E-ISAC. (2016). *Analysis of the Cyber Attack on the Ukrainian Power Grid*. Available at: https://ics.sans.org/media/E-ISAC_SANS_Ukraine_DUC_5.pdf

Sarı, A., Biricik, C. G., Keser, C., & Gündoğdu, E. (2014). Inspection of Malware Against the Ethics of Information Systems. *Management Information Systems Congress, at Istanbul Boğaziçi University*. Available at: https://www.researchgate.net/publication/273318222_Bilisim_Sistemleri_Etigine_Aykiri_Zar arli_Yazilimlarin_Incelenmesi Last accessed date: 16/06/2018

Şener, Ç. (2013). *Stuxnet attack and cyber war strategy of USA: An evaluation within the frame of principle of abstaining from using force in international law*. Available at: http://hukuk.deu.edu.tr/dosyalar/dergiler/dergimiz-15-1/senercelik.pdf

Solon, O., & Hern, A. (2017). *'Petya' ransomware attack: what is it and how can it be stopped?* Available at: https://www.theguardian.com/technology/2017/jun/27/petya-ransomware-cyber-attack-who-what-why-how

Sophos. (2018). *SamSam: The (Almost) Six Million Dollar Ransomware*. Available at: https://www.sophos.com/en-us/medialibrary/PDFs/technical-papers/SamSam-The-Almost- Six-Million-Dollar-Ransomware.pdf

STM. (2017). *Cyber Threat Report for the Period of October – December 2017*. Available at: https://www.stm.com.tr/documents/file/Pdf/siber-tehdit-durum-raporu-ekim-aralik-2017.pdf

STM. (2016). *Cyber Threat Report for the Period of October – December 2016*. Available at:https://farukcalikusu.files.wordpress.com/2016/10/siber-tehdit-durum-raporu-temmuz-eylul- 2016.pdf

Symantec. (2018). *Internet Security Threat Report*. Available at: https://www.symantec.com/content/dam/symantec/docs/reports/istr-23-2018-en.pdf

The 2nd Biggest Data Violation in History has Occurred. (2017). *CHIP ONLINE Haber bülteni*. Available at: https://www.chip.com.tr/haber/tarihin-en-buyuk-2-veri-ihlali-gerceklesti_71789.html

The Center for Strategic and International Studies (CSIS) and McAfee. (2014). *Net Losses: Estimating the Global Cost of Cybercrime*. Available at: https://csis-prod.s3.amazonaws.com/s3fs- public/legacy_files/files/attachments/140609_rp_economic_impact_cybercrime_report.pdf

The Center for Strategic and International Studies (CSIS) and McAfee. (2018). *The Economic Impact of Cybercrime—No Slowing Down*. Available at: https://csis-prod.s3.amazonaws.com/s3fs-public/publication/economic-impact- cybercrime.pdf?kab1HywrewRzH17N9wuE24soo1IdhuHdutm_source=Pressutm_campaign= bb9303ae70 EMAIL_CAMPAIGN_2018_02_21utm_medium=emailutm_term=0_7623d157be-bb9303ae70-194093869 Last accessed date: 25/06/2018

Thomas, A. (2017). *Zomato hacked: Security breach results in 17 million user data stolen*. Available at: https://economictimes.indiatimes.com/small-biz/security-tech/security/zomato-hacked- security-breach-results-in-17-million-user-data-stolen/articleshow/58729251.cms

Turner, N. (2018). *Under Armour Says 150 Million MyFitnessPal Accounts Hacked*. Available at: https://www.bloomberg.com/news/articles/2018-03-29/under-armour-says-150-million-myfitnesspal-accounts-were-hacked

Ventures, C. (2018). *Global Ransomware Damage Costs Predicted To Exceed $8 Billion In 2018*. Available at: https://cybersecurityventures.com/global-ransomware-damage-costs-predicted-to-exceed-8- billion-in-2018/

Zetter, K. (2016). *Everything we know about Ukraine's power plant hack*. Available at: https://www.wired.com/2016/01/everything-we-know-about-ukraines-power-plant-hack/

Zhioua, S. (2013). *The Middle East under Malware Attack Dissecting Cyber Weapons*. Available at: http://faculty.kfupm.edu.sa/ics/zhioua/Research/malwareSurvey-NFSP-2013.pdf

Compilation of References

A gentle introduction to how i2p works. (n.d.). Accessed on July 2018 https://geti2p.net/en/docs/how/intro

Abney, S. (1996a). Part-of-speech tagging and partial parsing. In S. Young & G. Bloothooft (Eds.), *Corpus-Based Methods in Language and Speech Processing* (pp. 118–136). Dordrecht: Kluwer Academic.

Abney, S. (1996b). Statistical methods and linguistics. The Balancing Act: Combining Symbolic and Statistical. *Linguistics*, *23*, 597–618.

Aboelela, E. (2003). Laboratory 7 - OSPF: Open Shortest Path First: A Routing Protocol Based on the Link-State Algorithm. In *Network Simulation Experiments Manual*. Morgan Kaufmann. doi:10.1016/B978-012042171-8/50022-

Abu Rajab, M., Zarfoss, J., Monrose, F., & Terzis, A. (2006, October). A multifaceted approach to understanding the botnet phenomenon. In *Proceedings of the 6th ACM SIGCOMM conference on Internet measurement* (pp. 41-52). ACM. 10.1145/1177080.1177086

Acer, Y., Aydınlı, E., Demirkan, O., Çelikpala, M., Ekinci, A. C., İpek, P., . . . Yüksel, H. (2012). *Final Report of Critical Energy Infrastructure Security Project*. Available at: https://books.google.com.cy/books?id=oYr4AgAAQBAJ&pg=PT14&lpg=PT14&dq=co%C4%9Frafyaya+g%C3%B6re+de%C4%9Fi%C5%9Fiklik+g%C3%B6stermektedir&source=bl& ots=p054yN3UaZ&sig=g1JN0Ztr9FcqTWa9f2DNT5yf6jI&hl=tr&sa=X&ved=2ahUKEwiRjJ yIirvdAhXSl4sKHclVB0oQ6AEwAHoECAAQAQ#v=onepage& q=co%C4%9Frafyaya%20g %C3%B6re%20de%C4%9Fi%C5%9Fiklik%20 g%C3%B6stermektedir&f=false

Ahmad, R., Yunos, Z., & Sahib, S. (2012). Understanding cyber terrorism: The grounded theory method applied. In *Cyber Security, Cyber Warfare and Digital Forensic (CyberSec), 2012 International Conference on* (pp. 323-328). IEEE.

Ahmad, R., & Yunos, Z. (2012). A dynamic cyber terrorism framework. *International Journal of Computer Science and Information Security, 10*(2), 149.

Ahmad, R., Yunos, Z., Sahib, S., & Yusoff, M. (2012). Perception on cyber terrorism: A focus group discussion approach. J. *Information Security, 3*(3), 231–237. doi:10.4236/jis.2012.33029

Akdag, P. (2009). *Siber Suçlar ve Türkiye'nin Ulusal Politikasi* (Master's thesis). Retrieved from file:///F:/email/2009-TEZ-Siber%20Su%C3%A7lar%20ve%20 T%C3%BCrkiye'nin%20Ulusal%20Politikas%C4%B1-Polis%20Akademisi. pdf

Akyazı, U. (2012). *Siber Harekât Ortamının Siber Güvenlik Tatbikatları Kapsamında Değerlendirilmesi*. İstanbul: Harp Akademileri Basımevi.

Akyıldız, A. M. (2013). *Siber Güvenlik Açısından Sızma Testlerinin Uygulamalar İle Değerlendirilmesi* (MSc thesis). Süleyman Demirel Üniversitesi Fen Bilimler Enstitüsü.

Akyıldız, M. A. (2016). *Uygulamalarla Siber Güvenliğe Giriş (2nd ed.)*. Ankara: Ltd. Şti.

Al Jazeera. (2018). *What is the Muslim Brotherhood?* Retrieved from https://www.aljazeera.com/indepth/features/2017/06/muslim-brotherhood-explained-170608091709865.html

Alazab, M., Layton, R., Venkataraman, S., & Watters, P. (2010). *Malware detection based on structural and behavioral features of API calls*. Academic Press.

Alejandre, F. V., Cortés, N. C., & Anaya, E. A. (2017, February). Feature selection to detect botnets using machine learning algorithms. In *Electronics, Communications and Computers (CONIELECOMP), 2017 International Conference on* (pp. 1-7). IEEE. 10.1109/CONIELECOMP.2017.7891834

Alenazi, A., Traore, I., Ganame, K., & Woungang, I. (2017, October). Holistic Model for HTTP Botnet Detection Based on DNS Traffic Analysis. In *International Conference on Intelligent, Secure, and Dependable Systems in Distributed and Cloud Environments* (pp. 1-18). Springer. 10.1007/978-3-319-69155-8_1

Alfifi, M., Kaghazgaran, P., Caverlee, J., & Morstatter, F. (2018). *Measuring the Impact of ISIS Social Media Strategy*. Retrieved from http://faculty.cs.tamu.edu/caverlee/pubs/alfifi2018mis2.pdf

Anderson, C., & Sadjadpour. (2018). *Iran's cyber threat espionage, sabotage and revenge*. Washington, DC: Carnegie Endowment for International Peace.

Andrés, S., Kenyon, B., & Birkholz, E. P. (2004). *Routing Devices and Protocols, Security Sage's Guide to Hardening the Network Infrastructure*. Syngress. doi:10.1016/B978-193183601-2/50010-5

Arif, S. (2017). *Analysis of Ransomware and Recent Derivatives WannaCry & Petya*. Available at: https://www.slideshare.net/CezeriSGACezeriSiber/ransomware-ve-son-varyantlar-analizi-wannacry-petya

Arimatsu, L. (2012). A Treaty for Governing Cyber-Weapons: Potential Benefits and Practical Limitations. In *4th International Conference on Cyber Conflict*. Talinn: NATO CCD COE Publications.

Armstrong, M. (2017). *The USA's Biggest Arms Export Partners*. Retrieved from https://www.statista.com/chart/12205/the-usas-biggest-arms-export-partners/

Aron, R. (1965). *Democratie et Totalitarisme*. Paris: Galliard.

Arora, M. (2012). E-Security Issues. *International Journal of Computers and Technology*, *3*(2), 301–305.

Assante, M. J. (2016). *Confirmation of a Coordinated Attack on the Ukrainian Power Grid*. Available at: https://ics.sans.org/blog/2016/01/09/confirmation-of-a-coordinated-attack-on-the-ukrainian-power-grid

Associated Press. (2004, June 11). U.S. Wrongly Reported Drop in World Terrorism in 2003. *The New York Times*, p. A9.

Atalay, A. H. (2012). *Kurumsal Bilgi Güvenliği*, Siber Güvenlik. *Mimar ve Mühendis Dergisi, 68*, 42–47.

Aydın, M. (Ed.). (2013). *21.Yüzyılda Siber Güvenlik, 1.Baskı.* İstanbul: İstanbul Bilgi Üniversitesi Yayınları.

Ayoub, M. M. (2011). *Redemptive suffering in islam: A study of the devotional aspects of ashura in twelver shi'ism* (Vol. 10). Walter de Gruyter.

Bacik, G., & Coskun, B. B. (2011). The PKK problem: Explaining Turkey's failure to develop a political solution. *Studies in Conflict and Terrorism, 34*(3), 248–265. doi:10.1080/1057610X.2011.545938

Back, A. (2002). Hashcash-a denial of service counter-measure. *Belkasoft.* Retrieved from https://belkasoft.com/

Bailey, M., Cooke, E., Jahanian, F., Xu, Y., & Karir, M. (2009, March). A survey of botnet technology and defenses. In Conference For Homeland Security, 2009. CATCH'09. Cybersecurity Applications & Technology (pp. 299-304). IEEE doi:10.1109/CATCH.2009.40

Bang for the buck. (n.d.). In *Wikipedia*. Available at: https://en.wikipedia.org/wiki/Bang_for_the_buck

Barkly. (2017). *Must-Know Ransomware Statistics 2017.* Available at: https://blog.barkly.com/ransomware-statistics-2017

Barkly. (2018). *Must-Know Ransomware Statistics 2018.* Available at: https://blog.barkly.com/ransomware-statistics-2018

Barnett, T. (2004). *The Pentagon's New Map: War and Peace in the Twentieth-First Century.* New York: Putnam and Sons.

Bar, S. (2004, June/July). The religious sources of Islamic terrorism. *Policy Review, 125*, 27–37.

Bayraktar, G. (2015). *Siber Savaş ve Ulusal Güvenlik Stratejisi.* İstanbul: Yeniyüzyıl Yayınları.

BBC. (2010). *Who are Hezbollah?* Retrieved from http://news.bbc.co.uk/2/hi/middle_east/4314423.stm

Beauchamp, Z. (2018). *What is Hamas?* Retrieved from https://www.vox.com/cards/israel-palestine/hamas

Beggs, C., & Warren, M. (2009). Safeguarding Australia from cyber-terrorism: a proposed cyber-terrorism SCADA risk framework for industry adoption. In *Australian information warfare and security conference* (p. 5). Academic Press.

Benedickt, M. (1991). *Cyberspace: first steps.* Cambridge, MA: MIT Press.

Bergman, M. K. (2001). White Paper: The Deep Web: Surfacing Hidden Value. *The Journal of Electronic Publishing: JEP, 7*(1). doi:10.3998/3336451.0007.104

Bethencourt, J., Franklin, J., & Vernon, M. K. (2005, August). Mapping Internet Sensors with Probe Response Attacks. In *USENIX Security Symposium* (pp. 193-208). USENIX.

Bican, C. (2008). *Sosyal Mühendislik Saldırıları - Ulusal Bilgi Güvenliği Kapısı.* Retrieved from https://www.bilgiguvenligi.gov.tr/sosyal-muhendislik/sosyal-muhendislik-saldirilari-3.html

Biddle, S. (2004). *Military Power: Explaining Victory and Defeat in Modern Battle.* Princeton, NJ: Princeton University Press.

Bilge, L., Balzarotti, D., Robertson, W., Kirda, E., & Kruegel, C. (2012, December). Disclosure: detecting botnet command and control servers through large-scale netflow analysis. In *Proceedings of the 28th Annual Computer Security Applications Conference* (pp. 129-138). ACM. 10.1145/2420950.2420969

Binkley, J. R., & Singh, S. (2006). An Algorithm for Anomaly-based Botnet Detection. *SRUTI, 6*, 7–7.

Bircan, B. (2012). *Gelişmiş Siber Silahlar ve Tespit Yöntemleri.* Tübitak Bilgem. Retrieved from http://docplayer.biz.tr/1142152-Gelismis-siber-silahlar-ve-tespit-yontemleri-bahtiyar-bircan uzman-arastirmaci-siber-guvenlik-enstitusu.html

Blockchain and Bitcoin Offer New Approach, Risks to Cyber Security. (n.d.). Accessed on July 2018, https://online.maryville.edu/blog/blockchain-and-bitcoin-offer-new-approach-risks-to-cyber-security/

Bodenheim. (2014). *Impact of the shodan computer search engine on internet-facing industrial control system devices.* Air Force Institute of Technology Air University Pompeu Casanovas. Open Source Intelligence, Open Social Intelligence and Privacy by Design Retrieved from: http://ceur-ws.org/Vol-1283/paper_24.pdf

Bogdanoski, M., & Petreski, D. (2013). Cyber terrorism–global security threat. Contemporary Macedonian Defense-International Scientific Defense. *Security and Peace Journal, 13*(24), 59–73.

Botnet. (2018, September 22). Retrieved from https://en.wikipedia.org/wiki/Botnet

Boukerche, A., Turgut, B., Aydin, N., Ahmad, M. Z., Bölöni, L., & Turgut, D. (2011). Routing protocols in ad hoc networks: A survey. *Computer Networks, 55*(13), 3032-3080. doi:10.1016/j.comnet.2011.05.010

Brown, B. (2009). *Beyond Downadup: Security expert worries about smart phone, TinyURL threats: Malware writers just waiting for financial incentive to strike, F-Secure exec warns.* Retrieved, February 11, 2012 from http://business.highbeam.com/409220/article-1G1-214585913/beyond-downadup-security-expert-worries-smart-phone

Brown, D. (2018). *15 years ago, the US invaded Iraq – here`s how it changed the Middle East country.* Retrieved from https://www.businessinsider.com/us-invasion-iraq-anniversary-how-it-changed-middle-east-country-2018-3#in-march-2004-a-few-months-after-saddam-hussein-was-captured-near-tikrit-four-blackwater-contractors-were-killed-and-hung-by-insurgents-from-a-bridge-in-fallujah-5

Brown, G. D., & Metcalf, A. O. (2014). Easier Said Than Done: Legal Reviews of Cyber Weapons. *Journal of National Security Law and Policy, 7*(115), 115–138.

BTK (Bilgi Teknolojileri ve İletişim Kurumu). (2009). *Siber Güvenliğin Sağlanması: Türkiye'deMevcut Durum ve Alınması Gereken Tedbirler.* Retrieved from https://www.btk.gov.tr/File/?path=ROOT%2F1%2FDocuments%2FSayfalar%2FSiberGuvenlik %2Fsg.pdf

Burke, J. (2004). Al Qaeda. *Foreign Policy*, (142), 18–26. doi:10.2307/4147572

Burlu, K. (2015). *Bilişimin Karanlık Yüzü (5ᵗʰ ed.)*. Ankara: Sinemis Yayın Grup.

Business of Apps. (2018). *App Download and Usage Statistics*. Retrieved from http://www.businessofapps.com/data/app-statistics/#1

Byman, D. (2016). ISIS Goes Global: Fight the Islamic State by Targeting Its Affiliates. *Foreign Affairs*, *95*, 76.

Çakmak, H., & Demir, C. K. (2009). Siber Dünyadaki Tehdit ve Kavramlar. In Suç, Terör ve Savaş Üçgeninde Siber Dünya (pp. 23-54). Ankara: Barış Platin Kitabevi.

Çakmak, H., & Soyoğlu, İ. K. (2009). Doğu Avrupa ve Asya'dan Siber Saldırı Örnekleri. In Suç, Terör ve Savaş Üçgeninde Siber Dünya (pp. 111-136). Ankara: Barış Platin Kitabevi.

Callimachi, R. (2015). Clues on Twitter Show Ties between Texas Gunman and ISIS Network. *New York Times*. Retrieved from https://www.nytimes.com/2015/05/12/us/twitter cluesshow-ties- between-isis-and-garland-texas-gunman.html

Callimachi, R. (2017). Not 'Lone Wolves' after All: How ISIS Guides World's Terror Plots from Afar. *New York Times*. Retrieved from https://www.nytimes.com/2017/02/04/ world/asia/isis-messaging-app-terror-plot.html?mtrref=t.co&gwh=EF42D2AC6FBB561

Cameron, R., Cantrell, C., Killion, D., Russell, K., & Tam, K. (2005). Routing. In Configuring NetScreen Firewalls. Syngress. doi:10.1016/B978-193226639-9/50011-6

Canavan, J. (2005, October). The evolution of malicious IRC bots. In *Virus Bulletin Conference* (pp. 104-114). Academic Press.

Canbek, G., & Sağıroğlu, Ş. (2006). *Information and Computer Security: Spyware and Protection Methods*. Ankara: Graphic Designer.

Canbek, G., & Sağıroğlu, Ş. (2007). Bilgisayar Sistemlerine Yapılan Saldırılar ve Türleri:Bir İnceleme. *Erciyes Üniversitesi Fen Bilimleri Enstitüsü Dergisi, 23*(1-2), 1–12.

Castillo, D., & Falzon, J. (2018). *An Analysis of the Impact of WannaCry Cyberattack on Cybersecurity Stock Returns.* Available at: http://www.bapress.ca/ref/ref-article/1923-7529-2018-03-93-08.pdf

Cavallaro, L., Saxena, P., & Sekar, R. (2008, July). On the limits of information flow techniques for malware analysis and containment. In *International Conference on Detection of Intrusions and Malware, and Vulnerability Assessment* (pp. 143-163). Springer. 10.1007/978-3-540-70542-0_8

Çelik, S., & Çeliktaş, B. (2018). *Current Cyber Security Threats: Ransomware.* Available at: http://dergipark.gov.tr/cyberj/issue/39157/460303

Çelikpala, M. (n.d.). *Cyber security and nuclear power plants: International framework* (Doctoral dissertation).

Çeliktaş, B. (2016). *Siber Güvenlik Kavraminin Gelişimi Ve Türkiye Özelinde Bir Değerlendirme* (MSc thesis). Karadeniz Technical University Social Sciences İnstitute.

Çeliktaş. (2016). *Siber güvenlik kavraminin gelişimi ve türkiye özelinde bir değerlendirme.* Available at: file:///C:/Users/DEO/Desktop/data/SBERGVENLK KAVRAMININGELMVETRKYEZELN DEBRDEERLENDRME.pdf

Çetin, H., Çetin, H. H., & Gündak, İ. (2015). A Research on E-Business Security and Cyber Attacks. *Çankırı Karatekin University Journal of Institute of Social Sciences, 6*(2), 229. Available at: http://dergipark.gov.tr/download/article-file/253880

Chan, P. P., & Song, W. K. (2014, July). Static detection of Android malware by using permissions and API calls. In *Machine Learning and Cybernetics (ICMLC), 2014 International Conference on* (Vol. 1, pp. 82-87). IEEE. 10.1109/ICMLC.2014.7009096

Chaudhuri, A. (2009). *Language-based security on Android.* Retrieved from http://www.cs.umd.edu/~avik/papers/lbsa.pdf

Chen, Li, Enck, Aafer, & Zhang. (2017). Analysis of SEAndroid Policies: Combining MAC and DAC in Android. In *Proceedings of the 33rd Annual Computer Security Applications Conference* (ACSAC 2017). ACM. 10.1145/3134600.3134638

Chen, X., Andersen, J., Mao, Z. M., Bailey, M., & Nazario, J. (2008, June). Towards an understanding of anti-virtualization and anti-debugging behavior in modern malware. In *2008 IEEE International Conference on Dependable Systems and Networks With FTCS and DCC (DSN)* (pp. 177-186). IEEE. 10.1109/DSN.2008.4630086

Chhillar, R. S. (n.d.). Extraction Transformation Loading – A Road to Data Warehouse. *2nd National Conference Mathematical Techniques: Emerging Paradigms for Electronics and IT Industries*, 384-388.

Cho, M. (2003). *Mixing Technology and Business: The Roles and Responsibilities of the Chief Information Security Officer.* Retrieved from SANS Institute: SANS Institute: https://www.sans.org/reading-room/whitepapers/assurance/mixing-technology-business-roles-responsibilities-chief-information-security-of-1044

Choi, H., Lee, H., Lee, H., & Kim, H. (2007, October). Botnet detection by monitoring group activities in DNS traffic. In *Computer and Information Technology, 2007. CIT 2007. 7th IEEE International Conference on* (pp. 715-720). IEEE. 10.1109/CIT.2007.90

Choucri, N., Madnick, S., & Ferwerda, J. (2014). Institutions for cyber security: International responses and global imperatives. *Information Technology for Development*, 20(2), 96–121. doi:10.1080/02681102.2013.836699

Chu, E. (2016). *Android Market: a user-driven content distribution system.* Retrieved February, 11, 2012 from http://android-developers.blogspot.com

Chuipka, A. (2017). *The Strategies of Cyberterrorism: Is Cyberterrorism an effective means to Achieving the Goals of Terrorists?* Academic Press.

Çifçi, H. (2012). Her Yönüyle Siber Savaş. TÜBİTAK Popüler Bilim Kitapları, 37, 134-135.

Çifçi, H. (2013). *Her Yönüyle Siber Savaş.* İstanbul: TÜBİTAK Popüler Bilim Kitapları.

Cisco Networking Academy. (2014). *Cisco Networking Academy's Introduction to Routing Dynamically.* Available at: http://www.ciscopress.com/articles/article.asp?p=2180210&seqNum=7

Cisco. (2005). *Cisco Networking Academy, Introduction to EIGRP, 2005.* Retrieved from: https://www.cisco.com/c/en/us/support/docs/ip/enhanced-interior-gateway-routing-protocol-eigrp/13669-1.html#intro

Cisco. (2007). *Cisco Networking Academy, Intermediate System-to-Intermediate System Protocol, White Paper, 2007.* Retrieved from: https://www.cisco.com/en/US/tech/tk365/technologies_white_paper09186a00800a3e6f.shtml

Cisco. (n.d.a). *Cisco Datasheets, Intermediate System-to-Intermediate System (IS-IS).* Retrieved from https://www.cisco.com/c/en/us/products/ios-nx-os-software/intermediate-system-to-intermediate-system-is-is/index.html

Cisco. (n.d.b). *Cisco Networking Academy, IS-IS Protocol and IP-Route and Configurations.* Retrieved from: https://content.cisco.com/chapter.sjs?uri=/searchable/chapter/content/en/us/td/docs/ios-xml/ios/iproute_isis/configuration/xe-16-6/irs-xe-16-6-book/

Clarke, A. R., & Knake, K. R. (2010). Cyber War: The Next Threat to National Security and What to do About It. New York: Academic Press.

Clarke, C. P. (2017). *How Hezbollah came to dominate information warfare.* Retrieved from https://www.jpost.com/Opinion/How-Hezbollah-came-to-dominate-information-warfare-505354

Clarke, J.A., Nelson, K.J., & Stoodley, I.D. (2013). *The place of higher education institutions in assessing student engagement, success and retention: A maturity model to guide practice.* Academic Press.

Colarik, A. M., & Janczewski, L. (2007). *Cyber warfare and cyber terrorism.* Yurchak Printing Inc.

Collins. (2018). *Definition of 'nation-state'.* Retrieved from https://www.collinsdictionary.com/dictionary/english/nation-state

Constitutional Rights Foundation. (2018). *The Bush Doctrine*. Retrieved from http://www.crf-usa.org/war-in-iraq/bush-doctrine.html

Conway, M. (2007). *Reality Bites: Cyberterrorism and Terrorist 'Use' of the Internet*. Retrieved from http://firstmonday.org/article/view/1001/922

Cooke, E., Jahanian, F., & McPherson, D. (2005). The Zombie Roundup: Understanding, Detecting, and Disrupting Botnets. *SRUTI, 5,* 6–6.

Corell, H. (2000). *The Challenge of Borderless Cyber-Crime*. Symposium On The Occasion of The Signing of The United Nations Convention Against Transnational Organized Crime, Palermo, Italy. Retrieved from http://legal.un.org/ola/media/info_from_lc/cybercrime.pdf

CSS Cyber Defense Project. (2017). *Hotspot Analysis: Stuxnet*. Available at: http://www.css.ethz.ch/content/dam/ethz/special-interest/gess/cis/center- for-securities-studies/pdfs/Cyber-Reports-2017-04.pdf

D'Arienzo, M., & Romano, S. P. (2016). GOSPF: An energy efficient implementation of the OSPF routing protocol. *Journal of Network and Computer Applications, 75,* 110-127. doi:10.1016/j.jnca.2016.07.011

Daemen, J., & Rijmen, V. (1999). *AES proposal: Rijndael*. Taher ElGamal.

Dagon, D. (2005, July). Botnet detection and response. In OARC workshop (Vol. 2005). Academic Press.

Daily Dot. (n.d.). *Huge Equifax data breach affects almost 148 million Americans*. Retrieved from https://www.dailydot.com/debug/equifax-data-breach/

Danford, N. (2015). *Forget Sykes-Picot. It's the Treaty of Sèvres That Explains the Modern Middle East*. Retrieved from https://foreignpolicy.com/2015/08/10/sykes-picot-treaty-of-sevres-modern-turkey-middle-east-borders-turkey/

Daniel, B. (2015). Big Data and analytics in higher education: Opportunities and challenges. *British Journal of Educational Technology, 46*(5), 904–920. doi:10.1111/bjet.12230

Dantas, Y. G., Lemos, M. O. O., Fonseca, I. E., & Nigam, V. (2016). *Formal Specification and Verification of a Selective Defense for TDoS Attacks*. Available at: https://link.springer.com/chapter/10.1007/978-3-319-44802-2_5

Davies, S. (2011). Still building the memex. *Communications of the ACM, 54*(2), 80–88. doi:10.1145/1897816.1897840

Davis, J. (2017). *Petya cyberattack cost Merck $135 million in revenue.* Available at: https://www.healthcareitnews.com/news/petya-cyberattack-cost-merck-135-million-revenue

Dean, M., & Herridge, C. (2016). Patriotic Hackers' Attacking on Behalf of Mother Russia. *Fox News*. Retrieved from http://www.foxnews.com/politics/2016/01/16/patriotic-hackers-attacking-on-behalf-mother -russia.html

Dehlawi, Z., & Abokhodair, N. (2013). *Saudi Arabia's response to cyber conflict: A case study of the Shamoon malware incident.* Available at: https://ieeexplore.ieee.org/abstract/document/6578789/authors

Dell Security Annual Threat Report. (2015). *Boom: A Journal of California, 5*(1), 12-13.

Demir, B. (2013). Yazılım Güvenliği Saldırı Ve Savunma. Dikeysen Yayın Dağıtım, 423.

Denning, D. E. (2001). Activism, hacktivism, and cyberterrorism: The Internet as a tool for influencing foreign policy. *Networks and netwars: The future of terror, crime, and militancy, 239*, 288.

Developers, A. (2016). *Android developer guide.* Retrieved February 11, 2012 from www.android.com

Dictionary.com. (2018). *Guerrilla Warfare.* Retrieved from https://www.dictionary.com/browse/guerrilla-warfare

Digital Attack Map. (2013). *What is a DDoS Attack?* Retrieved from https://www.digitalattackmap.com/understanding-ddos/

Dw.com. (2018). *The Middle East's complex Kurdish landscape.* Retrieved from https://www.dw.com/en/the-middle-easts-complex-kurdish-landscape/a-38863844

Edgington, T. M. (2011). Introducing text analytics as a graduate business school course. *Journal of Information Technology Education, 10*, 207–234.

Elbahadır, H. (2016). *Hacking Interface. In KODLAB Yayın Dağıtım Yazılım ve Eğitim Hizmetleri San.* İstanbul: Ve Tic. Ltd. Şti.

ElGamal, T. (1985). A public key cryptosystem and a signature scheme based on discrete logarithms. *IEEE Transactions on Information Theory, 31*(4), 469–472. doi:10.1109/TIT.1985.1057074

Elish, K., Yao, D., & Ryder, B. (2015). *User-Centric Dependence Analysis for Identifying Malicious Mobile Apps.* Retrieved from http://people.cs.vt.edu/~kelish/most-12.pdf

Emerson, S. (2018). *Hezbollah Hacked Into Mobile Devices Globally.* Retrieved from https://www.newsmax.com/emerson/catfishing-checkpoint-mares-masrayk/2018/10/11/id/885922/

Emin İslam, T. (2012). *Vulnerabilities Scan with Google.* Department of Computer Science, University of Mannheim.

Enck, W., Ongtang, M., & McDaniel, P. (2008). *Mitigating Android software misuse before it happens.* Retrieved from http://siis.cse.psu.edu

Enck, W., Ongtang, M., & McDaniel, P. (2009a). On lightweight mobile phone application certification. *Proceedings of Computer and Communications Security (CCS'09).* Retrieved from http://www.patrickmcdaniel.org/pubs/ccs09a.pdf

Ercan, M. (2015). *Kritik Altyapilarin Korunmasina İlişkin Belirlenen Siber Güvenlik Stratejileri* (MSc thesis). Gebze Technical University.

Eren, V. (2017). *Türk Korsan Gruplarının Siber Terörizmle Mücadelede Etkileri.* Retrieved from file:///F:/email/VahapEren.pdf

Ermiş, K. (2006). Sayısal İmza ve Elektronik Belge Yönetimi. *Bilgi Dünyası, 7*(1), 121–146.

Ersson, J., & Moradian, E. (2013). Botnet Detection with Event-Driven Analysis. *Procedia Computer Science, 22*, 662–671. doi:10.1016/j.procs.2013.09.147

EUROPOL Public Information. (n.d.). *Changes in Modus Operandi of Islamic State Terrorist Attacks.* Academic Press.

Eyal, I., & Sirer, E. G. (2018). Majority is not enough: Bitcoin mining is vulnerable. *Communications of the ACM*, *61*(7), 95–102. doi:10.1145/3212998

Feily, M., Shahrestani, A., & Ramadass, S. (2009, June). A survey of botnet and botnet detection. In *Emerging Security Information, Systems and Technologies, 2009. SECURWARE'09. Third International Conference on* (pp. 268-273). IEEE. 10.1109/SECURWARE.2009.48

Feng, Y., Anand, S., Dillig, I., & Aiken, A. (2014, November). Apposcopy: Semantics-based detection of Android malware through static analysis. In *Proceedings of the 22nd ACM SIGSOFT International Symposium on Foundations of Software Engineering* (pp. 576-587). ACM. 10.1145/2635868.2635869

Fernández-Luna, J. M., Huete, J. F., MacFarlane, A., & Efthimiadis, E. N. (2009). Teaching and learning in information retrieval. *Information Retrieval*, *12*(2), 201–226. doi:10.100710791-009-9089-9

Finklea, K. M. (2015). *Dark web*. Congressional Research Service. Accessed on July 2018 https://www.fas.org/sgp/crs/misc/R44101.pdf

Finklea, K. M. (2017). *Dark web*. Congressional Research Service.

Finklestone, J., & Obe, J. F. (2013). *Anwar Sadat: visionary who dared*. Routledge. doi:10.4324/9781315035864

Firdausi, I., Erwin, A., & Nugroho, A. S. (2010, December). Analysis of machine learning techniques used in behavior-based malware detection. In *Advances in Computing, Control and Telecommunication Technologies (ACT), 2010 Second International Conference on* (pp. 201-203). IEEE. 10.1109/ACT.2010.33

Fulbright, N. R. (2017). *WannaCry Ransomware Attack Summary*. Available at: https://www.dataprotectionreport.com/2017/05/wannacry-ransomware-attack-summary/

Fu, T., Abbasi, A., & Chen, H. (2010). A focused crawler for Dark Web forums. *Journal of the American Society for Information Science and Technology*, *61*(6), 1213–1231.

Gandhewar, N., & Sheikh, R. (2010). Google Android: An emerging software platform for mobile devices. *International Journal on Computer Science and Engineering, 1*(1), 12–17.

García, S. (2014). *Identifying, Modeling and Detecting Botnet Behaviors in the Network* (Unpublished doctoral dissertation). Universidad Nacional del Centro de la Provincia de Buenos Aires.

Garcia, S., Grill, M., Stiborek, J., & Zunino, A. (2014). An empirical comparison of botnet detection methods. *Computers & Security, 45*, 100-123.

Garetto, M., Gong, W., & Towsley, D. (2003, March). Modeling malware spreading dynamics. In *INFOCOM 2003. Twenty-Second Annual Joint Conference of the IEEE Computer and Communications. IEEE Societies* (Vol. 3, pp. 1869-1879). IEEE. 10.1109/INFCOM.2003.1209209

Gee, J. P. (2010). *An introduction to discourse analysis: Theory and method.* Routledge. doi:10.4324/9780203847886

Gennaro, R., & Rohatni, P. (2001). How to Sign Digital Streams. *Information and Computation, 165*(1), 100–116. doi:10.1006/inco.2000.2916

Giacomello, G. (2003). Measuring 'digital wars': Learning from the experience of peace research and arms control. *Infocon Magazine, 1.*

Giacomello, G. (2004). Bangs for the buck: A cost-benefit analysis of cyberterrorism. *Studies in Conflict and Terrorism, 27*(5), 387–408. doi:10.1080/10576100490483660

Glazer, E. (2014). *J.P. Morgan Says About 76 Million Households Affected By Cyber Breach.* Available at: https://www.marketwatch.com/story/jp-morgan-says-about-76-million-households-affected-by-cyber-breach-2014-10-02-17103316

Glenn, M., & D'Agostino, D. (2008). *The future of higher education: How technology will shape learning.* New Media Consortium.

Goharian, N., Grossman, D., Frieder, O., & Raju, N. (2004). Migrating information retrieval from the graduate to the undergraduate curriculum. *Journal of Information Systems Education, 15*(1), 55.

Going Dark. The Internet behind the Internet. (2014). Accessed August 30, 2016. http://www.npr.org/ sections/alltechconsidered/2014/05/25/315821415/ going-dark-the-internet-behind-the-internet

Gökhan, B. (n.d.). New Requirement of Harbin Fifth Dimension: Cyber Intelligence. *Security Strategies Magazine, 20.*

Goralski, W. (2009). IGPs: RIP, OSPF, and IS—IS. In The Illustrated Network. Morgan Kaufmann. doi:10.1016/B978-0-12-374541-5.50021-3

Goralski, W. (2017). IGPs: RIP, OSPF, and IS-IS. In The Illustrated Network (2nd ed.). Morgan Kaufmann. doi:10.1016/B978-0-12-811027-0.00015-1

Goralski, W. J., Gadecki, C., & Bushong, M. (2011). *JUNOS OS For Dummies: The IS-IS Protocol functionalities* (2nd ed.). Retrieved from https://www.dummies.com/store/product/JUNOS-OS-For-Dummies-2nd-Edition. productCd-0470891890.html

Goztepe, K. (2012). Designing fuzzy rule based expert system for cyber security. *International Journal of Information Security Science, 1*(1), 13–19.

Göztepe, K., Boran, S., & Yazgan, H. R. (2012). *Siber Saldırıların Tespiti ve Engellenmesi İçin Uzman Sistem (US) Tasarımı: Siber Savunma Uzman Sistemi (SİSU). Yöneylem Araştırması ve Endüstri Mühendisliği 32.* İstanbul: Ulusal Kongresi.

Grace, M., Zhou, Y., Zhang, Q., Zou, S. S., & Jiang, X. (2013). *RiskRanker: Scalable and Accurate Zero-day Android Malware Detection.* Retrieved from https://www.csc2.ncsu.edu/faculty/xjiang4/pubs/MOBISYS12.pdf

Greenberg, J. (2000). *Sharon Touches a Nerve, and Jerusalem Explodes.* Retrieved from https://www.nytimes.com/2000/09/29/world/sharon-touches-a-nerve-and-jerusalem-explodes.html

Grizzard, J. B., Sharma, V., Nunnery, C., Kang, B. B., & Dagon, D. (2007). Peer-to-Peer Botnets: Overview and Case Study. *HotBots, 7,* 1–1.

Gu, G., Perdisci, R., Zhang, J., & Lee, W. (2008). *Botminer: Clustering analysis of network traffic for protocol-and structure-independent botnet detection.* Academic Press.

Gu, G., Zhang, J., & Lee, W. (2008). *BotSniffer: Detecting botnet command and control channels in network traffic.* Academic Press.

Guinchard, A. (2011). Between Hype and Understatement- Reassessing Cyber Risks as a Security Strategy. *Journal of Strategic Security, 4*(2), 87. doi:10.5038/1944-0472.4.2.5

Gunes, C., & Lowe, R. (2015). *The impact of the Syrian War on Kurdish politics across the Middle East.* Chatham House.

Güngör, M. (2015). *Ulusal Bilgi Güvenliği: Strateji ve Kurumsal Yapılanma* (PhD thesis). Uzmanlık Tezi, T.C. Kalkınma Bakanlığı, Bilgi Toplumu Dairesi Başkanlığı.

Güntay, V. (2017). Uluslararası Sistem ve Güvenlik Açısından Değişen Savaş Kurgusu; Siber Savaş Örneği. *Güvenlik Bilimleri Dergisi, 6*(2), 81–108. doi:10.28956/gbd.354150

Gupta, P., & Narang, B. (2012). Role of Text Mining in Business Intelligence. *Gian Jyoti E-Journal, 1*(2).

Gupta, S. (2006). *Foundstone Hacme Bank v2.0™ Software Security Training Application User and Solution Guide.* Retrieved from http://www.mcafee.com/us/resources/whitepapers/foundstone/wp-hacmebank-v2-user-guide.pdf

Gupta, V., & Gosain, A. 2013, May. Tagging Facts and Dimensions in Unstructured Data. In *International Conference on Electrical, Electronics and Computer Science Engineering (EECS)* (pp. 1-6). Academic Press.

Gupta, V., & Lehal, G. (2009, August). A Survey of text mining techniques and applications. *Journal of Emerging Technologies in Web Intelligence, 1*(1), 60–76. doi:10.4304/jetwi.1.1.60-76

Gürkaynak, M., & İren, Â. A. (2011). Reel Dünyada Sanal Açmaz: Siber Alanda Uluslararası İlişkiler. *Süleyman Demirel Üniversitesi İktisadi ve İdari Bilimler Dergisi, 16*(2), 263–279.

Gurkaynak, M., & İren, A. A. (2011). Reel dünyada sanal açmaz: Siber alanda uluslararasi ilişkiler. *Suleyman Demirel University Journal of Faculty of Economics & Administrative Sciences, 16*(2), 264–276.

Gürsoy, A. K. Ç. A. (2007). Osmanli millet sisteminin dönüşümü. *Doğu Anadolu Bölgesi Araştırmaları*, 57-68.

Haaretz. (2018). *Hezbollah*. Retrieved from https://www.haaretz.com/misc/tags/TAG-hezbollah-1.5598890

Hachem, N., Mustapha, Y. B., Granadillo, G. G., & Debar, H. (2011, May). Botnets: lifecycle and taxonomy. In *Network and Information Systems Security (SAR-SSI), 2011 Conference on* (pp. 1-8). IEEE. 10.1109/SAR-SSI.2011.5931395

Hagerott, M. (2014). Stuxnet and the vital role of critical infrastructure operators and engineers. *International Journal of Critical Infrastructure Protection*, *7*(4), 244–246. doi:10.1016/j.ijcip.2014.09.001

Hakan, H., & Oğuzhan, B. (2013). *Turkey's Cybercrime and Cyber Security Policy*. Retrieved from http://www.acarindex.com/dosyalar/makale/acarindex-1423936102.pdf

Haley, C. (2013). A Theory of Cyber Deterrence. *Georgetown Journal of International Affairs*. Retrieved from http://journal.georgetown.edu/a-theory-of-cyberdeterrence-christopher-haley/

Hamas.ps. (2017). *About Hamas*. Retrieved from http://hamas.ps/en/page/2/

Harik, J. P. (2005). *Hezbollah: The changing face of terrorism*. Ib Tauris.

Harvard Divinity School, The Religious Literacy Project. (2018). *Hassan al-Banna*. Retrieved from https://rlp.hds.harvard.edu/faq/hassan-al-banna

Hatipoğlu, C. (2017). Teknolojik Savaşlar: Siber Terörizm Tehditleri. *ICPESS 2017 Proceedings Volume 1: Political Studies*.

Heickero, R. (2008). *Terrorism online and the change of modus operandi*. In *Proceedings of 13th International Command And Control Research and Technology Symposium* (pp. 1–13). Seattle, WA: ICCRTS.

Henderson, C. W. (2010). *Understanding International Law*. Blackwell.

Hernandez & Butler. (2018). Android Escalation Paths: Building Attack-Graphs from SEAndroid Policies. In *Proceedings of the 11th ACM Conference on Security & Privacy in Wireless and Mobile Networks* (WiSec '18). ACM.

Hernández, I., Rivero, C. R., & Ruiz, D. (2018). *World Wide Web (Bussum)*. doi:10.100711280-018-0602-1

Hildreth, S. A. (2001). *Cyberwarfare*. CRS Report for Congress, Congressional Research Service, *Order Code, RL30735*, 2.

History. (2018a). *Britain and France conclude Sykes-Picot agreement*. Retrieved from https://www.history.com/this-day-in-history/britain-and-france-conclude-sykes-picot-agreement

History. (2018b). *9/11 Attacks*. Retrieved from https://www.history.com/topics/9-11-attacks

History. (2018c). *Thirty Years War ends*. Retrieved from https://www.history.com/this-day-in-history/thirty-years-war-ends

Howden, S. (2015). *What was the cost of the JP Morgan Chase data breach?* Available at: https://www.morganmckinley.co.jp/en/article/what-was-cost-jp-morgan-chase-data-breach

Hua, J., & Bapna, S. (2013). The economic impact of cyber terrorism. *The Journal of Strategic Information Systems*, 22(2), 175–186. doi:10.1016/j.jsis.2012.10.004

Huang, J., Zhang, X., Tan, L., Wang, P., & Liang, B. (2014, May). Android: Detecting stealthy behaviors in android applications by a user interface and program behavior contradiction. In *Proceedings of the 36th International Conference on Software Engineering* (pp. 1036-1046). ACM. 10.1145/2568225.2568301

Hundley, R. O., & Anderson, R. H. (1997). Emerging Challenge: Security and Safety in Cyberspace. In Athena's Camp, Preparing for Conflict in the Information Age (pp. 231-251). Santa Monica, CA: RAND Corporation.

Hypponen, M. (2010). *Mobile security review. F-secure labs* [Video file]. Retrieved from http://www.youtube.com/watch?v=fJMLr8BDQq8

IBM 7 Ponemon Institute. (2018). *2018 Cost of a Data Breach Study: Global Overview*. Available at: https://databreachcalculator.mybluemix.net/assets/2018_Global_Cost_of_a_Data_Breac h_Report.pdf

ICS-CERT. (2016). *Cyber-attack against Ukrainian critical infrastructure.* Available at: https://ics-cert.us-cert.gov/alerts/IR-ALERT-H-16-056-01

IDF. (2018). *Hamas' online terrorism.* Retrieved from https://www.idf.il/en/minisites/hamas/hamas-online-terrorism

Iliou, C., Kalpakis, G., Tsikrika, T., Vrochidis, S., & Kompatsiaris, I. (2017). Hybrid focused crawling on the Surface and the Dark Web. *EURASIP Journal on Information Security, 2017*(1), 11

Internet Crime Complaint Center. (2017). *2017 Internet Crime Report.* Available at: https://pdf.ic3.gov/2017_IC3Report.pdf

Internet- deep web darknet. (n.d.). Accessed on July 2018, https://darkwebnews.com/wp-content/uploads/2017/11/internet-deep-web-darknet.png

Intoccia, F. G., & Moore, J. W. (2006). Communications Technology, Warfare, And The Law: Is The Network A Weapon System? *Houston Journal of International Law, 28*(2), 467–489.

Ioannidis, J., & Bellovin, S. M. (2002, February). Implementing Pushback: Router-Based Defense Against DDoS Attacks. In NDSS (Vol. 2). Academic Press.

Ise, O. A. (2016). Integration and Analysis of Unstructured Data for Decision Making: Text Analytics Approach. *International Journal of Open Information Technologies, 4*(10).

ITU. (2008). *Overview of Cybersecurity.* ITU-T Recommendations. Retrieved from http://handle.itu.int/11.1002/1000/9136-en?locatt=format:pdf&auth

Jane's Information Group. (1999). *Cyberterrorism hype.* Retrieved from http://www.iwar.org.uk/cyberterror/resources/janes/jir0525.htm

Javed, A., & Pandey, M. K. (2014). Advance Cyber Security System Using Fuzzy Logic. *ACME: Journal of Management &IT, 10*(1), 17–27.

Javelin, Identity Fraud Hits All Time High With 16.7 Million U.S. Victims in 2017, According to New Javelin Strategy & Research Study. (n.d.). Accessed on December 12 2018, https://www.javelinstrategy.com/press-release/identity-fraud-hits-all-time-high-167-million-us-victims-2017-according-new-javelin

Jenkins, J. P. (2018). *Terrorism*. Retrieved from https://www.britannica.com/topic/terrorism

JLT. (2017). *Notpetya attack disrupts infrastructure and business*. Available at: https://www.jltspecialty.com/our-insights/publications/cyber-decoder/notpetya-attack-disrupts-infrastructure-and-business

Johansen, D., Van Renesse, R., & Schneider, F. B. (1995, May). Operating system support for mobile agents. In *Hot Topics in Operating Systems, 1995. (HotOS-V), Proceedings., Fifth Workshop on* (pp. 42-45). IEEE. 10.1109/HOTOS.1995.513452

John, M. (2013). *Old Trick Threatens the Newest Weapons*. Retrieved from http://www.nytimes.com/2009/10/27/science/27trojan.html?_r=2&ref=science&pagewanted=al

Johnson, P. (2013). *History of the Jews*. Hachette, UK.

Jones, A. (2005). Cyber terrorism: Fact or fiction. *Computer Fraud & Security*, *2005*(6), 4–7. doi:10.1016/S1361-3723(05)70220-7

Juniper Networks. (2018). *IS-IS overview*. Retrieved from https://www.juniper.net/documentation/en_us/junos/topics/concept/is-is-routing-overview.html

Kara, M. (2013). *Cyber Attacks-Cyber Wars and their effects*. Available at: https://core.ac.uk/download/pdf/51099850.pdf

Kara, M. (2013). *Siber Saldirilar - Siber Savaşlar ve Etkileri* (MSc thesis). İstanbul Bilgi Üniversitesi.

Kara, O., Aydın, Ü., & Oğuz, A. (2013). *Ağ Ekonomisinin Karanlık Yüzü: Siber Terör*. Retrieved from http://kisi.deu.edu.tr/oguz.kara/Ag%20Ekonomisinin%20karanlik%20yuzu%20siber%20teror.pdf

Karaarslan, E., Akın, G., & Feath, V. (2008). *Kurumsal Ağlarda Zararlı Yazılımlarla Mücadele Klavuzu*. Ulusal Akademik Ağ ve Bilgi Merkezi, Döküman Kodu:ULAKCSIRT-2008-01, 1, 2.

Karakuş, C. (2011). *Cyber Attacks Against Critical Infrastructures*. Available at: http://ckk.com.tr/bilimsel/siber.pdf

Karakuş, C. (2013). *Kritik Alt Yapılara Siber Saldırı*. İstanbul Kültür Üniversitesi. Retrieved from http://ylt44.com/bilimsel/siber.html

Karame, G., Androulaki, E., & Capkun, S. (2012). Two Bitcoins at the Price of One? Double-Spending Attacks on Fast Payments in Bitcoin. *IACR Cryptology ePrint Archive, 2012*(248).

Karasaridis, A., Rexroad, B., & Hoeflin, D. A. (2007). Wide-Scale Botnet Detection and Characterization. *HotBots, 7*, 7–7.

Kaspersky Lab. (2016). *Kaspersky Lab Discovers Vulnerable Industrial Control Systems Likely Belonging to Large Organizations*. Available at: https://usa.kaspersky.com/about/press-releases/2016_kaspersky-lab-discovers-vulnerable-industrial-control-systems-likely-belonging-to-large-organizations

Kaspersky Lab. (2017). *2017 yılında simdiye kadar yasanan en büyük 5 veri sızıntısı*. Available at: https://www.kaspersky.com.tr/blog/data-leaks-2017/4261/

Kaspersky. (2018). *What is Cyber-Security?* Retrieved from https://www.kaspersky.com/resource-center/definitions/what-is-cyber-security

Katasonov, V. (2016). *The SWIFT System: A Potential Weapon in the Hybrid War*. Available at: http://www.voltairenet.org/article191715.html

Kaur, P., & Sharma, S. (2014, March). Google Android a mobile platform: A review. In Engineering and Computational Sciences (RAECS), 2014 Recent Advances in (pp. 1-5). IEEE. doi:10.1109/RAECS.2014.6799598

Kavitha, D., & Rani, S. K. (2015). Review of Botnet Attacks and its detection Mechanism. *International Journal of Innovative Research in Computer and Communication Engineering, 3*, 2377-2383.

Kaya, A., & Öğün, N. M. (2009). Siber Güvenliğin Milli Güvenlik Açısından Önemi ve Alınabilecek Tedbirler. *Güvenlik Stratejileri, 18*, 8–27.

Keddie, N. R. (1973). Is There a Middle East? *International Journal of Middle East Studies, 4*(3), 255–271. doi:10.1017/S0020743800031457

Keleştemur, A. (2015). *Siber İstihbarat*. İstanbul: Yazın Basın Yayınevi Matbaacılık Trz.Tic.Ltd.Şti.

Kim, D. H., Lee, T., Kang, J., Jeong, H., & In, H. P. (2012). Adaptive pattern mining model for early detection of botnet-propagation scale. *Security and Communication Networks*, *5*(8), 917–927. doi:10.1002ec.366

Kingsbury, A. (2010). *Documents Reveal Al Qaeda Cyberattacks*. Retrieved from https://www.usnews.com/news/articles/2010/04/14/documents-reveal-al-qaeda-cyberattacks

Kirk, J. (2018). *Banco de Chile Loses $10 Million in SWIFT-Related Attack*. Available at: https://www.bankinfosecurity.com/banco-de-chile-loses-10-million-in-swift-related-attack-a-11075

Knop, K. V. (2008). Institutionalization of a Web-Focused, Multinational Counter-Terrorism Campaign-Building a Collective Open Source Intelligent System. A Discussion Paper. *NATO Security Through Science Series E Human and Societal Dynamics*, *34*, 8.

Knox, P. (2017). *Cyber Jihadis Who are the United Cyber Caliphate and what do the pro-Isis hacking group believe in?* Retrieved from https://www.thesun.co.uk/news/3242477/united-cyber-caliphate-isis-hacking/

Koppes, C. R. (1976). Captain Mahan, General Gordon, and the origins of the term 'Middle East'. *Middle Eastern Studies*, *12*(1), 95–98. doi:10.1080/00263207608700307

Kovacs, E. (2017). *Hamas-Linked 'Gaza Cybergang' Has New Tools, Targets*. Retrieved from https://www.securityweek.com/hamas-linked-gaza-cybergang-has-new-tools-targets

Kugisaki, Y., Kasahara, Y., Hori, Y., & Sakurai, K. (2007, October). Bot detection based on traffic analysis. In *Intelligent Pervasive Computing, 2007. IPC. The 2007 International Conference on* (pp. 303-306). IEEE. 10.1109/IPC.2007.91

Kurnaz, İ. (2017). Siber Güvenlik ve İlintili Kavramsal Çerçeve. *Cyberpolitik Journal*, (1), 62-83.

Kushwaha, A., & Kushwaha, V. (2011). Location-based services using the Android mobile operating system. *International Journal of Advances in Engineering and Technology*, *1*(1), 14.

Kwon, Y., Kim, D., Son, Y., Vasserman, E., & Kim, Y. (2017, October). Be selfish and avoid dilemmas: Fork after withholding (faw) attacks on bitcoin. In *Proceedings of the 2017 ACM SIGSAC Conference on Computer and Communications Security* (pp. 195-209). ACM. 10.1145/3133956.3134019

Lee, J. S., Jeong, H., Park, J. H., Kim, M., & Noh, B. N. (2008, December). The activity analysis of malicious http-based botnets using degree of periodic repeatability. In *Security Technology, 2008. SECTECH'08. International Conference on* (pp. 83-86). IEEE. 10.1109/SecTech.2008.52

Lefkowitz, J. (2007). *The 1993 Philadelphia Meeting: A Roadmap for Future Muslim Brotherhood Actions in the US*. NEFA Foundation.

Letsch, C., & Khomami, N. (2015). *Turkey terror attack: mourning after scores killed in Ankara blasts*. Retrieved from https://www.theguardian.com/world/2015/oct/10/turkey-suicide-bomb-killed-in-ankara

Lewis, B. (2004). *The crisis of Islam: Holy war and unholy terror*. Random House Incorporated.

Liang, C. S. (2015). Cyber Jihad: Understanding and Countering Islamic State Propaganda. *GSCP Policy Paper*, (2), 4.

Libicki, M. C. (2009). *Cyberdeterrence and Cyberwar*. Santa Monica, CA: RAND Cooperation.

Lin, K. C., Chen, S. Y., & Hung, J. C. (2014). Botnet detection using support vector machines with artificial fish swarm algorithm. *Journal of Applied Mathematics*.

Lipovsky, R. (2014). *Back in BlackEnergy: 2014 Targeted Attacks in Ukraine and Poland*. Retrieved from http://www.welivesecurity.com/2014/09/22/back-in-blackenergy-2014/

Liu, D., Barber, B., & DiGrande, L. (2009). Routing Protocols: RIP, RIPv2, IGRP, EIGRP, OSPF. In Cisco CCNA/CCENT Exam 640-802, 640-822, 640-816 Preparation Kit. Syngress. doi:10.1016/B978-1-59749-306-2.00009-9

Liu, E. (2015). *Al Qaeda Electronic: A Sleeping Dog*. Academic Press.

Liu, J., Xiao, Y., Ghaboosi, K., Deng, H., & Zhang, J. (2009). Botnet: Classification, attacks, detection, tracing, and preventive measures. *EURASIP Journal on Wireless Communications and Networking, 2009*(1), 692654. doi:10.1155/2009/692654

Long, J., Gardner, B., & Brown, J. (2016). *Google Hacking for Penetration Testers* (3rd ed.). Elsevier.

Lupovici, A. (2011). Cyber Warfare and Deterrence. *Military and Strategic Affairs, 3*(3), 49–62.

Lv, J., Wang, X., Zhang, Q., & Huang, M. (2018). LAPGN: Accomplishing information consistency under OSPF in General Networks (an extension). *Journal of Network and Computer Applications, 119*, 57-69. doi:10.1016/j.jnca.2018.06.014

Magnani, D. B., Carvalho, I. A., & Noronha, T. F. (2016). Robust Optimization for OSPF Routing. *IFAC-PapersOnLine, 49*(12), 461-466. doi:10.1016/j.ifacol.2016.07.654

Maia, C., Nogueira, L. M., & Pinho, L. M. (2010, July). Evaluating android os for embedded real-time systems. In *6th international workshop on operating systems platforms for embedded real-time applications* (pp. 63-70). Academic Press.

Malhotra, Y. (2013). *Bitcoin Protocol: Model of 'Cryptographic Proof' Based Global Crypto-Currency & Electronic Payments System. Monic Thudja, The Impact of Blockchain (and Bitcoin) on Cybersecurity.* Accessed on July 2018, https://www.incapsula.com/blog/impact-of-blockchain-bitcoin-on-cybersecurity.html

Manyika, J., Chui, M., Brown, B., Bughin, J., Dobbs, R., Roxburgh, C., & Byers, A.H. (2011). *Big data: The next frontier for innovation, competition, and productivity.* Academic Press.

Margaret, R. (n.d.). *Cybersecurity.* Retrieved 14th December 2018. Available at: https://searchsecurity.techtarget.com/definition/cybersecurity

Marpaung, J. A., Sain, M., & Lee, H. J. (2012, February). Survey on malware evasion techniques: State of the art and challenges. In *Advanced Communication Technology (ICACT), 2012 14th International Conference on* (pp. 744-749). IEEE.

Martey, A. (2002b). *Integrated IS-IS Routing Protocol Concepts*. Retrieved from http://www.ciscopress.com/articles/article.asp?p=26850&seqnum=5

Martey, A. (2002a). *IS-IS Network Design Solutions*. Indianapolis, IN: Cisco Press.

Martorella, C. (2014). *Metagoofil*. Retrieved from http://tools.kali.org/information-gathering/metagoofil

Marx, M. (2014). *The Extension and Customisation of the Maltego Data-Mining Environment into an Anti-Phishing System*. Rhodes University.

Masud, M. M., Al-Khateeb, T., Khan, L., Thuraisingham, B., & Hamlen, K. W. (2008, October). Flow-based identification of botnet traffic by mining multiple log files. In *Distributed Framework and Applications, 2008. DFmA 2008. First International Conference on* (pp. 200-206). IEEE. 10.1109/ICDFMA.2008.4784437

Matherly. (2017). *Complete Guide to Shodan*. Leanpub.

Mathur, K., & Hiranwal, S. (2013). A survey of techniques in detection and analyzing malware executables. *International Journal of Advanced Research in Computer Science and Software Engineering*, *3*(4).

Mattei, T. A. (2017). *Privacy, Confidentiality, and Security of Health Care Information: Lessons from the Recent WannaCry Cyberattack*. Available at: https://www.worldneurosurgery.org/article/S1878-8750(17)30996-8/abstract

McAfee. (2011). *Revealed: Operation Shady RAT*. Retrieved from http://www.mcafee.com/us/resources/white-papers/wp -operation-shady-rat.pdf

McCarty, B. (2003). Botnets: Big and bigger. *IEEE Security and Privacy*, *99*(4), 87–90. doi:10.1109/MSECP.2003.1219079

McMillan, R. (2009). *Android security chief: mobile-phone attacks coming*. Retrieved from www.computerworld.com

Medhi, D., & Ramasamy, K. (2018a). IP Routing and Distance Vector Protocol Family. In Network Routing (2nd ed.). Morgan Kaufmann. doi:10.1016/B978-0-12-800737-2.00007-7

Medhi, D., & Ramasamy, K. (2018b). Routing Protocols: Framework and Principles. In Network Routing (2nd ed.). Morgan Kaufmann. doi:10.1016/B978-0-12-800737-2.00004-1

Medhi, D., & Ramasamy, K. (2018c). OSPF and Integrated IS–IS, Editor(s): Deep Medhi, Karthik Ramasamy. In Network Routing (2nd ed.). Morgan Kaufmann. doi:10.1016/B978-0-12-800737-2.00008-9

Mele, S. (2013). *Cyber-Weapons: Legal and Strategic Aspects, Version 2.0.* Machiavelli Editions. Retrieved from http://www.strategicstudies.it/wp-content/uploads/2013/07/Machiavelli-Editions-Cyber- Weapons-Legal-and-Strategic-Aspects-V2.0.pdf

Meral, M. (2015). *Importance of protection of critical infrastructures within the scope of cyber security.* Available at: http://afyonluoglu.org/PublicWebFiles/Reports-TR/Akademi/2015-Siber%20g%C3%BCvenlik%20kapsam%C4%B1nda%20kritik%20altyap%C4%B1lar%C4%B1n%20korunmas%C4%B1n%C4%B1n%20%C3%B6nemi.pdf

Merrick, K., Hardhienata, M., Shafi, K., & Hu, J. (2016). A survey of game theoretic approaches to modelling decision-making in information warfare scenarios. *Future Internet*, *8*(3), 34. doi:10.3390/fi8030034

Michallef, J. V. (2017). *Turkey and the Kurdish Corridor: Why the Islamic State Survives.* Retrieved from https://www.huffingtonpost.com/joseph-v-micallef/turkey-and-the-kurdish-co_b_7994540.html

Micro, T. (2018). *SAMSAM Ransomware Hits US Hospital, Management Pays $55K Ransom.* Available at: https://www.trendmicro.com/vinfo/my/security/news/cyber-attacks/samsam-ransomware-hits-us-hospital-management-pays-55k-ransom

Middle East Monitor. (2017). *Remembering the First Intifada.* Retrieved from https://www.middleeastmonitor.com/20171209-remembering-the-first-intifada-2

Middle East Monitor. (2018). *What is behind the US' support of the YPG?* Retrieved from https://www.middleeastmonitor.com/20180130-what-is-behind-the-us-support-of-the-ypg/

Miller, C., Daniel, M., & Honoroff, J. (2009). *Exploiting Android*. Retrieved February 11, 2012 from http://securityevaluators.com

Mohammad, M., & Kankale, A. P. (2016). Designing Forward Chaining Inference Engine For Fuzzy Rule Based Expert System For Cyber Security. *International Journal of Pure and Applied Research in Engineering and Technology*, *4*(9), 725–730.

Mohd Sani, M. (2016). *ISIS Recruitment of Malaysian Youth: Challenge and Response*. Middle East Institute. Retrieved from http://www.mei.edu/content/map/isis-recruitment-malaysianyouth-challenge-and-response

Mosakheil, J. H. (2018). *Security Threats Classification in Blockchains*. Academic Press.

Moser, A., Kruegel, C., & Kirda, E. (2007, December). Limits of static analysis for malware detection. In Computer security applications conference, 2007. ACSAC 2007. Twenty-third annual (pp. 421-430). IEEE. doi:10.1109/ACSAC.2007.21

Mueller, P., & Yadegari, B. (2012). *The Stuxnet Worm*. Retrieved from http://www.cs.arizona.edu/~collberg/Teaching/466566/2012/Resources/presentations/2012/topic 9-final/report. pdf

Munson, Z. (2001). Islamic mobilization: Social movement theory and the Egyptian Muslim Brotherhood. *The Sociological Quarterly*, *42*(4), 487–510. doi:10.1111/j.1533-8525.2001.tb01777.x

Mustafa, Ü. (2014). *Awareness Study on National Cyber Security,* Academic Press.

Mustafa, Ü., & Cafer, C. (2010). *Cyber Security with National and International Dimensions*. Academic Press.

Mustafa, Ü., Cafer, C., & Ayşe Gül, M. (2009). *Ensuring Cyber Security: Current Situation and Cautions in Turkey*. Retrieved from https://www.btk.gov.tr/uploads/undefined/sg.pdf

Muthumanickam, K., Ilavarasan, E., & Dwivedi, S. K. (2014). A Dynamic Botnet Detection Model based on Behavior Analysis. *International Journal on Recent Trends in Engineering & Technology*, *10*(1), 104.

MwrInfosecurity. (n.d.). *Threat Analysis SWIFT Systems and the SWIFT Customer Security Program*. Available at: https://www.mwrinfosecurity.com/assets/swift-whitepaper/mwr-swift-payment-systems-v2.pdf

Nakamoto, S. (2008). *Bitcoin: A peer-to-peer electronic cash system*. Academic Press.

Narayanan, A., Bonneau, J., Felten, E., Miller, A., & Goldfeder, S. (2016). *Bitcoin and cryptocurrency technologies: a comprehensive introduction*. Princeton University Press.

Nasa, D. (2012, April). Text Mining Techniques - A Survey. *International Journal of Advanced Research in Computer Science and Software Engineering*, *2*(4), 50–54.

Nebil, F. S. (2016). *Swift attack had occurred in 3 Turkish banks, BDDK warned the banks*. Available at: http://t24.com.tr/yazarlar/fusun-sarp-nebil/swift-saldirisi-3-turk-bankasinda-yasanmis-bddk-bankalari-uyardi,16136

Networks, J. (2015). *Empowering Mobile Productivity*. Retrieved from http://www.walkerfirst.com/wa_files/File/tech/Juniper_Empowering_Mobile_Productivity.pdf?PHPSESSID=v6ocd0ep1lv71414v1ecie4ek6

Nicholson, A., Webber, S., Dyer, S., Patel, T., & Janicke, H. (2012). SCADA security in the light of Cyber-Warfare. *Computers & Security*, *31*(4), 418–436. doi:10.1016/j.cose.2012.02.009

Nogueira, A., Salvador, P., & Blessa, F. (2010, June). A botnet detection system based on neural networks. In *Digital Telecommunications (ICDT), 2010 Fifth International Conference on* (pp. 57-62). IEEE. 10.1109/ICDT.2010.19

Noll, K. L. (2012). *Canaan and Israel in antiquity: A textbook on history and religion*. A&C Black.

Northrup, T., & Mackin, J. (2011). *Configuring Windows Server 2008 Network Infrastructure*. Washington, DC: Microsoft Press.

Norton, A. R. (2014). *Hezbollah: A Short History-Updated Edition* (Vol. 53). Princeton University Press. doi:10.1515/9781400851447

Nosrati, M., Karimi, R., & Hasanvand, H. A. (2012). Mobile computing: Principles, devices, and operating systems. *World Applied Programming*, 2(7), 399–408.

Ntoulas, A., Zerfos, P., & Cho, J. (2005, June). Downloading textual hidden web content through keyword queries. In *Proceedings of the 5th ACM/IEEE-CS joint conference on Digital libraries* (pp. 100-109). ACM. 10.1145/1065385.1065407

Oikarinen, J., & Reed, D. (1993). *Internet relay chat protocol* (No. RFC 1459).

Olivia. (2018). *Bitcoin and Cyber Security: Digital Frenemies.* Accessed on July 2018, https://www.cybrary.it/2018/01/bitcoin-cyber-security-digital-frenemies/

Ollmann, G. (2009). *Botnet communication topologies.* Academic Press.

Ongtang, M., McLaughlin, S., Enck, W., & McDaniel, P. (2009b). Semantically rich application-centric security in Android. In *Proceedings of the 25th Annual Computer Security Applications Conference (ACSAC'09).* Retrieved from http://dl.acm.org

Ourfali, E. (2015). Comparison between Western and Middle Eastern Cultures: Research on Why American Expatriates Struggle in the Middle East. *Otago Management Graduate*, 33-40. Retrieved from https://www.otago.ac.nz/management/otago632081.pdf

Oxford Dictionaries. (2018a). *Terrorism.* Retrieved from https://en.oxforddictionaries.com/definition/terrorism

Oxford Dictionaries. (2018b). *Intifada.* Retrieved from https://en.oxforddictionaries.com/definition/intifada

Oxford Islamic Studies. (2018a). *Hadith.* Retrieved from http://www.oxfordislamicstudies.com/article/opr/t125/e758

Oxford Islamic Studies. (2018b). *Jihad.* Retrieved from http://www.oxfordislamicstudies.com/article/opr/t125/e1199

Özalp, A. N., & Asker, A. (2017). *Devletin Güvenlik Politikalarında Siber İstihbaratın Rolü ve Önemi, Akademik Bilişim Konferansları, 2017.* Aksaray Üniversitesi.

Özcan, M. (2018). *Siber Terörizm ve Ulusal Güvenliğe Tehdit Boyutu.* Retrieved from http://www.turkishweekly.net/turkce/makale.php?id=87

Özdemir, B. (2007). Zararlı Yazılıma Karşı Korunma Kılavuzu. *Tübitak Uekae, 12.*

Özkan, T. (2006). *Siber Terörizm Bağlamında Türkiye'ye Yönelik Faaliyet Yürüten Terör Örgütlerinin İnternet Sitelerine Yönelik Bir İçerik Analizi.* Yüksek Lisans Tezi, Anadolu Üniversitesi Sosyal Bilimler Enstitüsü.

Pappas, K. (2008). *Back to basics to fight botnets.* Academic Press.

Park, J., Levy, J., Son, M., Park, C., & Hwang, H. (2018). Advances in Cybersecurity Design: An Integrated Framework to Quantify the Economic Impacts of Cyber-Terrorist Behavior. In *Security by Design* (pp. 317–339). Cham: Springer. doi:10.1007/978-3-319-78021-4_15

Pederson, S. (2013). *White Paper: Understanding the deep Web in 10 MinUtes.* Birghtplanet.

Pekkaya, M., Temli, M., & Ozturk, Z. (2017). *Siber Saldırıların Firmalara etkileri: Zonguldak Ornegi.* Available at: https://www.researchgate.net/publication/322250063_SIBER_SALDIRILARIN_FIRMALARA_ETKILERI_ZONGULDAK_ORNEGI

Perdisci, R., Lee, W., & Feamster, N. (2010, April). *Behavioral Clustering of HTTP-Based Malware and Signature Generation Using Malicious Network Traces* (Vol. 10). NSDI.

Perez, C. (2009). *Metadata Enumeration with FOCA.* Retrieved from https://www.darkoperator.com/blog/2009/4/24/metadata-enumeration-with-foca.html

Peters, R. (1980). Idjtihād and taqlīd in 18th and 19th Century Islam. *Die welt des Islams, 20*(3-4), 131-145.

Petsas, T., Voyatzis, G., Athanasopoulos, E., Polychronakis, M., & Ioannidis, S. (2014, April). Rage against the virtual machine: hindering dynamic analysis of Android malware. In *Proceedings of the Seventh European Workshop on System Security* (p. 5). ACM. 10.1145/2592791.2592796

Pinheiro, M. (2017). Know Thy Enemies. *IOSR Journal Of Humanities And Social Science, 22*(10), 39–44.

Ponemon Institute. (2012). *Cyber Security on the Offense: A Study of IT Security Experts.* Available at: https://security.radware.com/uploadedfiles/resources_and_content/attack_tools/cybersecurityo ntheoffense.pdf

Portokalidis, G., Homburg, P., Anagnostakis, K., & Bos, H. (2009). *Paranoid Android: Zero-day protection for smartphones using the cloud.* Retrieved from www.cs.vu.nl/~herbertb/papers/trpa10.pdf

Poulsen, K. (2007). FBI's secret spyware tracks down teen who made bomb threats. *Priv. Secur. Crime Online, 1,* 40–44.

Pressman, J. (2006). The second intifada: Background and causes of the Israeli-Palestinian conflict. *Journal of Conflict Studies, 23*(2).

Pricop, E., & Mihalache, S. F. (2015). Fuzzy approach on modelling cyber-attacks patterns on data transfer in industrial control systems. In *Electronics, Computers and Artificial Intelligence (ECAI), 2015 7th International Conference on.* IEEE. 10.1109/ECAI.2015.7301200

Quick & Choo. (2018). *Digital Forensic Data and Open Source Intelligence.* Big Digital Forensic Data.

Rapheal, J. R. (2010). *Will Android Honeycomb come to smartphones?* Retrieved January, 25, 2012 from http://blogs.computerworld.com/17642/android_honeycomb_smartphones

Rash, W. (2004). *Latest skulls Trojan foretells risky smartphone future.* Retrieved January, 25, 2012 from www.eweek.com

Rathod, D. (2017). Darknet Forensics. *International Journal of Emerging Trends and Technology in Computer Science, 4*(6).

Rees, L. P., Deane, J. K., Rakes, T. R., & Baker, W. H. (2011). Decision support for cybersecurity risk planning. *Decision Support Systems, 51*(3), 493–505. doi:10.1016/j.dss.2011.02.013

Reeve, S., & Koca, G. (2001). *Yeni çakal'lar: Remzi Yusuf, Usame Bin Ladin ve terörizmin geleceği*. Everest.

Richet, J. L. (Ed.). (2015). Cybersecurity Policies and Strategies for Cyberwarfare Prevention. IGI Global. doi:10.4018/978-1-4666-8456-0

Rid, T., & McBurney, P. (2012). Cyber-Weapons. *The RUSI Journal, 157*(1), 6–13. doi:10.1080/03071847.2012.664354

Riley, C., Flannagan, M. E., Fuller, R., Khan, U., Lawson, W. A., O'Brien, K., & Walshaw, M. (2003). IP Routing. In The Best Damn Cisco Internetworking Book Period. Syngress.

Ritchey, D. (2015). *Data Breach Directions: What to Do After an Attack.* Available at: https://www.securitymagazine.com/articles/86071-data-breach-directions-what-to-do-after-an-attack

Robillard, N. (2004). *Global Information Assurance Certification Paper, 1*(4), 2.

Roldán-Molina, G., Almache-Cueva, M., Silva-Rabadão, C., Yevseyeva, I., & Basto-Fernandes, V. (2017). A Decision Support System for Corporations Cybersecurity Management. *Proceedings of 2017 12th Iberian Conference on Information Systems and Technologies (CISTI)*, 1-6. 10.23919/CISTI.2017.7975826

Roman, J. (2014). *eBay Breach: 145 Million Users Notified.* Available at: https://www.bankinfosecurity.com/ebay-a-6858

Rood, J. M. (2006). The Time the Peasants Entered Jerusalem: The revolt against Ibrahim Pasha in the Islamic court sources. *The Jerusalem Quarterly*, 27.

Rouse, M., & Ward, M. (2007). *IS-IS (Intermediate System-to-Intermediate System protocol)*. TechTarget. Retrieved from: https://searchnetworking.techtarget.com/definition/IS-IS

Sağıroğlu, Ş. (2011). *Siber Güvenlik ve Türkiye*. Ankara: Siber Güvenlik Çalıştayı.

Said, E. W. (1995). Orientalism: Western conceptions of the Orient. Harmondsworth, UK: Penguin.

Samson, O. F., Serdar, S., & Vanduhe, V. (2014). Advancing Big Data for Humanitarian Needs. *Procedia Engineering*, 78, 88–95. doi:10.1016/j.proeng.2014.07.043

SANS & E-ISAC. (2016). *Analysis of the Cyber Attack on the Ukrainian Power Grid*. Available at: https://ics.sans.org/media/E-ISAC_SANS_Ukraine_DUC_5.pdf

Santos, I., Penya, Y. K., Devesa, J., & Bringas, P. G. (2009). N-grams-based File Signatures for Malware Detection. *ICEIS*, 9(2), 317–320.

Sarı, A., Biricik, C. G., Keser, C., & Gündoğdu, E. (2014). Inspection of Malware Against the Ethics of Information Systems. *Management Information Systems Congress, at Istanbul Boğaziçi University*. Available at: https://www.researchgate.net/publication/273318222_Bilisim_Sistemleri_Etigine_Aykiri_Zar arli_Yazilimlarin_Incelenmesi Last accessed date: 16/06/2018

Sari, A. (2018). Context-Aware Intelligent Systems for Fog Computing Environments for Cyber-Threat Intelligence. In *Fog Computing* (pp. 205–225). Cham: Springer. doi:10.1007/978-3-319-94890-4_10

Sari, A. (2019). Turkish national cyber-firewall to mitigate countrywide cyber-attacks. *Computers & Electrical Engineering*, 73, 128–144. doi:10.1016/j.compeleceng.2018.11.008

Schaefer, B. (2018). *The Cyber Party of God: How Hezbollah Could Transform Cyberterrorism*. Retrieved from http://georgetownsecuritystudiesreview.org/2018/03/11/the-cyber-party-of-god-how-hezbollah-could-transform-cyberterrorism/#_edn11

Schmidt, A.-D., Bye, R., Schmidt, H.-G., Clausen, J., & Kiraz, O. (2009). *Static analysis of executables for collaborative malware detection on Android*. Retrieved from www.dai-labor.de

Schmitz, R. (2009). *Mobile malware evolution and the Android security model*. Retrieved January, 25, 2012 from www.kriha.de

Sedat, A., Hamdi Murat, Y., & Zeliha, Y.T. (2011). *Cryptology and Application Areas: Open Key Structure and Registered Electronic Mail*. Academic Press.

Seda, Y., & Şeref, S. (2013). *Cyber Security Risk Analysis*. Threat and Preparatory Levels.

Sela, Y. (2016). *U.S. Patent No. 9,521,705*. Washington, DC: U.S. Patent and Trademark Office.

Şener, Ç. (2013). *Stuxnet attack and cyber war strategy of USA: An evaluation within the frame of principle of abstaining from using force in international law*. Available at: http://hukuk.deu.edu.tr/dosyalar/dergiler/dergimiz-15-1/senercelik.pdf

Serkan, S., & Nurettin, T. (2016). *A New Dimension in Cyber Security: Social Media Intelligence*. Academic Press.

Seth, H. (2018). *Evolving Tech, Evolving Terror*. Center for Strategic & International Studies. Available at: https://www.csis.org/npfp/evolving-tech-evolving-terror

Shabtai, A., & Elovici, Y. (2010). *Applying behavioral detection on Android-based devices*. Retrieved January, 25, 2012 from http://www.arnetminer.org/viewpub.do?pid=2955537

Shabtai, A., Fledel, Y., Kanonov, U., Elovici, Y., Dolev, S., & Glezer, C. (2010, March/April). Android: A comprehensive security assessment. *IEEE Security and Privacy*, 8(2), 35–44. doi:10.1109/MSP.2010.2

Shakarian, P., Shakarian, J., & Ruef, A. (2013). *Introduction To Cyberwarfare A Multidisciplinary Approach*. Elsevier, Inc.

Shamah, D. (2015). *Official: Iran, Hamas conduct cyber-attacks against Israel*. Retrieved from https://www.timesofisrael.com/official-iran-hamas-conduct-cyber-attacks-against-israel/

Sheikh, A. A., Ganai, P. T., Malik, N. A., & Dar, K. A. (2013). Smartphone: Android Vs IOS. *The SIJ Transactions on Computer Science Engineering & its Applications (CSEA)*, 1(4), 141-148.

Shin, J., Son, H., & Heo, G. (2015). Development of a cyber security risk model using Bayesian networks. *Reliability Engineering & System Safety*, *134*, 208–217. doi:10.1016/j.ress.2014.10.006

Shin, W., Kiyomoto, S., Fukushima, K., & Tanaka, T. (2009) Towards formal analysis of the permission-based security model for Android. *Fifth International Conference on Wireless and Mobile Communications*, 87-92. 10.1109/ICWMC.2009.21

Silberschatz, A., Galvin, P. B., & Gagne, G. (2014). *Operating system concepts essentials*. John Wiley & Sons, Inc.

Singer, P. W., & Friedman, A. (2014). Cybersecurity And Cyberwar What Everyone Needs To Know. Oxford University Press.

Singer, P. W., & Friedman, A. (2015). Siber Güvenlik ve Siber Savaş. Ankara: Buzdağı Yayınevi.

Small, W., & Singer, D. J. (1982). *Resort to arms: international and civil wars, 1816-1980*. Sage Publications.

Smith, C. S. (2001). 6-12; The First World Hacker War. *The New York Times*. Retrieved from http://www.nytimes.com/2001/05/13/weekinreview/may-6-12-the-first-worldhacker-war.html

Snort - Network Intrusion Detection & Prevention System. (n.d.). Retrieved from http://www.snort.org/

Sökmen, A. İ. (2015). *Dünya'da Siber Terör Örnekleri*. Retrieved from http://www.academia.edu/20041386/D%C3%BCnyadaki_Siber_Ter%C3%B6r_%C3%96rnekleri

Solon, O., & Hern, A. (2017). *'Petya' ransomware attack: what is it and how can it be stopped?* Available at: https://www.theguardian.com/technology/2017/jun/27/petya-ransomware-cyber-attack-who-what-why-how

Sophos. (2018). *SamSam: The (Almost) Six Million Dollar Ransomware*. Available at: https://www.sophos.com/en-us/medialibrary/PDFs/technical-papers/SamSam-The-Almost- Six-Million-Dollar-Ransomware.pdf

Sozcu. (2016). *Son dakika: Kayseri'de hain saldırı*. Retrieved from https://www.sozcu.com.tr/2016/gundem/son-dakika-kayseride-patlama-1570850/

Speckmann, B. (2008). *The Android Google platform*. Retrieved January, 25, 2012 from http://www.emich.edu

Spencer, B., Benedikt, M., & Senellart, P. (2018, June). Form filling based on constraint solving. In *International Conference on Web Engineering* (pp. 95-113). Springer. 10.1007/978-3-319-91662-0_7

Sputnik News. (2018). *A Kurdish fighter from the People's Protection Units (YPG) looks at a smoke after an coalition airstrike in Raqqa, Syria June 16, 2017 Kurdish Forces Use NATO Weapons Against Turkey – Military Analysts*. Retrieved from https://sputniknews.com/analysis/201802021061298505-kurds-nato-weapons-turkey-afrin/

Stanford Encyclopedia of Philosophy. (2014). *Nationalism*. Retrieved from https://plato.stanford.edu/entries/nationalism/

Stefany. (n.d.). *Electronic Civil Disobedience and the World Wide Web of Hacktivism: A Mapping of Extraparliamentarian*. Retrieved from https://www.webpagefx.com/research/electronic-civil-disobedience-hacktivism.html

Stewart, D. J. (2005). The greater Middle East and reform in the Bush administration's ideological imagination. *Geographical Review*, *95*(3), 400–424. doi:10.1111/j.1931-0846.2005.tb00373.x

STM. (2016). *Cyber Threat Report for the Period of October – December 2016*. Available at: https://farukcalikusu.files.wordpress.com/2016/10/siber-tehdit-durum-raporu-temmuz-eylul- 2016.pdf

STM. (2017). *Cyber Threat Report for the Period of October – December 2017*. Available at: https://www.stm.com.tr/documents/file/Pdf/siber-tehdit-durum-raporu-ekim-aralik-2017.pdf

Stohl, M. (2006). Cyber terrorism: A clear and present danger, the sum of all fears, breaking point or patriot games? *Crime, Law, and Social Change*, *46*(4-5), 223–238. doi:10.100710611-007-9061-9

Stueckle, J. (2011) *Android Protection Mechanism: A Signed Code Security Mechanism for Smartphone Applications*. Retrieved January, 25,2012 from http://www.dtic.mil

Stuttard, D., & Pinto, M. (2011). *The Web Application Hackers Handbook*. Indianapolis, IN: John Wiley & Sons, Inc.

Sudhir, M. R. (2008). Asymmetric War: A Conceptual Understanding. *CLAWS Journal*, 58-66.

Sui, D., Caverlee, J., & Rudesill, D. (2015). T*he deep web and the darknet: a look inside the internet's massive black box*. Google Scholar.

Sukumaran, S., & Sureka, A. (2006). Integrating structured and unstructured data using text tagging and annotation. *Business Intelligence Journal*, *1*(2), 8.

Sulin, O. (2018). *Cyber Attack Campaigns in Political Conflicts: A case study of Anonymous hacktivists' campaign against ISIS* (Master's thesis).

Sullivan, M. (2014). *Middle East Security Report 19-Hezbollah in Syria*. Academic Press.

Symantec. (2011). *Symantec Report on Attack Kits and Malicious Websites*. Retrieved from http://www.symantec.com/content/en/us/enterprise/other_resources/b- symantec_report_on_attack_kits_and_malicious_websites_exec_summary_21169172_WP.enus. pdf

Symantec. (2018). *Internet Security Threat Report*. Available at: https://www.symantec.com/content/dam/symantec/docs/reports/istr-23-2018-en.pdf

Tabansky, L. (2012). Cybercrime- A National Security Issue? *Military and Strategic Affairs*, *4*(3), 117.

Tanenbaum, A. S. (2009). *Modern operating system*. Pearson Education, Inc.

Tanış, T. (2016). US-Turkey relations at a breaking point over the Kurds. *Turkish Policy Quarterly*, *14*(4), 67–75.

Tapscott, D., & Tapscott, A. (2017, June). *Realizing the Potential of Blockchain. A Multistakeholder Approach to the Stewardship of Blockchain and Cryptocurrencies*. World Economic Forum White Paper. Tor Project. Accessed on July 2018 https://www.torproject.org/about/overview.html

Temizel, M. (2011). Terörizmde Yeni Milad: 11 Eylül 2001. *Selçuk Üniversitesi Sosyal Bilimler MYO Dergisi, 14*(1-2), 311–348.

Terrorism. (n.d.). Available at: https://www.google.com/search?q=terror+meaning&rlz=1C1CHBF_enCY821CY821&o q=terror+meaning&aqs=chrome.69i57j0l5.3245j1j9&sourceid=chrome&ie=UTF-8#dobs=terrorism

The 2nd Biggest Data Violation in History has Occurred. (2017). *CHIP ONLINE Haber bülteni*. Available at: https://www.chip.com.tr/haber/tarihin-en-buyuk-2-veri-ihlali-gerceklesti_71789.html

The Center for Strategic and International Studies (CSIS) and McAfee. (2014). *Net Losses: Estimating the Global Cost of Cybercrime*. Available at: https://csis-prod.s3.amazonaws.com/s3fs- public/legacy_files/files/attachments/140609_rp_economic_impact_cybercrime_report.pdf

The Center for Strategic and International Studies (CSIS) and McAfee. (2018). *The Economic Impact of Cybercrime—No Slowing Down*. Available at: https://csis-prod.s3.amazonaws.com/s3fs-public/publication/economic-impact- cybercrime.pdf?kab1HywrewRzH17N9wu E24soo1IdhuHdutm_source=Pressutm_campaign= bb9303ae70 EMAIL_CAMPAIGN_2018_02_21utm_medium=emailutm_term=0_7623d157be-bb9303ae70-194093869 Last accessed date: 25/06/2018

The Treaty of Sevres. (1920). *The allied and associated powers and turkey*. Retrieved from http://sam.baskent.edu.tr/belge/Sevres_ENG.pdf

The World Factbook. (2018). *Middle East*. Retrieved from https://www.cia.gov/library/publications/the-world-factbook/wfbExt/region_mde.html

Thomas, A. (2017). *Zomato hacked: Security breach results in 17 million user data stolen*. Available at: https://economictimes.indiatimes.com/small-biz/security-tech/security/zomato-hacked- security-breach-results-in-17-million-user-data-stolen/articleshow/58729251.cms

Tibi, B. (1990). The simultaneity of the unsimultaneous: Old tribes and imposed nation-states in the modern Middle East. *Tribes and State Formation in the Middle East*, 127-152.

Tor Project. (n.d.). *Tor at the Heart: The Ahmia project\ The Tor Blog*. Retrieved June 12, 2018, from https://blog.torproject.org/tor-heart-ahmia-project

Tracy, K. W. (2012). Mobile Application Development Experiences on Apple¿s iOS and Android OS. *IEEE Potentials, 31*(4), 30–34. doi:10.1109/MPOT.2011.2182571

Turhan, M. (2010). Siber Güvenliğin Sağlanması, Dünya Uygulamaları ve Ülkemiz İçin Çözüm Önerileri. *Bilgi Teknolojileri ve İletişim Kurumu, 42.*

Türkay, Ş. (2013). *Siber Savaş Hukuku ve Uygulanma Sorunsalı. İstanbul Üniversitesi Hukuk Fakültesi Mecmuası, 71*(1), 1177–1228.

Turner, N. (2018). *Under Armour Says 150 Million MyFitnessPal Accounts Hacked*. Available at: https://www.bloomberg.com/news/articles/2018-03-29/under-armour-says-150-million-myfitnesspal-accounts-were-hacked

Ulaşanoğlu, M. E. (2010). *Bilgi Güvenliği: Riskler ve Öneriler*. Bilgi Teknolojileri ve İletişim Kurumu. Retrieved from http://docplayer.biz.tr/632957-Bilgiguvenligi-riskler-ve-oneriler.html

United States Government. The Secretary of Air Force. (2014). *Air Force Policy Directive 10-7, Information Operations* (Operation No: OPR: AF/A3O-QI). Retrieved from http://static.e-publishing.af.mil/production/1/af_a3_5/publication/afpd10-7/afpd10-7.pdf

University U. L. M. Germany. (2011). *Catching authtokens in the wild. The insecurity of Google's clientlogin protocol*. Retrieved from http://www.uni-ulm.de/in/mi/mitarbeiter/koenings/catching-authtokens.html

Uraz, Y., Şeref, S., & İlhami, Ç. (2012). Information Security Threats and Measures to be Taken in Social Networks. *Journal of Polytechnic Volume, 15*(1).

Vallet, J., & Brun, O. (2014). Online OSPF weights optimization in IP networks. *Computer Networks, 60*, 1-12. doi:10.1016/j.bjp.2013.12.014

van Hardeveld, G. J., Webber, C., & O'Hara, K. (2017). Deviating From the Cybercriminal Script: Exploring Tools of Anonymity (Mis) Used by Carders on Cryptomarkets. *The American Behavioral Scientist, 61*(11), 1244–1266. doi:10.1177/0002764217734271

Van Ruitenbeek, E., & Sanders, W. H. (2008, September). Modeling peer-to-peer botnets. In *Quantitative Evaluation of Systems, 2008. QEST'08. Fifth International Conference on* (pp. 307-316). IEEE. 10.1109/QEST.2008.43

Vasilescu C., (2012). Cyber Attacks-Emerging Threats to the 21st Century Critical Information Infrastructures. *Pobrana a Strategie/Defence & Strategy, 1*. 7199.12.2012.01.053-062 doi:10.3849/1802

Vatis, M. A. (2001). *Cyber attacks during the war on terrorism: A predictive analysis*. Dartmouth Coll Hanover Nh Inst For Security. doi:10.21236/ADA386280

Veerasamy, N. (2009). *Towards a Conceptual Framework for Cyber-terrorism. 4th International Conference on Information Warfare and Security*, Pretoria, South Africa.

Venkatesh, G. K., & Nadarajan, R. A. (2012, June). HTTP botnet detection using adaptive learning rate multilayer feed-forward neural network. In *IFIP International Workshop on Information Security Theory and Practice* (pp. 38-48). Springer.

Vennon, T. (2010). *Android malware, 2010*. Retrieved January, 25, 2012 from http://threatcenter.smobilesystems.com

Vennon, T., & Stroop, D. (2010). *Android market analysis, 2010*. Retrieved January, 25, 2012 from http://threatcenter.smobilesystems.com

Ventures, C. (2018). *Global Ransomware Damage Costs Predicted To Exceed $8 Billion In 2018*. Available at: https://cybersecurityventures.com/global-ransomware-damage-costs-predicted-to-exceed-8- billion-in-2018/

Villamarín-Salomón, R., & Brustoloni, J. C. (2008, January). Identifying botnets using anomaly detection techniques applied to DNS traffic. In *Consumer Communications and Networking Conference, 2008. CCNC 2008. 5th IEEE* (pp. 476-481). IEEE. 10.1109/ccnc08.2007.112

Virtual Museum of Protestantism. (2018). *Dechristianisation during the Reign of Terror (1793-1794)*. Retrieved from https://www.museeprotestant.org/en/notice/dechristianisation-during-the-reign-of-terror-1793-1794/

Vormayr, G., Zseby, T., & Fabini, J. (2017). Botnet communication patterns. *IEEE Communications Surveys and Tutorials, 19*(4), 2768–2796. doi:10.1109/COMST.2017.2749442

Vyas, C. A., & Lunagaria, M. (2014). Security concerns and issues for bitcoin. *Proceedings of National Conference cum Workshop on Bioinformatics and Computational Biology.*

Wagemakers, J. (2016). Religion. *Oxford Research Encyclopedias.*

Wagener, G., & Dulaunoy, A. (2008). Malware behavior analysis. *Journal in Computer Virology, 4*(4), 279-287.

Wang, A., Chang, W., Chen, S., & Mohaisen, A. (2018). Delving into internet DDoS attacks by botnets: Characterization and analysis. *IEEE/ACM Transactions on Networking, 26*(6), 2843–2855. doi:10.1109/TNET.2018.2874896

Wang, P., Aslam, B., & Zou, C. C. (2010). Peer-to-peer botnets. In *Handbook of Information and Communication Security* (pp. 335–350). Berlin: Springer. doi:10.1007/978-3-642-04117-4_18

Warren, H. (2000). Should you use distance vector or link state routing protocols? *Networking.* Available at: https://www.techrepublic.com/article/should-you-use-distance-vector-or-link-state-routing-protocols/

Wei, X., Gomez, L., Neamtiu, I., & Faloutsos, M. (2012, August). ProfileDroid: multi-layer profiling of android applications. In *Proceedings of the 18th annual international conference on Mobile computing and networking* (pp. 137-148). ACM.

Wiktorowicz, Q. (2006). Anatomy of the Salafi movement. *Studies in Conflict and Terrorism, 29*(3), 207–239. doi:10.1080/10576100500497004

Wilkins, S., & Smith, F. (2011). *CCNP Security Offical Exam Cert Guide.* Indianapolis, IN: Cisco Press.

Willems, C., Holz, T., & Freiling, F. (2007). Toward automated dynamic malware analysis using cwsandbox. *IEEE Security and Privacy, 5*(2), 32–39. doi:10.1109/MSP.2007.45

Williams, H. J., & Blum, I. (2018). *Defining Second Generation Open Source Intelligence (OSINT) for the Defense Enterprise.* Santa Monica, CA: Published by the RAND Corporation. doi:10.7249/RR1964

Wilson, C. (2005). *Computer Attack and Cyberterrorism: Vulnerabilities and Policy Issues for Congress.* Library of Congress. Washington, DC: Congressional Research Service.

Wilson, C. (2008). *Botnets, cybercrime, and cyberterrorism: Vulnerabilities and policy issues for congress.* Library of Congress. Washington, DC: Congressional Research Service.

Wong, L. (2005). *Potential Bluetooth vulnerabilities in smartphones.* Retrieved, February 11, 2012, from http://citeseerx.ist.psu.edu

Xie, Y., Yu, F., Achan, K., Panigrahy, R., Hulten, G., & Osipkov, I. (2008). Spamming botnets: Signatures and characteristics. *Computer Communication Review*, *38*(4), 171–182. doi:10.1145/1402946.1402979

Yayla M. (2013). Hukuki Bir Terim Olarak —Siber Savaş —Cyber War As A Legal Term. *TBB Dergisi*, (104), 177-202.

Yazıcı, A. (2011). *Siber Güvenlik ve SAHAB*, Retrieved from http://www.emo.org.tr/ekler/fad64faae21db53_ek.pdf

Yeni Akit. (2017). *YPG'nin kullandığı silah şoke etti!* Retrieved from https://www.yeniakit.com.tr/haber/ypgnin-kullandigi-silah-soke-etti-275642.html

Yıldız, M. (2014). *Siber Suçlar ve Kurum Güvenliği* (Thesis). Republic of Turkey Ministry Of Transport Maritime Affairs And Communications, Department of Information Technologies.

Yıldız, S. Ö. (n.d.). Makarenko'nun "Kara Delik Sendromu" Teorisi ve Terörizmin Finansmanında Sınıraşan Organize Suçlar. *Güvenlik Stratejileri Dergisi*, *13*(25), 27-64.

Yılmaz, S. (2012). Türkiye'nin İç Güvenlik Yapılanmasında Değişim İhtiyacı. *Çukurova Üniversitesi Sosyal Bilimler Enstitüsü Dergisi, 21*(3).

Yılmaz, S., & Salcan, O. (2008). *Siber Uzay'da Güvenlik ve Türkiye.* İstanbul: Milenyum Yayınları.

Yunos, Z., & Ahmad, R. (2014). Evaluating cyber terrorism components in Malaysia. In *Information and Communication Technology for The Muslim World (ICT4M), 2014 The 5th International Conference on* (pp. 1-6). IEEE. 10.1109/ICT4M.2014.7020582

Yunos, Z., Ahmad, R., & Mohd Sabri, N. A. (2015). A qualitative analysis for evaluating a cyber terrorism framework in Malaysia. *Information Security Journal: A Global Perspective, 24*(1-3), 15-23.

Yunos, Z., Ahmad, R., Suid, S. H., & Ismail, Z. (2010). Safeguarding malaysia's Critical National Information Infrastructure (CNII) against cyber terrorism: Towards development of a policy framework. In *Information Assurance and Security (IAS), 2010 Sixth International Conference on* (pp. 21-27). IEEE.

Yunos, Z., Ahmad, R., & Yusoff, M. (2014). Grounding the component of cyber terrorism framework using the grounded theory. In *Science and Information Conference (SAI)*, 2014 (pp. 523-529). IEEE. 10.1109/SAI.2014.6918237

ZDNet. (2010). *Google fixes android root-access flaw*. Retrieved January, 25, 2012 from www.zdnetasia.com

Zelin, A. Y. (2014). The war between ISIS and al-Qaeda for supremacy of the global jihadist movement. The Washington Institute for Near East Policy, 20(1), 1-11.

Zetter, K. (2016). *Everything we know about Ukraine's power plant hack*. Available at: https://www.wired.com/2016/01/everything-we-know-about-ukraines-power-plant-hack/

Zhao, D., Traore, I., Sayed, B., Lu, W., Saad, S., Ghorbani, A., & Garant, D. (2013). Botnet detection based on traffic behavior analysis and flow intervals. *Computers & Security, 39*, 2–16. doi:10.1016/j.cose.2013.04.007

Zhioua, S. (2013). *The Middle East under Malware Attack Dissecting Cyber Weapons*. Available at: http://faculty.kfupm.edu.sa/ics/zhioua/Research/malwareSurvey-NFSP-2013.pdf

Zhou, W., Zhou, Y., Jiang, X., & Ning, P. (2014). *Detecting Repackaged Smartphone Applications in Third-Party Android Marketplaces*. Retrieved from https://www.csc2.ncsu.edu/faculty/xjiang4/pubs/CODASPY12.pdf

Zhou, Y., Wang, Z., Zhou, W., & Jiang, X. (2016). *Detecting Malicious Apps in Official and Alternative Android Markets*. Retrieved from http://www.csd.uoc.gr/~hy558/papers/mal_apps.pdf

Zou, C. C., & Cunningham, R. (2006, June). Honeypot-aware advanced botnet construction and maintenance. In Null (pp. 199-208). IEEE. doi:10.1109/DSN.2006.38

Related References

To continue our tradition of advancing information science and technology research, we have compiled a list of recommended IGI Global readings. These references will provide additional information and guidance to further enrich your knowledge and assist you with your own research and future publications.

Abbas, R., Michael, K., & Michael, M. G. (2017). What Can People Do with Your Spatial Data?: Socio-Ethical Scenarios. In A. Marrington, D. Kerr, & J. Gammack (Eds.), *Managing Security Issues and the Hidden Dangers of Wearable Technologies* (pp. 206–237). Hershey, PA: IGI Global. doi:10.4018/978-1-5225-1016-1.ch009

Abulaish, M., & Haldar, N. A. (2018). Advances in Digital Forensics Frameworks and Tools: A Comparative Insight and Ranking. *International Journal of Digital Crime and Forensics*, 10(2), 95–119. doi:10.4018/IJDCF.2018040106

Ahmad, F. A., Kumar, P., Shrivastava, G., & Bouhlel, M. S. (2018). Bitcoin: Digital Decentralized Cryptocurrency. In G. Shrivastava, P. Kumar, B. Gupta, S. Bala, & N. Dey (Eds.), *Handbook of Research on Network Forensics and Analysis Techniques* (pp. 395–415). Hershey, PA: IGI Global. doi:10.4018/978-1-5225-4100-4.ch021

Ahmed, A. A. (2017). Investigation Approach for Network Attack Intention Recognition. *International Journal of Digital Crime and Forensics*, 9(1), 17–38. doi:10.4018/IJDCF.2017010102

Akhtar, Z. (2017). Biometric Spoofing and Anti-Spoofing. In M. Dawson, D. Kisku, P. Gupta, J. Sing, & W. Li (Eds.), Developing Next-Generation Countermeasures for Homeland Security Threat Prevention (pp. 121-139). Hershey, PA: IGI Global. doi:10.4018/978-1-5225-0703-1.ch007

Akowuah, F. E., Land, J., Yuan, X., Yang, L., Xu, J., & Wang, H. (2018). Standards and Guides for Implementing Security and Privacy for Health Information Technology. In Y. Maleh (Ed.), *Security and Privacy Management, Techniques, and Protocols* (pp. 214–236). Hershey, PA: IGI Global. doi:10.4018/978-1-5225-5583-4.ch008

Akremi, A., Sallay, H., & Rouached, M. (2018). Intrusion Detection Systems Alerts Reduction: New Approach for Forensics Readiness. In Y. Maleh (Ed.), *Security and Privacy Management, Techniques, and Protocols* (pp. 255–275). Hershey, PA: IGI Global. doi:10.4018/978-1-5225-5583-4.ch010

Aldwairi, M., Hasan, M., & Balbahaith, Z. (2017). Detection of Drive-by Download Attacks Using Machine Learning Approach. *International Journal of Information Security and Privacy*, *11*(4), 16–28. doi:10.4018/IJISP.2017100102

Alohali, B. (2017). Detection Protocol of Possible Crime Scenes Using Internet of Things (IoT). In M. Moore (Ed.), *Cybersecurity Breaches and Issues Surrounding Online Threat Protection* (pp. 175–196). Hershey, PA: IGI Global. doi:10.4018/978-1-5225-1941-6.ch008

AlShahrani, A. M., Al-Abadi, M. A., Al-Malki, A. S., Ashour, A. S., & Dey, N. (2017). Automated System for Crops Recognition and Classification. In N. Dey, A. Ashour, & S. Acharjee (Eds.), *Applied Video Processing in Surveillance and Monitoring Systems* (pp. 54–69). Hershey, PA: IGI Global. doi:10.4018/978-1-5225-1022-2.ch003

Anand, R., Shrivastava, G., Gupta, S., Peng, S., & Sindhwani, N. (2018). Audio Watermarking With Reduced Number of Random Samples. In G. Shrivastava, P. Kumar, B. Gupta, S. Bala, & N. Dey (Eds.), *Handbook of Research on Network Forensics and Analysis Techniques* (pp. 372–394). Hershey, PA: IGI Global. doi:10.4018/978-1-5225-4100-4.ch020

Anand, R., Sinha, A., Bhardwaj, A., & Sreeraj, A. (2018). Flawed Security of Social Network of Things. In G. Shrivastava, P. Kumar, B. Gupta, S. Bala, & N. Dey (Eds.), *Handbook of Research on Network Forensics and Analysis Techniques* (pp. 65–86). Hershey, PA: IGI Global. doi:10.4018/978-1-5225-4100-4.ch005

Aneja, M. J., Bhatia, T., Sharma, G., & Shrivastava, G. (2018). Artificial Intelligence Based Intrusion Detection System to Detect Flooding Attack in VANETs. In G. Shrivastava, P. Kumar, B. Gupta, S. Bala, & N. Dey (Eds.), *Handbook of Research on Network Forensics and Analysis Techniques* (pp. 87–100). Hershey, PA: IGI Global. doi:10.4018/978-1-5225-4100-4.ch006

Antunes, F., Freire, M., & Costa, J. P. (2018). From Motivation and Self-Structure to a Decision-Support Framework for Online Social Networks. In V. Ahuja & S. Rathore (Eds.), *Multidisciplinary Perspectives on Human Capital and Information Technology Professionals* (pp. 116–136). Hershey, PA: IGI Global. doi:10.4018/978-1-5225-5297-0.ch007

Atli, D. (2017). Cybercrimes via Virtual Currencies in International Business. In M. Moore (Ed.), *Cybersecurity Breaches and Issues Surrounding Online Threat Protection* (pp. 121–143). Hershey, PA: IGI Global. doi:10.4018/978-1-5225-1941-6.ch006

Baazeem, R. M. (2018). The Role of Religiosity in Technology Acceptance: The Case of Privacy in Saudi Arabia. In J. McAlaney, L. Frumkin, & V. Benson (Eds.), *Psychological and Behavioral Examinations in Cyber Security* (pp. 172–193). Hershey, PA: IGI Global. doi:10.4018/978-1-5225-4053-3.ch010

Bailey, W. J. (2017). Protection of Critical Homeland Assets: Using a Proactive, Adaptive Security Management Driven Process. In M. Dawson, D. Kisku, P. Gupta, J. Sing, & W. Li (Eds.), Developing Next-Generation Countermeasures for Homeland Security Threat Prevention (pp. 17-50). Hershey, PA: IGI Global. doi:10.4018/978-1-5225-0703-1.ch002

Bajaj, S. (2018). Current Drift in Energy Efficiency Cloud Computing: New Provocations, Workload Prediction, Consolidation, and Resource Over Commitment. In S. Aljawarneh & M. Malhotra (Eds.), *Critical Research on Scalability and Security Issues in Virtual Cloud Environments* (pp. 283–303). Hershey, PA: IGI Global. doi:10.4018/978-1-5225-3029-9.ch014

Balasubramanian, K. (2018). Hash Functions and Their Applications. In K. Balasubramanian & M. Rajakani (Eds.), *Algorithmic Strategies for Solving Complex Problems in Cryptography* (pp. 66–77). Hershey, PA: IGI Global. doi:10.4018/978-1-5225-2915-6.ch005

Balasubramanian, K. (2018). Recent Developments in Cryptography: A Survey. In K. Balasubramanian & M. Rajakani (Eds.), *Algorithmic Strategies for Solving Complex Problems in Cryptography* (pp. 1–22). Hershey, PA: IGI Global. doi:10.4018/978-1-5225-2915-6.ch001

Balasubramanian, K. (2018). Secure Two Party Computation. In K. Balasubramanian & M. Rajakani (Eds.), *Algorithmic Strategies for Solving Complex Problems in Cryptography* (pp. 145–153). Hershey, PA: IGI Global. doi:10.4018/978-1-5225-2915-6.ch012

Balasubramanian, K. (2018). Securing Public Key Encryption Against Adaptive Chosen Ciphertext Attacks. In K. Balasubramanian & M. Rajakani (Eds.), *Algorithmic Strategies for Solving Complex Problems in Cryptography* (pp. 134–144). Hershey, PA: IGI Global. doi:10.4018/978-1-5225-2915-6.ch011

Balasubramanian, K. (2018). Variants of the Diffie-Hellman Problem. In K. Balasubramanian & M. Rajakani (Eds.), *Algorithmic Strategies for Solving Complex Problems in Cryptography* (pp. 40–54). Hershey, PA: IGI Global. doi:10.4018/978-1-5225-2915-6.ch003

Balasubramanian, K., & K., M. (2018). Secure Group Key Agreement Protocols. In K. Balasubramanian, & M. Rajakani (Eds.), *Algorithmic Strategies for Solving Complex Problems in Cryptography* (pp. 55-65). Hershey, PA: IGI Global. doi:10.4018/978-1-5225-2915-6.ch004

Balasubramanian, K., & M., R. (2018). Problems in Cryptography and Cryptanalysis. In K. Balasubramanian, & M. Rajakani (Eds.), *Algorithmic Strategies for Solving Complex Problems in Cryptography* (pp. 23-39). Hershey, PA: IGI Global. doi:10.4018/978-1-5225-2915-6.ch002

Balasubramanian, K., & Abbas, A. M. (2018). Integer Factoring Algorithms. In K. Balasubramanian & M. Rajakani (Eds.), *Algorithmic Strategies for Solving Complex Problems in Cryptography* (pp. 228–240). Hershey, PA: IGI Global. doi:10.4018/978-1-5225-2915-6.ch017

Balasubramanian, K., & Abbas, A. M. (2018). Secure Bootstrapping Using the Trusted Platform Module. In K. Balasubramanian & M. Rajakani (Eds.), *Algorithmic Strategies for Solving Complex Problems in Cryptography* (pp. 167–185). Hershey, PA: IGI Global. doi:10.4018/978-1-5225-2915-6.ch014

Balasubramanian, K., & Mathanan, J. (2018). Cryptographic Voting Protocols. In K. Balasubramanian & M. Rajakani (Eds.), *Algorithmic Strategies for Solving Complex Problems in Cryptography* (pp. 124–133). Hershey, PA: IGI Global. doi:10.4018/978-1-5225-2915-6.ch010

Balasubramanian, K., & Rajakani, M. (2018). Secure Multiparty Computation. In K. Balasubramanian & M. Rajakani (Eds.), *Algorithmic Strategies for Solving Complex Problems in Cryptography* (pp. 154–166). Hershey, PA: IGI Global. doi:10.4018/978-1-5225-2915-6.ch013

Balasubramanian, K., & Rajakani, M. (2018). The Quadratic Sieve Algorithm for Integer Factoring. In K. Balasubramanian & M. Rajakani (Eds.), *Algorithmic Strategies for Solving Complex Problems in Cryptography* (pp. 241–252). Hershey, PA: IGI Global. doi:10.4018/978-1-5225-2915-6.ch018

Barone, P. A. (2017). Defining and Understanding the Development of Juvenile Delinquency from an Environmental, Sociological, and Theoretical Perspective. In S. Egharevba (Ed.), *Police Brutality, Racial Profiling, and Discrimination in the Criminal Justice System* (pp. 215–238). Hershey, PA: IGI Global. doi:10.4018/978-1-5225-1088-8.ch010

Beauchere, J. F. (2018). Encouraging Digital Civility: What Companies and Others Can Do. In R. Luppicini (Ed.), *The Changing Scope of Technoethics in Contemporary Society* (pp. 262–274). Hershey, PA: IGI Global. doi:10.4018/978-1-5225-5094-5.ch014

Behera, C. K., & Bhaskari, D. L. (2017). Malware Methodologies and Its Future: A Survey. *International Journal of Information Security and Privacy*, *11*(4), 47–64. doi:10.4018/IJISP.2017100104

Benson, V., McAlaney, J., & Frumkin, L. A. (2018). Emerging Threats for the Human Element and Countermeasures in Current Cyber Security Landscape. In J. McAlaney, L. Frumkin, & V. Benson (Eds.), *Psychological and Behavioral Examinations in Cyber Security* (pp. 266–271). Hershey, PA: IGI Global. doi:10.4018/978-1-5225-4053-3.ch016

Berbecaru, D. (2018). On Creating Digital Evidence in IP Networks With NetTrack. In G. Shrivastava, P. Kumar, B. Gupta, S. Bala, & N. Dey (Eds.), *Handbook of Research on Network Forensics and Analysis Techniques* (pp. 225–245). Hershey, PA: IGI Global. doi:10.4018/978-1-5225-4100-4.ch012

Berki, E., Valtanen, J., Chaudhary, S., & Li, L. (2018). The Need for Multi-Disciplinary Approaches and Multi-Level Knowledge for Cybersecurity Professionals. In V. Ahuja & S. Rathore (Eds.), *Multidisciplinary Perspectives on Human Capital and Information Technology Professionals* (pp. 72–94). Hershey, PA: IGI Global. doi:10.4018/978-1-5225-5297-0.ch005

Bhardwaj, A. (2017). Ransomware: A Rising Threat of new age Digital Extortion. In S. Aljawarneh (Ed.), *Online Banking Security Measures and Data Protection* (pp. 189–221). Hershey, PA: IGI Global. doi:10.4018/978-1-5225-0864-9.ch012

Bhattacharjee, J., Sengupta, A., Barik, M. S., & Mazumdar, C. (2018). An Analytical Study of Methodologies and Tools for Enterprise Information Security Risk Management. In M. Gupta, R. Sharman, J. Walp, & P. Mulgund (Eds.), *Information Technology Risk Management and Compliance in Modern Organizations* (pp. 1–20). Hershey, PA: IGI Global. doi:10.4018/978-1-5225-2604-9.ch001

Bruno, G. (2018). Handling the Dataflow in Business Process Models. In V. Ahuja & S. Rathore (Eds.), *Multidisciplinary Perspectives on Human Capital and Information Technology Professionals* (pp. 137–151). Hershey, PA: IGI Global. doi:10.4018/978-1-5225-5297-0.ch008

Carneiro, A. D. (2017). Defending Information Networks in Cyberspace: Some Notes on Security Needs. In M. Dawson, D. Kisku, P. Gupta, J. Sing, & W. Li (Eds.), *Developing Next-Generation Countermeasures for Homeland Security Threat Prevention* (pp. 354-375). Hershey, PA: IGI Global. doi:10.4018/978-1-5225-0703-1.ch016

Chakraborty, S., Patra, P. K., Maji, P., Ashour, A. S., & Dey, N. (2017). Image Registration Techniques and Frameworks: A Review. In N. Dey, A. Ashour, & S. Acharjee (Eds.), *Applied Video Processing in Surveillance and Monitoring Systems* (pp. 102–114). Hershey, PA: IGI Global. doi:10.4018/978-1-5225-1022-2.ch005

Chaudhari, G., & Mulgund, P. (2018). Strengthening IT Governance With COBIT 5. In M. Gupta, R. Sharman, J. Walp, & P. Mulgund (Eds.), *Information Technology Risk Management and Compliance in Modern Organizations* (pp. 48–69). Hershey, PA: IGI Global. doi:10.4018/978-1-5225-2604-9.ch003

Cheikh, M., Hacini, S., & Boufaida, Z. (2018). Visualization Technique for Intrusion Detection. In Y. Maleh (Ed.), *Security and Privacy Management, Techniques, and Protocols* (pp. 276–290). Hershey, PA: IGI Global. doi:10.4018/978-1-5225-5583-4.ch011

Chen, G., Ding, L., Du, J., Zhou, G., Qin, P., Chen, G., & Liu, Q. (2018). Trust Evaluation Strategy for Single Sign-on Solution in Cloud. *International Journal of Digital Crime and Forensics*, *10*(1), 1–11. doi:10.4018/IJDCF.2018010101

Chen, J., & Peng, F. (2018). A Perceptual Encryption Scheme for HEVC Video with Lossless Compression. *International Journal of Digital Crime and Forensics*, *10*(1), 67–78. doi:10.4018/IJDCF.2018010106

Chen, K., & Xu, D. (2018). An Efficient Reversible Data Hiding Scheme for Encrypted Images. *International Journal of Digital Crime and Forensics*, *10*(2), 1–22. doi:10.4018/IJDCF.2018040101

Chen, Z., Lu, J., Yang, P., & Luo, X. (2017). Recognizing Substitution Steganography of Spatial Domain Based on the Characteristics of Pixels Correlation. *International Journal of Digital Crime and Forensics*, *9*(4), 48–61. doi:10.4018/IJDCF.2017100105

Cherkaoui, R., Zbakh, M., Braeken, A., & Touhafi, A. (2018). Anomaly Detection in Cloud Computing and Internet of Things Environments: Latest Technologies. In K. Munir (Ed.), *Cloud Computing Technologies for Green Enterprises* (pp. 251–265). Hershey, PA: IGI Global. doi:10.4018/978-1-5225-3038-1.ch010

Chowdhury, A., Karmakar, G., & Kamruzzaman, J. (2017). Survey of Recent Cyber Security Attacks on Robotic Systems and Their Mitigation Approaches. In R. Kumar, P. Pattnaik, & P. Pandey (Eds.), *Detecting and Mitigating Robotic Cyber Security Risks* (pp. 284–299). Hershey, PA: IGI Global. doi:10.4018/978-1-5225-2154-9.ch019

Cortese, F. A. (2018). The Techoethical Ethos of Technic Self-Determination: Technological Determinism as the Ontic Fundament of Freewill. In R. Luppicini (Ed.), *The Changing Scope of Technoethics in Contemporary Society* (pp. 74–104). Hershey, PA: IGI Global. doi:10.4018/978-1-5225-5094-5.ch005

Crosston, M. D. (2017). The Fight for Cyber Thoreau: Distinguishing Virtual Disobedience from Digital Destruction. In M. Korstanje (Ed.), *Threat Mitigation and Detection of Cyber Warfare and Terrorism Activities* (pp. 198–219). Hershey, PA: IGI Global. doi:10.4018/978-1-5225-1938-6.ch009

da Costa, F., & de Sá-Soares, F. (2017). Authenticity Challenges of Wearable Technologies. In A. Marrington, D. Kerr, & J. Gammack (Eds.), *Managing Security Issues and the Hidden Dangers of Wearable Technologies* (pp. 98–130). Hershey, PA: IGI Global. doi:10.4018/978-1-5225-1016-1.ch005

Dafflon, B., Guériau, M., & Gechter, F. (2017). Using Physics Inspired Wave Agents in a Virtual Environment: Longitudinal Distance Control in Robots Platoon. *International Journal of Monitoring and Surveillance Technologies Research*, 5(2), 15–28. doi:10.4018/IJMSTR.2017040102

Dash, S. R., Sheeraz, A. S., & Samantaray, A. (2018). Filtration and Classification of ECG Signals. In C. Pradhan, H. Das, B. Naik, & N. Dey (Eds.), *Handbook of Research on Information Security in Biomedical Signal Processing* (pp. 72–94). Hershey, PA: IGI Global. doi:10.4018/978-1-5225-5152-2.ch005

Dhavale, S. V. (2018). Insider Attack Analysis in Building Effective Cyber Security for an Organization. In J. McAlaney, L. Frumkin, & V. Benson (Eds.), *Psychological and Behavioral Examinations in Cyber Security* (pp. 222–238). Hershey, PA: IGI Global. doi:10.4018/978-1-5225-4053-3.ch013

Dixit, P. (2018). Security Issues in Web Services. In G. Shrivastava, P. Kumar, B. Gupta, S. Bala, & N. Dey (Eds.), *Handbook of Research on Network Forensics and Analysis Techniques* (pp. 57–64). Hershey, PA: IGI Global. doi:10.4018/978-1-5225-4100-4.ch004

Doraikannan, S. (2018). Efficient Implementation of Digital Signature Algorithms. In K. Balasubramanian & M. Rajakani (Eds.), *Algorithmic Strategies for Solving Complex Problems in Cryptography* (pp. 78–86). Hershey, PA: IGI Global. doi:10.4018/978-1-5225-2915-6.ch006

E., J. V., Mohan, J., & K., A. (2018). Automatic Detection of Tumor and Bleed in Magnetic Resonance Brain Images. In C. Pradhan, H. Das, B. Naik, & N. Dey (Eds.), *Handbook of Research on Information Security in Biomedical Signal Processing* (pp. 291-303). Hershey, PA: IGI Global. doi:10.4018/978-1-5225-5152-2.ch015

Escamilla, I., Ruíz, M. T., Ibarra, M. M., Soto, V. L., Quintero, R., & Guzmán, G. (2018). Geocoding Tweets Based on Semantic Web and Ontologies. In M. Lytras, N. Aljohani, E. Damiani, & K. Chui (Eds.), *Innovations, Developments, and Applications of Semantic Web and Information Systems* (pp. 372–392). Hershey, PA: IGI Global. doi:10.4018/978-1-5225-5042-6.ch014

Farhadi, M., Haddad, H. M., & Shahriar, H. (2018). Compliance of Electronic Health Record Applications With HIPAA Security and Privacy Requirements. In Y. Maleh (Ed.), *Security and Privacy Management, Techniques, and Protocols* (pp. 199–213). Hershey, PA: IGI Global. doi:10.4018/978-1-5225-5583-4.ch007

Fatma, S. (2018). Use and Misuse of Technology in Marketing: Cases from India. *International Journal of Technoethics*, 9(1), 27–36. doi:10.4018/IJT.2018010103

Fazlali, M., & Khodamoradi, P. (2018). Metamorphic Malware Detection Using Minimal Opcode Statistical Patterns. In Y. Maleh (Ed.), *Security and Privacy Management, Techniques, and Protocols* (pp. 337–359). Hershey, PA: IGI Global. doi:10.4018/978-1-5225-5583-4.ch014

Filiol, É., & Gallais, C. (2017). Optimization of Operational Large-Scale (Cyber) Attacks by a Combinational Approach. *International Journal of Cyber Warfare & Terrorism*, 7(3), 29–43. doi:10.4018/IJCWT.2017070103

Forge, J. (2018). The Case Against Weapons Research. In R. Luppicini (Ed.), *The Changing Scope of Technoethics in Contemporary Society* (pp. 124–134). Hershey, PA: IGI Global. doi:10.4018/978-1-5225-5094-5.ch007

G., S., & Durai, M. S. (2018). Big Data Analytics: An Expedition Through Rapidly Budding Data Exhaustive Era. In D. Lopez, & M. Durai (Eds.), *HCI Challenges and Privacy Preservation in Big Data Security* (pp. 124-138). Hershey, PA: IGI Global. doi:10.4018/978-1-5225-2863-0.ch006

Gammack, J., & Marrington, A. (2017). The Promise and Perils of Wearable Technologies. In A. Marrington, D. Kerr, & J. Gammack (Eds.), *Managing Security Issues and the Hidden Dangers of Wearable Technologies* (pp. 1–17). Hershey, PA: IGI Global. doi:10.4018/978-1-5225-1016-1.ch001

Gamoura, S. C. (2018). A Cloud-Based Approach for Cross-Management of Disaster Plans: Managing Risk in Networked Enterprises. In S. Aljawarneh & M. Malhotra (Eds.), *Critical Research on Scalability and Security Issues in Virtual Cloud Environments* (pp. 240–268). Hershey, PA: IGI Global. doi:10.4018/978-1-5225-3029-9.ch012

Gao, L., Gao, T., Zhao, J., & Liu, Y. (2018). Reversible Watermarking in Digital Image Using PVO and RDWT. *International Journal of Digital Crime and Forensics*, *10*(2), 40–55. doi:10.4018/IJDCF.2018040103

Geetha, S., & Sindhu, S. S. (2016). Audio Stego Intrusion Detection System through Hybrid Neural Tree Model. In B. Gupta, D. Agrawal, & S. Yamaguchi (Eds.), *Handbook of Research on Modern Cryptographic Solutions for Computer and Cyber Security* (pp. 126–144). Hershey, PA: IGI Global. doi:10.4018/978-1-5225-0105-3.ch006

Geethanjali, P. (2018). Bio-Inspired Techniques in Human-Computer Interface for Control of Assistive Devices: Bio-Inspired Techniques in Assistive Devices. In D. Lopez & M. Durai (Eds.), *HCI Challenges and Privacy Preservation in Big Data Security* (pp. 23–46). Hershey, PA: IGI Global. doi:10.4018/978-1-5225-2863-0.ch002

Ghany, K. K., & Zawbaa, H. M. (2017). Hybrid Biometrics and Watermarking Authentication. In S. Zoughbi (Ed.), *Securing Government Information and Data in Developing Countries* (pp. 37–61). Hershey, PA: IGI Global. doi:10.4018/978-1-5225-1703-0.ch003

Hacini, S., Guessoum, Z., & Cheikh, M. (2018). False Alarm Reduction: A Profiling Mechanism and New Research Directions. In Y. Maleh (Ed.), *Security and Privacy Management, Techniques, and Protocols* (pp. 291–320). Hershey, PA: IGI Global. doi:10.4018/978-1-5225-5583-4.ch012

Hadlington, L. (2018). The "Human Factor" in Cybersecurity: Exploring the Accidental Insider. In J. McAlaney, L. Frumkin, & V. Benson (Eds.), Psychological and Behavioral Examinations in Cyber Security (pp. 46-63). Hershey, PA: IGI Global. doi:10.4018/978-1-5225-4053-3.ch003

Haldorai, A., & Ramu, A. (2018). The Impact of Big Data Analytics and Challenges to Cyber Security. In G. Shrivastava, P. Kumar, B. Gupta, S. Bala, & N. Dey (Eds.), *Handbook of Research on Network Forensics and Analysis Techniques* (pp. 300–314). Hershey, PA: IGI Global. doi:10.4018/978-1-5225-4100-4.ch016

Hariharan, S., Prasanth, V. S., & Saravanan, P. (2018). Role of Bibliographical Databases in Measuring Information: A Conceptual View. In J. Jeyasekar & P. Saravanan (Eds.), *Innovations in Measuring and Evaluating Scientific Information* (pp. 61–71). Hershey, PA: IGI Global. doi:10.4018/978-1-5225-3457-0.ch005

Hore, S., Chatterjee, S., Chakraborty, S., & Shaw, R. K. (2017). Analysis of Different Feature Description Algorithm in object Recognition. In N. Dey, A. Ashour, & P. Patra (Eds.), *Feature Detectors and Motion Detection in Video Processing* (pp. 66–99). Hershey, PA: IGI Global. doi:10.4018/978-1-5225-1025-3.ch004

Hurley, J. S. (2017). Cyberspace: The New Battlefield - An Approach via the Analytics Hierarchy Process. *International Journal of Cyber Warfare & Terrorism*, 7(3), 1–15. doi:10.4018/IJCWT.2017070101

Hussain, M., & Kaliya, N. (2018). An Improvised Framework for Privacy Preservation in IoT. *International Journal of Information Security and Privacy*, 12(2), 46–63. doi:10.4018/IJISP.2018040104

Ilahi-Amri, M., Cheniti-Belcadhi, L., & Braham, R. (2018). Competence E-Assessment Based on Semantic Web: From Modeling to Validation. In V. Ahuja & S. Rathore (Eds.), *Multidisciplinary Perspectives on Human Capital and Information Technology Professionals* (pp. 246–267). Hershey, PA: IGI Global. doi:10.4018/978-1-5225-5297-0.ch013

Jambhekar, N., & Dhawale, C. A. (2018). Cryptography in Big Data Security. In D. Lopez & M. Durai (Eds.), *HCI Challenges and Privacy Preservation in Big Data Security* (pp. 71–94). Hershey, PA: IGI Global. doi:10.4018/978-1-5225-2863-0.ch004

Jansen van Vuuren, J., Leenen, L., Plint, G., Zaaiman, J., & Phahlamohlaka, J. (2017). Formulating the Building Blocks for National Cyberpower. *International Journal of Cyber Warfare & Terrorism*, 7(3), 16–28. doi:10.4018/IJCWT.2017070102

Jaswal, S., & Malhotra, M. (2018). Identification of Various Privacy and Trust Issues in Cloud Computing Environment. In S. Aljawarneh & M. Malhotra (Eds.), *Critical Research on Scalability and Security Issues in Virtual Cloud Environments* (pp. 95–121). Hershey, PA: IGI Global. doi:10.4018/978-1-5225-3029-9.ch005

Jaswal, S., & Singh, G. (2018). A Comprehensive Survey on Trust Issue and Its Deployed Models in Computing Environment. In S. Aljawarneh & M. Malhotra (Eds.), *Critical Research on Scalability and Security Issues in Virtual Cloud Environments* (pp. 150–166). Hershey, PA: IGI Global. doi:10.4018/978-1-5225-3029-9.ch007

Javid, T. (2018). Secure Access to Biomedical Images. In C. Pradhan, H. Das, B. Naik, & N. Dey (Eds.), *Handbook of Research on Information Security in Biomedical Signal Processing* (pp. 38–53). Hershey, PA: IGI Global. doi:10.4018/978-1-5225-5152-2.ch003

Jeyakumar, B., Durai, M. S., & Lopez, D. (2018). Case Studies in Amalgamation of Deep Learning and Big Data. In D. Lopez & M. Durai (Eds.), *HCI Challenges and Privacy Preservation in Big Data Security* (pp. 159–174). Hershey, PA: IGI Global. doi:10.4018/978-1-5225-2863-0.ch008

Jeyaprakash, H. M. K., K., & S., G. (2018). A Comparative Review of Various Machine Learning Approaches for Improving the Performance of Stego Anomaly Detection. In G. Shrivastava, P. Kumar, B. Gupta, S. Bala, & N. Dey (Eds.), Handbook of Research on Network Forensics and Analysis Techniques (pp. 351-371). Hershey, PA: IGI Global. doi:10.4018/978-1-5225-4100-4.ch019

Jeyasekar, J. J. (2018). Dynamics of Indian Forensic Science Research. In J. Jeyasekar & P. Saravanan (Eds.), *Innovations in Measuring and Evaluating Scientific Information* (pp. 125–147). Hershey, PA: IGI Global. doi:10.4018/978-1-5225-3457-0.ch009

Jones, H. S., & Moncur, W. (2018). The Role of Psychology in Understanding Online Trust. In J. McAlaney, L. Frumkin, & V. Benson (Eds.), *Psychological and Behavioral Examinations in Cyber Security* (pp. 109–132). Hershey, PA: IGI Global. doi:10.4018/978-1-5225-4053-3.ch007

Jones, H. S., & Towse, J. (2018). Examinations of Email Fraud Susceptibility: Perspectives From Academic Research and Industry Practice. In J. McAlaney, L. Frumkin, & V. Benson (Eds.), *Psychological and Behavioral Examinations in Cyber Security* (pp. 80–97). Hershey, PA: IGI Global. doi:10.4018/978-1-5225-4053-3.ch005

Joseph, A., & Singh, K. J. (2018). Digital Forensics in Distributed Environment. In G. Shrivastava, P. Kumar, B. Gupta, S. Bala, & N. Dey (Eds.), *Handbook of Research on Network Forensics and Analysis Techniques* (pp. 246–265). Hershey, PA: IGI Global. doi:10.4018/978-1-5225-4100-4.ch013

K., I., & A, V. (2018). Monitoring and Auditing in the Cloud. In K. Munir (Ed.), *Cloud Computing Technologies for Green Enterprises* (pp. 318-350). Hershey, PA: IGI Global. doi:10.4018/978-1-5225-3038-1.ch013

Kashyap, R., & Piersson, A. D. (2018). Impact of Big Data on Security. In G. Shrivastava, P. Kumar, B. Gupta, S. Bala, & N. Dey (Eds.), *Handbook of Research on Network Forensics and Analysis Techniques* (pp. 283–299). Hershey, PA: IGI Global. doi:10.4018/978-1-5225-4100-4.ch015

Kastrati, Z., Imran, A. S., & Yayilgan, S. Y. (2018). A Hybrid Concept Learning Approach to Ontology Enrichment. In M. Lytras, N. Aljohani, E. Damiani, & K. Chui (Eds.), *Innovations, Developments, and Applications of Semantic Web and Information Systems* (pp. 85–119). Hershey, PA: IGI Global. doi:10.4018/978-1-5225-5042-6.ch004

Kaur, H., & Saxena, S. (2018). UWDBCSN Analysis During Node Replication Attack in WSN. In C. Pradhan, H. Das, B. Naik, & N. Dey (Eds.), *Handbook of Research on Information Security in Biomedical Signal Processing* (pp. 210–227). Hershey, PA: IGI Global. doi:10.4018/978-1-5225-5152-2.ch011

Kaushal, P. K., & Sobti, R. (2018). Breaching Security of Full Round Tiny Encryption Algorithm. *International Journal of Information Security and Privacy*, *12*(1), 89–98. doi:10.4018/IJISP.2018010108

Kavati, I., Prasad, M. V., & Bhagvati, C. (2017). Search Space Reduction in Biometric Databases: A Review. In M. Dawson, D. Kisku, P. Gupta, J. Sing, & W. Li (Eds.), Developing Next-Generation Countermeasures for Homeland Security Threat Prevention (pp. 236-262). Hershey, PA: IGI Global. doi:10.4018/978-1-5225-0703-1.ch011

Kaye, L. K. (2018). Online Research Methods. In J. McAlaney, L. Frumkin, & V. Benson (Eds.), *Psychological and Behavioral Examinations in Cyber Security* (pp. 253–265). Hershey, PA: IGI Global. doi:10.4018/978-1-5225-4053-3.ch015

Kenekar, T. V., & Dani, A. R. (2017). Privacy Preserving Data Mining on Unstructured Data. In S. Tamane, V. Solanki, & N. Dey (Eds.), *Privacy and Security Policies in Big Data* (pp. 167–190). Hershey, PA: IGI Global. doi:10.4018/978-1-5225-2486-1.ch008

Khaire, P. A., & Kotkondawar, R. R. (2017). Measures of Image and Video Segmentation. In N. Dey, A. Ashour, & S. Acharjee (Eds.), *Applied Video Processing in Surveillance and Monitoring Systems* (pp. 28–53). Hershey, PA: IGI Global. doi:10.4018/978-1-5225-1022-2.ch002

Knibbs, C., Goss, S., & Anthony, K. (2017). Counsellors' Phenomenological Experiences of Working with Children or Young People who have been Cyberbullied: Using Thematic Analysis of Semi Structured Interviews. *International Journal of Technoethics*, 8(1), 68–86. doi:10.4018/IJT.2017010106

Ko, A., & Gillani, S. (2018). Ontology Maintenance Through Semantic Text Mining: An Application for IT Governance Domain. In M. Lytras, N. Aljohani, E. Damiani, & K. Chui (Eds.), *Innovations, Developments, and Applications of Semantic Web and Information Systems* (pp. 350–371). Hershey, PA: IGI Global. doi:10.4018/978-1-5225-5042-6.ch013

Kohler, J., Lorenz, C. R., Gumbel, M., Specht, T., & Simov, K. (2017). A Security-By-Distribution Approach to Manage Big Data in a Federation of Untrustworthy Clouds. In S. Tamane, V. Solanki, & N. Dey (Eds.), *Privacy and Security Policies in Big Data* (pp. 92–123). Hershey, PA: IGI Global. doi:10.4018/978-1-5225-2486-1.ch005

Korstanje, M. E. (2017). English Speaking Countries and the Culture of Fear: Understanding Technology and Terrorism. In M. Korstanje (Ed.), *Threat Mitigation and Detection of Cyber Warfare and Terrorism Activities* (pp. 92–110). Hershey, PA: IGI Global. doi:10.4018/978-1-5225-1938-6.ch005

Korstanje, M. E. (2018). How Can World Leaders Understand the Perverse Core of Terrorism?: Terror in the Global Village. In C. Akrivopoulou (Ed.), *Global Perspectives on Human Migration, Asylum, and Security* (pp. 48–67). Hershey, PA: IGI Global. doi:10.4018/978-1-5225-2817-3.ch003

Krishnamachariar, P. K., & Gupta, M. (2018). Swimming Upstream in Turbulent Waters: Auditing Agile Development. In M. Gupta, R. Sharman, J. Walp, & P. Mulgund (Eds.), *Information Technology Risk Management and Compliance in Modern Organizations* (pp. 268–300). Hershey, PA: IGI Global. doi:10.4018/978-1-5225-2604-9.ch010

Ksiazak, P., Farrelly, W., & Curran, K. (2018). A Lightweight Authentication and Encryption Protocol for Secure Communications Between Resource-Limited Devices Without Hardware Modification: Resource-Limited Device Authentication. In Y. Maleh (Ed.), *Security and Privacy Management, Techniques, and Protocols* (pp. 1–46). Hershey, PA: IGI Global. doi:10.4018/978-1-5225-5583-4.ch001

Kukkuvada, A., & Basavaraju, P. (2018). Mutual Correlation-Based Anonymization for Privacy Preserving Medical Data Publishing. In C. Pradhan, H. Das, B. Naik, & N. Dey (Eds.), *Handbook of Research on Information Security in Biomedical Signal Processing* (pp. 304–319). Hershey, PA: IGI Global. doi:10.4018/978-1-5225-5152-2.ch016

Kumar, G., & Saini, H. (2018). Secure and Robust Telemedicine using ECC on Radix-8 with Formal Verification. *International Journal of Information Security and Privacy, 12*(1), 13–28. doi:10.4018/IJISP.2018010102

Kumar, M., & Bhandari, A. (2017). Performance Evaluation of Web Server's Request Queue against AL-DDoS Attacks in NS-2. *International Journal of Information Security and Privacy, 11*(4), 29–46. doi:10.4018/IJISP.2017100103

Kumar, M., & Vardhan, M. (2018). Privacy Preserving and Efficient Outsourcing Algorithm to Public Cloud: A Case of Statistical Analysis. *International Journal of Information Security and Privacy, 12*(2), 1–25. doi:10.4018/IJISP.2018040101

Kumar, R. (2018). A Robust Biometrics System Using Finger Knuckle Print. In G. Shrivastava, P. Kumar, B. Gupta, S. Bala, & N. Dey (Eds.), *Handbook of Research on Network Forensics and Analysis Techniques* (pp. 416–446). Hershey, PA: IGI Global. doi:10.4018/978-1-5225-4100-4.ch022

Kumar, R. (2018). DOS Attacks on Cloud Platform: Their Solutions and Implications. In S. Aljawarneh & M. Malhotra (Eds.), *Critical Research on Scalability and Security Issues in Virtual Cloud Environments* (pp. 167–184). Hershey, PA: IGI Global. doi:10.4018/978-1-5225-3029-9.ch008

Kumari, R., & Sharma, K. (2018). Cross-Layer Based Intrusion Detection and Prevention for Network. In G. Shrivastava, P. Kumar, B. Gupta, S. Bala, & N. Dey (Eds.), *Handbook of Research on Network Forensics and Analysis Techniques* (pp. 38–56). Hershey, PA: IGI Global. doi:10.4018/978-1-5225-4100-4.ch003

Lapke, M. (2018). A Semiotic Examination of the Security Policy Lifecycle. In Y. Maleh (Ed.), *Security and Privacy Management, Techniques, and Protocols* (pp. 237–253). Hershey, PA: IGI Global. doi:10.4018/978-1-5225-5583-4.ch009

Liang, Z., Feng, B., Xu, X., Wu, X., & Yang, T. (2018). Geometrically Invariant Image Watermarking Using Histogram Adjustment. *International Journal of Digital Crime and Forensics*, *10*(1), 54–66. doi:10.4018/IJDCF.2018010105

Liu, Z. J. (2017). A Cyber Crime Investigation Model Based on Case Characteristics. *International Journal of Digital Crime and Forensics*, *9*(4), 40–47. doi:10.4018/IJDCF.2017100104

Loganathan, S. (2018). A Step-by-Step Procedural Methodology for Improving an Organization's IT Risk Management System. In M. Gupta, R. Sharman, J. Walp, & P. Mulgund (Eds.), *Information Technology Risk Management and Compliance in Modern Organizations* (pp. 21–47). Hershey, PA: IGI Global. doi:10.4018/978-1-5225-2604-9.ch002

Long, M., Peng, F., & Gong, X. (2018). A Format-Compliant Encryption for Secure HEVC Video Sharing in Multimedia Social Network. *International Journal of Digital Crime and Forensics*, *10*(2), 23–39. doi:10.4018/IJDCF.2018040102

M., S., & M., J. (2018). Biosignal Denoising Techniques. In C. Pradhan, H. Das, B. Naik, & N. Dey (Eds.), *Handbook of Research on Information Security in Biomedical Signal Processing* (pp. 26-37). Hershey, PA: IGI Global. doi:10.4018/978-1-5225-5152-2.ch002

Mahapatra, C. (2017). Pragmatic Solutions to Cyber Security Threat in Indian Context. In R. Kumar, P. Pattnaik, & P. Pandey (Eds.), *Detecting and Mitigating Robotic Cyber Security Risks* (pp. 172–176). Hershey, PA: IGI Global. doi:10.4018/978-1-5225-2154-9.ch012

Majumder, A., Nath, S., & Das, A. (2018). Data Integrity in Mobile Cloud Computing. In K. Munir (Ed.), *Cloud Computing Technologies for Green Enterprises* (pp. 166–199). Hershey, PA: IGI Global. doi:10.4018/978-1-5225-3038-1.ch007

Maleh, Y., Zaydi, M., Sahid, A., & Ezzati, A. (2018). Building a Maturity Framework for Information Security Governance Through an Empirical Study in Organizations. In Y. Maleh (Ed.), *Security and Privacy Management, Techniques, and Protocols* (pp. 96–127). Hershey, PA: IGI Global. doi:10.4018/978-1-5225-5583-4.ch004

Malhotra, M., & Singh, A. (2018). Role of Agents to Enhance the Security and Scalability in Cloud Environment. In S. Aljawarneh & M. Malhotra (Eds.), *Critical Research on Scalability and Security Issues in Virtual Cloud Environments* (pp. 19–47). Hershey, PA: IGI Global. doi:10.4018/978-1-5225-3029-9.ch002

Mali, A. D. (2017). Recent Advances in Minimally-Obtrusive Monitoring of People's Health. *International Journal of Monitoring and Surveillance Technologies Research*, *5*(2), 44–56. doi:10.4018/IJMSTR.2017040104

Mali, A. D., & Yang, N. (2017). On Automated Generation of Keyboard Layout to Reduce Finger-Travel Distance. *International Journal of Monitoring and Surveillance Technologies Research*, *5*(2), 29–43. doi:10.4018/IJMSTR.2017040103

Mali, P. (2018). Defining Cyber Weapon in Context of Technology and Law. *International Journal of Cyber Warfare & Terrorism*, *8*(1), 43–55. doi:10.4018/IJCWT.2018010104

Malik, A., & Pandey, B. (2018). CIAS: A Comprehensive Identity Authentication Scheme for Providing Security in VANET. *International Journal of Information Security and Privacy*, *12*(1), 29–41. doi:10.4018/IJISP.2018010103

Manikandakumar, M., & Ramanujam, E. (2018). Security and Privacy Challenges in Big Data Environment. In G. Shrivastava, P. Kumar, B. Gupta, S. Bala, & N. Dey (Eds.), *Handbook of Research on Network Forensics and Analysis Techniques* (pp. 315–325). Hershey, PA: IGI Global. doi:10.4018/978-1-5225-4100-4.ch017

Manogaran, G., Thota, C., & Lopez, D. (2018). Human-Computer Interaction With Big Data Analytics. In D. Lopez & M. Durai (Eds.), *HCI Challenges and Privacy Preservation in Big Data Security* (pp. 1–22). Hershey, PA: IGI Global. doi:10.4018/978-1-5225-2863-0.ch001

Mariappan, P. B. P., & Teja, T. S. (2016). Digital Forensic and Machine Learning. In S. Geetha & A. Phamila (Eds.), *Combating Security Breaches and Criminal Activity in the Digital Sphere* (pp. 141–156). Hershey, PA: IGI Global. doi:10.4018/978-1-5225-0193-0.ch009

Marques, R., Mota, A., & Mota, L. (2016). Understanding Anti-Forensics Techniques for Combating Digital Security Breaches and Criminal Activity. In S. Geetha & A. Phamila (Eds.), *Combating Security Breaches and Criminal Activity in the Digital Sphere* (pp. 233–241). Hershey, PA: IGI Global. doi:10.4018/978-1-5225-0193-0.ch014

Mbale, J. (2018). Computer Centres Resource Cloud Elasticity-Scalability (CRECES): Copperbelt University Case Study. In S. Aljawarneh & M. Malhotra (Eds.), *Critical Research on Scalability and Security Issues in Virtual Cloud Environments* (pp. 48–70). Hershey, PA: IGI Global. doi:10.4018/978-1-5225-3029-9.ch003

McAvoy, D. (2017). Institutional Entrepreneurship in Defence Acquisition: What Don't We Understand? In K. Burgess & P. Antill (Eds.), *Emerging Strategies in Defense Acquisitions and Military Procurement* (pp. 222–241). Hershey, PA: IGI Global. doi:10.4018/978-1-5225-0599-0.ch013

McKeague, J., & Curran, K. (2018). Detecting the Use of Anonymous Proxies. *International Journal of Digital Crime and Forensics, 10*(2), 74–94. doi:10.4018/IJDCF.2018040105

Meitei, T. G., Singh, S. A., & Majumder, S. (2018). PCG-Based Biometrics. In C. Pradhan, H. Das, B. Naik, & N. Dey (Eds.), *Handbook of Research on Information Security in Biomedical Signal Processing* (pp. 1–25). Hershey, PA: IGI Global. doi:10.4018/978-1-5225-5152-2.ch001

Menemencioğlu, O., & Orak, İ. M. (2017). A Simple Solution to Prevent Parameter Tampering in Web Applications. In M. Korstanje (Ed.), *Threat Mitigation and Detection of Cyber Warfare and Terrorism Activities* (pp. 1–20). Hershey, PA: IGI Global. doi:10.4018/978-1-5225-1938-6.ch001

Minto-Coy, I. D., & Henlin, M. G. (2017). The Development of Cybersecurity Policy and Legislative Landscape in Latin America and Caribbean States. In M. Moore (Ed.), *Cybersecurity Breaches and Issues Surrounding Online Threat Protection* (pp. 24–53). Hershey, PA: IGI Global. doi:10.4018/978-1-5225-1941-6.ch002

Mire, A. V., Dhok, S. B., Mistry, N. J., & Porey, P. D. (2016). Tampering Localization in Double Compressed Images by Investigating Noise Quantization. *International Journal of Digital Crime and Forensics*, 8(3), 46–62. doi:10.4018/IJDCF.2016070104

Mohamed, J. H. (2018). Scientograph-Based Visualization of Computer Forensics Research Literature. In J. Jeyasekar & P. Saravanan (Eds.), *Innovations in Measuring and Evaluating Scientific Information* (pp. 148–162). Hershey, PA: IGI Global. doi:10.4018/978-1-5225-3457-0.ch010

Mohan Murthy, M. K., & Sanjay, H. A. (2018). Scalability for Cloud. In S. Aljawarneh & M. Malhotra (Eds.), *Critical Research on Scalability and Security Issues in Virtual Cloud Environments* (pp. 1–18). Hershey, PA: IGI Global. doi:10.4018/978-1-5225-3029-9.ch001

Moorthy, U., & Gandhi, U. D. (2018). A Survey of Big Data Analytics Using Machine Learning Algorithms. In D. Lopez & M. Durai (Eds.), *HCI Challenges and Privacy Preservation in Big Data Security* (pp. 95–123). Hershey, PA: IGI Global. doi:10.4018/978-1-5225-2863-0.ch005

Mountantonakis, M., Minadakis, N., Marketakis, Y., Fafalios, P., & Tzitzikas, Y. (2018). Connectivity, Value, and Evolution of a Semantic Warehouse. In M. Lytras, N. Aljohani, E. Damiani, & K. Chui (Eds.), *Innovations, Developments, and Applications of Semantic Web and Information Systems* (pp. 1–31). Hershey, PA: IGI Global. doi:10.4018/978-1-5225-5042-6.ch001

Moussa, M., & Demurjian, S. A. (2017). Differential Privacy Approach for Big Data Privacy in Healthcare. In S. Tamane, V. Solanki, & N. Dey (Eds.), *Privacy and Security Policies in Big Data* (pp. 191–213). Hershey, PA: IGI Global. doi:10.4018/978-1-5225-2486-1.ch009

Mugisha, E., Zhang, G., El Abidine, M. Z., & Eugene, M. (2017). A TPM-based Secure Multi-Cloud Storage Architecture grounded on Erasure Codes. *International Journal of Information Security and Privacy*, 11(1), 52–64. doi:10.4018/IJISP.2017010104

Nachtigall, L. G., Araujo, R. M., & Nachtigall, G. R. (2017). Use of Images of Leaves and Fruits of Apple Trees for Automatic Identification of Symptoms of Diseases and Nutritional Disorders. *International Journal of Monitoring and Surveillance Technologies Research, 5*(2), 1–14. doi:10.4018/IJMSTR.2017040101

Nagesh, K., Sumathy, R., Devakumar, P., & Sathiyamurthy, K. (2017). A Survey on Denial of Service Attacks and Preclusions. *International Journal of Information Security and Privacy, 11*(4), 1–15. doi:10.4018/IJISP.2017100101

Nanda, A., Popat, P., & Vimalkumar, D. (2018). Navigating Through Choppy Waters of PCI DSS Compliance. In M. Gupta, R. Sharman, J. Walp, & P. Mulgund (Eds.), *Information Technology Risk Management and Compliance in Modern Organizations* (pp. 99–140). Hershey, PA: IGI Global. doi:10.4018/978-1-5225-2604-9.ch005

Newton, S. (2017). The Determinants of Stock Market Development in Emerging Economies: Examining the Impact of Corporate Governance and Regulatory Reforms (I). In M. Ojo & J. Van Akkeren (Eds.), *Value Relevance of Accounting Information in Capital Markets* (pp. 114–125). Hershey, PA: IGI Global. doi:10.4018/978-1-5225-1900-3.ch008

Nidhyananthan, S. S. A., J. V., & R., S. S. (2018). Wireless Enhanced Security Based on Speech Recognition. In C. Pradhan, H. Das, B. Naik, & N. Dey (Eds.), Handbook of Research on Information Security in Biomedical Signal Processing (pp. 228-253). Hershey, PA: IGI Global. doi:10.4018/978-1-5225-5152-2.ch012

Norri-Sederholm, T., Huhtinen, A., & Paakkonen, H. (2018). Ensuring Public Safety Organisations' Information Flow and Situation Picture in Hybrid Environments. *International Journal of Cyber Warfare & Terrorism, 8*(1), 12–24. doi:10.4018/IJCWT.2018010102

Nunez, S., & Castaño, R. (2017). Building Brands in Emerging Economies: A Consumer-Oriented Approach. In Rajagopal, & R. Behl (Eds.), Business Analytics and Cyber Security Management in Organizations (pp. 183-194). Hershey, PA: IGI Global. doi:10.4018/978-1-5225-0902-8.ch013

Odella, F. (2018). Privacy Awareness and the Networking Generation. *International Journal of Technoethics, 9*(1), 51–70. doi:10.4018/IJT.2018010105

Ojo, M., & DiGabriele, J. A. (2017). Fundamental or Enhancing Roles?: The Dual Roles of External Auditors and Forensic Accountants. In M. Ojo & J. Van Akkeren (Eds.), *Value Relevance of Accounting Information in Capital Markets* (pp. 59–78). Hershey, PA: IGI Global. doi:10.4018/978-1-5225-1900-3.ch004

P, P., & Subbiah, G. (2016). Visual Cryptography for Securing Images in Cloud. In S. Geetha, & A. Phamila (Eds.), *Combating Security Breaches and Criminal Activity in the Digital Sphere* (pp. 242-262). Hershey, PA: IGI Global. doi:10.4018/978-1-5225-0193-0.ch015

Pandey, S. (2018). An Empirical Study of the Indian IT Sector on Typologies of Workaholism as Predictors of HR Crisis. In V. Ahuja & S. Rathore (Eds.), *Multidisciplinary Perspectives on Human Capital and Information Technology Professionals* (pp. 202–224). Hershey, PA: IGI Global. doi:10.4018/978-1-5225-5297-0.ch011

Pattabiraman, A., Srinivasan, S., Swaminathan, K., & Gupta, M. (2018). Fortifying Corporate Human Wall: A Literature Review of Security Awareness and Training. In M. Gupta, R. Sharman, J. Walp, & P. Mulgund (Eds.), *Information Technology Risk Management and Compliance in Modern Organizations* (pp. 142–175). Hershey, PA: IGI Global. doi:10.4018/978-1-5225-2604-9.ch006

Prachi. (2018). Detection of Botnet Based Attacks on Network: Using Machine Learning Techniques. In G. Shrivastava, P. Kumar, B. Gupta, S. Bala, & N. Dey (Eds.), *Handbook of Research on Network Forensics and Analysis Techniques* (pp. 101-116). Hershey, PA: IGI Global. doi:10.4018/978-1-5225-4100-4.ch007

Pradhan, P. L. (2017). Proposed Round Robin CIA Pattern on RTS for Risk Assessment. *International Journal of Digital Crime and Forensics*, 9(1), 71–85. doi:10.4018/IJDCF.2017010105

Prentice, S., & Taylor, P. J. (2018). Psychological and Behavioral Examinations of Online Terrorism. In J. McAlaney, L. Frumkin, & V. Benson (Eds.), *Psychological and Behavioral Examinations in Cyber Security* (pp. 151–171). Hershey, PA: IGI Global. doi:10.4018/978-1-5225-4053-3.ch009

Priyadarshini, I. (2017). Cyber Security Risks in Robotics. In R. Kumar, P. Pattnaik, & P. Pandey (Eds.), *Detecting and Mitigating Robotic Cyber Security Risks* (pp. 333–348). Hershey, PA: IGI Global. doi:10.4018/978-1-5225-2154-9.ch022

R., A., & D., E. (2018). Cyber Crime Toolkit Development. In G. Shrivastava, P. Kumar, B. Gupta, S. Bala, & N. Dey (Eds.), *Handbook of Research on Network Forensics and Analysis Techniques* (pp. 184-224). Hershey, PA: IGI Global. doi:10.4018/978-1-5225-4100-4.ch011

Raghunath, R. (2018). Research Trends in Forensic Sciences: A Scientometric Approach. In J. Jeyasekar & P. Saravanan (Eds.), *Innovations in Measuring and Evaluating Scientific Information* (pp. 108–124). Hershey, PA: IGI Global. doi:10.4018/978-1-5225-3457-0.ch008

Ramadhas, G., Sankar, A. S., & Sugathan, N. (2018). The Scientific Communication Process in Homoeopathic Toxicology: An Evaluative Study. In J. Jeyasekar & P. Saravanan (Eds.), *Innovations in Measuring and Evaluating Scientific Information* (pp. 163–179). Hershey, PA: IGI Global. doi:10.4018/978-1-5225-3457-0.ch011

Ramani, K. (2018). Impact of Big Data on Security: Big Data Security Issues and Defense Schemes. In G. Shrivastava, P. Kumar, B. Gupta, S. Bala, & N. Dey (Eds.), *Handbook of Research on Network Forensics and Analysis Techniques* (pp. 326–350). Hershey, PA: IGI Global. doi:10.4018/978-1-5225-4100-4.ch018

Ramos, P., Funderburk, P., & Gebelein, J. (2018). Social Media and Online Gaming: A Masquerading Funding Source. *International Journal of Cyber Warfare & Terrorism*, 8(1), 25–42. doi:10.4018/IJCWT.2018010103

Rao, N., & Srivastava, S., & K.S., S. (2017). PKI Deployment Challenges and Recommendations for ICS Networks. *International Journal of Information Security and Privacy*, 11(2), 38–48. doi:10.4018/IJISP.2017040104

Rath, M., Swain, J., Pati, B., & Pattanayak, B. K. (2018). Network Security: Attacks and Control in MANET. In G. Shrivastava, P. Kumar, B. Gupta, S. Bala, & N. Dey (Eds.), *Handbook of Research on Network Forensics and Analysis Techniques* (pp. 19–37). Hershey, PA: IGI Global. doi:10.4018/978-1-5225-4100-4.ch002

Ricci, J., Baggili, I., & Breitinger, F. (2017). Watch What You Wear: Smartwatches and Sluggish Security. In A. Marrington, D. Kerr, & J. Gammack (Eds.), *Managing Security Issues and the Hidden Dangers of Wearable Technologies* (pp. 47–73). Hershey, PA: IGI Global. doi:10.4018/978-1-5225-1016-1.ch003

Rossi, J. A. (2017). Revisiting the Value Relevance of Accounting Information in the Italian and UK Stock Markets. In M. Ojo & J. Van Akkeren (Eds.), *Value Relevance of Accounting Information in Capital Markets* (pp. 102–113). Hershey, PA: IGI Global. doi:10.4018/978-1-5225-1900-3.ch007

Rowe, N. C. (2016). Privacy Concerns with Digital Forensics. In R. Cropf & T. Bagwell (Eds.), *Ethical Issues and Citizen Rights in the Era of Digital Government Surveillance* (pp. 145–162). Hershey, PA: IGI Global. doi:10.4018/978-1-4666-9905-2.ch008

Sabillon, R., Serra-Ruiz, J., Cavaller, V., & Cano, J. J. (2017). Digital Forensic Analysis of Cybercrimes: Best Practices and Methodologies. *International Journal of Information Security and Privacy*, *11*(2), 25–37. doi:10.4018/IJISP.2017040103

Sample, C., Cowley, J., & Bakdash, J. Z. (2018). Cyber + Culture: Exploring the Relationship. In J. McAlaney, L. Frumkin, & V. Benson (Eds.), *Psychological and Behavioral Examinations in Cyber Security* (pp. 64–79). Hershey, PA: IGI Global. doi:10.4018/978-1-5225-4053-3.ch004

Sarıgöllü, S. C., Aksakal, E., Koca, M. G., Akten, E., & Aslanbay, Y. (2018). Volunteered Surveillance. In J. McAlaney, L. Frumkin, & V. Benson (Eds.), *Psychological and Behavioral Examinations in Cyber Security* (pp. 133–150). Hershey, PA: IGI Global. doi:10.4018/978-1-5225-4053-3.ch008

Shahriar, H., Clincy, V., & Bond, W. (2018). Classification of Web-Service-Based Attacks and Mitigation Techniques. In Y. Maleh (Ed.), *Security and Privacy Management, Techniques, and Protocols* (pp. 360–378). Hershey, PA: IGI Global. doi:10.4018/978-1-5225-5583-4.ch015

Shet, S., Aswath, A. R., Hanumantharaju, M. C., & Gao, X. (2017). Design of Reconfigurable Architectures for Steganography System. In N. Dey, A. Ashour, & S. Acharjee (Eds.), *Applied Video Processing in Surveillance and Monitoring Systems* (pp. 145–168). Hershey, PA: IGI Global. doi:10.4018/978-1-5225-1022-2.ch007

Shrivastava, G., Sharma, K., Khari, M., & Zohora, S. E. (2018). Role of Cyber Security and Cyber Forensics in India. In G. Shrivastava, P. Kumar, B. Gupta, S. Bala, & N. Dey (Eds.), *Handbook of Research on Network Forensics and Analysis Techniques* (pp. 143–161). Hershey, PA: IGI Global. doi:10.4018/978-1-5225-4100-4.ch009

Singh, N. (2016). Cloud Crime and Fraud: A Study of Challenges for Cloud Security and Forensics. In S. Geetha & A. Phamila (Eds.), *Combating Security Breaches and Criminal Activity in the Digital Sphere* (pp. 68–84). Hershey, PA: IGI Global. doi:10.4018/978-1-5225-0193-0.ch005

Singh, N., Mittal, T., & Gupta, M. (2018). A Tale of Policies and Breaches: Analytical Approach to Construct Social Media Policy. In M. Gupta, R. Sharman, J. Walp, & P. Mulgund (Eds.), *Information Technology Risk Management and Compliance in Modern Organizations* (pp. 176–212). Hershey, PA: IGI Global. doi:10.4018/978-1-5225-2604-9.ch007

Singh, R., & Jalota, H. (2018). A Study of Good-Enough Security in the Context of Rural Business Process Outsourcing. In J. McAlaney, L. Frumkin, & V. Benson (Eds.), *Psychological and Behavioral Examinations in Cyber Security* (pp. 239–252). Hershey, PA: IGI Global. doi:10.4018/978-1-5225-4053-3.ch014

Sivasubramanian, K. E. (2018). Authorship Pattern and Collaborative Research Productivity of Asian Journal of Dairy and Food Research During the Year 2011 to 2015. In J. Jeyasekar & P. Saravanan (Eds.), *Innovations in Measuring and Evaluating Scientific Information* (pp. 213–222). Hershey, PA: IGI Global. doi:10.4018/978-1-5225-3457-0.ch014

Somasundaram, R., & Thirugnanam, M. (2017). IoT in Healthcare: Breaching Security Issues. In N. Jeyanthi & R. Thandeeswaran (Eds.), *Security Breaches and Threat Prevention in the Internet of Things* (pp. 174–188). Hershey, PA: IGI Global. doi:10.4018/978-1-5225-2296-6.ch008

Sonam, & Khari, M. (2018). Wireless Sensor Networks: A Technical Survey. In G. Shrivastava, P. Kumar, B. Gupta, S. Bala, & N. Dey (Eds.), *Handbook of Research on Network Forensics and Analysis Techniques* (pp. 1-18). Hershey, PA: IGI Global. doi:10.4018/978-1-5225-4100-4.ch001

Soni, P. (2018). Implications of HIPAA and Subsequent Regulations on Information Technology. In M. Gupta, R. Sharman, J. Walp, & P. Mulgund (Eds.), *Information Technology Risk Management and Compliance in Modern Organizations* (pp. 71–98). Hershey, PA: IGI Global. doi:10.4018/978-1-5225-2604-9.ch004

Sönmez, F. Ö., & Günel, B. (2018). Security Visualization Extended Review Issues, Classifications, Validation Methods, Trends, Extensions. In Y. Maleh (Ed.), *Security and Privacy Management, Techniques, and Protocols* (pp. 152–197). Hershey, PA: IGI Global. doi:10.4018/978-1-5225-5583-4.ch006

Srivastava, S. R., & Dube, S. (2018). Cyberattacks, Cybercrime and Cyberterrorism. In G. Shrivastava, P. Kumar, B. Gupta, S. Bala, & N. Dey (Eds.), *Handbook of Research on Network Forensics and Analysis Techniques* (pp. 162–183). Hershey, PA: IGI Global. doi:10.4018/978-1-5225-4100-4.ch010

Stacey, E. (2017). Contemporary Terror on the Net. In *Combating Internet-Enabled Terrorism: Emerging Research and Opportunities* (pp. 16–44). Hershey, PA: IGI Global. doi:10.4018/978-1-5225-2190-7.ch002

Sumana, M., Hareesha, K. S., & Kumar, S. (2018). Semantically Secure Classifiers for Privacy Preserving Data Mining. In Y. Maleh (Ed.), *Security and Privacy Management, Techniques, and Protocols* (pp. 66–95). Hershey, PA: IGI Global. doi:10.4018/978-1-5225-5583-4.ch003

Suresh, N., & Gupta, M. (2018). Impact of Technology Innovation: A Study on Cloud Risk Mitigation. In M. Gupta, R. Sharman, J. Walp, & P. Mulgund (Eds.), *Information Technology Risk Management and Compliance in Modern Organizations* (pp. 229–267). Hershey, PA: IGI Global. doi:10.4018/978-1-5225-2604-9.ch009

Survey, A. K. Balasubramanian & M. Rajakani (Eds.), *Algorithmic Strategies for Solving Complex Problems in Cryptography* (pp. 111–123). Hershey, PA: IGI Global. doi:10.4018/978-1-5225-2915-6.ch009

Tank, D. M. (2017). Security and Privacy Issues, Solutions, and Tools for MCC. In K. Munir (Ed.), *Security Management in Mobile Cloud Computing* (pp. 121–147). Hershey, PA: IGI Global. doi:10.4018/978-1-5225-0602-7.ch006

Thackray, H., & McAlaney, J. (2018). Groups Online: Hacktivism and Social Protest. In J. McAlaney, L. Frumkin, & V. Benson (Eds.), *Psychological and Behavioral Examinations in Cyber Security* (pp. 194–209). Hershey, PA: IGI Global. doi:10.4018/978-1-5225-4053-3.ch011

Thandeeswaran, R., Pawar, R., & Rai, M. (2017). Security Threats in Autonomous Vehicles. In N. Jeyanthi & R. Thandeeswaran (Eds.), *Security Breaches and Threat Prevention in the Internet of Things* (pp. 117–141). Hershey, PA: IGI Global. doi:10.4018/978-1-5225-2296-6.ch006

Thota, C., Manogaran, G., Lopez, D., & Vijayakumar, V. (2017). Big Data Security Framework for Distributed Cloud Data Centers. In M. Moore (Ed.), *Cybersecurity Breaches and Issues Surrounding Online Threat Protection* (pp. 288–310). Hershey, PA: IGI Global. doi:10.4018/978-1-5225-1941-6.ch012

Thukral, S., & Rodriguez, T. D. (2018). Child Sexual Abuse: Intra- and Extra-Familial Risk Factors, Reactions, and Interventions. In R. Gopalan (Ed.), *Social, Psychological, and Forensic Perspectives on Sexual Abuse* (pp. 229–258). Hershey, PA: IGI Global. doi:10.4018/978-1-5225-3958-2.ch017

Tidke, S. (2017). MonogDB: Data Management in NoSQL. In S. Tamane, V. Solanki, & N. Dey (Eds.), *Privacy and Security Policies in Big Data* (pp. 64–91). Hershey, PA: IGI Global. doi:10.4018/978-1-5225-2486-1.ch004

Tierney, M. (2018). #TerroristFinancing: An Examination of Terrorism Financing via the Internet. *International Journal of Cyber Warfare & Terrorism*, 8(1), 1–11. doi:10.4018/IJCWT.2018010101

Topal, R. (2018). A Cyber-Psychological and Behavioral Approach to Online Radicalization. In J. McAlaney, L. Frumkin, & V. Benson (Eds.), *Psychological and Behavioral Examinations in Cyber Security* (pp. 210–221). Hershey, PA: IGI Global. doi:10.4018/978-1-5225-4053-3.ch012

Tripathy, B. K., & Baktha, K. (2018). Clustering Approaches. In *Security, Privacy, and Anonymization in Social Networks: Emerging Research and Opportunities* (pp. 51–85). Hershey, PA: IGI Global. doi:10.4018/978-1-5225-5158-4.ch004

Tripathy, B. K., & Baktha, K. (2018). De-Anonymization Techniques. In *Security, Privacy, and Anonymization in Social Networks: Emerging Research and Opportunities* (pp. 137–147). Hershey, PA: IGI Global. doi:10.4018/978-1-5225-5158-4.ch007

Tripathy, B. K., & Baktha, K. (2018). Fundamentals of Social Networks. In *Security, Privacy, and Anonymization in Social Networks: Emerging Research and Opportunities* (pp. 1–22). Hershey, PA: IGI Global. doi:10.4018/978-1-5225-5158-4.ch001

Tripathy, B. K., & Baktha, K. (2018). Graph Modification Approaches. In *Security, Privacy, and Anonymization in Social Networks: Emerging Research and Opportunities* (pp. 86–115). Hershey, PA: IGI Global. doi:10.4018/978-1-5225-5158-4.ch005

Tripathy, B. K., & Baktha, K. (2018). Social Network Anonymization Techniques. In *Security, Privacy, and Anonymization in Social Networks: Emerging Research and Opportunities* (pp. 36–50). Hershey, PA: IGI Global. doi:10.4018/978-1-5225-5158-4.ch003

Tsimperidis, I., Rostami, S., & Katos, V. (2017). Age Detection Through Keystroke Dynamics from User Authentication Failures. *International Journal of Digital Crime and Forensics*, *9*(1), 1–16. doi:10.4018/IJDCF.2017010101

Wadkar, H. S., Mishra, A., & Dixit, A. M. (2017). Framework to Secure Browser Using Configuration Analysis. *International Journal of Information Security and Privacy*, *11*(2), 49–63. doi:10.4018/IJISP.2017040105

Wahlgren, G., & Kowalski, S. J. (2018). IT Security Risk Management Model for Handling IT-Related Security Incidents: The Need for a New Escalation Approach. In Y. Maleh (Ed.), *Security and Privacy Management, Techniques, and Protocols* (pp. 129–151). Hershey, PA: IGI Global. doi:10.4018/978-1-5225-5583-4.ch005

Wall, H. J., & Kaye, L. K. (2018). Online Decision Making: Online Influence and Implications for Cyber Security. In J. McAlaney, L. Frumkin, & V. Benson (Eds.), *Psychological and Behavioral Examinations in Cyber Security* (pp. 1–25). Hershey, PA: IGI Global. doi:10.4018/978-1-5225-4053-3.ch001

Xylogiannopoulos, K. F., Karampelas, P., & Alhajj, R. (2017). Advanced Network Data Analytics for Large-Scale DDoS Attack Detection. *International Journal of Cyber Warfare & Terrorism*, *7*(3), 44–54. doi:10.4018/IJCWT.2017070104

Yan, W. Q., Wu, X., & Liu, F. (2018). Progressive Scrambling for Social Media. *International Journal of Digital Crime and Forensics*, *10*(2), 56–73. doi:10.4018/IJDCF.2018040104

Yang, L., Gao, T., Xuan, Y., & Gao, H. (2016). Contrast Modification Forensics Algorithm Based on Merged Weight Histogram of Run Length. *International Journal of Digital Crime and Forensics*, 8(2), 27–35. doi:10.4018/IJDCF.2016040103

Yassein, M. B., Mardini, W., & Al-Abdi, A. (2018). Security Issues in the Internet of Things: A Review. In S. Aljawarneh & M. Malhotra (Eds.), *Critical Research on Scalability and Security Issues in Virtual Cloud Environments* (pp. 186–200). Hershey, PA: IGI Global. doi:10.4018/978-1-5225-3029-9.ch009

Yassein, M. B., Shatnawi, M., & l-Qasem, N. (2018). A Survey of Probabilistic Broadcast Schemes in Mobile Ad Hoc Networks. In S. Aljawarneh, & M. Malhotra (Eds.), *Critical Research on Scalability and Security Issues in Virtual Cloud Environments* (pp. 269-282). Hershey, PA: IGI Global. doi:10.4018/978-1-5225-3029-9.ch013

Yue, C., Tianliang, L., Manchun, C., & Jingying, L. (2018). Evaluation of the Attack Effect Based on Improved Grey Clustering Model. *International Journal of Digital Crime and Forensics*, 10(1), 92–100. doi:10.4018/IJDCF.2018010108

Zhang, P., He, Y., & Chow, K. (2018). Fraud Track on Secure Electronic Check System. *International Journal of Digital Crime and Forensics*, 10(2), 137–144. doi:10.4018/IJDCF.2018040108

Zhao, J., Wang, Q., Guo, J., Gao, L., & Yang, F. (2016). An Overview on Passive Image Forensics Technology for Automatic Computer Forgery. *International Journal of Digital Crime and Forensics*, 8(4), 14–25. doi:10.4018/IJDCF.2016100102

Zhao, X., Zhu, J., & Yu, H. (2016). On More Paradigms of Steganalysis. *International Journal of Digital Crime and Forensics*, 8(2), 1–15. doi:10.4018/IJDCF.2016040101

Zhou, L., Yan, W. Q., Shu, Y., & Yu, J. (2018). CVSS: A Cloud-Based Visual Surveillance System. *International Journal of Digital Crime and Forensics*, 10(1), 79–91. doi:10.4018/IJDCF.2018010107

Zhu, J., Guan, Q., Zhao, X., Cao, Y., & Chen, G. (2017). A Steganalytic Scheme Based on Classifier Selection Using Joint Image Characteristics. *International Journal of Digital Crime and Forensics*, 9(4), 1–14. doi:10.4018/IJDCF.2017100101

Zoughbi, S. (2017). Major Technology Trends Affecting Government Data in Developing Countries. In S. Zoughbi (Ed.), *Securing Government Information and Data in Developing Countries* (pp. 127–135). Hershey, PA: IGI Global. doi:10.4018/978-1-5225-1703-0.ch008

Zubairu, B. (2018). Security Risks of Biomedical Data Processing in Cloud Computing Environment. In C. Pradhan, H. Das, B. Naik, & N. Dey (Eds.), *Handbook of Research on Information Security in Biomedical Signal Processing* (pp. 177–197). Hershey, PA: IGI Global. doi:10.4018/978-1-5225-5152-2.ch009

About the Contributors

Arif Sari is a full time Associate Professor and Chairman of the department of Management Information Systems at the Girne American University, North Cyprus. He received his BS degree - in Computer Information Systems and MBA degree - (2008 and 2010) at European University of Lefke, and Ph.D. degree (2013) in Management Information Systems at The Girne American University. He has been granted as Visiting Scholar of Sapienza University of Rome in Italy (2012). He is an IEEE, ACM, and IEICE Member since Sept. 2012 and has published various papers, book chapters, participated in variety of conferences in the fields of Network Security, Cyber Security, Network Simulation, Mobile Networks, Information Communication Technologies, Mobile Network Security and Mobile Security Systems. After investigation of national firewall systems in different countries such as China, Russia, United Kingdom, USA/NSA and Israel, Dr. Sari is currently working on national cyber-security firewall project named "SeddülBahir", which presented at Yıldız Technic University, Istanbul in December 2015. He is co-author of additional three textbooks in field of network, cryptography and cyber security.

* * *

Murat Akkaya is a full time Associate Professor of MIS in Girne American University. He is currently working as Acting Dean of Faculty of Business and Director of School of Social and Applied Sciences at Girne American University, where he is teaching Programming, Operating Systems, Hardware, Computer Graphics, Animations, Technical Drawing, Databases, IT Security, IT Law, Artificial Intelligence, Software Engineering, Computer Networks and Management Information Systems courses. He studied BSc. Computer Science and received his Master of Science degree of Computer Engineering at Girne American University in 2004. He completed his Ph.D. studies at Girne American University in 2013. His Ph.D. dissertation entitled

"Analysis of the Relation Between Several Group of Factors and Job Satisfaction of Academicians in Higher Education Through the Use of Artificial Neural Networks". His research areas are Neural Network Applications, Robotics, Automation Systems. He is Editorial Board member of Journal of Automation and Control, Science and Education Publishing, Science Board member of Kıbrıs Bilim Teknik and executive board member of Girne American University.

Ugur Can Atasoy is an Information Security Specialist, Lecturer and International Editor. He consults business owners and organizations in offensive and defensive aspects for better information security and privacy structure. He has university level teaching experience and hands-on field experience including defence industry, media and education. He holds BA degree in Computer and Instructional Technologies Teacher Education and MSc degree in Management Information Systems from European University of Lefke, Cyprus. He is currently a Ph.D. candidate at the Girne American University, Cyprus. Additionally, he holds an OSCP (Certified Professional) certification in the area of offensive security. He is a member of ACM and international editorial boards and also published various papers along with book chapters in variety of conferences in the fields of Information Security, Cyber Security, Mobile Security, Social Engineering, Cyber Intelligence, Privacy, Cyber Warfare and Information Communication Technologies. He is currently working as Cyber Security Specialist and Training Coordinator in the defence industry.

Mubarak Banisakher is an Associate professor of computer science at Saint Leo University, Tampa, FL, USA. His research interest is Big Data, Cloud Computing, Disaster Management, Networks and Security.

O. Ayhan Erdem was born in Ankara. He received his B.Sc., M.Sc. and Ph.D. degrees from Gazi University Institute of Science and Technology, Turkey. He is currently a Prof. Dr. at Gazi University Technology Faculty Department of Computer Engineering. His research focus is open source programming, unixbased systems, industrial network equipment, computer networks, wireless networks, mobile ad-hoc networks, fuzzy logic, computer programming language and computer software. He is married and has three children.

Samson Fadiya is an Information Systems Expert, Lecturer and International Editor. He helps business owners build compliant defined Information Security and Business Systems to automate business processes and retain top-notch employees. He believes the key to a successful job is to build a plan with flexible Design, development and administration of systems, performance monitoring, reporting, and tuning of processes. He has over 4 years of classroom teaching experience at the university level and 6 over years experience in the private sector, helping small business clients with defined contribution provision of support and assistance to their IT development teams in the design, development, testing, tuning and implementation of database applications. Dr. Samson holds a B.Sc. Degree in Information Systems, MSc and PhD Degree in Management Information System from Girne American University, Cyprus. Additionally, he holds an OCA (Certified Associate), OCP (Certified Professional), and has obtained eleven certifications at Texas A&M University in the area of Information Technology and Project Management. He is a member of many professional bodies and is currently Editor in Chief for International Journal of Scientific Research in Information Systems and Engineering. (IJSRISE). Courses and papers taught by him include Artificial Intelligence, Algorithm and Computer Programming, Computer Applications, System Analysis and Design, Management Information System, Computer Organization Architecture, Operating System, Electronic Commerce, Fundamental of Information System.

Ibrahim Firat has completed his high school studies in Cyprus and he has moved to United Kingdom in order to pursue his educational goals. Currently, he is an undergraduate Computer Science student at the University of Reading and looking forward to increasing his knowledge in Computer Science field. He is interested in making new contributions and as well as reading new studies and investigations related to his subject. He is interested in cyber security (specifically botnets and malware detection mechanisms), programming languages (C, C++, java) and other kinds of software development (web development, mobile application development and so on).

Mustafa Fırat was born in September 15 1995 in Nicosia. He has graduated from the Levent College (6th form) in 2013. From 2013 September to May 2014 he has attended to an English foundation program in the Southampton University. In 2014-2015 academic year he enrolled to the Eastern Mediterranean University`s International Relations program and graduated in 3 and half years with an honor degree. Firat continued his further education by attending International Relations master`s program at the same University. At the Same time he is also attending Middle Eastern Studies Master`s program at Lund university`s Center of Middle Eastern Studies. Throughout his university time, Firat did internships in the several ministries of his own state.

Van Nguyen is an Assistant Professor of Computer Science at Saint Leo University. He received his BS degree from University of Western Sydney, MS degree from McNeese University, and Ph.D. degree from the Center for Advanced Computer Studies at University of Louisiana at Lafayette. His BS and Ph.D. degrees are in Computer Science and his MS is in Math and Science. He has experience in the following areas: network security for inbound/outbound traffic, IDS/IPS, access control, internal and external routing protocols (OSPF, EIGRP, BGP, MPLS and others), VoIP architectures, IoT, network performance, and network protocol design. His research areas are in computer security, computer management, wireless networks, protocol design (TCP/IP, MAC/Link-layer), performance analysis, IoT, and performance enhancements. His vision of a future computer is that there would be one single secured computer, which consists of all the networked devices in the world, to solve any problem presented to it in a timely manner.

Acheme Odeh is currently a Ph.D. candidate and Graduate teaching assistant at the Girne American University, Cyprus in the Department of Management Information System. I completed a bachelor of Physics (Ed) from the Benue State University, Nigeria and a Masters of Business Administration in Management Information Systems from Girne American University in 2015.

Marwan Omar is an Assistant Professor of Computer Science and Information Systems School of Business University Campus. Dr. Marwan Omar is also a member of the Saint Leo Community since 2015. Dr. Omar received a Master's degree in Information Systems and Technology from the University of Phoenix, 2009 and a Doctorate Degree in Digital Systems Security from Colorado Technical University, 2012. Dr. Omar has been working in Academia for six years; his most recent academic position was an Adjunct Faculty, ITT-Technical Institute-Houston, Texas. Dr. Omar teaches Cyber security classes at Saint Leo University. Dr. Omar recently co-edited and published a book with IGI-Global titled "Security Solutions for Hyperconnectivity and the Internet of Things".

Onder Onursal is a full-time instructor in Department of Management Information Systems at European University of Lefke. He has received his BSc. and MSc.in Computer Engineering and currently pursuing for PhD degree at American University of Cyprus.

Merve Sener was born on 26 November, 1989 in Mugla province of Turkey. She completed her elementary education at Sakarya Primary School and her high school education at Milas Anatolian High School in Milas district of Mugla. She graduated from the Department of Management Information Systems in Girne American University in 2017. She worked as IT Technical Support Specialist at Girne American University between 2017-2018. She continues her Masters with Thesis program which she started in 2017 in the Department of Business Management in the Institute of Social Sciences in Girne American University.

Esra Söğüt was born in Eskişehir. She graduated from Eskişehir Osmangazi University Department of Computer Engineering. She received her master degree from Gazi University Institute of Science and Technology and, she started her doctorate education. She is working as a research assistant at Gazi University Department of Computer Engineering. Areas of interests: cyber security, computer networks, malware, data mining.

Joshua Sopuru works with a wide variety of information systems to achieve technology-aided transformations for organizational growth and profit. He is an experienced Business Analyst, a Project Management Professional and has experience in Supply Chain management and CRM. He offers IT solutions to businesses, help businesses seamlessly transit from their current technology to more recent technologies. With a specialization in Information Systems, He implements intelligent systems without interrupting current business processes. With foundations in computer science and mathematics, Management Information Systems, and Engineering. As a Ph.D. student, he has conducted himself accordingly to contribute in the fields of cybersecurity, Computer Science and Engineering.

Sabu Thampi is a Professor at Indian Institute of Information Technology and Management - Kerala (IIITM-K), Technopark Campus, Trivandrum, Kerala State, India. He has completed a Ph.D in Computer Engineering under the supervision of Dr. K. Chandrasekaran from National Institute of Technology Karnataka. Sabu has several years of teaching and research experience in various institutions in India. His research interests include sensor networks, Internet of Things (IoT), authorship analysis, social networks, nature inspired computing, image forensics and video surveillance. He has authored and edited few books published by reputed international publishers and published papers in academic journals and international and national proceedings. Sabu has served as Guest Editor for special issues in few international journals and program committee member for many international conferences and workshops. He has co-chaired several international workshops and conferences. He has initiated and is also involved in the organization of several annual conferences/symposiums: International Conference on Advances in Computing, Communications and Informatics (ICACCI), Symposium on Intelligent Systems Technologies and Applications (ISTA), Symposium on Security in Computing and Communications (SSCC), Symposium on Intelligent Informatics (ISI), Symposium on Signal Processing and Intelligent Recognition Systems (SIRS) etc. Sabu is currently serving as Editor for Journal of Network and Computer Applications (JNCA), Elsevier and Journal of Applied Soft Computing, Elsevier; and Associate Editor for IEEE Access and International Journal of Embedded Systems, Inderscience, UK; and reviewer for several reputed international journals. Sabu is a Senior Member of IEEE and member of IEEE Communications Society, IEEE SMCS, and Senior Member of ACM. He is the founding Chair of ACM Trivandrum Professional Chapter.

Athira U. is a research scholar pursuing research leading to PhD degree in computer science and engineering. She is a SPEED-IT research scholarship recipient. She received her M.Tech in computer science and Engineering from Amrita Vishwavidyapeetham Amritapuri.

Onurhan Yilmaz graduated from Girne American University Management Information Systems. worked as a research assistant for a year at the university. During this period, he served as an instructor in various conferences and published 7 international articles. He is the founder of Tridea Cyber Security and Information Technologies Ltd. Ltd. Şti., and is working as an Penetration Test and Information Security Consultant.

Index

Purchase Print, E-Book, or Print + E-Book

IGI Global books can now be purchased from three unique pricing formats:
Print Only, E-Book Only, or Print + E-Book. Shipping fees apply.

www.igi-global.com

Recommended Reference Books

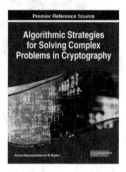

Premier Reference Source

Algorithmic Strategies for Solving Complex Problems in Cryptography

ISBN: 978-1-5225-2915-6
© 2018; 302 pp.
List Price: $245

Research Insights

Combating Internet-Enabled Terrorism
Emerging Research and Opportunities

Emily Stacey

ISBN: 978-1-5225-2190-7
© 2017; 133 pp.
List Price: $115

Research Insights

Decentralized Computing using Blockchain Technologies and Smart Contracts
Emerging Research and Opportunities

S. Asharaf and S. Adarsh

ISBN: 978-1-5225-2193-8
© 2017; 128 pp.
List Price: $120

Premier Reference Source

Managing Security Issues and the Hidden Dangers of Wearable Technologies

ISBN: 978-1-5225-1016-1
© 2017; 345 pp.
List Price: $200

Premier Reference Source

Threat Mitigation and Detection of Cyber Warfare and Terrorism Activities

ISBN: 978-1-5225-1938-6
© 2017; 315 pp.
List Price: $190

Premier Reference Source

Police Brutality, Racial Profiling, and Discrimination in the Criminal Justice System

ISBN: 978-1-5225-1088-8
© 2017; 372 pp.
List Price: $195

Looking for free content, product updates, news, and special offers?
Join IGI Global's mailing list today and start enjoying exclusive perks sent only to IGI Global members.
Add your name to the list at **www.igi-global.com/newsletters.**

Publisher of Peer-Reviewed, Timely, and Innovative Academic Research

IGI Global
DISSEMINATOR OF KNOWLEDGE

www.igi-global.com   Sign up at www.igi-global.com/newsletters   facebook.com/igiglobal   twitter.com/igiglobal

Ensure Quality Research is Introduced to the Academic Community

Become an IGI Global Reviewer for Authored Book Projects

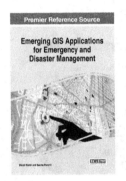

The overall success of an authored book project is dependent on quality and timely reviews.

In this competitive age of scholarly publishing, constructive and timely feedback significantly expedites the turnaround time of manuscripts from submission to acceptance, allowing the publication and discovery of forward-thinking research at a much more expeditious rate. Several IGI Global authored book projects are currently seeking highly qualified experts in the field to fill vacancies on their respective editorial review boards:

Applications may be sent to:
development@igi-global.com

Applicants must have a doctorate (or an equivalent degree) as well as publishing and reviewing experience. Reviewers are asked to write reviews in a timely, collegial, and constructive manner. All reviewers will begin their role on an ad-hoc basis for a period of one year, and upon successful completion of this term can be considered for full editorial review board status, with the potential for a subsequent promotion to Associate Editor.

If you have a colleague that may be interested in this opportunity, we encourage you to share this information with them.

www.igi-global.com

Celebrating 30 Years of Scholarly
Knowledge Creation & Dissemination

InfoSci®-Books

A Collection of 4,000+ Reference Books Containing Over
87,000 Full-Text Chapters Focusing on Emerging Research

This database is a collection of over 4,000+ IGI Global single and
multi-volume reference books, handbooks of research, and encyclopedias,
encompassing groundbreaking research from prominent experts worldwide.
These books are highly cited and currently recognized in prestigious indices
such as: Web of Science™ and Scopus®.

Librarian Features:
• No Set-Up or Maintenance Fees
• Guarantee of No More Than A
  5% Annual Price Increase
• COUNTER 4 Usage Reports
• Complimentary Archival Access
• Free MARC Records

Researcher Features:
• Unlimited Simultaneous Users
• No Embargo of Content
• Full Book Download
• Full-Text Search Engine
• No DRM

To Find Out More or To Purchase This Database:
www.igi-global.com/infosci-books

eresources@igi-global.com • Toll Free: 1-866-342-6657 ext. 100 • Phone: 717-533-8845 x100

www.igi-global.com

IGI Global Proudly Partners with

Enhance Your Manuscript with
eContent Pro International's Professional
Copy Editing Service

Expert Copy Editing

eContent Pro International copy editors, with over 70 years of combined experience, will provide complete and comprehensive care for your document by resolving all issues with spelling, punctuation, grammar, terminology, jargon, semantics, syntax, consistency, flow, and more. In addition, they will format your document to the style you specify (APA, Chicago, etc.). All edits will be performed using Microsoft Word's Track Changes feature, which allows for fast and simple review and management of edits.

Additional Services

eContent Pro International also offers fast and affordable proofreading to enhance the readability of your document, professional translation in over 100 languages, and market localization services to help businesses and organizations localize their content and grow into new markets around the globe.

IGI Global Authors Save 25% on eContent Pro International's Services!

Scan the QR Code to Receive Your 25% Discount

The 25% discount is applied directly to your eContent Pro International shopping cart when placing an order through IGI Global's referral link. Use the QR code to access this referral link. eContent Pro International has the right to end or modify any promotion at any time.

Email: customerservice@econtentpro.com

econtentpro.com

ARE YOU READY TO
PUBLISH YOUR RESEARCH?

IGI Global offers book authorship and editorship opportunities across 11 subject areas, including business, healthcare, computer science, engineering, and more!

Benefits of Publishing with IGI Global:

- Free one-to-one editorial and promotional support.
- Expedited publishing timelines that can take your book from start to finish in less than one (1) year.
- Choose from a variety of formats including: Edited and Authored References, Handbooks of Research, Encyclopedias, and Research Insights.
- Utilize IGI Global's eEditorial Discovery® submission system in support of conducting the submission and blind-review process.

- IGI Global maintains a strict adherence to ethical practices due in part to our full membership to the Committee on Publication Ethics (COPE).
- Indexing potential in prestigious indices such as Scopus®, Web of Science™, PsycINFO®, and ERIC – Education Resources Information Center.
- Ability to connect your ORCID iD to your IGI Global publications.
- Earn royalties on your publication as well as receive complimentary copies and exclusive discounts.

Get Started Today by Contacting the Acquisitions Department at:
acquisition@igi-global.com

Available to Order Now

Order through www.igi-global.com with __Free Standard Shipping__.

The Premier Reference for Information Science & Information Technology

100% Original Content
Contains 705 new, peer-reviewed articles with color figures covering over 80 categories in 11 subject areas

Diverse Contributions
More than 1,100 experts from 74 unique countries contributed their specialized knowledge

Easy Navigation
Includes two tables of content and a comprehensive index in each volume for the user's convenience

Highly-Cited
Embraces a complete list of references and additional reading sections to allow for further research

Included in:

InfoSci°-Books

Encyclopedia of Information Science and Technology Fourth Edition
A Comprehensive 10-Volume Set

Mehdi Khosrow-Pour, D.B.A. (Information Resources Management Association, USA)
ISBN: 978-1-5225-2255-3; © 2018; Pg: 8,104; Release Date: July 2017

For a limited time, receive the complimentary e-books for the First, Second, and Third editions with the purchase of the *Encyclopedia of Information Science and Technology, Fourth Edition* e-book.*

The **Encyclopedia of Information Science and Technology, Fourth Edition** is a 10-volume set which includes 705 original and previously unpublished research articles covering a full range of perspectives, applications, and techniques contributed by thousands of experts and researchers from around the globe. This authoritative encyclopedia is an all-encompassing, well-established reference source that is ideally designed to disseminate the most forward-thinking and diverse research findings. With critical perspectives on the impact of information science management and new technologies in modern settings, including but not limited to computer science, education, healthcare, government, engineering, business, and natural and physical sciences, it is a pivotal and relevant source of knowledge that will benefit every professional within the field of information science and technology and is an invaluable addition to every academic and corporate library.

Scan for Online Bookstore

Pricing Information

Hardcover: **$5,695**   E-Book: **$5,695**   Hardcover + E-Book: **$6,895**

Both E-Book Prices Include:
- Encyclopedia of Information Science and Technology, First Edition E-Book
- Encyclopedia of Information Science and Technology, Second Edition E-Book
- Encyclopedia of Information Science and Technology, Third Edition E-Book

*Purchase the Encyclopedia of Information Science and Technology, Fourth Edition e-book and receive the first, second, and third e-book editions for free. Offer is only valid with purchase of the fourth edition's e-book through the IGI Global Online Bookstore.

Recommend this Title to Your Institution's Library: www.igi-global.com/books

www.igi-global.com/infosci-ondemand

InfoSci®-OnDemand

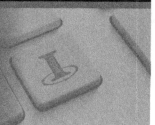

Continuously updated with new material on a weekly basis, InfoSci®-OnDemand offers the ability to search through thousands of quality full-text research papers. Users can narrow each search by identifying key topic areas of interest, then display a complete listing of relevant papers, and purchase materials specific to their research needs.

Comprehensive Service

- Over 81,600+ journal articles, book chapters, and case studies.
- All content is downloadable in PDF format and can be stored locally for future use.

No Subscription Fees

- One time fee of $37.50 per PDF download.

Instant Access

- Receive a download link immediately after order completion!

"It really provides an excellent entry into the research literature of the field. It presents a manageable number of highly relevant sources on topics of interest to a wide range of researchers. The sources are scholarly, but also accessible to 'practitioners'."

- Lisa Stimatz, MLS, University of North Carolina at Chapel Hill, USA

"It is an excellent and well designed database which will facilitate research, publication and teaching. It is a very very useful tool to have."

- George Ditsa, PhD, University of Wollongong, Australia

"I have accessed the database and find it to be a valuable tool to the IT/IS community. I found valuable articles meeting my search criteria 95% of the time."

- Lynda Louis, Xavier University of Louisiana, USA

Recommended for use by researchers who wish to immediately download PDFs of individual chapters or articles.

www.igi-global.com/e-resources/infosci-ondemand

IGI Global
DISSEMINATOR OF KNOWLEDGE

www.igi-global.com

Printed in the United States
By Bookmasters